AA

explorer

NEW ZEALAND

Nick Hanna

Hodder Moa Beckett

Published in 1997
by Hodder Moa Beckett Publishers Limited
[a member of the Hodder Headline Group]
4 Whetu Place, Mairangi Bay, Auckland,
New Zealand

Written by Nick Hanna
Original photography by Paul Kenward
Edited, designed and produced by AA Publishing

Published in the United Kingdom by AA Publishing

ISBN 1-86958-458-9

Colour separation by Fotographics Ltd
Printed and bound in Italy by Printers Trento srl

Cover (front): Lake Pukaki, Mt Cook
Mike Hollman /Visual Impact Pictures Ltd
Cover (back flap): Pohotu Geyser, Rotorua
Page 2(a): Maori warrior, Concert, Queenstown
Page 2(b): Carving, Waitangi Meeting House
Page 3: White-water rafting, Rotorua
Page 4(a): Picton air taxi
Page 4 (b): Auckland pedicab
Page 5(a): Sheep market
Page 5(b): Lake Wakatipu, South Island
Pages 6/7: Kiwifruit
Page 8: Milford Sound

KAITUNA
CASCADES
3
KAITUNA
CASCADES

How to use this book

This book is divided into five main sections:

- ❑ Section 1: ***New Zealand Is***
  discusses aspects of life and living today, from farming to inventiveness

- ❑ Section 2: ***New Zealand Was***
  places the country in its historical context and explores those past events whose influences are felt to this day

- ❑ Section 3: ***A to Z Section***
  covers places to visit, arranged by region within North and South Islands, with suggested walks and drives. Within this section fall the Focus-on articles, which consider a variety of topics in greater detail

- ❑ Section 4: ***Travel Facts***
  contains the strictly practical information that is vital for a successful trip

- ❑ Section 5: ***Hotels and Restaurants***
  lists recommended establishments in New Zealand, giving a brief résumé of what they offer

How to use the star rating
Most places described in this book have been given a separate rating:

▶▶▶ **Do not miss**

▶▶ **Highly recommended**

▶ **Worth seeing**

Not essential viewing

Map references
To make the location of a particular place easier to find, every main entry in this book is given a map reference, such as 81A2. The first number (81) indicates the page on which the map can be found; the letter (A) and the second number (2) pinpoint the square in which the main entry is located. The maps on the inside front cover and inside back cover are referred to as IFC and IBC respectively.

Contents

Dinghy racing on Lake Wakatipu, South Island

Quick reference

This quick-reference guide highlights the elements of the book you will use most often: the maps; the introductory features; the Focus-on articles; the walks and the drives.

Maps

New Zealand Is

Quick reference

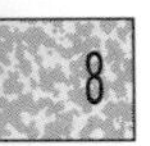

My New Zealand by Nick Hanna

Like many visitors to New Zealand, my first impressions were of the warmth and friendliness of the people, many of whom went out of their way to be helpful and hospitable during my travels around the country. Another thing which strikes you as soon as you head out of the cities – the great open spaces, the empty road rolling onwards and isolated farmsteads nestling in valleys in the middle of nowhere.

Kiwis themselves are inveterate lovers of the Great Outdoors and thousands now work in tourism as adventure guides – their enthusiasm and dedication make them amongst the most professional guides to be found anywhere in the world.

Contrary to the stereotype, Kiwis have a lively sense of humour. Another myth which is demolished as soon as you hit a town or city of any size is that the country is a cultural backwater; the sheer variety of arts, entertainment, crafts and music that's on offer may come as something of a surprise. I found myself spoilt for choice, as well, when eating out, with standards of food and wine which compare well with more exalted gourmet destinations. That doesn't mean you won't occasionally find yourself stuck in the wopwops where Mom & Pop's tearooms have got nothing left but a stale meat pie – but at least you can compensate for it later elsewhere.

Kiwis are acutely conscious of their colonial heritage and with only 200 years of European settlement behind them, every plough, Victorian utensil, or other material scrap of history has been preserved. Most of these are in rural museums which are something of a cultural cliché: I shan't mind if I never have to look at another vintage tractor again. At the opposite extreme, the heritage sector has produced some outstanding attractions which are at the cutting edge of museum design internationally: two fine examples which I particularly enjoyed were Auckland's National Maritime Museum and Kelly Tarlton's Antarctic World.

Above all, New Zealand gives the impression of openness: openness of opportunity for those who have settled there, openness from Kiwis towards visitors, and open spaces to roam in. These are rare qualities in an increasingly crowded world.

Nick Hanna

NEW ZEALAND IS

■ For its modest size, New Zealand has an astonishing diversity of landscapes and natural attractions, ranging from geysers to glaciers, rugged peaks to rushing rivers, and endless beaches to ancient beech forests. In this beautiful country, it is impossible for visitors to resist the call of the wild. ■

❑ Highest mountain
Mount Cook (3,764m)
Longest river
Waikato River (425km)
Largest lake
Lake Taupo (606 sq km)
Largest glacier
Tasman Glacier (29km) ❑

Distant islands Over 2,000km away from the nearest continent, Australia, the islands of New Zealand have the South Pacific on the north and east, the Tasman Sea on the west and the the Southern Ocean to the south.

The two major land masses are the North Island (115,777 sq km) and the South Island (151,215 sq km), with Stewart Island (1,746 sq km) lying off the southern tip of the South Island. To the south and east there are also six remote and uninhabited island groups (many now wildlife refuges) plus the inhabited Chatham Islands.

The North Island is the more heavily populated of the two main islands and the chief centre for commerce and business, while the South Island has the lion's share of majestic scenery and unspoiled wilderness. With about three-quarters of the population of 3.6 million living in urban areas, there is no shortage of space.

❑ In order of popularity, the most frequently visited natural attractions in New Zealand are:

1. Whakarewarewa Thermal Reserve, Rotorua
2. Waiţomo Caves
3. Milford Sound
4. Mount Cook National Park
5. Fox and Franz Josef Glaciers ❑

New Zealand is both volcanic and sedimentary in origin, with geothermal springs and geysers (as well as active volcanoes) found mostly in the North Island. Mountain ranges and rugged hills are characteristic of both main islands; the Southern Alps (South Island) are the most impressive mountain chain, with 223 named peaks rising above 2,300m. The country's high rainfall combined with the steep landforms has created numerous fast-flowing rivers, many of which are used to generate hydroelectric power. There are also many superb inland lakes.

New Zealand's 15,811km of coastline encompasses everything from mighty fiords to semi-tropical beaches, as well as hundreds of bays and harbours.

The Bay of Islands

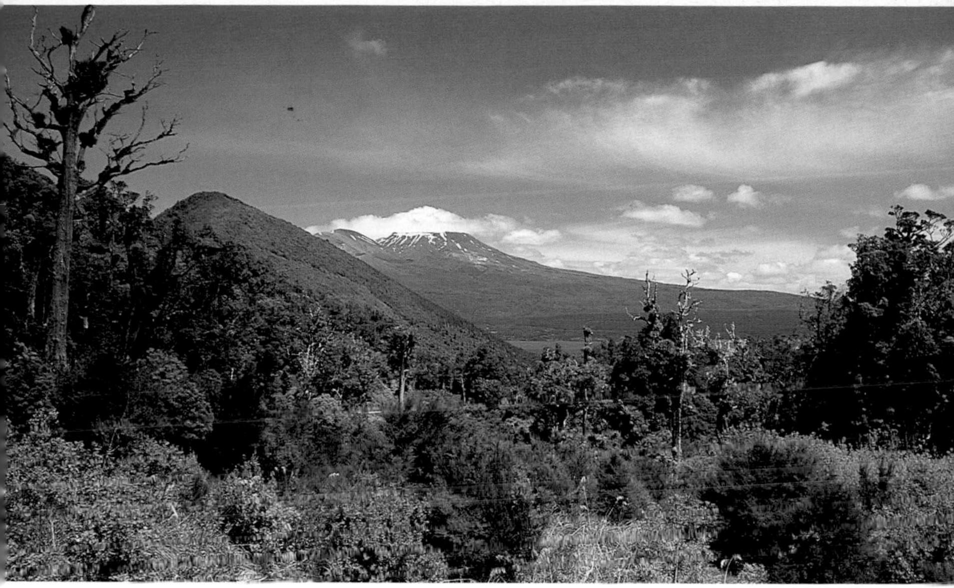

Moa's Ark This group of islands drifted away from the ancient supercontinent of Gondwanaland somewhere between 80 and 100 million years ago, long before the appearance of mammals on other land masses. In this isolated environment (which naturalist David Bellamy has dubbed 'Moa's Ark'), numerous species of flightless bird evolved; the moa is now extinct, but kiwi, takahe and other flightless species still exist. Also to be seen are many visiting waders and the royal albatross. Around the shoreline seals, dolphins and even whales abound.

❑ New Zealand's Department of Conservation is acknowledged as one of the top environment conservation authorities in the world. Operating through a network of field centres and 14 conservancy offices, it uses its annual budget of just NZ$100 million to look after and protect some three million hectares. Vital recovery programmes are focused on rare and threatened species such as tuatara, kiwi, native frogs, kakapo, giant weta and land snails. ❑

Much of New Zealand is volcanic; the snow-capped cone of North Island's Mount Ruapehu began to erupt again in 1995

Originally 80 per cent of New Zealand was covered in forest; just under a quarter of this is now left, most of it protected. The majority of native trees are evergreens, including giant conifers such as kauri, totara and rimu. There are some 2,500 native plant species (including 1,450 flowering plants). Some of the more common and distinctive plants include nikau palms, tree ferns, and the 'cabbage tree', which is a lily though it looks like a palm. In coastal areas native flax and pampas grass are common; and this is also the favoured environment of the 'New Zealand Christmas Tree', or pohutukawa, which blooms deep crimson in December.

Around one-third of the country comes under the control of the Department of Conservation (DoC) Te Papa Atawhai, which administers 13 national parks, three maritime parks, 20 forest parks and more than a thousand regional parks or reserves. Among these are two natural World Heritage Areas: Tongariro and South West New Zealand.

The world's biggest farm

■ Sometimes referred to as 'the world's biggest farm', New Zealand is heavily dependent on agriculture and horticulture. Around 10 per cent of the labour force is employed in agriculture, which has become remarkably efficient since the removal of subsidies in the 1980s. ■

Scientific farming Dairy products, meat and wool are among the principal export-earners in New Zealand and, despite diversification into other areas, agriculture and horticulture still account for around 60 per cent of export earnings and 11.5 per cent of gross domestic product. As befits a farming nation, agricultural research is well established, and efficient management of grasslands enables even sparse, hilly terrain to support high stock numbers. In order to achieve this, New Zealand pioneered the use of aircraft for spreading fertilisers and seed; it was also one of the first countries to develop mechanical milking for dairy herds.

Sheep, sheep, sheep There are some 24,000 sheep farms in New Zealand, stocked with approximately 50 million sheep. This rises to 76 million at the height of the lambing season, with some 90 per cent of the 26 million lambs born each year being exported.

❑ Horticulture is a boom area for exports, with overseas sales rising from NZ$30 million in the 1970s to over NZ$1,500 million in the 1990s. Apart from the famous kiwifruit, the other principal earners are apples, pears and fresh and processed vegetables. Exotics such as ginseng, valerian and angelica are also exported to meet the growing demand for medicinal herbs. ❑

The first flocks in New Zealand were of merinos, introduced in the 1830s for their fine fleeces, but these were gradually replaced with other breeds which adapted better to the warm, humid climate. Refrigerated shipping (which started in 1882) led to a shift of emphasis towards breeds which produced both meat and wool,

There are 17 sheep to each New Zealander

such as the more hardy Romneys from Britain. Cross-breeding has produced sheep suitable for different areas, and a wide variety of sheep is now farmed – even the merino has made a comeback.

New Zealand wool is noted for its length and colour as well as for its high yields. The country is the second largest producer in the world (after Australia) of clean, scoured wool, about 90 per cent of which is exported. But the high cost of sheep farming is forcing farmers to turn to cattle or deer farming and forestry; the national flock has in fact fallen from its peak of some 70 million sheep in 1981.

Milk and cheese Dairy farming is concentrated mainly in the North Island, with around 14,500 dairy herds (approximately 2.8 million cattle) in the country as a whole. Herds are large compared to those elsewhere (averaging about 140 milking cows), and most farmers belong to dairy co-operatives which manufacture and market dairy products.

New Zealand has been exporting cheese since the 1840s and now manufactures over 60 varieties, including some developed in New Zealand (such as blue supreme, aorangi and akronia) as well as high-quality versions of European cheeses (such as cheddar, brie, parmesan, edam and mozzarella). Other dairy exports include milk powders, butter and ghee. The country accounts for about 25 per cent of world trade in dairy products, and the industry provides 11 per cent of New Zealand's export earnings.

Deer farming Deer are considered a pest, and until the 1970s it was official policy to kill them because of the damage they caused to upland grazing areas. Helicopters were used extensively to hunt them in the wild, with the venison then being exported (principally to Germany). When deer farming started in the 1970s, the hunters switched to capturing live animals which were kept in enclosures with strong, high fences. Now there are around 1.1 million farmed deer, although they are still classified as noxious animals and special licences are needed to farm them. As well as venison, antler velvet is also exported, principally to the Far East.

Venison and antler velvet are now farm produce

❑ Fur farming includes possum skins, rex and chinchilla rabbit fur and ferret fur. Possums (visible in squashed form on almost every road in the country), like deer, are classed as noxious pests, and are subject to an official eradication programme. Around two million possum skins are exported annually. ❑

■ It is a sad paradox that while New Zealand enjoys a high-profile environmental image, it also has one of the worst records in the world for wiping out native species. More than 500 plants, birds and animals are said to be still under threat. ■

❑ It is known that moa were still alive in Fiordland when the first Europeans arrived on the West Coast, because a bone from a bush moa recently found in a midden in Takahe Valley had a mark on it made by a steel implement. The Maori used to split the bones to get at the marrow, and the steel tool was probably obtained from sealers camping in nearby Dusky Sound. ❑

The end of the moa These colossal flightless birds (rather like ostriches, up to four metres tall) were wiped out by hunting (the early Maori were referred to as 'the Moa Hunters'), along with another 20 species of birds. One of these was the New Zealand eagle (*Harpagornis moorei*), the largest eagle ever known, with a wingspan of 2.5m: it vanished because its prey, including the moa, was also disappearing. The burning and clearing of forests by early Maori, and the introduction of predators such as the Polynesian rat (*kiore*) and the Maori dog (now also extinct) likewise had a significant effect on native species.

Disastrous introductions Worse was to come with the arrival of the Europeans, who began bringing animals into the country at an unprecedented rate. Some were liberated for sport, others were introduced for their fur or simply as pets. By the first decade of the century over 50 species had been introduced, including rabbits, possums, hares, weasels, stoats, deer, goats and even wallabies.

Some introduced species (such as cows and sheep) now form a mainstay of the nation's economy, but other animals had devastating effects. Possums ate kiwi eggs, stoats ate their young chicks, and dogs attacked the adults. Rabbits, deer, goats and possums gnawed away at native trees and plants, drastically altering the vegetation and soil ecology. The clearing of farmlands led to the loss of yet more native habitat and the extinction of a further nine species of bird.

Threatened birds Around 57 native bird species are currently considered threatened, including the kiwi, the national emblem (see pages 236-7). Other flightless birds currently under threat include the kakapo, a strange nocturnal parrot which retains a

precarious hold on Little Barrier Island and Codfish Island and of which only 48 individuals are still known to exist. Another Fiordland native, the bright blue and green takahe, was regarded as extinct before a small colony was discovered in 1948; just 150 of these birds are now left. The taiko, a large white-bellied sea-bird, was also thought to be extinct until an amateur ornithologist spotted two of them on Chatham Island; around 100 taiko have now been 'refound', but their survival is dependent on the offspring from just a few nesting burrows. The native black stilt, or kaki, is another threatened species, with under a hundred left in the wild. And the inquisitive kea, the world's only alpine parrot, is declining in numbers.

Mammals and insects The only native land mammals in New Zealand are bats. One species became extinct as recently as 1965, and the other two (the long-tailed and short-tailed bat) are both uncommon and under threat. The country's largest insects are the weta (a group of wingless crickets) and these too are in retreat, with the giant weta (which can grow up to 10cm long) currently found only in off-shore sanctuaries and one mainland site. The huge black ground beetle (*Mecodema punctellum*) is similarly endangered. Thousands of insects in the country have yet to be classified, and many more may be disappearing without our even knowing it.

The native kea parrot (right) is under threat but the introduced possum (below) is a pest

It is no exaggeration to claim that New Zealand is probably the best country in the world for adventure tourism. The choice of activities is enormous – and growing all the time.

Outdoor attractions Kiwis themselves prefer to spend much of their recreational time in the open air, and given that most overseas visitors are also drawn to the country by outdoor attractions (such as lakes, mountains, glaciers and forests), it is perhaps only to be expected that New Zealand should have developed a sophisticated infrastructure for adventure tourism. Nearly three-quarters of the 1.2 million visitors to the country each year take part in some kind of outdoor adventure, and there are now well over a thousand guides or companies in the adventure tourism business. For many New Zealanders, making a living from sharing their natural environment with visitors has become a way of life. Courteous, well-trained and enthusiastic guides add enormously to the enjoyment of exploring wilderness areas.

Try rafting for a thrill

Bush walks to bungee-jumping One of the most popular outdoor activities for visitors is a short bush walk (usually lasting less than half a day), and nearly every Visitor Information Centre or Department of Conservation centre provides helpful leaflets on local walking tracks. Longer tramps on some of New Zealand's famous long-distance paths (such as the Abel Tasman, Routeburn, Heaphy, Milford and Hollyford tracks) are also popular.

Ballooning is a great way to see the countryside, and is mainly centred around Christchurch. Jet-boating gives you a noisier, faster perspective on the great outdoors (see pages 210–11), and is the third most popular activity for visitors (after short walks and scenic boat cruises). With its mountainous terrain and high rainfall, New Zealand is a perfect location for white-water rafting and as many as 50 companies operate on rivers in both the North and South Islands. Recently, black-water rafting has also taken off in a big way: this mostly takes place around the Waitomo region.

Tandem hang-gliding, tandem parapenting and tandem parachuting are all good ways of experiencing these sports with little or no training, and bungee-jumping (see page 245) has become virtually synonymous with wacky adventures in New Zealand.

Flightseeing Helicopter sightseeing is also very popular, with the busiest areas being in the Mount Cook

National Park, Fiordland, Fox and Franz Josef Glaciers, and around the Queenstown Lakes. Heli-fishing, heli-skiing and heli-rafting are all popular. A spate of recent air crashes has prompted a review by the Civil Aviation Authority (CAA) into aircraft safety in New Zealand, however, with a crackdown on operators who have been flying below minimum heights: this review is probably long overdue, given that in the last decade a total of 43 people died on sightseeing flights over the South Island. For tourists cruising around the Milford Sound by boat, noise pollution from the constant procession of light planes and helicopters above can be annoying – but there have been far more catastrophic consequences for those who have chosen to view the fiord from the air. In 1989, two Cessnas collided over the Sound, killing all on board: on that fateful December day, no fewer than 40 flights had taken off from the Milford airstrip in the 20 minutes between 3.15 and 3.35pm.

Sky-high parapenting gives a superb view of the country

Dare-devil stunts While bungee-jumping and tandem parachuting are now so common as to be almost mundane, operators are seeking even more daring skills to tempt the brave. Among the new thrills recently proposed are 'wing-walking' (in which passengers are strapped to the top wing of a Tiger Moth plane) and a simulated, low-level aerial top-dressing run. One operator in Taupo even set up a stunt in which passengers were suspended from 12m-long chains beneath his helicopter and taken for a tour around the Huka Falls. A short item on television had passengers queuing up, but the CAA drew the line and closed it down.

If there is a new experience out there waiting to be invented, there is a good chance it will happen first in New Zealand!

❏ New Zealand is said to have more helicopters per head of population than any other country in the world. They were first used on a large scale during the 1960s for deer-culling, with up to 50 culling as many as 200 deer each in a day; in the 1970s the pilots switched to recovering the deer for farming. In many remote areas, helicopters are used as daily work-horses for moving materials, surveying, fire control, drilling work and crop spraying. ❏

■ The resumption of nuclear testing by the French in the South Pacific in 1995 and 1996 caused outrage in New Zealand, which has for a long time been recognised as the standard-bearer of the movement for a nuclear-free Pacific. ■

ANZUS and the USA Despite the loosening of colonial ties, New Zealand dutifully supported Britain in foreign policy in the first half of this century, sending 100,000 troops to Europe and the Middle East during World War I. During World War II it became clear that Britain was unable to reciprocate in defence matters, and politicians recognised the need to re-align with the USA, whose Pacific fleet was at least closer to home. In 1951 (during the Korean War) Australia, New Zealand and the USA together signed the ANZUS defence alliance.

As a result of this policy New Zealand sent troops to support the USA in Vietnam in 1965, which led to widespread anti-war protests. With the election of a nationalistic Labour Government in 1972 the troops were withdrawn, and New Zealand adopted an anti-nuclear stance, sending two warships to protest against French testing in the Mururoa atoll. This was partly a result of the greater role played by New Zealand in its Pacific backyard. At the same time, there was an outcry against nuclear-armed or nuclear-powered US warships using New Zealand ports, with a flotilla of 'peace boats' blockading Auckland harbour to prevent nuclear submarines from entering it.

Further protests followed in the early 1980s, contributing to the election in 1984 of a Labour Government which pledged to set up a 320-km 'nuclear-free zone' around the country's shores. With the USA stating that it would 'neither confirm nor deny' whether its naval vessels were carrying nuclear weapons, it was unable to use New Zealand ports, and suspended its obligations to New Zealand under the ANZUS treaty.

The *Rainbow Warrior* In July 1985 the *Rainbow Warrior*, flagship of the

Protestors keep up the pressure for a nuclear-free New Zealand

international protest group Greenpeace, sailed into Auckland's Waitemata Harbour to join a flotilla of vessels on a protest voyage to the French nuclear-testing site in Mururoa. Just before midnight on 10 July a bomb blasted a hole in the ship; while most of the crew jumped to safety, a Greenpeace photographer, Fernando Pereira, went back to retrieve equipment. A second bomb exploded, and Pereira was drowned as the *Rainbow Warrior* sank.

It was the first ever act of international terrorism on New Zealand soil. Within two weeks the police had arrested two suspects, who proved to be agents for the French secret service (DGSE).

Resumed testing Given the anger and resentment caused by this act of murder and sabotage by a foreign government in New Zealand territory, it was to be expected that New Zealand (with Australia) would lead the way in protesting against the resumption of French nuclear tests on Mururoa in 1995. The naval research ship *Tui* was sent to Mururoa in August 1995, one of only two government-backed vessels to take part in the protests (the other was a ceremonial canoe sent by the tiny Cook Islands). Although tests were still carried out in 1995 and 1996, worldwide protests have forced France to concede that these will be the last, and to sign the Comprehensive Test Ban Treaty.

Meanwhile, relations between the USA and New Zealand had improved with a visit to Washington by Prime Minister Jim Bolger in 1995. But diplomatic differences remain. With the hardening of attitudes caused by the French testing, it looks unlikely that New Zealand will now abandon its nuclear-free policy.

❑ In November 1985 the two French agents responsible for the *Rainbow Warrior* bombing were sentenced to ten years' imprisonment, but the French pressed for their return and imposed a trade ban on New Zealand products in retaliation. The row eventually led to United Nations arbitration, under which France agreed to pay $13 million compensation and New Zealand handed over the agents. They subsequently spent just two years 'imprisoned' on the Pacific island of Hao before being repatriated to France. ❑

The bombing of Rainbow Warrior *hardened public opinion against nuclear weapons*

■ The inherent flaws and misunderstandings over land ownership enshrined in the Treaty of Waitangi have led the Maori to protest almost since the day it was signed. Bitter disputes over land rights still continue today, to the detriment of good race relations. ■

A dubious legacy Constitutionally, New Zealand is perhaps unique in the world in that the legal basis for sovereignty and ownership over land is enshrined in a single controversial document, the Treaty of Waitangi (see pages 36–7). However, even if the Maori who 'sold' their land to the early settlers were fully aware of the consequences, the moral validity of these transactions has always been questionable. Disputes flared up from 1843 onwards, culminating in the New Zealand Wars and the Maori King Movement. A recent spate of occupations, sit-ins and other protests has once again brought the issue of land rights to the fore.

❑ During a visit to New Zealand to attend the 1995 Commonwealth summit, the Queen formally signed legislation which apologised to the Waikato Maori for the 'wrongful and unjust' land grab carried out by the whites in the name of her great-great-grandmother, Queen Victoria. On 2 November 1995, in the presence of the Maori Queen, Dame Te Atairangikaahu, and the Governor-General, Dame Katherine Tizzard, she gave the Royal Assent to an Act of Parliament compensating the Tainui tribe for its suffering 130 years ago, when they were wrongly branded rebels and troops were sent to fight them and confiscate their land. The bill admits that the British violated the Treaty of Waitangi and offers 'profound regret and apologies for the loss of lives'. Under the bill, the Crown will hand back nearly 16,000 hectares of land, valued at NZ$100 million, with around 30,000 Tainui benefiting from the settlement. ❑

The Waitangi Tribunal For much of this century the Maori have mounted peaceful challenges to the provisions of the treaty, with numerous petitions to Parliament, court cases, and even pilgrimages to London (in 1914 the Maori king Te Rata met King George V and Queen Mary at Buckingham Palace, but his deputation met with no response). In 1975 the Government set up the Waitangi Tribunal to investigate land claims, but this was largely ineffectual until 1985, when its terms of reference were extended to include the investigation of grievances dating back to 1840. Critics claim it is too slow, and in fact by 1990 the tribunal had ruled on only seven substantial claims. Since then it has dealt with around

90 more cases, but another 400 still await a ruling.

The fiscal envelope The backlog of outstanding claims and growing frustration amongst the Maori led the Government, in 1994, to propose an all-embracing package which (it was hoped) would resolve all outstanding claims before the end of the decade, with a ceiling of a billion NZ dollars on the cost of all future settlements. Since then, they have struggled to win acceptance for this 'fiscal envelope' package. To some Maori the idea of putting a ceiling on payments before claims have been heard is equivalent to putting the cart before the horse; they also fail to see the logic in proposing a pan-Maori settlement when claims are dealt with on a tribal basis.

Protests and sit-ins Anger over Government proposals boiled over in 1995, with protests in front of the Governor-General at the Waitangi Day celebrations marking the start of a round of sit ins and occupations throughout the country. Confrontations ensued in Hamilton, Tamaki (Auckland) and even the tourist-oriented Whakarewarewa thermal reserve in Rotorua; one of the most controversial occupations was that of the Moutoa Gardens in Wanganui, which dominated news headlines for several weeks as protestors squared up to the local council and refused to leave land which they claimed had been sold to the Crown illegally in 1848. In another confrontation, demonstrators burned down a school building near Kaitaia in protest at the time taken to hear their case.

Race relations The 1995 protests played a crucial role in bringing the issue of land rights once again to the fore, although they did little for race relations in a country which generally prides itself on its harmonious biculturalism. It was a reminder to New Zealanders that good race relations cannot be taken for granted, and that (bearing in mind their warrior past) the Maori have so far shown considerable restraint in their attempts to get their 156-year-old grievances addressed. Economic and social hardship amongst the Maori have also fanned the flames of protest, and some radicals have used the protests as a platform to push the idea of Maori sovereignty – with their own judicial and political systems. One thing is certain – land claims are likely to continue for some years yet.

Protestors disrupted the 1995 Waitangi Day celebrations

■ Given New Zealand's abundant natural produce and the different flavours and dishes introduced by immigrant groups, it comes as no surprise to discover that a new generation of chefs is creating a culinary revolution in the nation's eating habits. ■

From stodge to sashimi Having inherited a tradition of stodgy, British Empire cooking, culinary culture in New Zealand has for a long time been epitomised by solid, no-nonsense fare such as steak, chips and coleslaw, pies, fish and chips, and roast meats. Even now, this may be all that is offered in country pubs or rural towns, but in the major cities and resort areas there is an abundance of new restaurants, bistros and urban cafés offering a range of mouth-watering dishes drawing on a cosmopolitan array of regional styles from around the world.

This restaurant revolution has been driven partly by the demands of an increasingly sophisticated tourist industry, partly by growing expectations as a result of wider international travel by Kiwis themselves, and partly by the use of aromatic herbs, spices and different cooking styles introduced by immigrants from Asia and elsewhere.

In the 1960s good restaurants – and good chefs – were so few and far between that the Tourist Hotel Corporation was obliged to bring a squadron of chefs from Europe to work in local resorts. Now it is the Kiwi chefs who are in demand in places such as London, and New Zealand can boast over 2,500

Crayfish are amongst the superb ingredients of New Zealand cuisine

restaurants – Wellington is said to have more restaurants per head of population than New York.

There are few 'national dishes' as such, although *paua* (abalone) patties and whitebait fritters are certainly unique. Drawing on many different styles, the best Kiwi cooking today tends to lean towards the Mediterranean or alternatively the Pacific rim, a fashionable fusion of East and West in a style perhaps best described as 'Californian'.

From farm to restaurant New Zealand's farms produce superb beef and lamb (fed on pasture – rather than grain – which gives meat a richer flavour), and venison is now becoming increasingly popular. Fresh seafood, good-quality dairy produce and an abundance of exotic fruits are just a few of the other natural ingredients available.

Some regions do have their specialities, and while most of the raw ingredients are available everywhere, these specialities are likely to be that much fresher in local restaurants. Oysters and mussels are farmed around the Coromandel Peninsula, and the Firth of Thames is noted for its scallops, flounder and rock lobster. In the Bay of Islands, smoked kingfish and marlin are delicacies available during the game fishing season, and feijoas, passion fruit and tamarillos ('tree tomatoes') are grown in the Kerikeri area. Peaches, apples and pears are produced in abundance in Hawke's Bay, as are kiwifruit in the Bay of Plenty. The rich dairylands of the Taranaki region provide numerous excellent cheeses, and Lake Taupo is famous for its massive trout – although you will have to hook it yourself, since restaurants are not permitted to sell trout.

Tasty greenshell mussels, exported worldwide

❑ Traditional Maori delicacies include freshwater eels, muttonbird (the young of the sooty petrel, with a strong, fishy taste), and seafood such as pipi and tuatua shellfish and kina (prickly sea urchins). A *hangi* is a feast of meat, seafood and vegetables (including the staple root crop, kumara), steamed over hot rocks in an earth oven (the *hangi*). Like many Polynesian foods, it is high in carbohydrates but well worth sampling. ❑

In the South Island, the Marlborough Sounds are noted for their farmed mussels (which are exported worldwide), and oysters and scallops are perennial favourites in the port of Nelson. Blenheim produces garlic, cherries, apples, pears and much more besides, while the local crayfish in the seaside town of Kaikoura are not to be missed. Canterbury is famed for its lamb, and is also known for its numerous duck farms. On the other side of the Alps, whitebait are a local delicacy along much of the West Coast from September to November. Bluff oysters, Fiordland crayfish and blue cod are specialities in the south of the South Island.

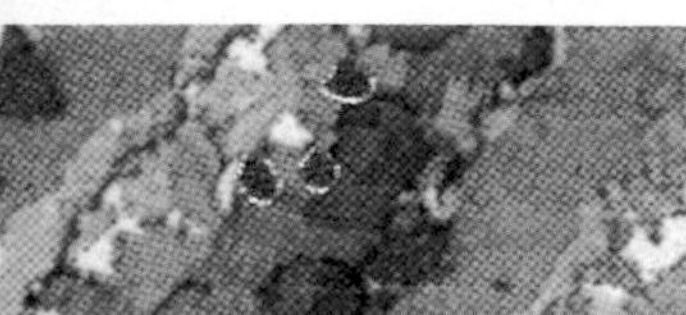

■ In just two decades, New Zealand has moved from producing ghastly 'plonk' to internationally acclaimed table wines. Over 100 wineries (most of which can be visited) now produce some 45 million litres of wine annually. ■

❑ The first vines in New Zealand were planted over 150 years ago by James Busby, the British Resident, who grew grapes in the back garden of his house in Waitangi. He was complimented on his 'delicious' white wine by the French explorer Dumont d'Urville in 1846, but fought a losing battle against intrusion by 'horses, sheep, cattle and pigs'. His little vineyard was finally destroyed by British soldiers during one of their battles with the rebel leader Hongi Hika. ❑

Early days As well as the vineyards around Auckland (see panel), other long-established wine-making areas include Gisborne, Nelson and Hawke's Bay, but output was traditionally small. The opening up of New Zealand to international influences in the 1960s led to a much greater demand for table wines, and the search began for fresh areas suitable for vineyards.

New vineyards In addition to the new vineyards planted in the older wine-growing areas, other possible areas were also sought – principally in the Wairarapa, Canterbury and Marlborough regions. Of the numerous varieties of grape planted, one of the trail-blazers was the Sauvignon Blanc, which is ideally suited to the New Zealand climate with its long, warm autumn days (helping to concentrate the sugar in the grape) and cool nights (providing a suitable acidic balance).

Among the pioneers in Marlborough were the Montana wineries, whose Sauvignon Blancs were the first New Zealand wines to gain international recognition. Another more recent winery in the area is Cloudy Bay (established in 1985 by Australian wine-makers), whose skilfully crafted Sauvignon Blancs are undoubtedly some of the best of each vintage. Sauvignon Blanc is produced in almost every wine-growing district, with those from the north being more lush and fruity and those from the south providing classic herbaceous overtones.

Chardonnay has also done exceptionally well in New Zealand, particularly in the Gisborne area. The Millton Vineyard, on the banks of the Te Arai River in Gisborne (the only certified organic producer in the country) produces some award-winning Chardonnays.

Whilst wine-making in the Auckland region waned during the 1970s, it made something of a comeback in the 1980s with new plantings at Huapai, Ihumatao (near Mangere) and on Waiheke Island. Michael Brajkovich, whose family was one of the original producers in the area, took a giant leap from the old sherries and table wines in the

Kiwi wines hold their own with the world's best

❑ For most of this century wine-making was dominated by sweet, highly alcoholic versions of fortified wines (such as sherry, port and Madeira) produced around the clay hills of West Auckland. Made largely by Dalmatian immigrants, they were referred to as 'Dally plonk'. ❑

mid 1980s to produce a series of top Chardonnays of great flair and individuality; his Kumeu River Chardonnays and Sauvignons are of consistently high quality. The 1993 vintages from around Auckland are also outstanding.

Neudorf Vineyard, near Nelson, is another great name to watch out for in Chardonnays, Sauvignons and Rieslings.

Red wines The most famous reds are those produced at the Te Mata Estate in Hawke's Bay, revitalised by John Buck in the 1980s. Their Cabernet Sauvignon-based reds have been winning awards ever since: outstanding vintages include the 1982, 1989, and 1991 Coleraines. Other top producers in Hawke's Bay include Mission Bay and Kemblefield Estate. Waiheke Island in the Hauraki Gulf and the Martinborough district north-east of Wellington are also good for reds.

Blenheim's sun and sparse soils are ideal for sparkling wines

Sparkling wines When Australia developed its first sparkling wines in the 1970s it did not take long for New Zealand to follow suit, although for many years the Montana vine yards were the only producers of *méthode champenoise* wines. Their Lindauer (which was first released in 1980) remains a classic. In 1989 Montana teamed up with the famous French Champagne house of Deutz and Geldermann, and their Deutz Marlborough Cuvée has now established itself as a thoroughbred.

Cloudy Bay has followed a similar path, teaming up with the prestigious Champagne house of Veuve Clicquot Ponsardin to produce the stylish Pelorus sparkling wines, named after nearby Pelorus Sound.

■ **From the earliest days New Zealanders have had to 'mend and make do', a tradition which has led to numerous inventions. Today, New Zealand is said to have more inventors per head of population than any other country.** ■

A replica of Richard Pearce's first plane

Home-made repairs There is a popular saying that given a length of no.8 wire (4mm fencing wire), New Zealanders can make anything. The do-it-yourself mentality arrived with the first European settlers, who had to learn to fix imported machinery themselves since the nearest spare parts depot was probably 20,000km away in Britain. Frequently they redesigned it as an improvement on the original.

Great inventions Pride of place for Kiwi inventors goes to Richard Pearce, the South Island farmer who allegedly flew before the Wright Brothers (see page 216). As well as designing his own planes, he also developed a machine for threading needles, a motorised plough, and a bicycle which pumped up its own tyres as it went along. Another South Island farmer, Bill Hamilton, was responsible for inventing the jet-boat (see pages 210–11). The physicist Ernest Rutherford could be said to have 'invented' modern nuclear physics when he split the atom in 1919. New Zealanders also invented the first automatic milking, franking and stamp-vending machines, and the wrinkle in the humble hair-grip. An Auckland student, Edward Smith, invented the world's first mechanical railway crossing.

Modern times A South Aucklander, Terry Roycroft, recently unveiled the ultimate amphibian car, with retractable wheels which allow it to achieve speeds of 30 knots (the previous maximum speed was 5 knots).

Another recent introduction is a solar-powered car driven by a revolutionary motor capable of producing speeds of up to 40kph invented by a Hamilton engineer.

More off-beat is a device called the NightStar, a deflated star globe which fits in your pocket and functions as a miniature planetarium.

❑ The inventiveness of New Zealanders is celebrated in *Kiwi Ingenuity, A Book of New Zealand Ideas and Inventions* by Bob Riley (Auckland Institute of Technology Press, 1995). ❑

NEW ZEALAND WAS

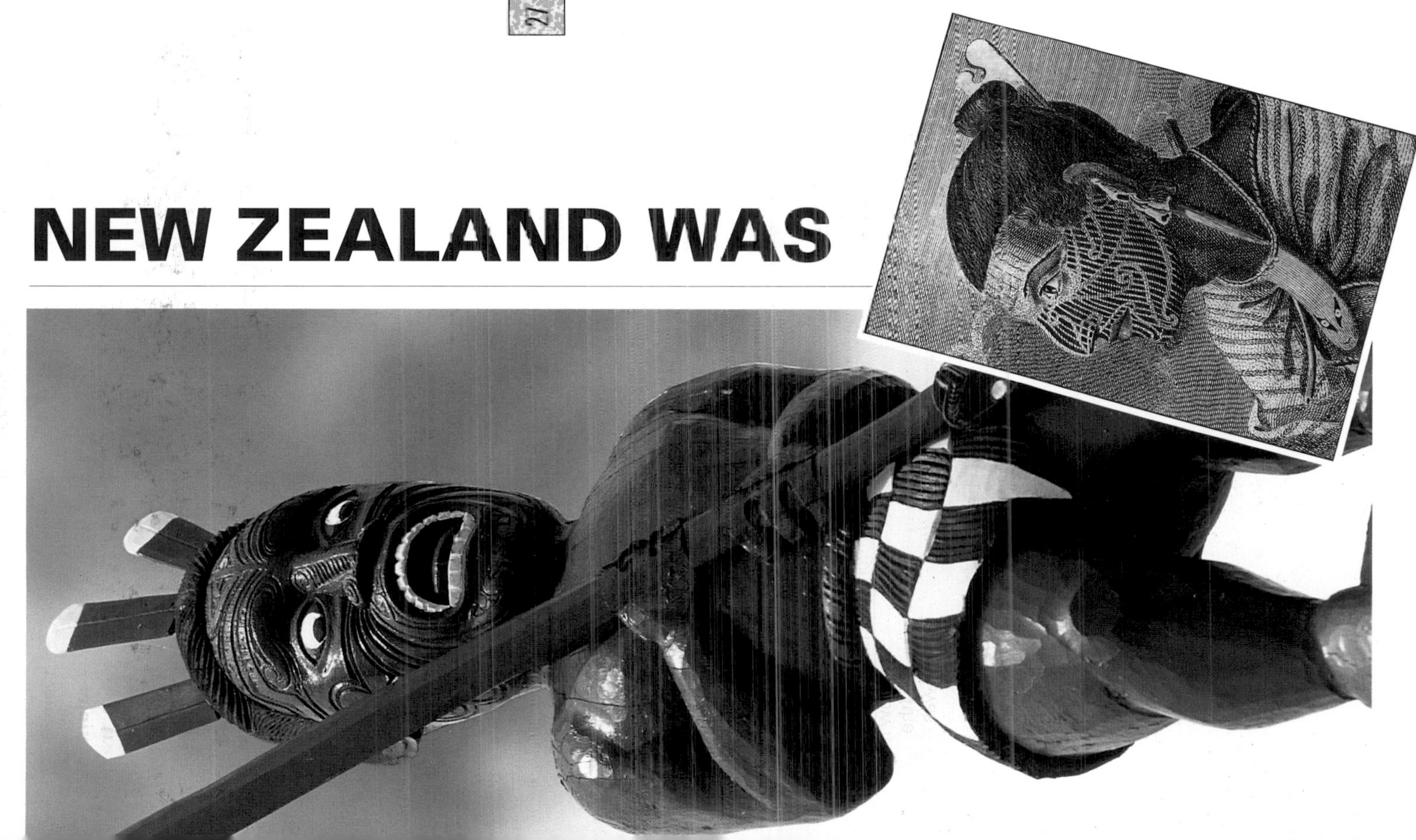

Arrival of the Polynesians

One consequence of New Zealand's geographic isolation was that it was one of the last countries of any size to be colonised by people. The first people to reach New Zealand were the Polynesians, who had originated in Asia and spread out across the Pacific some 3,000–4,000 years ago.

❑ The homeland of 'Hawaiki', venerated in Maori culture, does not necessarily refer to a specific place. 'Hawaiki' is a general term used throughout Polynesia to describe the ancestral homeland left behind in an onward migration, although in the case of Hawaii they may also have used it for the land they arrived in. Anthropologists believe the Maori originated in eastern Polynesia, possibly from the Marquesas in the Society Islands. ❑

The explorer Kupe The Polynesians were expert sailors and often made long sea voyages, sometimes discovering new lands by accident and sometimes setting off on migrations in order to relieve pressure on their homeland. According to tradition it was the Polynesian explorer Kupe who first discovered New Zealand in about AD 950, sailing from 'Hawaiki' (see box). He explored the coast and sailed inland up the Whanganui River, before returning to Hawaiki with information on how to reach the land which his wife may have named Aotearoa, or 'Land of the Long White Cloud'.

The great migrations Some canoes undoubtedly landed in New Zealand after Kupe, but legend has it that the first great migrations took place during the 14th century, with a fleet of 12 canoes setting off from Hawaiki to escape overpopulation in the homelands. The existence of such a 'fleet' has never been proved, but the names of all the canoes, with their occupants and landing places, form an important part of Maori genealogical history. Some of the canoes may have been lashed together to give greater stability on the ocean crossing, which would explain why they landed so close together. The voyagers brought food plants (including taro, yam and the sweet potato, kumara) as well as the rat and dog: pigs and domestic fowl were either eaten or lost overboard on the way.

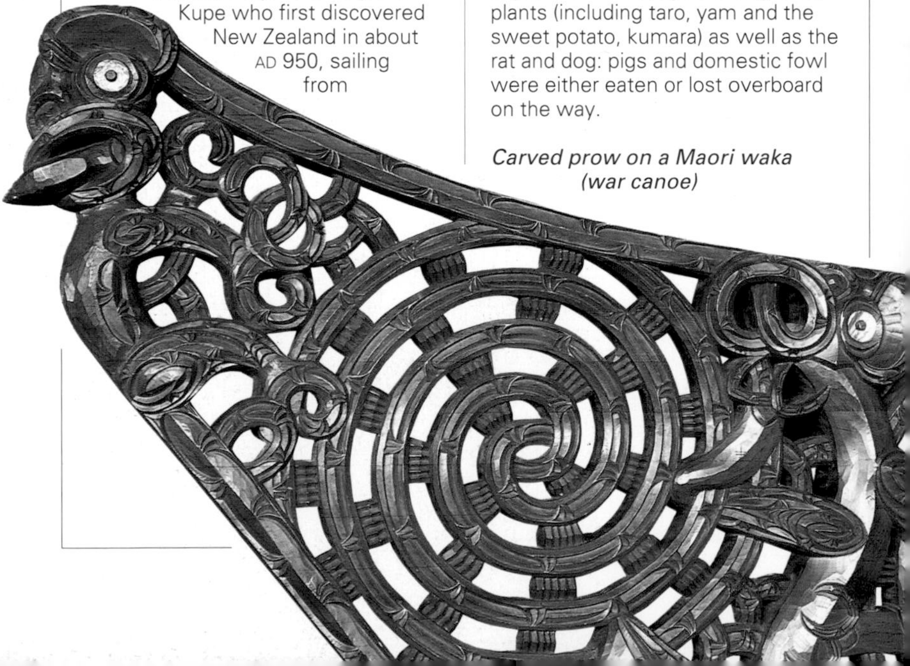

Carved prow on a Maori waka (war canoe)

Adaptation The people who arrived in Aotearoa had to adapt to a completely different climate from that of the tropical islands they had left. Food was at first plentiful: fish, shellfish, seals, and an abundance of edible birds provided protein; one of the most easily tapped food supplies was the flightless moa, which was defenceless against hunters.

Kumara, which is highly susceptible to frost, was difficult to grow as a perennial in New Zealand's temperate climate. Widespread cultivation only became possible with the discovery that kumara tubers could be lifted in the autumn and overwintered in pits (*rua*) in the earth for planting out in the spring.

Other aspects of life also changed. The settlers brought the paper mulberry plant for making tapa cloth, but it grew only in the warmer north, so they learned to plait flax into fibre for clothes, cords and baskets. Rain capes were also made from flax, often decorated with feathers or dog skin. The country's forests provided huge trees for building much bigger canoes, and elaborate woodcarving became an established tradition. Bones were used for fish-hooks, ornaments and spear heads, stone for tools such as adzes and axes, and volcanic stone such as obsidian for flake knives and other kinds of sharp tools.

In adapting to their new homeland, the Maori developed one of the most sophisticated neolithic cultures in the ancient world, with an elaborate social structure and a widespread trading system.

❑ Studies of teeth and skeletons have shown that in the early days the Maori had a varied and plentiful diet, but from the 15th century onwards the climate cooled considerably and populations became larger, with food becoming more scarce. People ate more shellfish such as pipi (which usually contains some sand) and fern roots, both of which wore down teeth, so that by the time they were in their mid-20s their teeth were often worn down to the gum. With the introduction of the potato by Europeans, plentiful food supplies were once more assured. ❑

Idols in an elaborate carving protect a* marae *entrance

Classic Maori society

■ Over the centuries, Maori society evolved from the 'archaic' culture of the early moa-hunters into the sophisticated social system of the 'classic Maori' period. Kinship was of fundamental importance in Maori society, and inter-tribal warfare was a constant feature of this period. ■

Social hierarchy Maori society was organised along strictly hierarchical lines, headed by the chiefs (*rangatira*), followed by the priests (*tohunga*), the commoners (*tūtūā*) and finally slaves (members of other tribes captured in battle). The family (*whānau*) and the sub-tribe (*hapū*) were part of the wider tribe (*iwi*), with this established social structure determining marriage and settlement patterns and, just as important, who fought whom.

The genealogy of the ancestors (*whakapapa*) was an essential element in the knitting together of tribes, and oral history played an important part in passing on information about the surrounding environment. A unified cosmology which venerated the gods of the natural elements was woven into the fabric of life, along with a series of concepts such as *tapu* (sacredness), *mana* (spiritual authority or prestige) and *mākutu* (sorcery) which governed behaviour. Imaginative legends formed an important part of the Maori oral heritage, and many of today's place names derive from incidents taken from these elaborate and colourful tales.

Inter-tribal wars The Maori people were constantly feuding, usually over territory or access to food sources, but also in order to avenge insults and extract *utu* (retribution). Sometimes these feuds would fester down the generations, but the consequent loss of life in pre-European times was probably negligible, as weapons were rudimentary and wars were usually only fought when the vital kumara crops did not need attention.

Young men sought honour in assaults with the *patu* (war club), gaining *mana* as warriors with each victory. The vanquished became slaves or were eaten. Although *hapū* would usually join forces to fight other *iwi*, there were also sometimes battles between *hapū* of the same *iwi*.

Tattoos and a greenstone pendant were Maori fashion in 1880

❑ Personal adornment in the form of tattooing (*tā moko*) was a striking feature of the classic period. The intricate patterns were purely for decoration, and tattooing had no relation to rank. It was a long, painful process undertaken with a bone chisel, with pigment rubbed into the incision afterwards. Men were often heavily tattooed on the face, body, buttocks and thighs; on women tattoos were usually confined to the chin and lips, and sometimes the ankles, wrists and forehead. ❑

Village life Most families lived in small huts (*whare*), grouped together into villages (*kāinga*) which could range in size from a handful of individuals to more than 500 households, usually all members of the same *hapū*.

The focus of the community was (and still is) the *marae*, including an open space or village green where meetings and councils are held. Visitors are ceremonially bade welcome or farewell on the *marae*. An integral part of the *marae* is the *whare runanga*, or meeting house, which serves as both a meeting place for amusement and gossip at night or in bad weather and as a hostel for accommodating visitors. It is usually decorated with elaborate carvings representing the ancestors, woven flax panels and symbolic paintings.

A sentry guards a fortified meeting house against other tribes

Within the village there would also be food storage pits (*rua*) and grain stores (*pātaka*), as well as bigger houses for the *tohunga* and *rangatira*, and sometimes a 'house of learning' or school (*whare wānanga*).

Often *kāinga* were grouped around a fortified hilltop village (*pā*). These hilltop forts were constructed using an elaborate system of ditches, banks and palisades, and in many cases proved impregnable to later attacks by European soldiers.

■ The first European to sail to New Zealand was the Dutchman, Abel Tasman, but after a bloody encounter with the Maori he never set foot on land. Another 130 years passed before James Cook arrived, 'rediscovering' the country and placing it, literally, on the world map. ■

Abel Tasman

Geographers in Europe were convinced that somewhere in the South Pacific there must be a huge land mass (which they termed *Terra australis incognita*) to 'balance' the continents of the Northern Hemisphere. The explorers were to prove them wrong, but it was with the intention of discovering this unknown continent that Abel Janszoon Tasman set out from the Dutch trading post of Batavia (present-day Jakarta, Indonesia) in 1642. In command of two small ships, the *Heemskerck* and the *Zeehaen*, he sailed first to Mauritius and then doubled back eastwards to discover Tasmania (which he named Van Diemen's Land).

After another seven days' sailing, on 13 December 1642, he sighted 'a land uplifted high' (the Alps in the South Island), but heavy seas precluded a landing. Instead he proceeded northwards along the coast, rounding Cape Farewell and anchoring in the shelter of what is today called Golden Bay. Although he had been hoping to establish friendly relations with the Maori, a fight broke out (see page 159) and he sailed on eastwards. Battling against head winds in what was later to be known as Cook Strait, he turned around and headed up the west coast of the North Island; if he had continued a little further he would have found that this new land was two islands, and not the great *Terra australis incognita*.

❑ Tasman at first christened the country he discovered Staten Landt, since he believed it to be connected to an island of that name off South America. But other explorers soon proved that the new land was an island, and the name was changed to 'Nieuw Zeeland', after the coastal province of Zeeland in Holland. It was probably an anonymous map-maker of the Dutch East India Company who thus gave the country its name, which was eventually anglicised to become New Zealand. ❑

Tasman then made another attempt to land, this time on what is now the Three Kings Islands (off Cape Reinga), but was again driven off by the Maori. His journal and incomplete chart nevertheless helped to establish the new country on explorers' maps.

James Cook Setting off from England in 1768 on the *Endeavour*, Cook's first goal was to sail to Tahiti to observe the transit of the sun by Venus (which helped astronomers to determine for the first time the distance from the earth to the sun). From there, he was to sail south in search of the unknown continent.

The coastline of New Zealand was first sighted on 6 October 1769, near Gisborne in the North Island. Cook eventually circumnavigated both islands (see pages 116–17), making charts of the coastline which were highly accurate, with two glaring exceptions: he thought that Banks Peninsula was an island, and that Stewart Island was attached to the mainland. His accounts of his voyage, the detailed descriptions of the flora and fauna (compiled by the ship's botanists Joseph Banks and Daniel Solander), and the artist Sydney Parkinson's sketches of the land and its peoples, brought New Zealand to the attention of the world. Cook returned to New Zealand in 1773 and again in 1777.

Later explorers The French navigator Jean-François Marie de Surville anchored in Doubtless Bay just two months after Cook had arrived in New Zealand, but after a violent clash with the Maori he sailed away after doing no more than chart the bay. He was followed two years later by a compatriot, Marion du Fresne, who believed that he was the first to rediscover the country after Tasman (Cook's data had not yet been published), and claimed it for France. After several weeks of friendly relations with the Maori, du Fresne and 13 of his crew were killed and eaten – probably because of a careless infringement of the Maori system of behaviour (see pages 30–1). The remaining crew butchered nearly 300 Maori in revenge. Several other expeditions followed, and by the end of the 18th century sealers and whalers were also arriving on New Zealand's shores.

Abel Tasman (left) was the first European to sight New Zealand but Cook (right) was the first to land. Below: Cook's ships

Traders and missionaries

■ Hard on the heels of the explorers came the European traders, intent on profiting from natural resources such as flax, timber, seal skins and whale oil in this rich land. By the beginning of the 19th century, missionaries had also begun to settle in New Zealand. ■

❑ Cook had first introduced potatoes to New Zealand, and the Maori quickly learned to cultivate them: they were easier to grow than kumara and gave bigger yields. Ironically, the time saved by growing potatoes also meant there was more time to spend fighting. Pigs (likewise introduced by Cook) were also reared for barter. Nails, blankets, axes and of course muskets were trading priorities for the Maori. Woodcarvings and shrunken human heads were much in demand by trading Pakeha (the Maori term for Europeans). ❑

Sealers and whalers From the 1790s onwards ships started landing shore parties around the coast of the South Island to hunt for fur seals. Often these men were marooned for months (sometimes years) in the harshest of conditions, but the seals were easy to kill and they could collect thousands of skins in a season. Within 30 years the seal population had been decimated and the trade was no longer profitable.

By the turn of the century whaling ships, hunting sperm whale offshore, were calling in at the Bay of Islands for reprovisioning. In the 1820s this led to the establishment of the first permanent European settlement in the country, at Kororareka (Russell). Around this time shore-based whaling stations were also being established, most of them in the South Island.

Flax and timber New Zealand flax was much in demand for making ropes and cordage, and the flax fibre prepared by the Maori was of good quality and attracted a high price. These traditional methods (which involved scraping away the fleshy part with a mussel shell) were unable to keep pace with demand, however, and mass production proved impractical. The trade lasted into the 20th century and was to prove far-reaching in its effects: it was largely through bartering flax for muskets that the Maori first acquired firearms. Europeans had already introduced diseases (such as gonorrhoea, measles and smallpox) to which the Maori had no resistance and which had a devastating effect

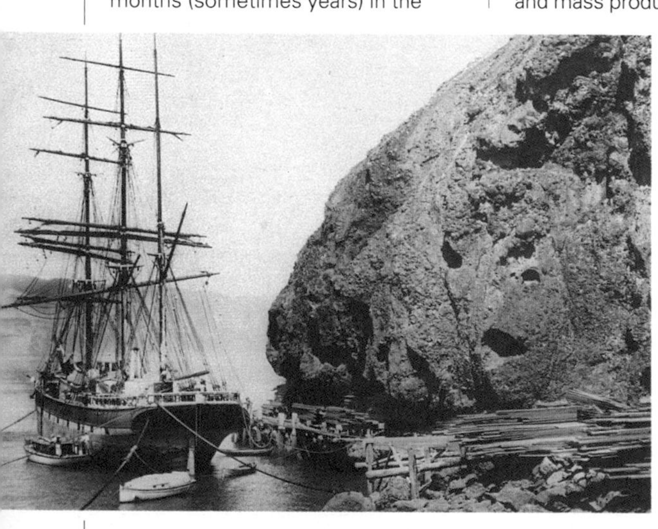

Loading kauri near Auckland in 1909

on the population. But worse was to come: the introduction of the musket added a lethal dimension to traditional inter-tribal warfare.

A longer-lived trade was provided by New Zealand's forests, which over more than a century of intensive exploitation yielded vast quantities of high-quality timber (see pages 76-7).

The missionaries Although there were never large numbers of missionaries in New Zealand at any one time, their influence was considerable – not necessarily in converting the Maori, but in protecting them from the worst excesses of unlawful adventurers and teaching them new skills, and in helping to influence the introduction of British jurisdiction and, eventually, sovereignty

The first Anglican mission station was established in 1814 by the Reverend Samuel Marsden in the Bay of Islands, although it was well over a decade before any converts were made. Wesleyan and Roman Catholic missionaries soon followed. The first printing press was set up by William Colenso, and the Bible, prayer books and hymns were translated into Maori. The missionaries

New Zealand's first missionary, the Reverend Samuel Marsden, lands at the Bay of Islands

had some success in discouraging polygamy and cannibalism, but in changing Maori society they inevitably destroyed much that was of value in the traditional culture.

❑ In 1820, the Ngapuhi chief Hongi Hika sailed to England to help scholars compile a Maori dictionary. Whilst there, he was presented to King George IV and showered with gifts, which he exchanged in Sydney on the return journey for 300 muskets. Once home, he embarked on a series of devastating campaigns against his old enemies in the Thames area and then the Waikato. The other tribes soon realised that they too must have muskets and a series of battles to settle old scores left some 60,000 dead. By 1830 the fighting had died down and most tribes were once more at peace with each other. ❑

■ Despite the rich resources of New Zealand, the British Crown was reluctant to take it on as a colony. However, with the signing of the Treaty of Waitangi in 1840, Britain assumed sovereignty over the land. This turning point in New Zealand's history is still a source of contention today. ■

Towards annexation The increasing lawlessness of many settlers led to calls for the imposition of law and order, and in 1823 the jurisdiction of the New South Wales courts was extended to New Zealand – though, given the difficulty of trying cases even in Sydney, this was largely a meaningless gesture. In 1833 the British Government appointed James Busby as the first British Resident, but he had limited legal powers and no military back-up; the Maori dubbed him 'the man-o'-war without guns'.

Maori chiefs sign the Treaty of Waitangi, which they understood as a pact with Queen Victoria

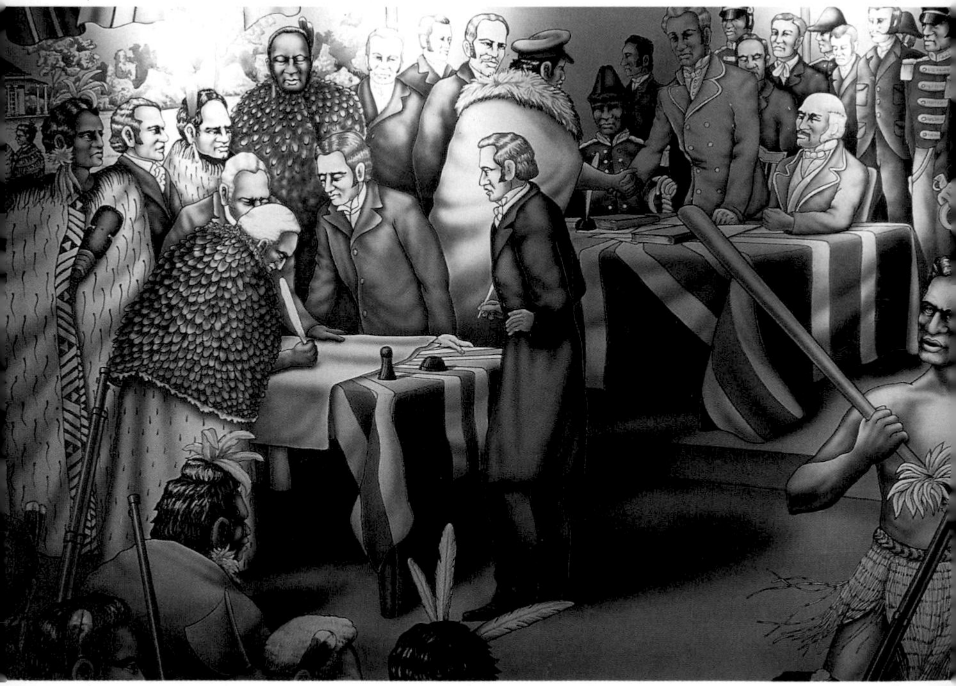

❑ On 5 February 1840, over 400 Maori gathered on the lawns of Busby's house (now the Treaty House) in the Bay of Islands to hear the Treaty of Waitangi read out. Many powerful chiefs opposed it, and after some changes had been made, the Maori withdrew to debate the issues. The next day they returned and, despite initial reluctance, 45 Maori chiefs eventually signed. Over the following months the treaty was carried throughout the land and signed by over 500 Maori chiefs. ❑

❑ French navy ships sometimes visited New Zealand to support the Roman Catholic missionaries. Anti-French fears were fuelled by a bizarre incident in 1837, when the self-styled Baron Charles Philip Hippolytus de Thierry proclaimed himself the Sovereign Chief of New Zealand and raised his own colourful flag on land he had bought at Hokianga. The threat soon receded, however, when he ran out of money. ❑

Captain Hobson oversaw the transfer of sovereignty to the British

During this period immigration (particularly from New South Wales) was increasing, and speculators were 'buying' vast tracts of land in dubious deals with the Maori; the threat from the French (however insignificant) and the initiation of mass settlement schemes fuelled the call for action. Busby was replaced by Captain William Hobson, who arrived in the Bay of Islands on 29 January 1840 with orders to negotiate with the Maori for the transfer of sovereignty to the British Crown.

The Treaty of Waitangi Hobson and his staff quickly drafted an agreement which they hoped would protect the rights of both the Maori and the settlers. The result was the Treaty of Waitangi, which was signed on 6 February 1840. Although this day has ever since been celebrated as the birth date of the nation, in fact the treaty was little more than a legal fraud. The ramifications of the errors contained in this document are still being felt in New Zealand today.

The text of the treaty was in English with a rough translation into Maori (signed by most of the chiefs), with considerable differences between the two. Essentially it assigned sovereignty (for which the Maoris had no concept and which therefore could not be translated) over the country to the British Crown. In exchange, the Maori would receive protection, full rights as British subjects, and the full possession of their lands. The treaty also established a policy on land sales, granting the Crown exclusive rights to buy land and sell it on to settlers. This attempt at even-handedness went badly wrong as the Government had only meagre resources at its disposal, and the agreement was in any case rarely honoured by land-hungry settlers.

Land tenure To the Maori, land was Papa, the Earth Mother, and closely tied in to their spiritual well-being. Land was held by the *hapū* or *iwi* rather than any one individual, and the concept of 'selling' territory was completely unknown (it could only be taken by conquest). It is clear that early land deals were considered by the Maori more as leases. As settlers started arriving in large numbers they wanted more and more land, but the Maori were becoming increasingly reluctant to sell. And the fact that land was soon changing hands at 20 times the price paid to the Maori not unnaturally caused huge resentment.

Planned utopias

Even before the Treaty of Waitangi had been signed, ships were setting sail from England with the first colonists destined for a series of 'planned communities' in New Zealand. These idealistic schemes brought a flood of new immigrants to the country.

Wakefield was a visionary who wanted planned communities

The New Zealand Company The first of these schemes was organised by Edward Gibbon Wakefield, who in 1838 set up the New Zealand Company, with the aim of re-creating genteel farming communities in which labourers knew their place and landowners were gentlemen of status and privilege. The plan was to buy up land cheaply from the Maori and sell it on to capitalist investors, using the profits to pay the fares of the labourers who would work the newly established farms.

As rumours grew of the British Government's intention to conclude a treaty with the Maori, the New Zealand Company dispatched the *Tory* and its crew to buy land before the Crown acquired the sole rights to do so. One of their principal targets was Wellington, which was tipped to become the capital. But long before the *Tory* had reached New Zealand, Wakefield was already 'selling' land, recruiting settlers, and sending off the first passenger ships

Decline and fall Between 1839 and 1843 the New Zealand Company sent 57 ships with over 18,000 immigrants from England. Settlements were established at Wellington, Nelson, Wanganui and New Plymouth, but many were beset by problems such as poor land, absentee landlords and disputes with the Maori over ownership. Speculation eventually led to the collapse of the company in 1850; its remaining land was taken over by the Government.

Although Wakefield's schemes did not work out exactly as planned (and he had not reckoned with the labourers' desire to move out of the communities and farm their own plots), they did at least ensure a more orderly pattern of settlement than had been achieved earlier in Australia and Canada.

❑ Inspired by Wakefield's example (and in some cases supported by the New Zealand Company) other groups also tried to establish 'ideal communities'. Thus the Free Church of Scotland founded Dunedin in 1848, and the Canterbury Association established the Anglican community of Christchurch in 1850. ❑

The New Zealand Wars

■ Outwardly peaceful at the beginning of the 1840s, New Zealand was soon in the throes of a civil war (known variously as the Land Wars, the Maori Wars, or the New Zealand Wars – now the accepted term) which lasted for over two decades and led to over 1,000 deaths on each side. ■

❑ The injustices of land sales led directly to the formation of the Maori King Movement in 1858. Traditionally, Maori owed their allegiance to their *hapū* or *iwi*, but they hoped that by uniting under a paramount chief they would be able to protect their lands. Several North Island tribes proclaimed Te Wherowhero as their first king, Potatau I, but the movement was defeated in 1864. The Maori Queen is still an important figure, however. ❑

Trouble ahead Following the signing of the Treaty of Waitangi in 1840, it was not long before the weakness of the agreement and its ineffective enforcement led to inevitable clashes over land.

The fighting broke out in the Wairau Valley near Blenheim in 1843, when settlers from the New Zealand Company started surveying land still under dispute with the Lands Commissioner. The chiefs, Te Ruaparaha and Rangihaeata, burned the survey huts and then repelled an armed party sent after them, killing 22 men.

Bloody conflicts Full-scale war broke out in June 1860, when the Government attempted to support a fraudulent land purchase in the Waitara. The British troops were roundly defeated by the Maori tribe Te Ati Awa at Puketakauere, a battle which marked the start of 21 years of conflict – and which confirmed to the Maori that the Government could not be trusted in land disputes.

War quickly spread across the central North Island. The outcome would have been far worse for the Government but for the fact that many tribes joined the Government forces in order to settle old scores. Troops were brought from Sydney, and although the Maori fought ferociously and won many battles, they were eventually defeated by the force of artillery ranged against them.

Although hostilities officially ceased in 1872, skirmishes continued until the formal surrender of the Maori king in 1881. To punish the rebel tribes, the Government confiscated huge areas of land, in complete disregard of the Treaty of Waitangi.

Rebel leader Hone Heke cuts down the British flagstaff at Kororareka

NEW ZEALAND WAS *a social laboratory*

■ At the end of the 19th century New Zealand was in the depths of recession, but as the economy improved, important social reforms were introduced, and it became the first country in the world to enfranchise women and introduce an old-age pension. ■

Hard times During the 1860s, gold rushes brought prosperity to New Zealand (particularly in the South Island), but by the 1880s the gold rush was over, wool prices were low, and the country was gripped by depression. Despite the introduction in 1882 of refrigerated shipping, which allowed meat and butter to be exported for the first time, farmers suffered. Unemployment was on the increase and factory conditions were appalling, with ruthless exploitation of child labour.

Reforms In 1890, the Liberal Party was voted into power under the leadership of John Ballance, with a new mandate to improve living conditions. Large land-holdings were bought by the Government and broken up into smaller farms in order to help more families to aquire land. Farmers were also lent money at low interest rates, and with a rise in overseas prices for farm products small family farms became profitable. Country towns began to flourish, and as new communities grew, libraries and schools were built (free compulsory education had already been introduced in 1877). New laws were passed regulating conditions in factories, and in 1894 the world's first compulsory arbitration system for industrial disputes was introduced.

Votes for women Alcohol was strong, cheap and widely available in the late 19th century, when it was said there were only two causes of death in New Zealand – alcohol poisoning and drowning as a result of riding home drunk from the pub. In 1885 the Women's Christian Temperance Union was formed; having successfully stopped the sale of alcohol to children, its members went on to campaign for votes for women. Petitions were organised and politicians lobbied, and in 1893 New Zealand became the first country in the world to extend the vote to women.

Women got the vote in New Zealand in 1893 – a world first

❑ In Christchurch in 1907, Dr Truby King and his wife formed the Plunket Society, with the principal aim of training women in proper child care. Although the infant mortality rate in New Zealand was half as high (75 per thousand births) as it was in Britain, it was still a matter of concern in a young nation with a small population. Plunket nurses established a unique support network which still exists in New Zealand today: you will see signs to the 'Plunket Rooms' in almost every town in the country. ❑

Pensions and health care Ballance was succeeded as leader of the Liberals by 'King Dick' Seddon, a popular politician whose concern for the lot of the poor led him in 1898 to introduce the world's first old-age pension for men (women's pensions followed in 1911). Other pioneering measures followed and New Zealand gained a reputation as an important innovator of social reforms.

Turn of the century At the beginning of the century conditions improved considerably for the Pakeha (whites). The small family farm (averaging 40 hectares) became the most common business. At the same time there was a drift to North Island (the population of which exceeded that of South Island in 1896), and into the towns.

The Maori population, meanwhile, was in decline. Most families lived apart from the Pakeha in their own villages, but most of their land had either been sold or illegally 'confiscated' after the New Zealand Wars, and much of what was left was too remote or too poor to farm. Life was hard and diseases introduced by immigrants took a heavy toll. The population fell from an estimated 100,000 at the time of Cook's first visit in 1769, to around 42,000 in the 1896 census, although by 1901 it had risen again to just over 45,000.

Above: the Dunedin *carried the first cargo of frozen meat to England from New Zealand. Below: clearing the forested land for farming was arduous work*

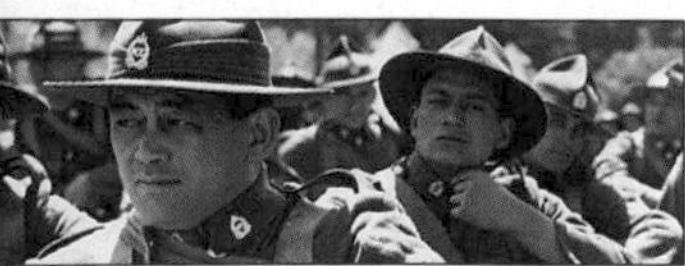

Although it was not to gain full independence until 1947, in the first half of the 20th century New Zealand was gradually gaining a sense of nationhood and of its own identity in the world.

First steps New Zealand was granted nominal self-government in 1852, but the British Crown still influenced legislation; it was not until the 1890s that the country gained proper control of its affairs (it would be another 50 years before full independence was achieved). In 1907, New Zealand was promoted from the rank of Colony to that of Dominion within the British Empire.

Birth of a nation In the 19th century the country was divided into six self-governing provinces (later expanded to ten), and people thought of themselves as 'Wellingtonians' or 'Aucklanders' rather than New Zealanders. The abolition of the provinces in 1876 broke down these barriers to some extent, but it was largely the introduction of telephones, the telegraph and roads and railways at the turn of the century that changed people's perception of New Zealand: from being a country of isolated coastal settlements it was now becoming a nation.

The first stirrings of nationhood came during the Boer War (1899–1902), when New Zealanders fought alongside British, Australian and Canadian troops. Used to long hours of riding and rough conditions, the New Zealanders made brilliant scouts and soon earned a reputation as 'the best soldiers in South Africa'.

World War I New Zealanders gained a new sense of identity and pride during World War I, when some 100,000 troops joined the Australia-New Zealand Army Corps (ANZAC) in Europe and the Middle East. Their finest hour (and greatest losses) came during the Battle of Gallipoli in April 1915, when 2,700 New Zealand troops were killed and 4,700 wounded

❑ After World War I, over 90 per cent of New Zealand's exports came from agriculture, but a dramatic drop in world prices for wool, meat and butter in the early 1920s hit farmers hard. The solution seemed to lie in increased production, and during this period New Zealand became one of the first countries in the world to apply scientific principles to farming, introducing top dressing for pasture and selective breeding of dairy herds. By the end of the 20s the average cow was producing 72 per cent more butterfat than it would have done at the beginning of the century. ❑

during an ill-fated but heroic attempt to capture the Gallipoli Peninsula. By the end of the war 16,317 had lost their lives and 41,262 more returned home wounded: the casualties were the highest per capita of any Allied country.

Troops landing at ANZAC Cove in 1915 during the ill-fated Gallipoli campaign

Labour Prime Minister 'Micky' Savage helped improve the lives of ordinary people

Inter-war years Despite increased agricultural production in the 1920s, the economy foundered and the Great Depression of the 1930s had a profound effect. Unemployment rose and work programmes were introduced under which thousands of hectares of pine forest were planted and many roads were built. In 1935, the new Labour Party swept to victory on a pledge of providing work, houses, schools and hospitals; as the world economy improved, bigger public projects (including hydroelectric schemes) were also funded. In 1938 Prime Minister Michael Savage announced the introduction of comprehensive health care and a social security system for those unable to work – another world first for New Zealand.

World War II At the outbreak of war in 1939, New Zealand readily joined the Allies again. New Zealanders, including some 17,000 Maori, many in the famous Maori Battalion, fought with distinction in the Pacific, Crete, Italy and North Africa. Of the 200,000 who fought, 11,600 died and a further 15,700 were wounded.

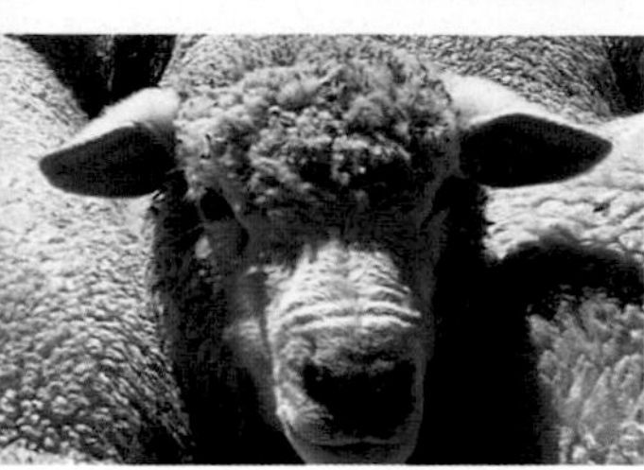

■ Heavily dependent on agricultural exports, New Zealand has had to learn some painful economic lessons in recent decades. The prosperity it enjoyed after World War II gave way in the 1970s to devastating recession. Despite drastic measures, this only deepened in the 1980s. If there are now signs of recovery, the profitable tourist industry is a major contributor. ■

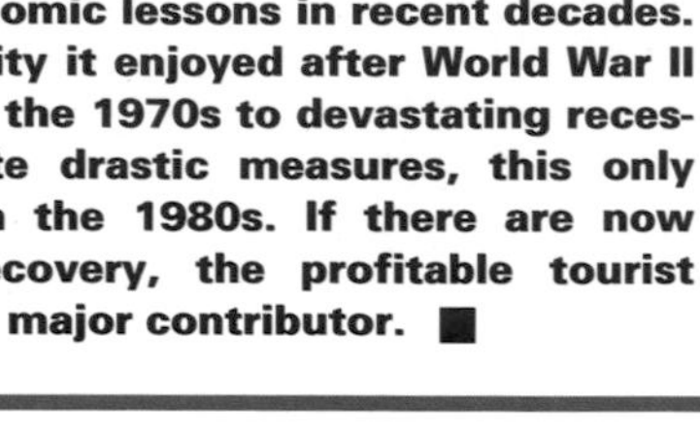

Post-war prosperity After World War II the economy prospered, with prices for meat, wool and butter at a premium, and New Zealand enjoyed one of the highest standards of living in the world.

Apart from a brief period (1957–60) when Labour was in power, post-war politics between 1949 and 1972 were dominated by the National Party. One of their first actions (1950) was to abolish the Legislative Council, Parliament's upper house, and although they promised to replace it with an elected body, this never happened.

Protest and survival Largely isolated and culturally stagnant in the 1950s, New Zealand was shaken out of its complacency in the following decade by the arrival of jet travel and television. The anti-war movement (calling for the withdrawal of NZ troops from Vietnam sent there in 1965) gathered strength. The country's first big environmental protest took place in the 1960s, prompted by a controversial plan to raise the level of Lake Manapouri in order to produce cheap hydroelectric power for the aluminium smelter at Bluff. In 1972 a nationalistic Labour government was elected under Norman Kirk. It gained instant popularity by withdrawing the troops from Vietnam, but the new mood of optimism was not to last long.

Recession Until the 1970s, Britain had been New Zealand's main export market (taking some 90 per cent of all produce), but when it joined the European Economic Community (EEC) in 1973, this market was effectively closed off. Combined with a steep rise in oil prices, this had a devastating effect on the economy. New markets had to be sought, but a

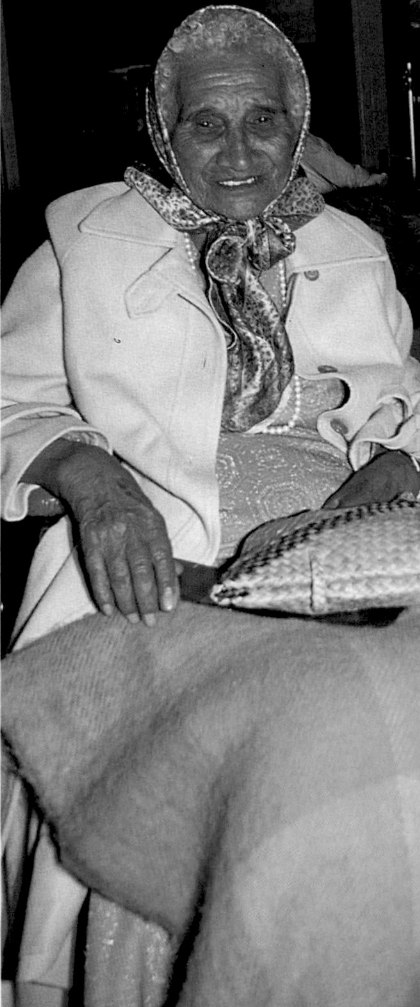

Maori Dame Whina Cooper was an inspirational leader of her people

Prime Minister David Lange oversaw extensive reforms

decade of recession followed and unemployment, violent crime, bad housing and other social problems resurfaced.

This fragmentation of society led to demands for change, and to the growth of movements for the rights of women, gays and Maoris. In 1975, Dame Whina Cooper (later affectionately dubbed 'the mother of the nation') led the Maori Land March from Northland to the capital in order to call attention to the injustices of the loss of ancestral lands, which resulted in the setting up of the Waitangi Tribunal by the Government.

Also in 1975, Labour was ousted by the National Party, led by the abrasive Robert Muldoon. Strict measures were imposed on immigration, imports and the dollar, but by the end of the decade inflation was running at 17 per cent and eventually the Government even subsidised farm prices. With registered unemployment reaching 66,534 by 1984, Muldoon was defeated in a snap election by a revitalised Labour Party, under the leadership of David Lange.

The Lange years New Zealand's youngest Prime Minister this century, David Lange initiated a wide-reaching programme of economic reforms designed to put the country back on its feet. These included floating the Kiwi dollar, deregulating the economy, reducing tariffs, selling nationalised industries and removing farm subsidies at a stroke. This painful medicine caused numerous business failures and, combined with the stock market crash of 1987, sent the New Zealand economy into a tailspin.

In August 1989 David Lange unexpectedly resigned and after the interim leadership of two of his deputies, Labour lost power once more to the National Party, led this time by Jim Bolger.

During the 1980s New Zealand was also re-orientating itself towards its Pacific neighbours, in particular Australia. A free trade agreement had been reached as early as 1965, but in 1983 this was replaced with the more far-reaching Closer Economic Relations Trade Agreement (CER). From 1 July 1990, this allowed unrestricted trade between the two countries.

Since the beginning of the 1990s there has been an overall growth in the country's economy, particularly in tourism, which now accounts for half of New Zealand's annual revenues from overseas.

The office blocks of Auckland's business area cheek by jowl with the marina

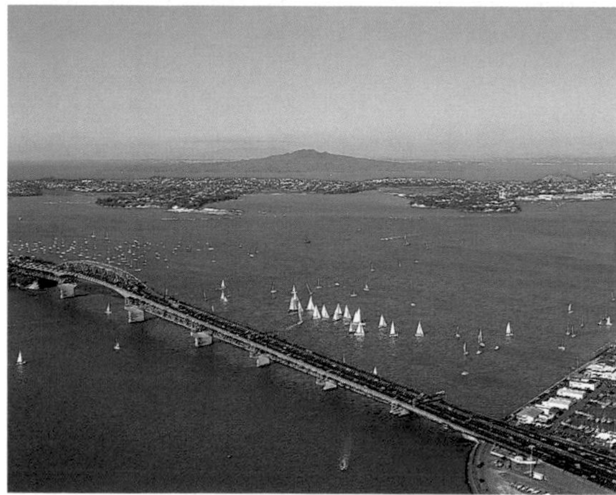

Start of a yacht race by the Auckland Harbour bridge

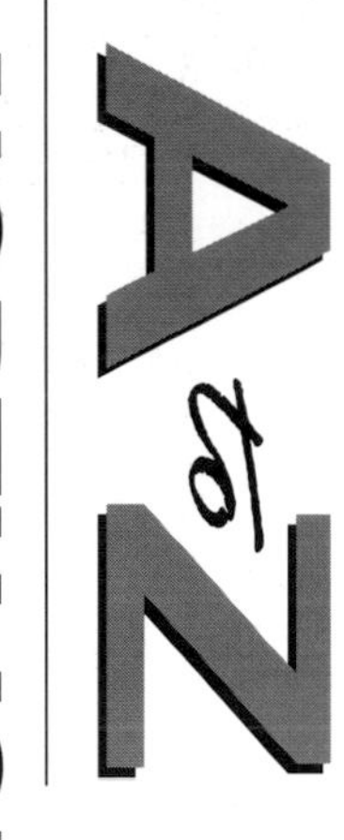

Auckland The gateway to New Zealand for most international visitors, Auckland is the country's largest and most cosmopolitan city, with a plethora of prestigious museums and galleries, smart restaurants and wine bars, excellent shops and numerous other attractions. Around a third of the country's population (just over a million people) live, work and play here. Aucklanders enjoy an undeniably appealing lifestyle in a city which combines sophisticated culture with proximity to sheltered harbours and islands, countless surf or swimming beaches, and outlying forests and parklands.

Auckland sprawls across a narrow volcanic isthmus facing two huge natural harbours, **Waitemata Harbour** to the east (which opens out into the Hauraki Gulf) and **Manukau Harbour** to the west. The isthmus was formed as a result of the eruption of over 50 volcanoes; the oldest dates back just 50,000 years, and the youngest erupted from the sea a mere 750 years ago.

The first Polynesians are said to have settled in the Hauraki Gulf after arriving in the canoe *Tainui* some 600 years ago. As other tribes descended on this fertile area they built numerous strongholds on the volcanic cones. By the 18th century nearly all of them were topped by *pa* sites, but by the mid-19th century inter-tribal warfare and epidemics of introduced diseases had wiped out most of the Maori population.

After the signing of the Treaty of Waitangi in 1840, Governor Hobson moved the capital of New Zealand south from Kororareka (Russell) to Auckland, partly because of the advantages offered by its vast harbours and fertile soil. That year, the British bought 1,200 hectares of land from the Ngati Whatua for a collection of blankets, clothes, pots, tobacco and pipes, plus a small cash sum; on 18 September 1840, the Union Jack was run up the flagpole and the settlement was proclaimed the capital. Hobson named the city after his former commander, Lord Auckland, then Viceroy of India. Auckland remained the capital until 1865, when the centre of government was moved further south again to the New Zealand Company settlement at Wellington.

Today Auckland's port handles much of the country's import and export trade and the city is one of its fastest-growing urban areas, with a highly cosmopolitan population that includes not only some 150,000 Pacific Islanders, but also a sizeable Asian community.

Orientation The main artery of downtown Auckland is **Queen Street**, which runs southwards from **Queen Elizabeth Square**. In and around Queen Street you will find many of the major shops, hotels, airline offices, cinemas and other facilities. Flanking Queen Elizabeth Square are **Customs Street** and **Quay Street**, both parallel to the waterfront. This is a lively area, with restaurants overlooking a constant procession of ferries and other craft; it is also home to the excellent **National Maritime Museum**. Arching across the harbour to the west is the harbour bridge, the main road link with the North Shore and the motorway up to Whangarei and Northland.

About halfway up Queen Street lies Aotea Square, the site of the massive **Aotea Centre** (with convention and theatre facilities), the main **Auckland Visitor Centre**, and

Pacific capital
In the 1950s Auckland began to attract thousands of Polynesian Islanders, drawn by opportunities for work and education. There are now some 100,000 Samoans in New Zealand, with more people from the Cook Islands and Nuie resident in the country than in their homelands. With good reason, Auckland has styled itself 'the hub of the Pacific'.

the city's original town hall (built in 1911 and currently undergoing restoration). One block to the east is the **City Art Gallery**, backing on to **Albert Park** and the main **Auckland University** campus.

To the east of the central downtown district are the undulating grounds of the **Auckland Domain**, dominated by the **Auckland Museum**. Beyond here are the trendy 'suburbs' of **Parnell** and **Remuera**, spreading back down to the waterfront, which offers attractions such as **Kelly Tarlton's Antarctic Encounter and Underwater World** and the popular beach at **Mission Bay**.

Auckland's skyline will have a dramatic new addition with the opening in 1997 of the **Sky Tower**, part of the Sky City casino, hotel and shopping complex. The 328m-high building will feature two enclosed observation decks

and a revolving bar and restaurant with 360-degree panoramas of the city.

Auckland is said to have more boats per head of population than any other city in the world, and on any sunny weekend (or even a rainy one) a fleet of yachts, speedboats, dinghies, cruisers and catamarans fans out from the marinas, bound for the **islands and beaches** of the **Hauraki Gulf** and elsewhere. For those without access to a boat, numerous public ferries also ply the harbour waters, and there are said to be over a hundred mainland beaches within an hour's drive of the city centre.

Auckland's attractions are fairly widely spread out across the city; fortunately there is a good bus network, including tourist buses which shuttle around the various sightseeing spots.

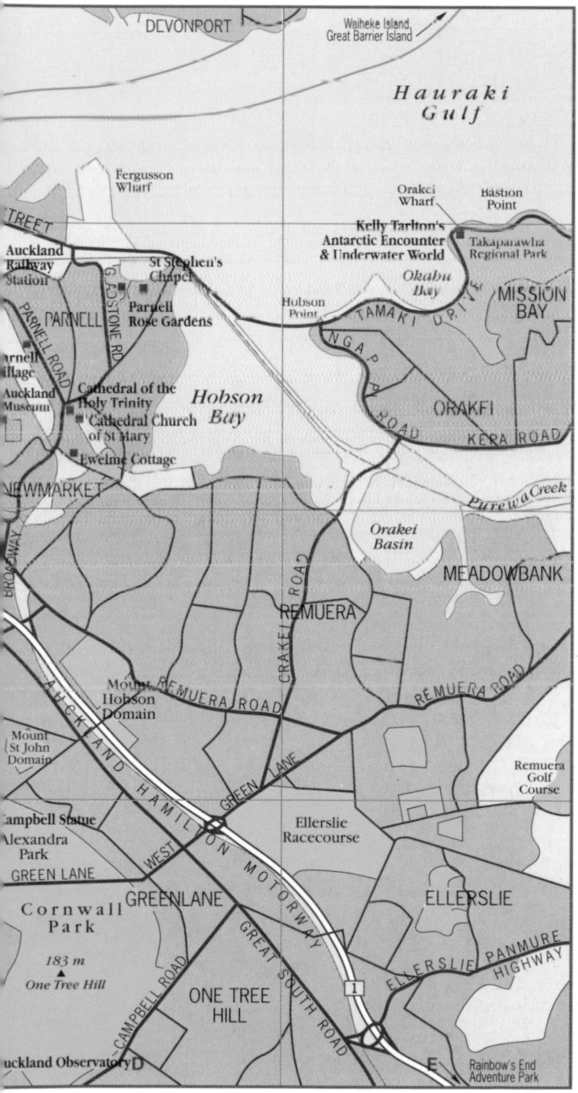

Auckland's Old Town Hall

Harbour sailing
Every visitor to the 'City of Sails' should go sailing on the harbour at least once. The Pride of Auckland Company (tel: 09 373 4557) has a fleet of five monohulls and catamarans which operate regular 'Experience Sailing' trips (*Open* daily 3pm) as well as various other options, including lunch or dinner cruises. The square-rigged brigantine *Soren Larsen* (tel: 09 445 9044) operates day trips during the summer. Confident sailors can hire a sailing boat from the Rangitoto Sailing Centre (tel: 09 358 2324) at Hobson's Wharf; the Centre also offers 12-hour learn-to-sail courses.

Visitor Information
The central Visitor Information Centre in Auckland is on Aotea Square (299 Queen Street, tel: 09 366 6888. *Open* daily 9–5); there is also an information kiosk in Queen Elizabeth Square at the bottom end of Queen Street, open the same hours.

Maori song and dance
Some of the best introductions to Maori culture are the regular shows held at the Auckland Museum. Preceded by a guided tour of the Maori exhibits, the half-hour shows (*Open* daily 11.15am and 12.45pm. *Admission charge* moderate) take place in front of the Hotunui meeting house and feature numerous *haka* (dances) with plenty of explanations and audience participation. The only tour company owned and operated by Maoris within the Auckland region is Maori Heritage Tours (tel: 09 235 1341) who run a range of interesting city and country tours from a Maori perspective, including 'twilight Maori experience' with a *hangi* and cultural show on a *marae*.

▶▶▶ Auckland Domain and Museum *49D3*

Auckland's biggest park, the Domain occupies a large wedge between the city centre and the eastern suburbs, with some 80 hectares of sports fields, landscaped gardens and wooded areas.

Crowning the central hilltop is the **Auckland Museum▶▶▶** (*Open* daily 10–5. *Admission free*/donation), housing extensive displays of Maori arts and culture, including the magnificent carved meeting house *Hotunui* (1878), elaborate gateways and store houses, and the great war canoe *Te Toki a Tapiri* ('Tapiri's battle-axe'). Built in about 1836, this was the last of the great Maori war canoes, capable of carrying up to a hundred warriors. There are also interesting displays on Pacific canoes and the decorative arts of Asia, an extensive natural history section, and a Weird and Wonderful children's discovery centre. The second-floor galleries devoted to New Zealand's military history include a new Spitfire and Zero gallery (with one of the few surviving Japanese Zero planes), an armoury display, and presentations on Kiwis at war.

The excellent range of items in the ground-floor shop includes hand-crafted jade, glass, ceramics and bone, as well as *paua* shell jewellery, knitwear and books.

Just near the museum, the **Winter Gardens▶** (*Open* daily 10–4. *Admission free*) are housed in a wonderful glass conservatory overflowing with tropical and sub-tropical plants and ferns.

▶▶▶ Auckland Zoo *48A3*

Western Springs
Open: daily 9.30–5.30, last admission 4.15. Admission charge: moderate.

Established in 1922, Auckland Zoo houses around 900 bird and animal species, ranging from Asian elephants to tuatara and other unique New Zealand fauna. Like all the best modern zoos, it has recently moved away from the 'animals in cages' formula to embrace a much wider perspective on the environment and to provide more naturalistic enclosures for the animals.

Recently developed exhibits include a meerkat enclosure (you can crawl through underground tunnels and pop up for a ground-level view of the enchanting meerkats), a new elephant enclosure, the Tui farm (hands-on farm activities for children), and the Qantas Aviary of the Forest. The latest project is a vast Rainforest exhibit, with five species of primate swinging free in the forest trees, and an adventure pathway including a platform in the tree canopy. Other future projects include a Night Forest exhibit (with bats, morepork, kiwi, tuatara, geckos, weta and glow-worms) and a Tiger River habitat for the Sumatran tigers.

The zoo is at Western Springs (bus 045 from downtown) and is linked by tramway and vintage bus to the nearby MOTAT (see page 53).

▶▶ City Art Gallery *48C3*

5 Kitchener Street
Open: daily 10–4.30; Friday until 8pm.

Opened in 1888, this was New Zealand's first permanent art gallery, and now houses one of the country's most significant collections of national and international art. The international collection spans European art (from the 13th century to Impressionism and after), Japanese prints and contemporary American works, while the national collection features some of the earliest Pakeha paintings in New Zealand (dating from Cook's voyages) together with works by C. F. Goldie, Gottfried Lindauer, Frances Hodgkins and other celebrated New Zealand artists. Exhibitions in the Heritage Gallery change frequently; the ground floor (free) exhibits are from the permanent collection; the first floor (usually a 'pay' area) has touring and international exhibitions.

In the City Art Gallery (below) Lindauer's Maori portraits chronicle the meeting of two cultures

Across the road from the main building, the New Gallery is a recent extension (opened in 1995) housed inside the former central Auckland telephone exchange building. This interesting project has been designed as a 'walk through' space linking Wellesley Street and Khartoum Place, with shops and cafés alongside the exhibition areas. The New Gallery focuses on contemporary New Zealand and international art and includes a gallery devoted to Colin McCahon, regarded by many as the country's foremost 20th-century artist.

Some scenes from the film The Piano *were shot inside Ewelme Cottage*

Market days
One of the best markets in the city is the Victoria Park Market (Victoria Street West. *Open* Mon–Sat 9–7; Sun 10–7), housed in a rambling old building with shops, cafés and stalls on several levels. At weekends there are outdoor performances and live music. Another good place for browsing is the China Oriental Markets warehouse (2 Britomart Place. *Open* daily 10–6) which has over 100 stalls with crafts, oriental herbs and so on, as well as an ethnic 'food street'. In the heart of Auckland's Polynesian community, the Otara Market (Newbury Street, Otara. *Open* Sat 6am–12 noon) has a lively atmosphere, with stalls selling food, clothing, arts and crafts and plenty more besides.

▶▶ Historic houses *48C2, 48B1, 49D3*

Open: daily 10.30–12, 1–4.30. Admission charge: inexpensive.

Auckland is not as well endowed with historic buildings as some other cities in the country, but it does have several historic homes under the protection of the Historic Places Trust. One of the finest of these houses is **Highwic▶▶** (40 Gillies Ave, Epsom), a 'colonial gentleman's residence' in the timber Gothic style built in 1862 by Alfred Buckland, a wealthy landowner and racing enthusiast.

Another impressive private mansion is **Alberton▶▶** (100 Mt Albert Rd) which was built in the same year and has exotic Indian-style verandas and towers. The more homely **Ewelme Cottage▶▶** (14 Ayr St, Parnell) is a fascinating cottage built in kauri wood which remained in the same family for 105 years and still contains many of their furnishings and personal effects.

▶▶▶ Kelly Tarlton's Antarctic Encounter and Underwater World *49E3*

23 Tamaki Drive

Open: daily 9am–9pm, last admissions 8pm. Admission charge: expensive.

Built in 1985 inside a series of underground storm-water storage tanks near Orakei Wharf to the east of the city centre, Underwater World was developed by the diver and wreck expert Kelly Tarlton. Its main feature is a vast aquarium with a moving walkway inside an acrylic tunnel, offering a fish-eye view of stingrays and reef fish, moray eels and several species of shark.

Linked to it is Antarctic Encounter, which opened in 1993. This starts with a replica – complete with sounds and smells – of the hut Scott used on his ill-fated expedition to the South Pole. A heated snow cat then carries visitors through a simulated snowstorm to an Antarctic landscape complete with a breeding colony of king penguins.

Antarctic Encounter and Underwater World is 6km from the city centre; several buses (including the Explorer Bus) run regularly from downtown.

►► Mount Eden 48C2

Auckland's highest volcanic cone (196m), Mount Eden used to be one of the best places to go for a panoramic view of the city and its isthmus and harbour – but in 1997 there will be the Sky Tower, not only over 130m higher but also centrally located downtown. Mount Eden is still worth a visit, however, principally to see the extensive earthworks and terracing which once protected this fortified site. The entrance is on Mount Eden Road, 15 minutes' drive from downtown (or take bus 274 or 275 from Customs Street East).

► Museum of Transport and Technology (MOTAT) 48B2

Western Springs
Open: weekdays 9–5; weekends 10–5. Admission charge: moderate.

Close to Auckland Zoo, the Museum of Transport and Technology contains a vast collection of vintage machinery and equipment, ranging from trucks, trains and trams to early computers, telephones, printing presses and much more. Of particular interest are the remains of the plane flown by Richard Pearce, the pioneering South Island aviator (see page 216).

The main site, MOTAT 1, is linked to MOTAT 2 (1km away) by a tramway to near the Auckland Zoo entrance where it connects with a vintage bus. MOTAT 2 houses the aviation collection, with a fascinating range of exhibits

The Auckland Card
The Auckland Card covers excursions and entry to a number of key attractions at an all-in price. Valid for three days, it includes Kelly Tarlton's Antarctic Encounter and Underwater World and, the National Maritime Museum, a Fullers harbour cruise, and a one-day Explorer bus pass: it also offers a number of discounts at other attractions and some shops and restaurants, but unless you take up all the offers, you may find it is cheaper to pay for everything separately. The Auckland Card costs $69 from Visitor Information Centres and selected travel agents.

Earthworks in Mount Eden's crater above the city

The marina at the National Maritime Museum

Thrills and spills
A big attraction for children in the Auckland area is the Rainbow's End Adventure Park, which features a rollercoaster, flume rides, a pirate ship, and numerous other rides and shows. Rainbow's End (*Open* daily 10–5. *Admission charge* expensive) is near the Manukau exit on the southern motorway, 15 mins from the centre of Auckland.

which includes the last Solent Mark IV flying boat left in the world.

MOTAT 1 is at Western Springs, on the Great North Road ten minutes' drive from downtown (bus 045 from Customs Street East).

▶▶▶ New Zealand National Maritime Museum, Hobson Wharf *48C4*

Eastern Viaduct, Quay Street
Open: daily 9–6 in summer; 9–5 in winter. Admission charge: moderate.

This excellent museum, right in the heart of the city on the harbour front, is a 'must see' for every visitor to Auckland, a dynamic and imaginative celebration of New Zealand's maritime heritage and the voyaging traditions and craft of the Pacific. You can easily spend several hours here watching craftsmen at work, admiring the many boats, taking a ride on a steam launch, listening to old mariners' tales in an oral history section, or exploring the interior of an immigrant ship. As well as a dockside restaurant, there is a nautical emporium with a good range of souvenirs.

Based around a marina, the museum includes displays on New Zealand yachting, whaling, Polynesian voyagers, seaports and much more. In the marina itself is a waterborne collection of Pacific Island canoes, veteran power and sail craft, and a massive 1926 steam crane-ship. Grouped around the marina are workshops for boatbuilders, sail-makers, riggers and wood-turners.

Outside the museum stands *KZ1*, the controversial contender for the 1988 America's Cup. You can take harbour cruises on board the scow *Ted Ashby* (daily 1pm. *Admission charge* moderate) or the steam launch *Puke* (Sun 11am. *Admission free*).

▶ One Tree Hill *49D1*

Nearly all the extinct volcanic cones in the Auckland area were used by the Maori as fortified hill settlements, but One Tree Hill was one of the biggest and most extensive, capable of sheltering up to 4,000 warriors. The volcanic crater was surrounded by a number of smaller 'satellite' *pā* sites, with the remains of the ditches and ramparts still visible today. The entrance is on Manukau Road (bus 302, 304, 305 or 312 from downtown).

▶▶ Parnell *49D3*

On the east side of the Domain from the downtown area, Parnell is one of Auckland's oldest inner city suburbs. At the beginning of the century it was one of the most desirable addresses in Auckland, but then fell into decline until it was redeveloped in the 1960s and 1970s, with the accent on restoration of the many old family houses and shops in the area. Today it is a hive of activity, with dozens of trendy boutiques, ethnic restaurants, wine bars, art galleries and craft and curio stores.

The main thoroughfare is **Parnell Road**, with restaurants and shops running all the way down the hill on both sides of the street. Halfway down on the west side is **Parnell Village**, with wooden bridges and old brick pavements linking a series of little shopping enclaves in and around restored Victorian houses.

Between November and March, it is worth wandering down to the **Parnell Rose Gardens**▶ (Gladstone Road. *Open* daylight hours. *Admission free*), where thousands of roses bloom. Just across from the rose gardens is **St Stephen's Chapel**▶ (Judge Street), in a lovely setting overlooking the harbour. Completed in 1857, this tiny wooden chapel is one of the best examples in the city of a 'Selwyn' church, built in a Gothic style which evolved under Bishop Selwyn (1809–78), characterised by steep-pitched shingle roofs, external timber buttresses and leaded windows.

At the top end of Parnell Road is the recently expanded **Cathedral of the Holy Trinity** (*Open* weekdays 9.30–4, weekends 2–5), which has been the subject of considerable controversy because of the use of virgin kauri wood (now extremely rare) in its construction. Just behind it is the lovely **Cathedral Church of Saint Mary**▶ (*Open* as above), another wooden church with some fine stained glass; built in 1888, it was moved here in 1982.

Bussing it

Auckland's biggest bus business, the Yellow Bus Company, has routes linking most major attractions, and a one-day Busabout pass gives you unlimited travel from 9am weekdays, any time at weekends; for details, call Buz-a-Bus (09 366 6400). An even easier option (although pricier) is the United Airlines Explorer Bus, which does a circuit of all the major attractions hourly, allowing visitors to hop on and off as they wish (departures on the hour 10am–4pm from the Ferry Building, tel: 09 360 0033).

Eat, drink and people-watch in trendy Parnell

A signal station on Mount Victoria above the waterfront suburb of Devonport

Auckland environs

▶▶ Devonport 49D4

One of the most enjoyable ways to spend a day or an afternoon in Auckland is to hop on one of the regular ferries to the historic suburb of Devonport, on the end of the North Shore peninsula.

Devonport was the landing place of the great canoe *Tainui* in the 14th century (commemorated by a bronze sculpture on the King Edward Parade foreshore); it was later one of the first areas to be settled by Europeans, and has many well-preserved old buildings.

Stepping ashore on the **Devonport Wharf** (recently redeveloped to include a host of shops and dockside eating places), you emerge at the bottom of **Victoria Road**, the main thoroughfare, lined with bookshops, craft galleries, outdoor cafés and antique and souvenir shops. Halfway up the road is **Brian Jackson's Museum of Automobilia, Sounds and Victoriana▶▶** (*Open* daily 10–5. *Admission charge* moderate), an eclectic private collection whose name is self-explanatory.

At the end of Victoria Road a pathway leads up to the top of **Mount Victoria▶▶**, an extinct volcanic cone with the outlines of ancient Maori fortifications clearly visible around the summit. There are terrific views of the **Hauraki Gulf**, with an orientation table identifying off-shore islands.

From the park at the bottom of Victoria Road it is a pleasant stroll along the seafront to the **North Head Historic Reserve▶** (*Open* daily 6am–10pm. *Admission free*) at the very tip of the peninsula. This is another volcanic cone, riddled with gun emplacements (including a rare 'disappearing gun') and tunnels which were dug during the 19th century, when there were fears of a Russian invasion. On the other side of the headland is the long sweep of **Cheltenham Beach**, overlooking Rangitoto Island.

In the other direction along the seafront is **Anne Street**, with quaint Victorian houses. Further along, Spring Street leads to the **Royal New Zealand Navy Museum** (*Open* daily 10–4.30. *Admission free*), which traces the Navy's development from the early days.

Ferries to Devonport
Fullers Ferries run to Devonport from the Downtown Ferry Terminal (Pier 1) every half-hour between 6.15am and 9.15am, and 10am to 6.30pm, and hourly from 7PM to 11pm Mon–Thu, 1am Sat and Sun mornings, 10pm Sun. The crossing takes 10–15 minutes and costs $7 return.

Urban Pacific chic

■ A movement that began quietly several years ago and was given impetus by the film *Once Were Warriors*, 'urban Pacific chic' is a fusion of cultures which represents an upsurge in pride in the Maori and Polynesian heritage of New Zealand. ■

From souvenirs to street cred Until recently, Kiwis (whether Maori or Pakeha) tended to look down on things with a Maori theme. Polynesian influences, too, seemed to be limited to bright floral shirts or shell necklaces. But now a new generation of young Maori and Polynesian designers, artists and musicians has sparked off a revival in traditional culture, interweaving conventional styles and textiles, high fashion, rap music and street wear to forge their own look and create a new style: 'urban Pacific chic'. The *lava-lava* (a Polynesian 'skirt' for men) may still take some bravado to wear, but *tapa* (a papery textile made from beaten tree bark) is increasingly being used for clothes, hats and bags.

Haka rap The ancient rhythms and chants of Maori or Polynesian music are being rediscovered and reworked into a distinctive contemporary sound. The arrival of hip-hop and rap music (which also rely on beats and chant-like deliveries) has been instrumental in the creation of a new hybrid, blending the beat with old songs, *poi* rhythms, and the melodic Maori flute. Artists such as Maree Sheehan and Emma Paki are part of this new Pacific sound, whilst the popular NZ band Crowded House used a group of Cook Island log drummers and a Maori choir on a recent album.

Tattoo you Tattooing is now in vogue again, a revival inspired partly by the film *Once Were Warriors*, which tells the stylised story of a Maori street gang, fully tattooed and proud to be Maori. Traditional curvilinear patterns are now combined with contemporary designs.

Pacific festival
The annual Pasifika Games, with their sporting events and dance festivals, are a melting pot of Auckland's Pacific community, with the sounds and colours of the Pacific mingling in a blur of cultures from Maori, Samoan, Chinese, Cook Island and Niuean peoples.

Maori design has gained impetus from Once Were Warriors

Island ferries
Marine transport throughout the Hauraki Gulf is dominated by the Fullers cruise and ferry company, with a fleet of vessels ranging from cargo and passenger monohulls to purpose-built cruise catamarans. Departures to Rangitoto are four times daily, to Motutapu and Motuihe three times weekly, to Waiheke seven times daily, and to Great Barrier Island four times weekly. There are many more sailings in summer. Fullers also offer a variety of packages including accommodation and tours on the islands. For full details contact: Fullers Cruise Centre, Ferry Building, Quay Street (tel: 09 367 9111/fax: 09 367 9116).

▶▶▶ Hauraki Gulf (south) *49E4*

It is no wonder that so many people in Auckland own boats, given the myriad of islands in the Hauraki Gulf within easy reach for beach barbecues, fishing jaunts, diving adventures, scenic walks and more. The islands are easily accessible for day trips or overnight stays, with regular ferry services to many of them and small charter boat companies providing other options.

Sheltered by the long arm of the Coromandel Peninsula to the east and by the mainland to the south and west, most of the Hauraki Gulf comes within the boundaries of the **Hauraki Gulf Maritime Park**, which embraces 47 islands and one mainland reserve (North Head in Devonport). Several of the islands are wildlife sanctuaries.

The nearest island to Auckland, and the youngest in the Gulf, is **Rangitoto▶▶▶**, which emerged from the sea in a series of volcanic explosions as recently as 750 years ago. Its distinctive cone is a familiar sight from downtown Auckland, and a climb to the top (2km: allow one hour each way) will be rewarded with a 360-degree panorama of the city and the Gulf from the hut at the summit (260m). The black basaltic lava rock of Rangitoto may seem like an inhospitable environment, but distinctive plant communities have developed here including mangroves, and the island hosts over 200 species of native trees and plants, 40 kinds of fern and several species of orchid. There are also lava caves, black back gull colonies, and pohutukawa groves, linked by tracks fanning out from the DoC Visitor Centre by the wharf.

Reached by a causeway from Rangitoto, **Motutapu▶** is two-thirds the size and completely different in character. Mainly farmland, it has some superb beaches and several

Rangitoto Reserve protects native trees, ferns and orchids

popular walking tracks, including the Motutapu Farm track from Islington Bay to Home Bay (90 minutes each way) across the south of the island, which is part of the New Zealand Walkway system. Just to the south of Motutapu, **Motuihe**▸ is a much smaller island (covering just 180 hectares) but it also has excellent beaches; dozens of boating enthusiasts anchor here at weekends for swimming and picnicking.

The largest and busiest island in the inner Gulf is **Waiheke**▸▸▸, just 35 minutes from Auckland by ferry. The most populous of the islands, it has a thriving arts and crafts community with many galleries and craft shops. A good starting point is the **Artworks Living Centre**▸ (Ocean View Road, tel: 09 372 6900. *Open* daily 10–5), which also offers crafts courses. The island is fringed by terrific beaches, while inland there are walkways through native bush and farmlands. One of the most popular walks is the 90-minute track to Stony Battery at the east end of the island, where there is a World War II gun emplacement overlooking the Gulf.

There is a wide choice of accommodation and plenty of restaurants and cafés. With average temperatures said to be five degrees warmer than the mainland, Waiheke also has no fewer than 14 vineyards and wineries. Mountain-biking, horseriding and sea-kayaking are other options on the island. Buses, taxis and rental cars are available, or you can bring your own vehicle on the car ferry. For visitors on foot, it is a pleasant 20-minute walk from the ferry wharf to Oneroa.

The distinctive volcanic cone of Rangitoto across Okahu Bay

From pā sites to picnic sites

Before the arrival of the Europeans, the islands of the Hauraki Gulf were extensively settled by the Maori, who called them *motu whakatere* ('the floating islands'), and the trenches and terraces of Maori *pā* sites can be seen on many island hill-sides. During the 19th century some of the islands were traded to the colonists in exchange for gold, guns, gunpowder and blankets. In the early 20th century the first ferry services started, bearing the families of Auckland city to the islands for Sunday picnics – Browns Island (Motukorea) and Motutapu were two of the most popular destinations.

A kauri dam on Great Barrier Island

Wildlife cruises
The *Te Aroha* is a wooden auxiliary schooner built in 1909 to service the small river settlements on the East Coast; it is now owned by Mike and Dee Pigneguy, who operate bird-watching and wildlife cruises around the Hauraki Gulf and further afield. During the summer (November to April) there are day trips to Waiheke, Little Barrier and Tiritiri Matangi, and three-day 'Bird Islands of the Gulf' tours. The boat is equipped for diving, snorkelling and fishing, and you can help out with the sailing if you feel so inclined. Contact: Adventure Cruising Company, P O Box 338, Auckland (tel/fax: 09 444 9342).

▶▶▶ Hauraki Gulf (north) *49E4*

Although slightly harder to reach, the islands in the north of the Hauraki Gulf are also worth visiting if you have the time. The most remote is **Great Barrier Island▶▶▶**, 80km from Auckland and the largest island in the Gulf. There is an enormous number of things to see and do on Great Barrier, which has just 572 residents distributed across its 280-sq-km area. Over half of the island is conservation land, with vast tracts of native bush containing several rare species of flora and fauna – including the largest populations of brown teal duck left in the country.

Great Barrier, so-named by Captain Cook in 1769 because it appeared to bar the entrance to the Gulf, was one of the first islands to be colonised by Europeans, who mined for gold and copper and milled its extensive kauri forests for timber. There are old kauri dams, hot springs, the remains of whaling stations and a network of tramping tracks to explore.

The west coast's sheltered beaches are good for swimming, while the more exposed east-coast beaches are popular for surfing, diving and fishing. Horse-trekking, kayaking and safari tours are also on offer, and with 200km of unsealed hill roads, the island is perfect for mountain-biking. Accommodation includes backpackers' hostels, motels, fishing lodges and homestays.

Great Barrier still has no mains electricity (power is supplied by generators, solar cells, windmills and gravity pumps), and the telephone system was modernised only recently, thus doing away with Barrier residents' main source of information – the party line.

To the west of Great Barrier, **Little Barrier Island** is an important nature reserve, containing the only area of rainforest in the country to have remained unaffected by introduced browsers (such as deer) or predators (such as possums). About a third of the island was logged in the past, but these areas are now regenerating bushland. Access to the island is strictly controlled: the only regular boat to call here is the *Te Aroha* (see panel opposite).

Close to the mainland shoreline, 25km south-west of Little Barrier Island, is **Kawau Island▶▶▶,** reached via ferries from Sandspit. Manganese was found here in the 1830s, and a Scottish company mined the deposits until a node of copper was discovered in 1842, when they switched to mining copper instead. In 1862 the island was bought by Sir George Grey (an early Governor and later Premier for a brief term), who converted and extended the former mine manager's house into a stately **Mansion House▶▶** which has recently been restored and opened to the public (*Open* daily 9.30–3.30. *Admission charge* moderate). Grey planted many exotic trees and introduced wallabies, peacocks, pheasants, quail, geese and even tree kangaroos to the island: peacocks still strut across the mansion's lawns and wallabies are a fairly common sight.

From the Mansion House walking tracks lead to beaches, Maori *pā* sites, and the remains of the old copper and manganese mines at Miners Bay.

To the north of Kawau Island, just 100m from the shore across a narrow channel, lies the scientific reserve of **Goat Island**. Access to the bush-clad island is restricted, but snorkellers and divers are allowed to explore the marine reserve which surrounds it.

To the south of Kawau is **Tiritiri Matangi▶** another scientific reserve, but this time run as an 'open sanctuary' in which visitors are free to wander the walkways around the island. It is particularly popular with bird watchers because of the large number of native birds (many of them endangered) which live here: you may be able to see or hear bellbirds, North Island saddlebacks, brown teal duck, black robins and red-crowned parakeets. The flightless takahe has also been introduced recently.

Ferries to Kawau
Ferries to Kawau Island operate from Sandspit, just outside Warkworth, one hour's drive north of Auckland. There are about six departures daily, journey time 45 minutes. You can also join the historic Mail Run, leaving Sandspit at 10.30am daily, which cruises around the bays delivering mail and supplies before reaching the Mansion House (there is time to visit the house and gardens before the return trip). Contact: The Ferry Boat Company, P O Box 931, Warkworth (tel: 09 425 8006; freephone 0800 888006).

Elegant Mansion House on Kawau Island

Drive and forest walk

Waitakere Ranges

The Waitakere Ranges Regional Park is a 10,000ha wilderness area within easy reach of the city centre, with waterfalls, beaches and rainforest walks. This tour takes you right through the park to the Tasman Coast and back, with opportunities for several short walks on the way. Allow the best part of a day.

From Auckland, follow SH16 to the north-west, taking the Waterview exit and then following Urban Routes 19 and 24 through Titirangi; 6km later you reach the Arataki Visitor Centre to the left.

You are now on the eastern fringes of the **Waitakere Ranges▶▶▶**. This hilly area, rising to a maximum of 470m above sea level, is volcanic in origin, and is most notable for its huge expanses of regenerating forest, criss-crossed by nearly 250km of walking and tramping tracks.

The **Arataki Visitor Centre▶▶**, opened in 1994, is superbly designed to blend into the surrounding bush; elevated platforms provide stunning **views▶▶** over the forest, with Manukau Harbour to the south-east of Auckland beyond.

Lion Rock at Piha Beach

The boardwalk leads past specimens of native trees (such as rimu, young kauri and maukoro) to displays inside the Visitor Centre (*Open* daily 9–5. *Admission free*) on the inhabitants of the rainforest, such as geckos, rare frogs, tui and kereru. On the lower level, an excellent wide-screen audio-visual presentation recounts the history and ecology of the ranges (*Open* daily 9–5, presentations every 20 min. *Admission charge* inexpensive).

As well as the distinctive architecture of Arataki (which means 'pathway to learning'), you will notice the powerful **carvings▶▶** of Maori ancestral figures. The *pou* ('guardian post') which fronts the building represents the ancestors of the local Kawerau a Maki, and is carved from two kauri which were felled with full protocol and *karakia* (rituals) offered to Tane, the god of the forest. Inside, four more carvings represent other ancestors.

From the Visitor Centre, follow the Nature Trail and then the Upper and Lower Loop Trail (a one-hour return walk) through the forest, where vines and climbers festoon trees and perching plants hang from every branch. At the far end of the Loop Track, steps lead up to a mature kauri plantation; although by no means as awesome as the tremendous forest giants of the Waipoua Kauri Forest (see pages 74–5), the biggest tree here still manages to impress (some 600 years old, it has a girth of nearly 8m and a height of 37m).

Leaving Arataki, follow the Scenic Drive signs, turning left at the first main junction down to **Piha**►►. As you crest the ridge, this huge black volcanic sand beach is laid out before you, with the 100m high Lion Rock proudly standing sentinel where the estuary meets the stream.

Piha is primarily a surfers' beach, so be extremely wary of rips and other hazards if you decide to swim; alternatively, you can climb and scramble up the track on Lion Rock (one hour return) or tackle the Tasman Look Out Track at the south end of the beach (40 minutes return).

Drive back up the Piha Road, turning left to rejoin Scenic Drive. After just under 1km you will come to the **Rose Hellaby House**, one of the earliest guest houses in the area, which now contains a display on the history of the region (*Open* Sun and public holidays 11–5 in summer; 1–4 in winter; Sat 1–4 all year round. *Admission charge* inexpensive). From the gardens (*Open* daily 9–6. *Admission free*) there is an astonishing **view**►► over West Auckland, Manukau Harbour, Waitemata Harbour and beyond to the Hauraki Gulf and the Coromandel.

Continue on to a short loop road, climbing up to the summit of Mount Pukematekeo (336m) which offers, as a fitting climax to this trip through the rainforest, a beautiful **panorama**►►, this time extending right up the West Coast to Kaipara Harbour and back across the city and its harbours.

Follow Scenic Drive until it ends on the outskirts of Swanson, continuing through the township to take the motorway back into Auckland.

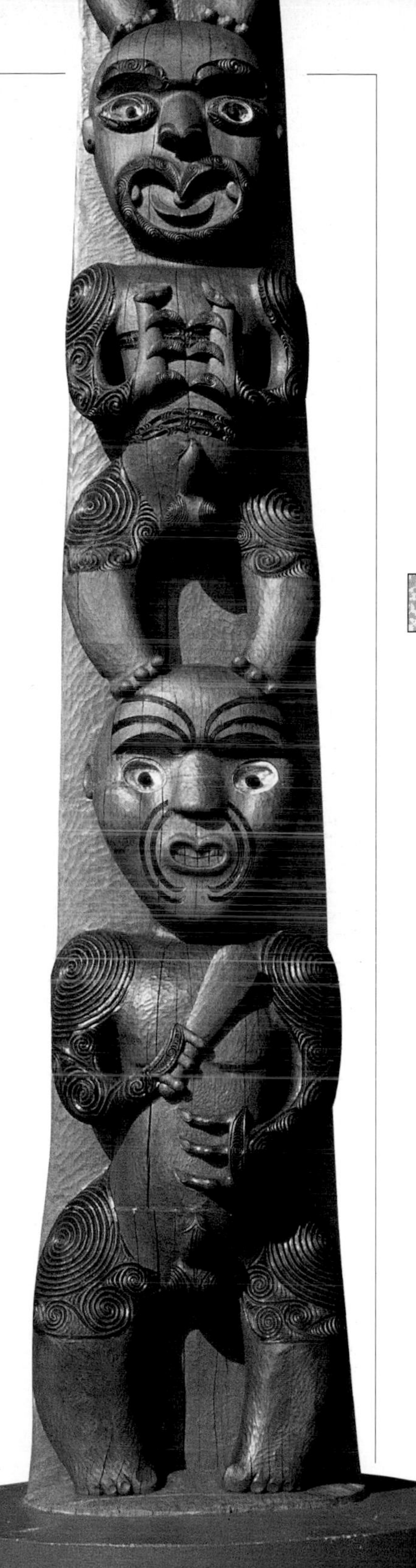

Maori ancestral figures at the Arataki Visitor Centre

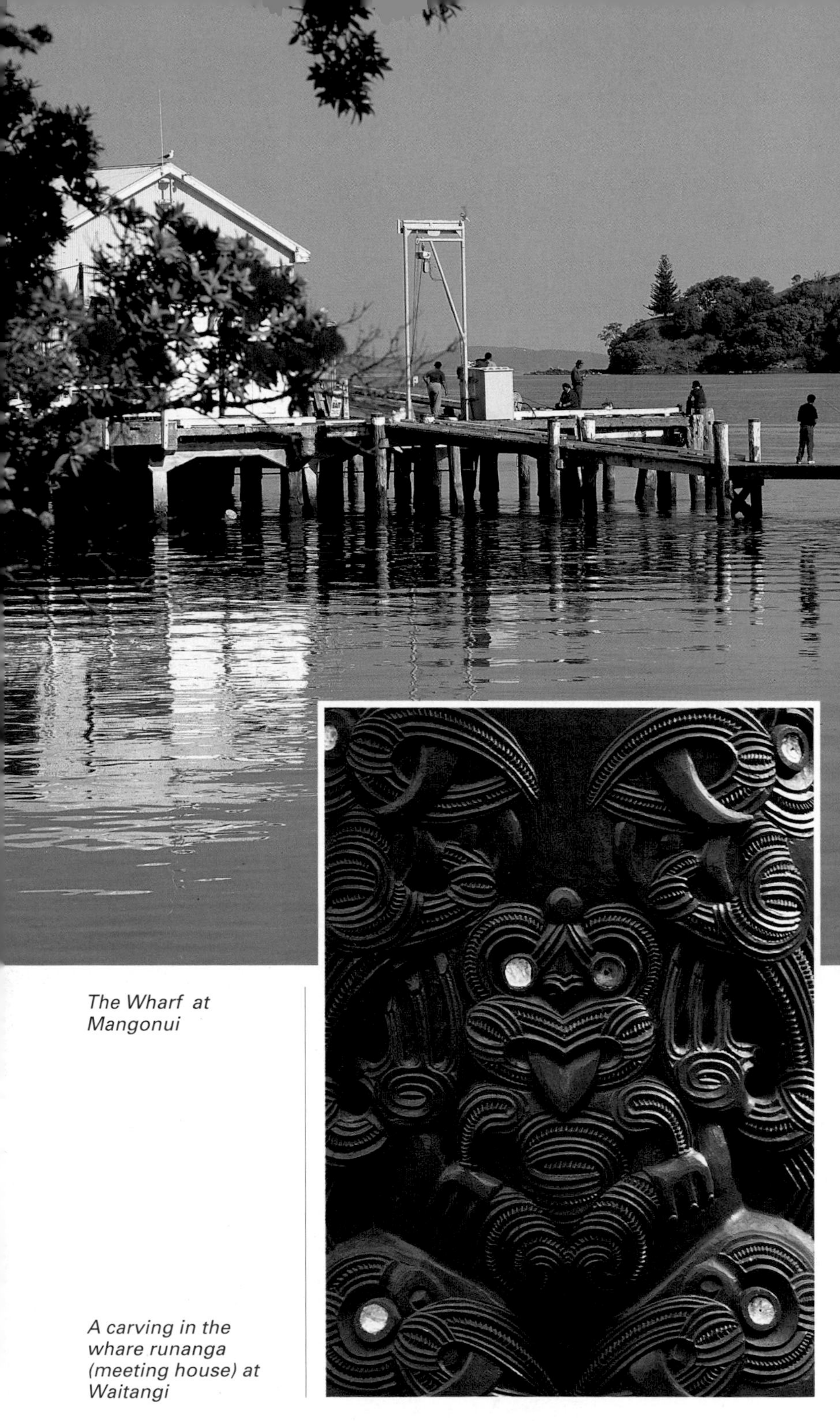

The Wharf at Mangonui

A carving in the whare runanga (meeting house) at Waitangi

NORTH ISLAND
NORTHLAND

Northland This 240km-long peninsula running northwards from Auckland towards the equator has a mild climate year-round which has earned it the sobriquet 'the winterless North'. The east coast is indented with numerous bays and harbours with islands, and its sandy beaches provide a base for adventure activities such as sailing, diving, sea-kayaking, swimming and surf-casting.

It is not just its climate that makes Northland a busy tourist region; it also has many historical attractions, including the **Waitangi National Reserve**, where the Treaty of Waitangi was signed in 1840. The reserve forms part of the **Bay of Islands Historic and Maritime Park**, a popular holiday area with most facilities concentrated in the seaside town of **Paihia**: it is advisable to book accommodation in advance for weekends or public holidays in high season. A short ferry ride across the bay from Paihia is the tranquil township of **Russell**, which takes great pride in its heritage as the earliest European settlement in the country.

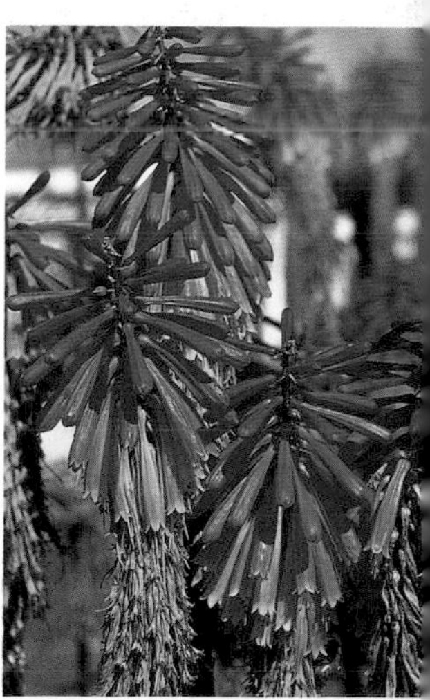

Departing souls
Cape Reinga was traditionally revered by the Maori as the last stepping stone for the spirits of the dead on their journey back to 'Hawaiki' starting from the gnarled roots of an ancient pohutukawa tree.

The west coast, by contrast, is characterised by sweeping beaches pounded by surf from the Tasman Sea – perfect for beach walks or surf-casting. Inland, the magnificent **kauri forests** are unmissable.

The bulk of Northland tapers off to a narrow finger jutting out into the ocean, with **Doubtless Bay** on the east coast providing a convenient base from which to explore. On the west coast, **Ninety Mile Beach** sweeps in a single unbroken stretch of shimmering sand up towards Cape Reinga, at the very tip of the peninsula.

►► Cape Reinga 66A3

Almost at the northernmost tip of the North Island, Cape Reinga offers breathtaking sea views, stretching as far as the Three Kings Islands on a clear day. To the right of the lighthouse you can also see the Surville Cliffs on the adjoining North Cape – the most northerly point on mainland New Zealand.

Trips to Cape Reinga (see panel) operate from the Bay of Islands, Doubtless Bay and Kaitaia, with one leg of the journey by road and the other travelling along **Ninety Mile Beach►►**, a huge expanse of sand (which is in reality 90 kilometres long).

On the east side of the peninsula is the lovely inlet of **Houhora Harbour**. On the edge of the bay is the **Wagener Museum►** (*Open* daily 9.30–4.30. *Admission charge* moderate) which includes a massive collection of Victoriana. Near by is the **Subritzky/Wagener Homestead** (entrance via the museum), an unusual pioneer cottage built in 1860–2.

►► Doubtless Bay 66B3

Doubtless Bay has plenty of good beaches and makes a convenient base for visiting the Far North and Cape Reinga. Sailing past in 1769, Cook declared it was 'Doubtless a bay', and continued on his circumnavigation.

The main settlement in Doubtless Bay is the charming and historic port of **Mangonui►►►**, a significant Maori settlement classified as a Conservation Zone. In the mid-18th century whaling ships called in here to pick up supplies, and by the end of the century it had become an important port for the shipping of kauri timber and kauri gum. Today it has a handful of hotels, craft shops, cafés, a bank and the famous Mangonui Fish Shop next to the wharf. Fishing, sailing, diving and other water-sports are popular here.

A good view of the harbour and sea can be had from the **Rangikapiti *Pā* Historic Reserve►**, just past the end of the village. Continuing westwards the next bay is **Coopers Beach►**, fringed by pohutukawa trees, followed by **Taipa**, where the explorer Kupe is said to have made his first landfall in about AD 950.

Cape Reinga trips
Both Fullers and Kings run trips to Cape Reinga from Paihia in the Bay of Islands, but this 500km round trip makes for a long, exhausting day. You will get more time to stop at other places of interest if you leave from Kaitaia or Doubtless Bay, and the service tends to be more personalised, with smaller buses. From Kaitaia tours are operated by Sand Safaris (tel: 09 408 1778) and Tu-Tu Seaspray Trail (09 408 0200); from Mangonui, Nor-East Coachlines (tel: 09 406 0244) run similar trips with daily departures.

Northland's Ninety-Mile-Beach is officially designated a road

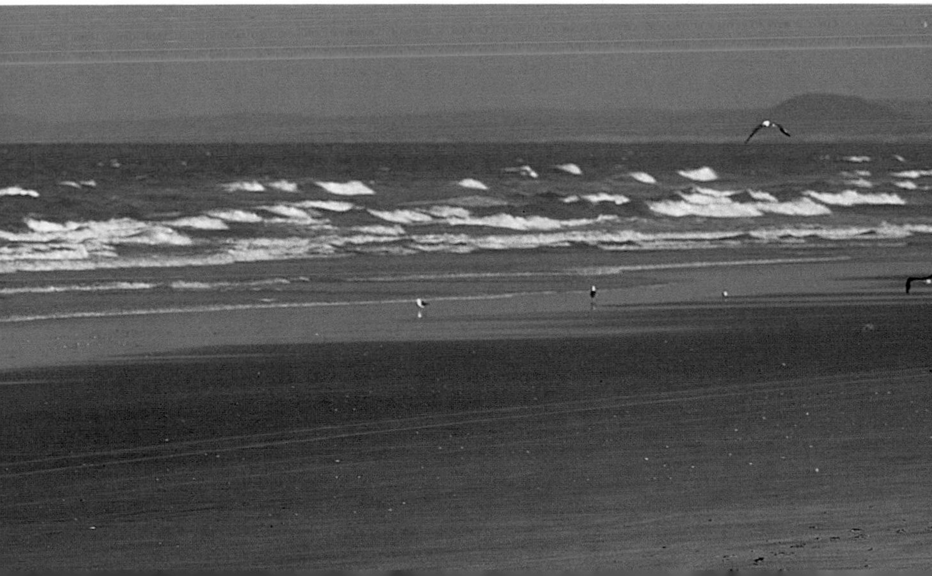

The first plough
The Kerikeri soil yielded an abundance of kumara and potatoes which the Maori traded (along with pigs and flax) with visiting whalers. In the early days of the mission station, Reverend Butler introduced the first plough and bullock team to the country, unloaded from the naval ship *Dromedary*. 'The agricultural plough was for the first time put into the land of New Zealand,' he wrote on 3 May 1820, 'and I felt much pleasure in holding it after a team of six bullocks.' The settlement thereafter acquired its name, *keri*, meaning to dig, and then *kerikeri* – 'to keep on digging'.

▶▶ Ka Iwi Lakes *66B1*

These three freshwater lakes 25km south-west of Dargaville have been developed as a recreation reserve with opportunities for swimming, boating, camping and fishing.

▶ Kaitaia *66B2*

One of the main commercial centres in the far north, Kaitaia is a busy centre for tours heading up to Cape Reinga, but its drab main street has limited appeal as somewhere to stay – Doubtless Bay is a much better prospect. Just off the main street, the **Far North Regional Museum** (*Open* Mon–Fri 10–5, weekends 1–5 in summer. *Admission charge* inexpensive) has many examples of polished and worked kauri gum, as well as displays on natural history and Maori artefacts.

To the east of Kaitaia (18km on the Peria Road) is **Sullivan's Nocturnal Park▶** (*Open* 9am–10pm summer, 9am–9pm winter. *Admission charge* moderate) which features a kiwi house and a glow-worm grotto.

▶▶▶ Kerikeri *66B2*

Kerikeri lies at the centre of a rich horticultural district and is surrounded by citrus and kiwifruit orchards. Around the main township there are also a number of workshops and cooperatives selling ceramics, woodcarvings, jewellery and other arts and crafts.

Just beyond the township is the delightful **Kerikeri Basin▶▶▶**, a picturesque inlet with numerous historical associations. It was here that the Reverend Samuel Marsden established the country's second mission station in 1819, with the Reverend John Butler appointed as superintendent. Three years later Butler had finished building his home, the oldest surviving building in New Zealand now known as the **Kemp House▶▶▶** (*Open* daily 10–4.30 in summer; closed Thu–Fri in winter. *Admission charge* moderate). The interior (restored in 1989) provides a fascinating insight into the lives of the early missionaries.

Next door to Kemp House is the **Stone Store▶▶** (the original being a wooden building), from which James Kemp dispensed rations to the other mission stations in the area. Completed in 1836, it is the oldest surviving stone building in New Zealand. A small museum contains the original plough (see panel), but in 1993 the store was closed indefinitely for urgent restoration work.

Also in the Basin, **Rewa's Village▶▶▶** (*Open* daily 10–4. *Admission charge* inexpensive) is well worth a visit.

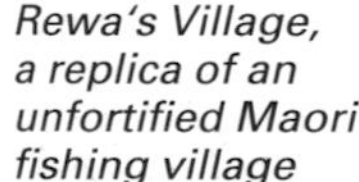

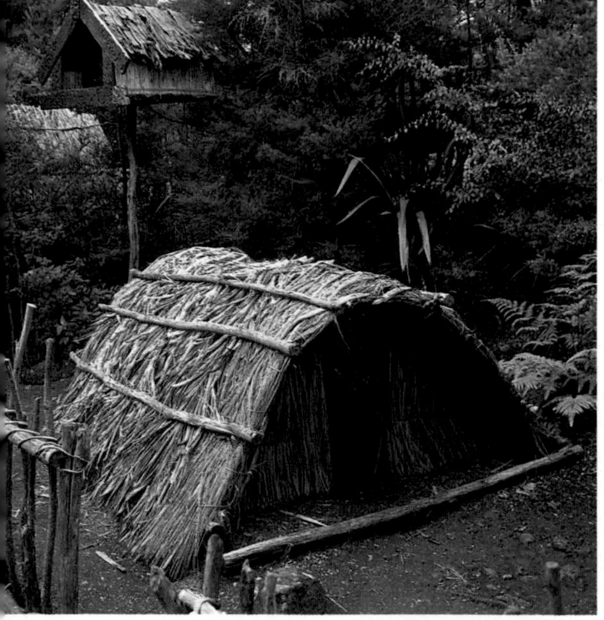

Rewa's Village, a replica of an unfortified Maori fishing village

It is a replica of a pre-European Maori fishing village (*kāinga*) on the river bank, built in 1969. The village has a chief's house, raised storehouses and typical thatched houses (*whare*). Access is via a Visitor Centre, where there is also an audio-visual display on the early history of the Kerikeri Basin (*Open on demand. Admission charge* donation).

Across the inlet from the village is the fortified *pā* site to which the villagers would have retreated when threatened by raiding parties. Now a historic reserve, **Kororipo** *Pā*▶▶▶ (*Open* at all times. *Admission free*) was the power base of the famous warrior chief Hongi Hika (see page 35). Signboards explain the various features of this elaborately terraced hilltop site, which is reached via a wooden footbridge from the tea-rooms opposite the Stone Store.

Missionaries built Kemp House (top); above: the church at Matakohe Museum

▶▶▶ Matakohe Kauri Museum *66C1*

Open: daily 9–5. Admission charge: moderate

Conveniently placed on the way to the Waipoua Kauri Forest when travelling north from Auckland, this wonderful museum covers absolutely everything to do with kauri, from the history of logging and gum-digging to superb items of kauri furniture. The kauri gum display in the basement is particularly noteworthy, featuring numerous elaborate carvings. A new wing is almost completely filled by the enormous trunk of the Balderston Kauri, a giant which was felled for the museum after it had been struck by lightning.

Hell-hole of the Pacific

When Captain Cook sailed into the Bay of Islands in 1769, there was a thriving Maori settlement here known as Kororareka. With the arrival of European whalers it degenerated. A visiting surveyor described it as a 'vile hole, full of impudent, half-drunken people' and its reputation earned it the title of 'Hell-hole of the Pacific'.

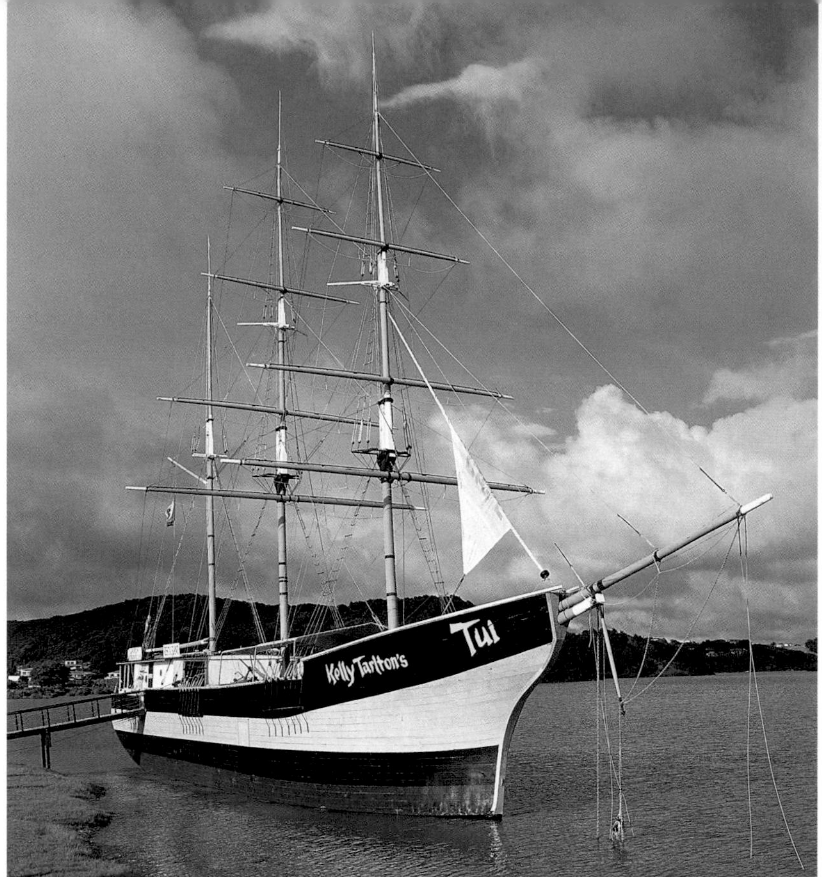

The barque Tui *contains a Museum of Shipwrecks*

Dolphins in the bay
Resident pods of bottlenose dolphins live in the bay throughout the year, and since 1991 Dolphin Discoveries has been taking small groups out to view them or (in calm conditions) swim with them. Snorkelling equipment and wetsuits are provided. Sei whales, Minke whales and Orcas can also be spotted along the coast at different times of year. Contact: Dolphin Discoveries, Williams Road, Paihia (tel: 09 402 8234; fax: 09 402 6058).

▶▶▶ Paihia *66B2*

The main tourist centre in the Bay of Islands, Paihia is the most convenient base for cruises or other activities in the Maritime and Historic Park and for visiting Russell, Kerikeri and Waitangi. It is not an especially attractive town but it does have a wide range of motels, hotels and other accommodation, as well as plenty of restaurants, cafés, and shops. Your first stop should be at the Maritime Building on the quayside, where there are several booking and information offices, including the Visitor Information Centre (tel: 09 402 7426. *Open* daily 8–5), Fullers Travel Centre, King's Tours and Cruises, and deep sea fishing operators. Behind the Maritime Building the Paihia wharf is busy with charter vessels, dolphin-watch boats, launches and the Russell ferries.

Just next to the wharf is a new aquarium, **Aquatic World▶** (*Open* daily 9.30–6; extended hours in summer. *Admission charge* moderate), which provides an insight into marine life in the Bay of Islands.

Heading north around the bay you come to the Waitangi River, where the barque *Tui* is beached alongside the road: this old sugar lighter (built in 1917) now houses the **Museum of Shipwrecks▶▶** (*Open* daily 9–5.30, extended hours in summer. *Admission charge* moderate), a fascinating collection of artefacts from wrecks around the coast put together by the late Kelly Tarlton.

▶▶▶ Russell *66B2*

This delightful tranquil town with a long history – just across the bay from Paihia, ten minutes or less away on the local ferries – is well worth visiting for the day to soak up its historic atmosphere.

Soon after the signing of the Treaty of Waitangi, Hobson purchased a block of land at nearby Okiato – renamed Russell after Lord John Russell, then British Colonial Secretary – with the aim of establishing the country's capital there. Just nine months later, in March 1841, the capital was transferred to Auckland, and in 1844 village of Kororareka was given the name of Russell.

The economic decline which followed the shift of the capital to Auckland fuelled resentment among the local Maori, who eventually sacked the town, led by chief Hongi Hika, in 1845. Rebuilt the following year, by the turn of the century it had become a quiet summer holiday destination. In 1930 a road between Whangarei and Russell was built, allowing access to the town by car for the first time.

Much of the colourful history of Russell is covered in the **Captain Cook Memorial Museum▶** (*Open* daily 10–5. *Admission charge* inexpensive). Next door, the **Bay of Islands Maritime and Historic Park Visitor Centre▶** (*Open* daily 8.30–5; 9–5 weekends. *Admission free*) has displays and an audio-visual presentation (every half-hour from 9am. *Admission free*) on the natural and human history of the park.

One block away is **Christ Church▶▶▶**, the oldest surviving church in the country, built in 1835 by the local citizenry who were horrified by Kororareka's debauched reputation (see panel page 69). The churchyard contains the graves of Maori chiefs, early whalers and six sailors from HMS *Hazard* who died in a pitched battle with Hongi Hika's forces (the outer walls of the church still bear the scars of musket shots and cannon balls).

Pompallier House▶▶▶ (*Open* daily 9.30–5; closed Thu–Fri in winter. *Admission charge* moderate), almost on the seafront, was built by French Roman Catholic Marist missionaries to house their printing press. For lack of funds they used the *pisé de terre* (rammed earth) technique which was common in their native town of Lyon, and the result is an elegant and unusual two-storey building, completed in 1842. Extensively restored, it now once more houses a printing press and book-bindery, as well as a display on the Marists and a small shop selling superb hand-crafted books and other items.

Bay of Plenty cruises
A bay cruise is a good way to see the islands and places of interest (such as the site where Cook landed in 1769). Fullers (tel: 09 402 7421) and King's (tel: 09 402 8288) both run a variety of trips. A popular one is the 64km (5-hour) Fullers 'cream trip', which began in the 20s to collect milk and cream from outlying farms (daily departures at 10am in summer; Mon, Wed, Thu and Sat in winter). Bay cruises also visit the 'Hole in the Rock' at Cape Brett at the mouth of the bay (weather permitting). You can also whizz through this in a fast open boat such as the *Reetrunner* (tel: 09 403-7596).

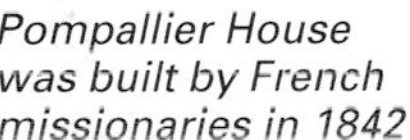

Pompallier House was built by French missionaries in 1842

Walk Historic Russell

This is an easy walk up to the top of Flagstaff Hill and then around historic Russell township, with lovely views from the top of the hill and many interesting places to visit. Allow around two to three hours, including visits to the Museum, Christ Church and Pompallier House.

From the ferry jetty turn left and follow The Strand. Immediately on your right is the **Duke of Marlborough Hotel▶**, the fourth hotel on this site (earlier ones were sacked or burned) and the proud possessor of New Zealand's oldest liquor licence, issued in August 1840. This is a good place to stop for coffee or refreshments on the outdoor terrace before heading up the hill.

Continue to the end of the beach and go on around the rocks into **Watering Bay** (at high tide, when this route is impassable, continue up Wellington Street and follow the high tide detour), used for reprovisioning ships in the early days. Take the sign-posted track up through the **Kororareka Scenic Reserve** to find a concrete dam. This is on the site of the original dam built by sailors so that they could collect water from the creek.

Emerging from the bush, follow the road until you see a track on the right up through the bush again to **Flagstaff Hill▶▶**. From here there are panoramic views across the Bay of Islands, with Cape Brett visible to the east. At the end of the peninsula you can see **Tapeka** *pā*, a fortified site which is now a historic reserve. A sea battle between rival tribes fighting for dominance in the region took place just off this point in the early 19th century.

Erected after the signing of the Treaty of Waitangi in 1840, the flagstaff itself has long been a symbol of English domination, and as such was cut down four times by the local Maori in 1844 and 1845. As a peace gesture organised as 'a voluntary act by those directly connected with cutting it down', it was replaced in 1857 with 'a noble spar, cut from the bush and dragged up the hill by four hundred men'. The following year the British flag was again hoisted on the mast, dubbed *Whakakotahitanga* ('being at one with the Queen'), the remains of which form the present flagstaff. On a hillock opposite is a **mosaic** of the Bay of Islands, commissioned in 1988. From Flagstaff Hill take the track signposted behind the car park, which cuts down through the bush to Wellington Street. On the corner of Wellington and Queen Street stands the **Baker's House**, built in the 1880s for Ernest Ford, merchant and son of New Zealand's first surgeon, Dr Samuel Ford. For almost a century since then it has been home to generations of the Baker family.

Bear left, following Wellington Street, then turn right into York Street. Immediately opposite the Methodist Church (built in 1913) is an **Immigrant Cottage**, the last of a group of five prefabricated cottages erected by the government in 1857; this one was the home of the signalman at the Flagstaff.

Turn left into Chapel Street and right into Church Street, at the end of which stands **Christ Church▶▶▶**, the oldest church in New Zealand. Head back down to the seafront along Robertson Street towards the **Captain Cook Museum▶**, turning left at the shore to reach **Pompallier House▶▶▶**.

As you return towards the wharf, the DoC Visitor Centre and headquarters of the Bay of Islands Maritime and Historic Park lies to the right, in a building which was Russell's post office and court house from 1875 to 1969. On the grassy foreshore just beyond it is an old cannon, one of two which were set up to defend the town against Hika's attack in 1847. Several historic buildings line the foreshore, amongst them the **Swordfish Club**, established in 1924.

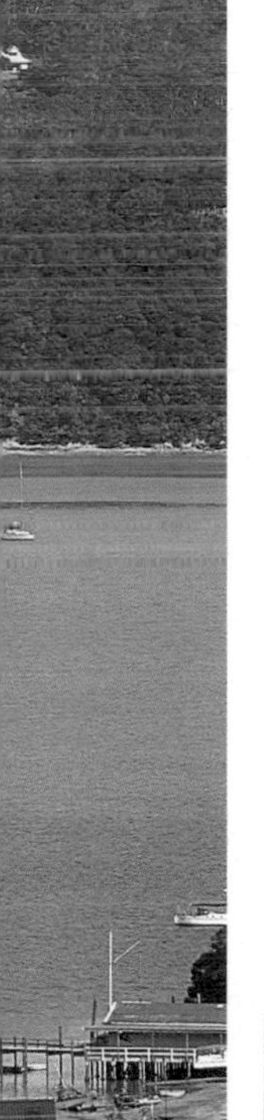

Left: the view from Flagstaff Hill. Below: cannon set up to defend Russell in 1847

The Poor Knights Marine Reserve
Located 24km off the east coast of Northland, the Poor Knights Islands Marine Reserve is New Zealand's most famous scuba diving destination. Established in 1981, the reserve consists of two main islands, Tawhiti Rahi and Aorangi, with a narrow passage between them. Warmed by currents from the Coral Sea, its sheer submarine cliffs, tunnels and caves are home to tropical and subtropical species not normally seen around New Zealand. Tutukaka (26km north-east of Whangarei) is the nearest port, but trips also depart from Paihia. Contact: Aqua Action, Marina Road, Tutukaka (tel: 09 434 3867) or Paihia Dive Centre, P O Box 210, Paihia (tel: 09 402 7551).

The war canoe Ngatokimatawhaorua *joins the annual Waitangi Day celebrations*

►►► Waitangi 66B2

The road bridge across the river from Paihia leads into the **Waitangi National Reserve►►►** (*Open* daily 9–5. *Admission charge* moderate). It was on the foreshore here that the signing of the Treaty of Waitangi took place between the Maori tribes and the British Crown on 6 February 1840, and this site is considered in effect the birthplace of modern New Zealand. The Visitor Centre contains portraits of many of the principal figures involved, copies of treaty documents and a theatre with an audio-visual presentation (*Open* every 30 minutes from 9am) on the events surrounding the treaty.

At the centre of the reserve is the **Treaty House►►►**, one of New Zealand's oldest surviving buildings (1834) and the home of James Busby, the British Resident at the time. A fine example of elegant Georgian design, it contains displays on the treaty and the Busby family.

In front of the house, extensive lawns sweep down to the water's edge, with a massive kauri **flagstaff** marking the spot where the treaty was signed. To one side is a splendid **Whare Runanga►►** (meeting house), built in 1940 to celebrate the centenary of the signing, which contains elaborate panels and carvings from all the major Maori tribes.

In the other direction from the Visitor Centre, on the foreshore at Hobson Beach, is a massive **war canoe►►►**, also built for the centenary in 1940. Called *Ngatokimatawhaorua*, this 35m-long canoe is one of the largest in the world, carrying 80 paddlers.

►►► Waipoua Kauri Forest 66B2

The last remnant of the extensive forests which once covered much of the North Island, the Waipoua Kauri Forest is well worth a visit to see some of the mightiest trees in New Zealand. Saved from the loggers at first by its very remoteness, the Waipoua Forest was purchased by the Crown in 1876, after which no one was sure what to do with it. The threat posed by the demand for wartime boat-building supplies in the 1940s sparked off a well-organised campaign to preserve these last remaining trees of the original forest. This was the country's first great conservation battle and resulted in the creation of the Waipoua Sanctuary in 1952.

The largest living tree in New Zealand is **Tane Mahuta** ('the God of the forest') in the northern section of the forest; this hugely impressive tree is thought to be around 1,200 years old and has a height of 51.5m and a girth of 13.7m. A few kilometres to the south, a side road leads to a car park with access to several more remarkable kauri, including the second largest in the forest.

There are extensive displays on kauri and forest flora and fauna in the **Waipoua Forest Visitor Centre** (*Open* daily 9–5. *Admission free*). Opposite is the historic **Maxwell's Cottage**► (*Open* daily 9–5. *Admission free*), built for the first ranger, which now contains artefacts used by the early kauri bushmen.

The Whangarei Falls, a popular picnic spot

► Whangarei *66C2*

New Zealand's northernmost city, Whangarei has a huge deep-water harbour with three separate port areas: the town's name in Maori means 'cherished harbour'.

The harbourside of the Town Basin has recently been redeveloped into an attractively landscaped complex with outdoor cafés and shops, as well as the new **Museum of Fishes**► (*Open* daily 10–4. *Admission charge* inexpensive), which has a small saltwater aquarium and a rock pool. The **Clapham Clock Museum** (*Open* daily 10–4. *Admission charge* inexpensive) has thousands of timepieces of all possible descriptions.

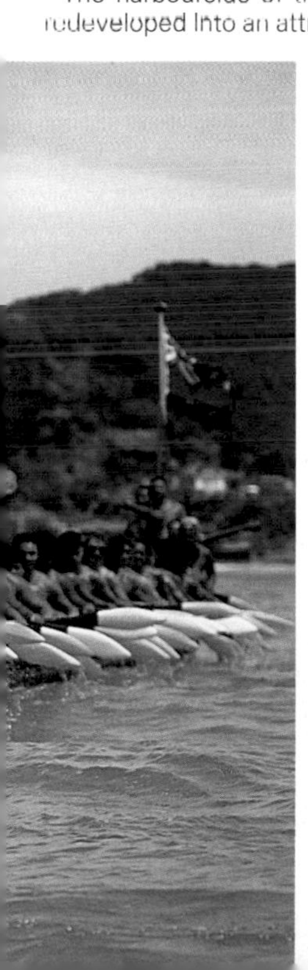

Other attractions in the vicinity include the **Whangarei Falls**►►, which cascade into a bush-fringed pool 25m below (on the Ngunguru Road, 6km north-east of the city centre). In the opposite direction (8km west of the city centre, on SH14 to Dargaville), the parklands of the **Whangarei Museum and Kiwi House**► (*Open* daily 10-4. *Admission charge* inexpensive) contain displays including a kiwi house, a pioneer homestead, vintage machinery and a good range of Maori artefacts, among them a rare burial chest (see panel).

Burial chests

In the Northland region in pre-European times the dead bodies of chiefs or other high-ranking Maori were exposed on atamira (platforms) until the flesh had rotted. Then certain bones were removed, cleaned, painted with red ochre and put in a waka-túpápaku (burial chest) before being placed in a cave or other sacred site. The burial chests often bore the likeness of Hine Nui Te Po, goddess of the underworld. The Whangarei Museum contains a rare example, unusually sculpted as a bird, perhaps to resemble the bird-god Hukerunui and thought to be 400–500 years old.

FOCUS ON *Kauri*

■ The magnificent kauri is one of the world's mightiest trees, often reaching heights of 50m or more with a trunk girth of up to 23m. Two hundred years ago kauri forests covered much of the warmer north half of the North Island, but today just four per cent of this forest remains. The felling and transporting of kauri timber, and the mining of the gum the trees produce, shaped the development of the Coromandel peninsula, Northland, and the Auckland region for well over a hundred years. ■

The growing tree The New Zealand species, *Agathis australis*, is just one of 13 species in the kauri family, a form of pine which bears male and female flowers each spring. Kauri seedlings grow to maturity in two stages: for the first century or so, they push upwards at the rate of around 30cm a year, sprouting numerous side branches and developing a distinctive conical crown. Then they start to shed the lower branches and develop a clean trunk with a crown of upper branches, although it may be another 200 to 300 years before a tree reaches full maturity. Some kauris in New Zealand are thought to be around 2,000 years old.

Shipbuilders and millers Early sailors were quick to realise that young kauri trunks (known as 'rickers') made excellent ships' masts and spars, and from the 1790s British naval supply vessels called in at the Firth of Thames to obtain timber – often after unloading convicts in Australia.

Shipbuilding began at Hokianga harbour in 1826, and shipbuilders and timber-millers were amongst the first to settle many of the coastal regions where kauri grows. They also discovered that kauri yielded sawn timber of unsurpassed quality, with the huge trunks producing clean lengths of timber which was easily worked. Each tree could provide enough to build three or four houses, and many of these distinctive 'kauri cottages' are still sound today.

Tane Mahuta, a kauri giant

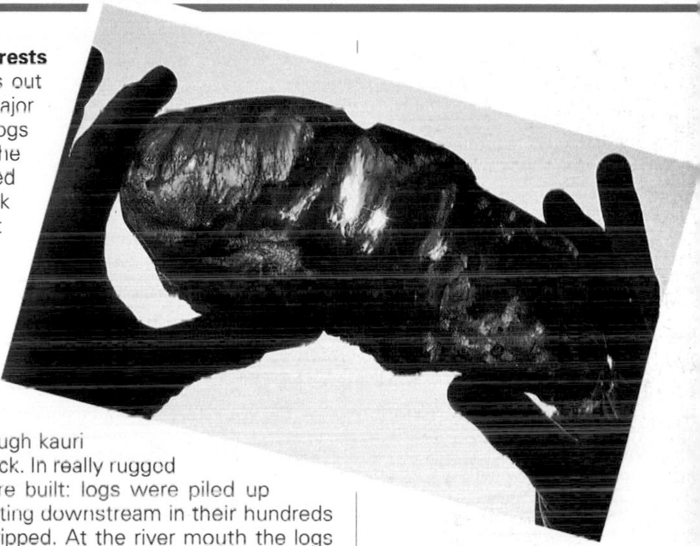

Working in the forests Moving the kauri logs out of the forest was a major operation. Massive logs were 'sniped' out of the bush and then dragged ('snigged') by bullock teams to the nearest mill. Bullocks were still in use until the 1920s, when they were succeeded by crawler tractors and lorries; bush tramways were also built into areas where there was enough kauri to justify laying the track. In really rugged areas kauri dams were built: logs were piled up behind the dam, shooting downstream in their hundreds when the dam was tripped. At the river mouth the logs which had not been broken up on the way were held in giant 'booms', a floating mass of timber which could then be towed to the mills or waiting ships.

In the early days kauri logs were sawn into planks using a pit saw, with one man standing above the log and the other pulling the saw downwards from underneath. In the 1840s steam-driven saws and water-powered mills took over; mechanisation greatly increased the rate of exploitation, with output reaching its peak in 1906.

Kauri gum Kauri gum, the solidified resin from the tree, was used by Maoris for chewing (when it was fresh and soft) and, because it burns easily, as a firelighter or torch, impregnated on a stick of flax. The kauri ash was then mixed with shark oil to make a pigment for tattooing.

The settlers soon discovered that this high-quality gum was ideal for making varnishes, and gum-diggers made up a second wave of settlers in the northern regions. In the second half of the 19th century, exports of kauri gum from Auckland were greater than those of wool, gold or kauri timber itself. In the 1930s synthetics took over in the manufacture of varnish, but the lower quality gums started to be used for making linoleum and false teeth.

Amber-coloured kauri gum, once used to make varnishes, was a valuable by-product

The gum diggers
At the peak of the kauri gum industry there were some 20,000 gum-diggers in the north, including Chinese, Malay and Maori workers. A gum-digger was generally equipped with a spear (to poke around in the bogs), a hurdy-gurdy (a cross between a washing machine and a sifter, to clean the gum), a spade and an axe. Gum was also bled from live trees, but this damaging process was banned in 1905.

Bubbling mud pools, geysers and other seething sulphurous features, all part of the volcanic activity around Rotorua

The Chinese gooseberry was renamed the kiwifruit when New Zealand began to export it commercially in the 1960s

NORTH ISLAND – FROM COROMANDEL TO THE WAIKATO

The Coromandel On the east side of the Hauraki Gulf from Auckland, the Coromandel is just a couple of hours' drive from that city and is a popular weekend retreat, with the rugged ranges which run down the centre of the peninsula providing a scenic backdrop to the deep blue sea. Once heavily exploited for kauri timber and gold, the peninsula's bush forests are now slowly regenerating and are fiercely protected by local residents. Many artists and craftspeople have settled here, and browsing in craft workshops is a popular option; more energetic activities include bush-walking, sailing, 'rock hounding' (looking for minerals) and horseriding, or you can simply take it easy on one of the many sheltered east-coast beaches.

The Bay of Plenty Aptly named by Cook, the Bay of Plenty is a fertile agricultural region where fruit (particularly kiwi and citrus fruit) flourishes in the rolling countryside. A busy holiday area, it has excellent beaches (particularly for surfing), plenty of adventure activities, and a smattering of historical

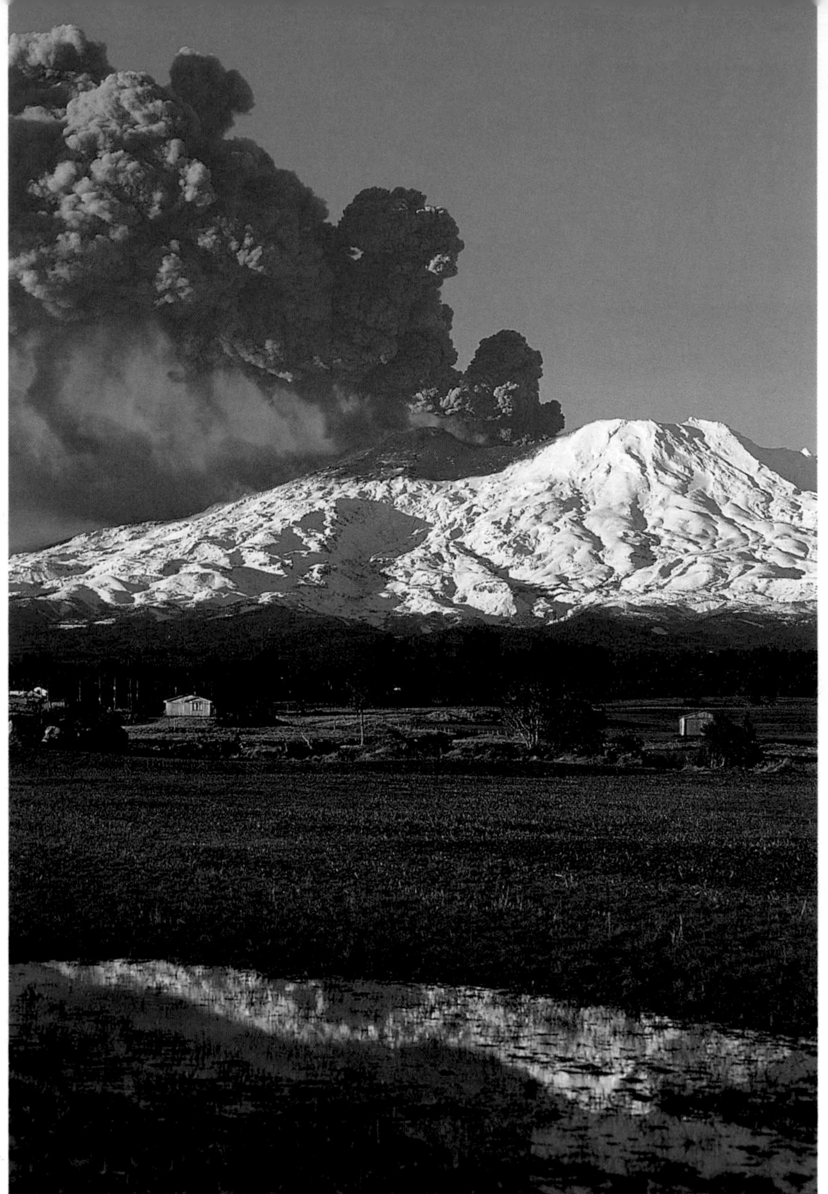

Mount Ruapehu burst into action in 1995 spreading debris up to 70km away

attractions. The biggest urban centre in the bay is **Tauranga,** a commercial harbour which is also quickly developing as a resort centre. Linked by the harbour bridge to the city, **Mount Maunganui** features an ancient Maori *pā* site, hot saltwater pools and good swimming and surfing beaches.

The main service centre for the eastern part of the Bay of Plenty is **Whakatane,** which lies at the mouth of the river of the same name. Here, too, there are superb beaches, the most famous of which is the 18km-long **Ohope Beach** to the west of town. Inland, vast areas of forest supply timber for the many board and paper mills around Whakatane.

White Island, one of the world's most accessible

continuously active volcanoes, lies 50km off-shore from Whakatane. Another volcanic creation, Whale Island (Motuhora), lies just 8km to the north of Whakatane.

Central North Island Bisected by a major fault in the earth's crust, the centre of the North Island is the most active volcanic area in the country. Volcanic lakes, geysers, mud pools and hot springs are just some of the manifestations of this underground turmoil beneath the Central Plateau. Travellers have been drawn to this region since Victorian times, and a well-developed tourist infrastructure now caters for every conceivable type of activity, from helicopter flights over volcanic craters to jet-boating, guided fishing, back-country horseriding, tramping and much more besides.

Between the Central Plateau and the Tasman Sea is the **Waikato**, one of the richest farming districts in the country thanks to its fertile volcanic topsoil and high rainfall. Winding through the heart of this evergreen countryside is the Waikato River, at 425km the longest river in New Zealand. The river gave its name (which means 'flowing waters') to this region and has been an important trading route from Maori times onwards. Today it is extensively exploited for hydroelectric power and features numerous dams and artificial lakes.

Maori country
Both the Waikato and the Central Plateau were heavily populated by Maori almost from the time of the first migrations. The Waikato was the scene of many bitterly fought battles during the New Zealand Wars, and was one of the last areas to be opened up to settlers in the North Island.

The small community of Colville, last chance to stock up before heading north along the dramatic Cape Road

Rock hounding
The Kauaeranga Valley is well known for its gemstones and rare rocks, and 'rock hounding' (fossicking) in and around the valley's streams is a popular pastime. Agates, jaspers, rhodonite and petrified wood of various kinds can all be found here by those with a keen eye. Geological hammers are allowed, but digging below the surface is not. Permits for fossicking are obtainable from the DoC Centre. Beaches along the west coast (particularly Te Mata Beach) are also good places for fossicking.

Coromandel

►► Colville and the Cape Road *81B3*

From Coromandel town the coast road wends its way along the western side of the peninsula past many scenic bays and inlets. **Colville**, 28km north of Coromandel, is a small rural village with just one café/store and a petrol station – the last one before the Cape. After Colville, the rugged interior is dominated by the bulk of **Mount Moehau** (892m), with the views along the coast opening out towards a succession of sandy beaches and campsites such as those at **Fantail Bay** and **Port Jackson**. Finally, after 36km of hair-raising road from Colville, you reach **Fletchers Bay►►**, the most northerly bay on the peninsula.

►► Coromandel Town *81B3*

The town of Coromandel is 56km north of Thames on the west coast of the peninsula. Named after HMS *Coromandel* which called here in 1820 to collect kauri spars for the British Navy, it was founded on the timber trade, but later boomed with the discovery of gold at nearby Driving Creek in 1852 (the first payable gold strike in New Zealand). During the peak gold rush years (the 1860s and 1870s) its population reached 10,000. Today it numbers around a 1,000 people and has a carefully nurtured 'village' atmosphere.

Most of Coromandel's craft shops, cafés and stores, as well as the Visitor Information Centre (*Open* Mon–Sat 9–4 in summer; Mon–Fri 10–3 in winter), are found on Kapanga Road, which runs at right angles to the harbour. Further along is the **Coromandel Mining Museum** (*Open* 10–12, 2–4 in summer only. *Admission charge* inexpensive) housed in the original School of Mines

(1897), which has mineralogical displays and, at the back, New Zealand's first ever jailhouse.

A short drive (3km) north of the town is the **Driving Creek Railway▶▶**, one of the most popular attractions on the peninsula. Local artist and railway enthusiast Barry Brickell set up a pottery at Driving Creek in 1974 and built the railway to bring clay and pinewood fuel for his kilns down from the hills. The 5km line features five viaducts, two spirals, a double switchback and two tunnels. As well as bringing materials downhill, the railway also carries tourists up and back again, and the one-hour round trip (daily 2pm; also 10.30am in summer. *Admission charge* moderate; bookings, tel: 07 866 8703) makes an enjoyable excursion through regenerating bushland.

▶▶ Coromandel Forest Park *81B2*

The Coromandel Forest Park covers 740 sq km of bush-clad hills and valleys in the Coromandel Range, with one of the most popular and easily accessible areas being the **Kauaeranga Valley▶▶** east of Thames. Heavily logged for kauri at the end of the last century, mostly because the gold boom fuelled the need for building timber in towns such as Thames, this is now regenerating bushland, with a few surviving patches of kauri here and there. Between 1870 and 1924 some 70 dams were built in the valley, and the remains of about a quarter of them form part of the historical attraction of the Kauaeranga; there are also more than 20 different walking tracks (and two overnight huts) in this scenic valley.

The DoC Visitors Centre (*Open* daily 8–4 in summer, Mon–Fri 8–4 in winter), 15km from Thames, at the lower end of the valley, has displays and leaflets on logging and the dams, and a short walk away (20 minutes return) is a one-third scale working replica of the Tarawaere Dam.

Oysters and mussels
The sheltered waters of the Coromandel and the high rate of water exchange between the Pacific Ocean and the Hauraki Gulf create perfect conditions for aquaculture. In the intertidal area, Pacific oysters are farmed on sticks held on racks, with around six million oysters harvested annually. The New Zealand green-shelled mussel is grown on long lines in deeper water, with some 12,000 tonnes produced annually. You may see the barges (there are 17 for the mussels and two for the oysters) working the aquaculture beds along the coast.

The Driving Creek railway snakes 5km up the hillside

▶▶▶ Mercury Bay 81B3

Mercury Bay is one of the most delightful coastal areas in the Coromandel, and with its superb beaches sheltered by bush-clad headlands it makes a pleasant base for visiting the peninsula. The explorer Kupe landed here some time between AD 800 and 950, and Cook anchored in the bay in November 1769 to make observations on the transit of Mercury, naming the bay after the planet. It was later a major kauri export port.

The main settlement in Mercury Bay is **Whitianga▶**, one of the most accessible anchorages on the coast thanks to the absence of a harbour bar (the name comes from *Te Whitianga a Kupe*, 'the crossing place of Kupe'). The port is a popular base for boating and deep-sea fishing, and the commercial fleet also hauls in catches of crayfish and scallops. With a good choice of accommodation, restaurants and other facilities, Whitianga attracts some 20,000 visitors during the summer season. Sea-kayaking, swimming with dolphins, bike rides, horseriding, fishing, boat trips and windsurfing are just some of the activities on offer.

The main beach in Whitianga is the 4km-long Buffalo Beach, named after the convict ship HMS *Buffalo* which was wrecked here in 1840. The town centre adjoins the harbour on the south side of the bay and the Visitor Information Centre (66 Albert Street, tel: 07 866 5555. *Open* daily 8–5, Sun 9–3 in summer; Mon–Fri 9.30–4.30, Sat 9.30–12.30 in winter) is conveniently located on the main street. On the harbour front, the **Mercury Bay Museum▶** (*Open* daily 10–4 in summer; Tue, Thu, Sun 11–2 in winter. *Admission charge* inexpensive) has numerous exhibits from the kauri milling days, as well as remnants of old shipwrecks and agricultural displays.

Opposite the museum is the main wharf, with a passenger ferry which shuttles across to **Ferry Landing▶▶** on the other side of the Narrows. This was the original site of the township, and the stone wharf (built in 1837) is said to be the oldest in the country. An enjoyable walk leads to a *pā* site at the top of the hill above the wharf, and you can hire bikes or walk to a string of excellent beaches.

Cathedral Cove▶▶▶ is a superb beach with sand tinted pink by crushed sea shells and framed by a massive rock arch at its southern end. The off-shore islands sheltering the beach form part of the Cathedral Cove Marine Reserve and are popular for diving and snorkelling. Cathedral Cove can be reached by boat (see panel) or via a walking track (two hours return) from **Hahei**; to the south of Hahei, **Hot Water Beach▶** features hot springs welling up through the sands.

▶ Thames 81B2

Lying at the base of the peninsula on the Firth of Thames, this sizeable town is the main gateway to the Coromandel. It gained its name indirectly when Captain Cook, visiting in 1769, named the Waihou River (which disgorges just

HOT WATER
AT LOW TIDE ONLY –
ADJACENT OUTCROP OF ROCKS.

Dig your own thermal pool at Hot Water Beach (right) where thermal activity heats the sand

Off-shore trips
Trips to Cathedral Cove and Hot Water Beach operate from both Whitianga and Hahei: from the wharf at Ferry Landing, Hot Water Beach ConneXion (tel: 07 866 2478) run daily excursions by road lasting 4–5 hours, while the Mercury Bay Scenic Jet (tel: 025 727 242) whizzes around the coast and back in one hour. From Hahei, the Hahei Explorer (tel: 07 866 3910) also incorporates snorkelling in the Cathedral Cove Marine Reserve. You can get to Cathedral Cove by kayak with Mercury Bay Sea Kayaks (tel: 07 866 2358). Dolphin swimming is organised by Dolphin Quest (tel: 07 866 2213).

south of the town) the 'Thames' because he felt it bore 'some resemblance to the river Thames in England'.

A massive gold strike was made on the nearby Kuranui Stream in 1867, and by the following year Thames had a population of 18,000, with 40 stamper batteries pounding away day and night to crush quartz for gold. Relics from that era include a **Stamper Battery and Gold Mine** (tours 10am and 4pm Mon–Sat, summer only. *Admission charge* inexpensive) on the outskirts of town, and the **Thames School of Mines and Mineralogical Museum** (cnr of Cochrane and Brown Streets. *Open* 11–4 daily in summer, 11–3 Tue–Sun in winter. *Admission charge* inexpensive).

Thames has a handful of characterful buildings, described in an *Urban Heritage Trail* leaflet available from the Visitor Information Centre (405 Queen Street, tel: 07 868 7284. *Open* Mon–Fri 9–5, Sat–Sun 10–3).

Range roads
The two coasts of the Coromandel are linked by four roads crossing the Coromandel Ranges. The longest (50km) is SH25, which crosses from Coromandel town to Whitianga via the beach at Kuaotunu; No 309 Road from Coromandel to Whitianga (33km) passes a Scenic Reserve; the newest crossing (also 33km) is the Kopu–Hikuai road. Perhaps the most scenic route is the Tapu–Coroglen road (29km), which passes the delightful Rapaura Water Gardens (*Open* daily 10–5, summer only. *Admission charge* moderate).

Wave action has created a rock arch at Cathedral Cove

Hauhau movement
This was a revivalist religion of the 1860s, whose supporters believed themselves to be immune from Paheka bullets. The Opotiki area was subject to repeated attacks by Hauhau, who would then retreat to the impenetrable wilderness of Te Urewera to seek sanctuary. Hauhauism finally fizzled out at the beginning of the 1870s.

Bay of Plenty

Opotiki *81C1*

At the eastern end of the Bay of Plenty, Opotiki is set on a harbour inlet formed by the junction of the Otara and Waioeka Rivers, with over 25km of sandy beaches. Opotiki is the main gateway to the wilderness of the Raukumara Ranges and the Motu River, and the beginning of the 342km-long East Cape Road to Gisborne.

Within the township, the **Church of St Stephen the Martyr▶** (Church Street) was the scene of the bloody murder in 1865 of a Lutheran missionary, the Reverend Carl Volkner, by followers of the Hauhau movement (see panel).

Outside Opotiki, the **Hukutaia Domain▶** (7km, signposted after turning south beyond Waioeka Bridge) is a lovely 5ha native plant reserve which includes one of New Zealand's most ancient trees, a massive puriri which is estimated to be some 2,000 years old.

The Pohutu geyser spouts forth at regular intervals

▶▶▶ Rotorua

81B1

Rotorua, at the heart of the volcanic Central Plateau, is one of the country's most popular and commercialised tourist resorts, with a range of large-scale attractions geared towards the incoming busloads. The city is built around (and on top of) a series of spouting geysers, hissing fumaroles and bubbling pools of mud and sulphur; these geothermal phenomena are more accessible here than almost anywhere else in New Zealand. The emissions of hydrogen sulphide from thermal areas have earned it the nickname 'sulphur city', and the pungent odour is highly noticeable when you first arrive: strangely, you soon get used to it!

Rotorua is located on the shores of the lake of the same name, and there are numerous other scenic lakes near by to visit. The area is an active centre for Maori culture, and traditional concerts are on offer in many hotels and outlying *marae* (see panel overleaf). The city was first developed as a spa town at the end of the last century, and the bath house (built in 1908) still exists, although today it is a museum: other popular attractions include soaking in hot pools, sheep shows, trout and wildlife parks, and scenic flights or cruises on the lake.

The main thermal area within the boundaries of the city is the extensive **Whakarewarewa**▶▶▶ (*Open* daily 8.30–5; guided tours hourly. *Admission charge* moderate) which features boiling mud pools, silica terraces, steam vents and other thermal phenomena. The main part of the reserve is the Geyser Flat, which has at least seven active geysers, including two which perform with almost clockwork reliability: the Prince of Wales Feathers, which shoots up as high as 12m, always precedes the mighty Pohutu (Maori for 'splashing'), which can reach as high as 30m and usually lasts about five to ten minutes (very occasionally it goes on for hours on end).

Whakarewarewa (or 'Whaka', as it is most often called) is well worth a visit for the geysers alone, but it is also the home of the **New Zealand Maori Arts and Crafts Institute**▶▶ (*Open* same hours, entrance on the same ticket as Whakarewarewa), which trains young craftspeople in the old traditions. You can watch them at work, and there is a gallery with recent carvings on display. Beyond the Geyser Flat is a replica Maori village with a daily cultural show (*Open* 12.15. *Admission charge* moderate).

Also near the city is the thermal zone called **Hell's Gate**▶▶▶, east of Lake Rotorua (see page 97), while other major areas of activity such as Waimangu, Waiotapu and Orakei Korako are some distance away.

Rotorua information
The purpose-built Tourism Rotorua complex (67 Fenton Street, tel: 07 348 5179. *Open* daily 8–5.30), centrally located downtown, houses not only the information centre but also a Department of Conservation office, an excellent map shop, toilet and shower facilities and a restaurant.

The mock-Tudor Tourism Rotorua complex, built to match the city's earliest buildings

Take the Skyline gondola up Mount Ngongotaha for panoramic views of the city and lake

On the lakeshore, the **Government Gardens** are an extensive park-like area issuing steam incongruously from the manicured croquet lawns and rose beds. At the centre of the gardens is the **Bath House**, a mock-Tudor structure whose orange-coloured half-timbering is either vulgar or charming, depending on your point of view. Built in 1908, it was once an actual bath house and was a deliberate attempt to emulate the elegance of a European spa. It had all the latest balneological equipment as well as thermal pools and massage cubicles and a foyer graced by thirteen classical marble sculptures. Although it was successful as a spa, by the 1920s faith in spa treatment was waning and the building was neglected. Rotorua City Council took it on in 1963 and it now houses the **Rotorua Art and History Museum▶▶** (*Open* daily 10–4.30. *Admission charge* inexpensive). This has some excellent exhibits displayed in rather cramped conditions. Permanent exhibitions include 'In the Shadow of the Volcano', which traces the story of the effects of the 1886 eruption on the people of the area; 'The Legacy of Houmaitawhiti', which deals with the history and *taonga* (treasures) of the Te Arawa Maori; and 'The Way We Were', which gives some idea about the beginnings of Rotorua as a spa town.

Just near the Bath House, the **Polynesian Pools▶** (*Open* daily 9am–10pm. *Admission charge* varies) contains a number of different mineral pools and hot springs to suit your ailment or state of fatigue – with total relaxation practically guaranteed by means of 'Aix massage' (administered under jets of hot water). Also within the grounds of Government Gardens, the **Orchid Gardens** (*Open* daily 8.30–5.30. *Admission charge* moderate) feature year-round displays of orchids, ferns

Maori concerts
Rotorua is one of the best places in New Zealand to experience a traditional Maori concert and hangi. Maori owned operators for these evening events include Rotoiti Tours (tel: 07 348 8969), Tamaki Tours (tel: 07 346 2823) and Waka Hikoi (tel: 07 362 7878). Ned's Café (tel: 07 348 8272), offers traditional foods from 11.30am.

and other exotic plants; there is also a water organ (on the hour 9–5) with synchronised lighting and music.

Several major attractions lie along the west shore of the lake, just a few minutes' drive from the city centre. The first of these is the **Skyline Skyride▸** (*Open* daily 9–5. *Admission charge* moderate), where a gondola whisks you 200m up the side of Mount Ngongotaha to a café/restaurant complex at the top. The young-at-heart can whizz back down again for part of the way on a luge (a sledge running down a purpose-built track) or a flying fox.

Just past the gondola base is **Rainbow Springs▸▸▸** (*Open* daily 8–5. *Admission charge* moderate), the largest and best-known of the trout springs in the area. The big tourist complex here includes a souvenir shop, photo processing facilities and a restaurant. Just inside the park entrance, the Rainbow Spring itself flows at a rate of 4.5 million litres a day, welling up into a series of crystal-clear pools where hundreds of trout come to feed and spawn (the trout are free to swim back to the lake via a small stream at any time). Spawning usually occurs in July, when pairs of trout can be seen laying and fertilising their eggs in the shingle bed of the stream. There is a large underwater viewing window for close-up views of the rainbow, brown and tiger trout in the pools. Beside the springs is a small zoo-type area which specialises in animals introduced to the country (such as deer, Himalayan thar and wild pigs), as well as native and introduced birds. It also has a nocturnal aviary housing kiwi and morepork.

Across the road (and linked by a tunnel) is the **Rainbow Farm▸▸**, part of the same complex. Here a huge barn is the setting for regular shows (at 10.30am, 11.45am, 1pm, 2.30pm. *Admission charge* moderate) featuring sheep-shearing, sheepdog mustering, a 'sheep auction' and plenty of other educational agricultural entertainment. There is also a shop incorporating a 'museum' with displays on pioneers and farming.

Continuing along the highway you will reach **Agrodome▸▸**, which has another show barn with regular demonstrations and sheep/cattle shows (daily at 9.15am, 11am and 2.30pm. *Admission charge* moderate). The Rainbow Farm setting is perhaps better, because the barn is open-ended and overlooks fields where the sheep are mustered, but otherwise the jokes and patter are remarkably similar in both shows.

Looping behind Mount Ngongotaha, Paradise Valley Road leads to **Paradise Valley Springs▸▸** (*Open* daily 9–5. *Admission charge* moderate). This is another trout-viewing area, with a dozen spring-fed pools strung out alongside the Ngongotaha stream; the 6ha park is home to a range of native New Zealand wildlife and a pride of African lions; in addition it contains a wetlands area with native birds.

The legend of the lake
Mokoia Island, in the middle of Lake Rotorua, is central to the romantic story of Hinemoa and Tutanekai. Hinemoa was a young girl living on the shore who fell in love with an illegitimate young chief, Tutanekai, who lived on the island. Her family opposed the union, and in despair, she lashed together calabash gourds and began the long swim over to Mokoia. The lovers' union was later accepted by their families, and their descendants still live in Rotorua today.

Top shearers demonstrate the art of fleecing at Rotorua Agrodome

When Mount Tarawera erupted in 1886, volcanic ash buried the Maori village at Te Wairoa, preserving the huts and their contents

Rotorua environs

Rotorua's other outlying attractions are scattered over a wider area to the south-east of the lake and the city. One of the most fascinating is **Te Wairoa Buried Village▶▶▶** (*Open* daily 9–5. *Admission charge* moderate), 15km along the Tarawera Road. The village was the main resort for trips to the Pink and White Terraces before the Tarewera eruption (see panel) and had two hotels, a store and numerous *whare* (Maori houses), all of which were buried beneath volcanic ash in 1886. Excavations began in 1936, and in this village the Maori huts, preserved beneath the ash, are the genuine article – unlike those you are likely to see almost everywhere else, which have been built specifically for tourists. A path tours the excavated huts and other interesting relics (including a storehouse with rare stone-carvings), culminating in a short bush walk alongside Te Wairoa falls. There is also a small gallery displaying old photographs and artefacts.

About 20 minutes' drive from the city centre, the **Waimangu Volcanic Valley** (*Open* daily 8.30–5. *Admission charge* moderate) is an extensive thermal area leading down to Lake Rotomahana, with many different geothermal phenomena visible on the one-hour downhill walk to the lakeshore; a bus carries you back up again, or you can combine it with a boat trip on the lake past the site of the former Pink and White Terraces. Hot springs and fumaroles, steaming cliffs and a boiling lake are among the attractions here.

Further south still (29km from Rotorua), the **Waiotapu Thermal Wonderland▶** (*Open* daily 8.30–5.30. *Admission charge* moderate) is another major thermal zone, with pathways between the blowholes and boiling mud pools. Highlights include colourful mineral deposits around the

The Tarawera eruption

The celebrated Pink and White Terraces beneath Mount Tarawera were one of the country's most famous natural attractions during the last century. Previously thought to be extinct, Mount Tarawera erupted without warning in the early hours of 10 June 1886, with Lake Rotomahana beneath it, exploding with a roar heard hundreds of miles away. Rescuers arriving from Rotorua the next day were met with scenes of 'utter distress and unimaginable desolation', with three Maori villages (including Te Wairoa) completely devastated and 153 people dead. Ash, lava and mud were scattered over an area of 16,000 sq km, and the Pink and White Terraces were totally destroyed.

Champagne Pool and Artist's Palette, vast sulphurous craters and the Lady Knox Geyser (which is primed with soap to foam out at 10.15am daily).

Tucked away in a 'hidden valley' between Taupo (32km) and Rotorua (72km), **Orakei Korako▶▶** is a fine thermal area well worth visiting for its colourful silica terraces, which – since the destruction of the famous Pink and White Terraces by the Tarawera eruption in 1886 – are considered to be the best remaining example of this geothermal phenomenon in the country.

Orakei Korako's hot springs bubble out from the north side of the valley on the other side of Lake Ohakuri, which was created in the 1960s by damming the Waikato. Entrance to Orakei Korako (tel: 07 378 3131. *Open* daily 8–4.30, extended hours in summer. *Admission charge* expensive) includes the short boat trip across the lake, from where you first see the Emerald Terrace. The largest in New Zealand, this silica terrace is around 20m thick and continues for 35m beneath the waters of the lake.

From the jetty next to the Emerald Terrace walking tracks continue up through the thermal zones, which include a number of geysers, mud pools, and further silica terraces. A bush walk leads eventually to Ruatapu Cave ('sacred cave'), which has an entrance framed by tree ferns leading down to a 'pool of mirrors' where Maori women are said to have groomed themselves – the valley takes its name from this custom (*orakei korako* means 'the place of adorning'). Passing by one last gusher, the Soda Fountain, the track leads gently back to the boat jetty. Amidst the fernery on the track, look out for examples of the silver fern, the country's national emblem.

Mural town
The small town of Katikati (40km north west of Tauranga) was in economic decline until someone had the bright idea of painting murals all over the place and turning the whole town into an outdoor art gallery. As the idea mushroomed, more and more murals appeared, so did the tourists – and this friendly town prospered once more. The high-quality murals are described in detail in a leaflet available from the Visitor Centre (Cherry Court. *Open* Mon–Fri 9.30–4.30; Sat 10–1).

The Rainbow Terrace, one of the unusual thermal formations at Orakei Korako

Mayor Island
During the main holiday period (25 December to the end of January), there are regular ferry trips (crossing time 2½ hours) to Mayor Island from Tauranga and Mount Maunganui on either the MV *Manutere* (tel: 07 544 3072) or the MV *Te Kuia* (tel: 07 578 7119). At other times private charters and fishing excursions can be arranged.

Mount Maunganui, an important pā *site, marks the eastern entrance to Tauranga harbour*

►► Tauranga *81B2*

The principal city in the Bay of Plenty, prosperous Tauranga is protected from the ocean by Mount Maunganui and Matakana Island, and its harbour has provided shelter for mariners for centuries (the name means 'safe anchorage'). Today it is the busiest export port in New Zealand, while the surrounding region produces an abundance of subtropical fruit. Its inhabitants enjoy an enviable lifestyle, with opportunities for a wide range of adventure sports and nautical activities.

Within the central waterfront area (a large chunk of which is being transformed into an imaginatively conceived pedestrian area) there are several historic sites, including the second-oldest mission station in the country, the **Elms Mission House►►** (Mission Street. *Open* Mon–Sat 2–6pm. *Admission free*). Completed in 1847, it has a tiny chapel, a fascinating library and a superb garden.

Near by on Cliff Road the **Monmouth Redoubt** was a fortified encampment (only the earthworks remain) built by British troops during the New Zealand Wars. Below Cliff Street, at the top of The Strand, is a fine war canoe, *Te Awanui*, carved from kauri wood in 1973.

A few minutes' drive from the city centre, the **Historic Village►►** (155 17th Avenue West. *Open* daily 9–5. *Admission charge* moderate) features a period 'Main Street', a Maori village and other attractions.

Attractive parks within the city centre include Robbins Park, Tauranga Domain and, 4km from the centre,

Historic Elms Mission House in its lovely garden

Yatton Park. Outside the centre, the lakeside **Mclaren Falls Park** (20 minutes along SH29, 11km westwards) is popular for picnics and trout-fishing; next door to it is **Marshalls Animal Park** (*Open* Oct–May daily 10–4.15; Jun–Sep weekends 10–4.15. *Admission charge* inexpensive), with unusual animals such as Tibetan yaks.

Mount Maunganui▶▶, linked to Tauranga city centre by a long harbour bridge, is an attractive resort area with an exceptionally long surfing beach. The Mount itself, at the tip of the peninsula, marks the eastern entrance to Tauranga harbour and offers a fine viewpoint. An important Maori defensive site, it still has many remains of fortifications. Several walking tracks wind their way up to the 232m summit (entrance on Adams Avenue, allow at least two hours return). At the bottom you can soothe aching muscles in the **Hot Salt Pools▶** (Adams Avenue. *Open* daily 8am–10pm. *Admission charge* inexpensive).

Mayor Island (Tuhua), 35km off-shore from Tauranga, is a famous big game fishing base (see panel opposite): it has an underwater marine reserve and some *pā* sites. Extinct craters hold two lakes (one green and one black).

Te Puke *81B2*

The largest inland town in the Bay of Plenty area (31km south-east of Tauranga), Te Puke lays claim to having launched New Zealand's kiwifruit industry, amply documented in **Kiwifruit Country▶** (*Open* daily 9–5. *Admission charge* inexpensive), 5km east of the town on SH2. In May and June, when the trees are in fruit, there is a tour (*Open* hourly 9.15–3.45. *Admission charge* moderate) of the orchards and packing sheds. There is also a children's playground. Next door is the **Vintage Auto Barn▶** (*Open* daily 9–5. *Admission charge* moderate), with over 50 classic and vintage vehicles.

On the shore 15km east of Te Puke is **Maketu**, where the Arawa canoe first landed over 600 years ago, marking the first migration from Hawaiki to Aotaroa. A **cairn** by the river mouth commemorates this event.

River rafting
Tauranga is the main base for rafting expeditions on the Motu River. The rapids are mostly grades three and four, and several adventure options (lasting from one to four days) are operated by the Wet'n'Wild Rafting Company (P O Box 1047, Tauranga, tel: 07 578 4093). Rafting on the Motu is also available through Woodrow Rafting Expeditions (P O Box 770, Tauranga, tel: 07 576 2628).

A replica of the canoe Mataatua, *which brought the first Maori to Whakatane, stands by the sacred rock arch* Pohaturoa

Dolphin swims
Dolphins frequent the Bay of Plenty off-shore from Whakatane, and three-hour trips to swim with resident pods are run on a daily basis between October and May by Dolphins Down Under (92 The Strand, Whakatane, tel: 07 308 4636). The Bay of Plenty is also on the migratory routes of several whale species, so there is a good chance of encountering these too.

▶ Whakatane *81C1*

Whakatane gained its name with the arrival of the *Mataatua* canoe from Hawaiki in the 14th century: as the menfolk stepped ashore to test the lie of the land, the canoe started drifting out to sea with all the women aboard. Although it was *tapu* (forbidden) for women to handle the paddles, the captain's daughter, Wairaka, grabbed a paddle and cried '*Kia Whakatane au i ahau*' ('I will be bold and act as a man') and the others followed suit, bringing the canoe back to shore. The settlement was thus christened Whakatane ('to be manly').

The main street of Whakatane is The Strand. Bisecting it is Boon Street, where you will find the Visitor Information Centre (*Open* daily 9–5) and the small **Whakatane Museum and Gallery▶** (*Open* Mon–Fri 10–4.30; Sat, Sun 1.30–4pm. *Admission charge* inexpensive) which has displays on the eastern Bay of Plenty and its people, as well as a gallery showing changing exhibitions of arts, craft and history.

In the town centre, Whakatane's origins are commemorated by a model of the canoe *Mataatua* next to an old rock arch known as ***Pohaturoa***; this once stood on the foreshore, and was a sacred place where *tohunga* performed tattooing and other ceremonies. Now it is the centrepiece of a small park (corner of The Strand and Commerce Streets), a memorial to the dead of World War I. Next to it stands a statue of Te Hurinui Apanui, a local Mataatua chief.

A statue of Wairaka stands on the Whakatane Heads at the mouth of the river, whilst a nearby plaque marks the landing place of the canoe.

Whale Island (Motuhora) *81C1*

Slightly smaller than White Island, Whale Island or Motuhora is also volcanic and has numerous fumaroles (particularly in the aptly named Sulphur Bay); the island is a major bird nesting site, with one colony of

grey-faced petrels numbering some 10,000 birds. Occupied in pre-European times by Maori, it was also the site of a whaling station in the 1830s: the English name, however, refers not to this but to its shape, which resembles a humpback whale (the Maori name also refers to this likeness). The island is privately owned and is now a wildlife refuge.

▶▶ White Island *81C2*

Lying at the northern end of the Taupo-Rotorua volcanic zone, White Island usually emits a visible plume of steam and often spurts clouds of ash which can be seen for miles around. Its Maori name is Whakaari ('to make visible') and Cook gave the volcano its English name in 1769, inspired by the dense clouds of smoke.

At the end of the 19th century there was a huge demand for sulphur to fertilise farmlands, and the first sulphur was mined on White Island in the 1880s. An eruption in September 1914 caused a mudflow which swept the mining settlement out to sea, leaving no trace of the 12 people who worked there. Parts of the abandoned workings can still be seen on the south-east side of the island. The bankrupt White Island Sulphur Company gave the island to the father of John Buttle, who owns it today. In 1953 it was declared a Private Scenic Reserve, administered by the Department of Conservation.

Organised boat trips run to the island; the journey out takes about an hour each way, with half an hour on shore to gaze at steaming fumaroles and peer into the crater itself. Scenic flights over the island are also popular (see panel).

Island trips
Tours to White Island from Whakatane can be made on board the *Peejay* (tel: 07 312 9075), the *Island Princess* (tel: 07 312 4236), and *Te Kahurangi* (tel: 07 323 7829). For scenic flights contact Vulcan Helicopters (tel: 0800 804 354) and Bell-Air (tel: 07 308 6656). Trips to Motuhora (Whale Island) operate only in December; details from Whakatane DoC (236 The Strand, tel: 07 308 7213).

White Island billows the steam that gave it its name

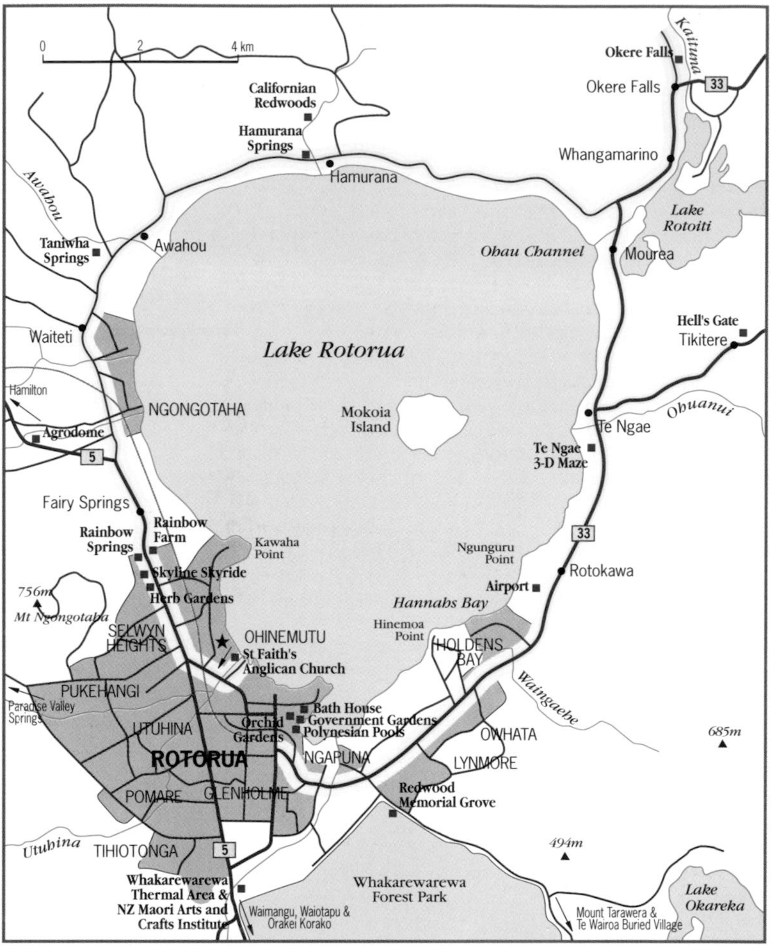

Around Lake Rotorua

This pleasant drive along the shores of Lake Rotorua offers several possible stops to see the original Maori village of the lake, trout springs, volcanic activity, waterfalls and a wildlife park. The distance is about 60km; allow the best part of a day.

Starting from the lakeside jetty, turn right into **Ohinemutu▶▶**, the original Maori village around which the city eventually developed. There is an elaborately carved meeting house, built in 1873, rebuilt 1941, with **St Faith's Anglican Church▶▶** (*Open* 8.30–5) opposite. Constructed in Tudor style in 1910, this features an unusual window depicting Christ draped in a *korowai* (chief's cloak) and has some particularly rich carvings and lattice panel work.

Head down Lake Road and turn right on to SH5 to Hamilton; after 2km you will see the turning on your left for the **Skyline Skyride▶** (see pages 88–9) up the slopes of Mount Ngongotaha, from which there is a fabulous panorama of the lake.

Immediately past the Skyline is **Rainbow Springs** with the **Rainbow**

Farm opposite (see page 89). At the roundabout where the Hamilton road forks left, carry straight on towards Ngongotaha. After passing through the village, the road diverts inland before rejoining the lakeshore at Hamurana; from here there are lovely views back across to Mokoia Island with Mount Tarawera dominating the far lakeside. There is a small strip of wildlife refuge on the shoreline, with the 80ha **Hamurana Springs▶▶** on the left of the road. Pull over into the car park and walk across the bridge which spans the picturesque springs.

Follow the path upstream to a mighty and unusual glade of Californian redwood trees planted in the 1920s. Rejoin the road, which now winds through a scenic part of the lakeshore (with the roadside verges shaded by numerous tree ferns) before joining SH33 at the Ohau Channel. On your right-hand side are the pretty bays and inlets of the western reaches of **Lake Rotoiti▶▶**, once used as a link by canoe between lakes further to the east and Lake Rotorua.

Continue on around the lake, turning left immediately after the Okere Falls Garage down a side road (unsignposted at the time of writing) before the next bridge. The **Okere Falls▶▶** can be reached via a walking track from the car park here: these spectacular falls drop some 100m over a series of falls and rapids in a relatively short distance; this is where the combined outflows from Lakes Rotorua and Rotoiti start their journey to the sea. A series of steps leads down the rock to a cave at the foot of one of the main falls where, according to legend, Maori women and children would hide when the *pā* site on top of the hill was under attack.

Return down the same road, continuing on through Mourea towards Rotorua. At the junction with SH30, make a detour to the left of 4km to **Hell's Gate▶▶▶** (*Open* daily 9–5. *Admission charge* moderate). Also known as 'Tikitere', this reserve covers some 10ha, with a 2.5km walking track around and between the bubbling mud pools, crystal formations, gas vents and other seething sulphurous features. Part of the track includes a bush walk which passes beside the Kakahi Falls; fed by hot lakes higher up, these falls are said to be the only hot thermal waterfall in the southern hemisphere.

Return down to the main road, following it back along the lakeshore to Rotorua city centre.

St Faith's Anglican Church, built in mock-Tudor style in 1910

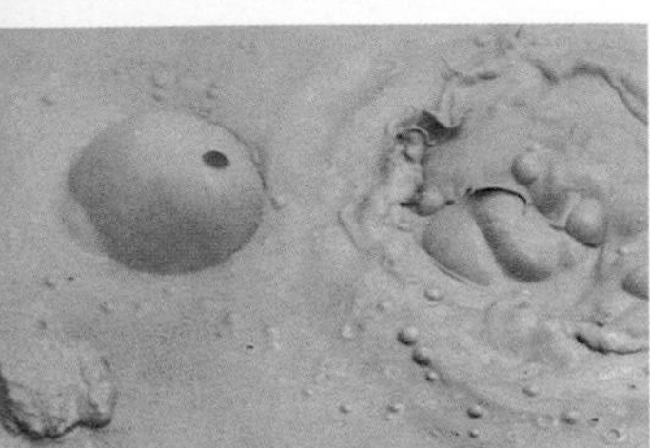

■ New Zealand is famed for its beautiful scenery, and in particular for its serenely spectacular mountains and lakes. Yet these tranquil panoramas mask enormous pressures underground (indeed they were created by them), and the country is still geologically highly active. New Zealanders may disregard the dangers, but the country's history is punctuated with natural disasters. ■

The Ring of Fire
The earth's surface is divided into vast, moving sheets known as tectonic plates. At places where these meet, 'fault lines' develop through which molten magma can force its way. In the Pacific Ocean, continental blocks press against the plate which holds the sea, and the volatile fault line which surrounds the ocean is known as the Pacific 'Ring of Fire'. The islands of New Zealand were thrust up from the ocean bed at the southern extremity of the Ring of Fire.

A fumarole in the crater of volcanic White Island

Shaping the landscape Many of the country's natural features have been created by volcanic activity. In the South Island the main mountain range, the Southern Alps, is still undergoing tectonic uplift, and hot springs bubble through fissures in the earth at Hamner and on the Lewis Pass. The harbours of Otago (Dunedin) and Lyttelton (Christchurch) have been created in the drowned craters of ancient volcanoes. In the North Island a major fault runs from the still active volcano of White Island in the Bay of Plenty down through Rotorua, where boiling mud pools and steaming vents have been a tourist attraction for well over a century. Further south, the crater in which Lake Taupo lies was created by several massive explosions.

The Taupo eruptions Some 250,000 years ago a huge eruption from Taupo spread rock debris and ash across 2,500 sq km of countryside, and material from the eruption has been located in the waters of Antarctica near South America. This monster explosion is the largest known in the southern hemisphere. About 26,500 years ago another vast blast spread ash over most of the country, and in the most recent eruption, 1,800 years ago, pumice and ash buried everything in the surrounding region.

Emerson Street in Napier immediately after the devastating earthquake of February 1931

Earthquake zone The same forces which produce volcanic activity also cause earthquakes, as the tectonic plates grind against each other. The first known earthquake in New Zealand occurred in the Wellington region in 1460, and is thought to have been of about magnitude 8 on the Richter scale. The first earthquake recorded by Europeans was in Queen Charlotte Sound in 1773.

The fledgling settlement of Wellington was awakened at 1.40am on 16 October 1848 by a big earthquake, which was followed by three more over the next eight days. The town was virtually destroyed, but happily only three people died. Seven years later another massive earthquake (8.1 on the Richter scale) rocked the Wellington and Wairarapa region, raising the shoreline by up to three metres in places. Over the next 90 years there were a further 10 severe earthquakes in the region.

The worst disaster in the last century in terms of lives lost was the Tarawera eruption of 10 June 1886, which killed 153 people. With no warning the entire side of the volcano blew out, shattering its base and in the process destroying the famous Pink and White Terraces (see page 90).

In this century One of the country's most powerful earthquakes this century struck the West Coast of the South Island on 16 June 1929: measuring 7.8 on the Richter scale, the Murchison earthquake was so strong that earth movements were noticed 1,600km away in Auckland. Huge tracts of land were uplifted, and 17 people lost their lives. But the worst disaster of all was the Napier earthquake in 1931, when in just two and a half minutes the two towns of Napier and Hastings were reduced to rubble, and 256 people died. During the two weeks that followed, 525 aftershocks were recorded.

On 24 June 1942, the Wellington and Wairarapa area was hit by two earthquakes, the second one (of magnitude 7 on the Richter scale) damaging some 8,000 homes. Two more severe earthquakes followed in August. The biggest recent earthquake was in the Bay of Plenty on 2 March 1987, when a magnitude 6.1 earthquake rocked the whole region. Miraculously, no one died.

The Earthquake Commission

During the 1942 Wellington and Wairarapa earthquakes hundreds of buildings collapsed, and most people found they had inadequate insurance to cover their rebuilding costs. Realising that something needed to be done, the Government set up the Earthquake and War Damage Commission, levying a premium on fire insurance to assist in rebuilding after earthquakes. In 1993 this became the Earthquake Commission (EQC) and cover was extended to other natural disasters. In 1994, the EQC successfully intervened for the first time to prevent a disaster before it happened, by stabilising a massive landslip which was threatening to engulf homes at Akaroa on Banks Peninsula.

Hamilton, commercial centre for the rich agricultural district around the Waikato River

Paddle steamer trips
Moored at Memorial Park directly across the Victoria Bridge from the centre of Hamilton, the MV *Waipa Delta* is modelled on the old paddle-steamers and has a fully licensed restaurant. There are four scenic cruises up-river daily, including a luncheon cruise and a moonlight dinner cruise. For reservations, tel: 07 854 9415.

The Waikato

▶ Cambridge *81B1*

Situated on the Waikato River 24km south-east of Hamilton, Cambridge was first a *pā* site and then a military base, chosen because it was as far upstream as the British gunboats could navigate in 1864. A large redoubt was built in Fort Street behind the present police station, but the town's military phase lasted less than a decade, and it soon developed into a flourishing market town. It is now also a major stud farm centre.

The town has a charming atmosphere, with fine parks and gardens (including a 'village green' at its centre), stately trees and old churches. One of these churches (dating from 1898) has been converted into the award-winning **Cambridge Country Store** (92 Victoria Street. *Open* daily 8.30–5), which claims to be New Zealand's largest retail centre for crafts. There are also half a dozen or more antique shops and galleries, and several craft workshops which you can visit; details from the Information Centre (corner of Queen and Victoria Streets, tel 07 827 6033. *Open* Mon–Fri 8–4.30).

▶▶ Hamilton *81B2*

The commercial and industrial hub of the Waikato region, Hamilton is the largest inland city in New Zealand. With a population of just over 156,000, it has prospered on the back of the dairy industry, forestry and manufacturing; since the beginning of the decade much of the city centre has been renovated to include extensive shopping malls, 'boulevard-style' streets, new office blocks, smart hotels and trendy cafés and restaurants. With its many attractions and a busy calendar of colourful events it is an attractive city for a stop-over.

The Waikato River winds through the heart of Hamilton, with several peaceful parks and gardens laid out on both banks and linked by footpaths and bridges. The city centre is on the west side of the river. Its heart lies half way down the main thoroughfare, **Victoria Street**, in **Garden Place**, a popular venue for street theatre, buskers and outdoor markets, and also the location of the Visitor

Information Centre (City Council Building, tel: 07 839 3360. *Open* Mon–Fri 9–4.45; weekends 10–2).

A couple of minutes' walk away is the **Waikato Museum of Art and History▶▶** (corner of Victoria and Grantham streets. *Open* daily 10–4.30. *Admission charge* inexpensive), with galleries (and a good café) overlooking the Waikato. Permanent exhibits include the 150-year-old war canoe *Te Winika*, and contemporary Tainui carvings and Tukutuku weavings commissioned for the opening of the museum in 1987. The majority of the display space is devoted to a varied programme of changing exhibitions, fine arts, Tainui cultural history, crafts, film and video, and music performances.

Hamilton Gardens▶ (Cobham Drive. *Open* continuous. *Admission free*) cover 58ha and feature numerous theme gardens, including a Chinese garden, English garden, Japanese garden and herb garden. They are also home to the Waikato Polytechnic horticultural school and there is a café/restaurant overlooking the Turtle Lake.

Outside the city centre, the **Hamilton Zoo▶▶** (Brymer Road, signposted from Avalon Drive on SH1. *Open* daily 9–5; last admission 4pm. *Admission charge* moderate) covers 14ha and has a strong conservation theme. Its new free-flight, walk-through aviary is the largest in New Zealand, and other displays include a new rainforest exhibit and a Waikato Wetlands area.

The **National Agricultural Heritage▶**, 10km to the south of the city, in the opposite direction (Mystery Creek Road. *Open* daily 9.30–4.30. *Admission charge* inexpensive), features an agricultural museum, dairy museum, Clydesdale horses, and a 'Down on the Farm' area where children can touch the animals. There are also farm animal demonstrations (daily 11.30am and 1.30pm).

Heritage walk
Amongst its gleaming malls and modern blocks, Hamilton also has a number of historic buildings. Although many are privately owned and not open to the public, some fascinating hidden corners are described in the *Architrek Heritage Trail*, an excellent illustrated booklet available free from the Visitor Centre.

The massive New Zealand Fieldays (sic), the biggest agricultural exposition in the southern hemisphere, is held at the National Agricultural Heritage site in June

A vast range of events takes place each year in and around the Waikato capital. Those worth watching out for include the Ngaruawahia Regatta (March) with Maori canoe races on the river; a hot-air balloon rally (April); the Warbirds fighter plane meet (April); the Waikato races (May); the Waikato Winter Show carnival (May/June); and the massive New Zealand Agricultural Fieldays (June), the largest agricultural expo in the southern hemisphere.

▶ Marokopa *81A1*

The road from Waitomo westwards towards Marakopa and the coast passes a number of scenic attractions, and the three to four-hour round trip makes a pleasant excursion from Waitomo. The first stop is at the remarkable **Mangapohue Natural Bridge▶**, 26km from Waitomo; this massive limestone arch high above the Mangapohue stream is the remnant of a collapsed cave. The bridge is a 15-minute walk from the main road (signposted). Just near by is the **Marokopa Tunnel**, another huge limestone formation; it has a 50m high roof and runs for 270m through the hillside (guided tours daily 10.30. *Admission charge* expensive; contact: Marokopa Tunnel Treks, tel: 07 876 7865).

Further on, the **Marokopa Falls▶▶** (31km from Waitomo) plummet a spectacular 36m over a fault in the limestone, and there are several tracks leading to impressive viewpoints.

Washing the bow carving before a war canoe (waka) race

Otorohanga *81A1*

Set on the fertile flats surrounding the Waipa River (the biggest tributary of the Waikato), Otorohanga was once the northern centre of the great Ngati Maniapoto tribe. Its name (which means 'place of food spun out to last a long journey') refers to the story of a chief who set out from here to Taupo, and who made a small amount of food last the whole journey by means of a magic chant.

Otorohanga was the earliest base for tourists visiting the Waitomo Caves (16km to the south-west) following their 'discovery' in 1887, a role which it has retained to this day: the town has several good-quality motels, tea-rooms, craft shops and other facilities. There is a small **Historical Museum** (Kakamutu Rd. *Open* Sun 2–4. *Admission charge* donation), but the main attraction in the town itself is the **Kiwi House and Native Bird Park►►** (Alex Telfer Drive. *Open* daily 9.30–5. *Admission charge* moderate). Guides are on hand to show you the kiwi in the kiwi house, where there is also a breeding colony of tuatara. An audio-visual presentation on kiwi in their natural environment is shown at regular intervals.

Outside is one of the largest walk-through aviaries in the country, containing some 300 species of native bird, including the tui, saddleback, kakariki and bellbird. Native waterfowl include the endangered blue duck, New Zealand shoveller, brown and grey teal duck, and Auckland Island teal. There is also a Raptor Walk, featuring harriers and owls.

Black-water rafting

This exciting adventure, which started in the 1980s, is now one of the most popular activities at the Waitomo Caves. Up to 20,000 people annually explore the caves (see page 104) in this way. Kitted out with wetsuit and caver's helmet, you set off on a magic journey through the cave (part of the way beneath twinkling glow-worms), floating placidly along on an inflated inner tube. This highly recommended 'soft adventure' is open to anyone. Tours take three hours (90 minutes in the cave) and depart several times daily; booking advised. Contact: Black Water Rafting (Box 13, Waitomo Caves, tel: 07 878 6219); Waitomo Down Under (Box 24, Waitomo, tel: 07 878 6577).

Crowded caves
Time your visit to see the main attraction, the Glow-worm Cave. Tourist buses from Auckland and Rotorua arrive between 10.30 and 3pm, during which time the site is jam-packed. Some sections (such as the Organ Loft) may also be shut off during this time in order to prevent a build-up of carbon dioxide. To enjoy the caves to the full, go early or late.

►►► Waitomo Caves *81A1*

The principal magnet for tourism in the Waikato, the Waitomo Caves have been attracting tourists since their 'discovery' by Europeans over a hundred years ago. The rugged hill country around Waitomo (*wai* = water, *tomo* = hole) is characterised by karst formations, with numerous caves, underground rivers, sink holes and other limestone features. The caves at Waitomo are simply the best-known of these wonderful natural phenomena.

The village at Waitomo Caves developed as a tourist base for the caves at the turn of the century, when the magnificent old Waitomo Caves Hotel was built. Today the activities on offer include numerous caving adventures, horse-trekking, mountain-biking and canoeing.

The Maori knew of the existence of the Waitomo Caves long ago, but they were first explored by Europeans when an English surveyor, Fred Mace, persuaded a local chief, Tane Tinorau, to take him inside in 1887. As the caves were mapped by the Government, visitors started arriving, and Tane and his wife Huti began the first tour business. But damage to the caves prompted the Government to take them over, and it was not until 1989 that they were returned to the descendants of the original owners.

First stop in Waitomo should be the exceptional **Museum of Caves►►** (*Open* daily 8.30–5.30. *Admission charge* inexpensive), with displays on all aspects of limestone caves, including their formation, flora and fauna and exploration, illustrated with videos on glow-worms and the Waitomo area, and an audio-visual presentation on caving. The museum also functions as an information and booking centre for all the nearby activities.

The most famous cave is the outstanding **Glow-worm Cave►►►** (tours depart every half-hour 9–4.30. *Admission charge* expensive). Outside the entrance (500m past the museum) a huge carving, *Te Poupou a Tane Mahuta*, commemorates the centenary of its first exploration. The 45-minute tour of the three-level cave starts off in the Banquet Chamber (where early tourists used to stop for a meal), before leading back up to the Organ Loft where there is a large stalactite formation. From here it descends to the Cathedral, a dramatic cave

The caves at Waitomo, formed in the limestone rock

with incredible acoustics. Finally, a small boat carries visitors through the most awesome part of the tour, a silent journey along an underground river with millions of glow-worms sparkling on the walls and ceiling.

The second most visited cave is **Aranui**►► (tours at 10am, 11am, 1pm, 2pm, 3pm. *Admission charge* expensive), 3km from the village centre. Discovered in 1910 by a young Maori, Ruruku Aranui, it has vast caverns up to 20m high, stalactites 6m tall, and many thousands of delicate 'straw' stalactites and other features. There are no glow-worms, but the limestone formations are possibly more spectacular than those in the main cave.

The third cave is **Ruakuri**► (tours hourly 9–4. *Admission charge* expensive), which has only recently opened to the public owing to a long-running land dispute. It has plenty of limestone formations and patches of glow-worms; the river that runs through it is one of the main locations for black-water rafting (see panel page 103).

Only experienced cavers are advised to descend into the 100m-deep *tomo* (limestone shaft), dubbed the **Lost World** (see panel), which leads down into a cave system (the Mangapu Cave) alive with mosses and ferns and thousands of glow-worms, with underground waterfalls, fossils and astonishing stalactites.

Outside Waitomo, the **Ohaki Maori Cultural Centre**►► (*Open* daily 10–4.30. *Admission charge* inexpensive) is well worth a visit, offering the opportunity to see two of the country's best-known weavers (Diggeress Te Kanawa and Dame Rangimarie Hetet) at work using traditional tools. There is also a contemporary art gallery with woodcarvings, paintings, prints and ceramics of high quality. On the hillside above the centre (which also has a café) is a replica Maori village. The centre is 2km from Waitomo on the road to SH3.

The nearby **Rabbit World** (tours daily 9.30–5. *Admission charge* inexpensive) has fluffy angora rabbits.

*Sparks of light in the Glow-worm Cave are produced by the New Zealand glow-worm (*Arachnocampa luminosa*), luminous at all stages in its life*

The Lost World

There are several options available for abseiling into the Lost World, the easiest of which is a tandem abseil tethered to a guide (four hours). A one-and-a-half-day option includes complete abseil training and an underground river journey. Contact: Lost World Adventures, c/o Caves Museum, tel: 07 878 7640.

Named by Captain Cook (far right: monument at Kaiti Hill, Gisborne) Cape Kidnappers (above) dramatically encloses the southern end of Hawke Bay

Grapes flourish in the Hawke's Bay region, home of some of New Zealand's most prestigious vineyards

NORTH ISLAND THE EAST COAST

Eastland Beyond Whakatane, at the southern edge of the Bay of Plenty, stretch the vast wilderness areas, bush-clad mountains and long deserted beaches of Eastland, a remote corner of the North Island which bulges out into the Pacific half-way down the eastern coastline.

Captain (then Lieutenant) Cook made his first landings here, astutely (if unimaginatively) naming the easternmost promontory East Cape, even though he had yet to complete his circumnavigation of the island. But the rugged hinterland (in particular the Raukumara Range, running along the spine of Eastland) discouraged early settlers, who flocked instead to the fertile lands and warm climate of the Hawke Bay hinterland. This pattern of settlement by newcomers meant that the Maori were left more or less in peace. Much of Eastland is still Maori-owned, with Maori culture much in evidence in the many small communities that dot the area. The principal tribe is the Ngati Porou, centred mostly on Tikitiki and Ruatoria.

Running through the Raukumara Range is the **Motu River**, which rushes through a spectacular 100km gorge

bordered by virgin native forest. '*Motu*' means 'isolated', and it is an apt description for this mysterious river. The Motu remained unexplored by Europeans until 1919, when four local lads set off in two wooden boats for what they thought was a three-day adventure down river: ten harrowing days later they arrived at the Pacific Ocean, after battling rapids and negotiating precipitous gorges. In 1970, a special Act of Parliament designated the river and a large part of the Raukumura as a Wilderness Zone.

The northern gateway to Eastland is **Opotiki** in the Bay of Plenty. From here there are two routes across Eastland, the first of which cuts across inland to **Gisborne** (148km), passing through fern-lined **Waioeka Gorge** and the **Raukumara Forest Park**. The second and more compelling option is to take the coastal route along the **East Cape Road** (see page 111). Gisborne, on the southern side of the Eastland promontory, is the region's

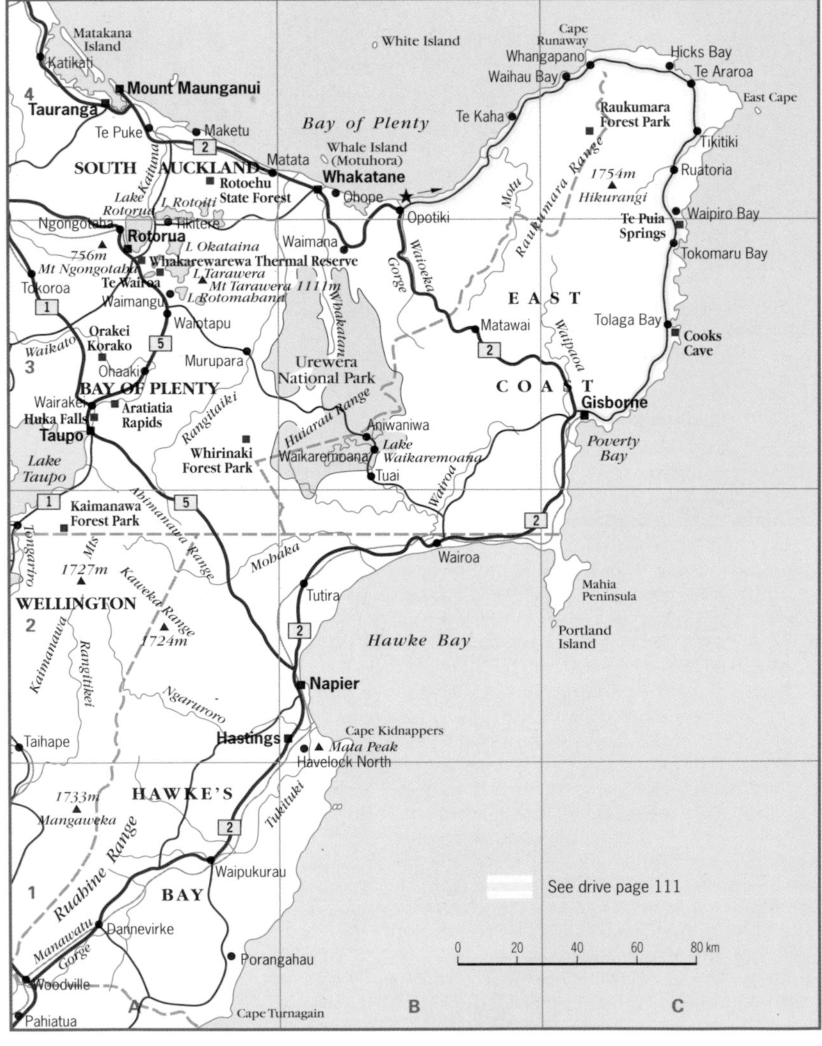

capital. Thanks to its orientation towards the International Date Line, it is also the first city in the world to witness the sunrise every day.

Hawke's Bay One of the country's prime wine regions, the fertile Hawke's Bay region lies round Hawke Bay itself. The largest resort in the area is Napier, an unusual and interesting city which makes an ideal base for visiting the region. Flattened by a massive earthquake in 1931, it was rebuilt almost entirely in Art Deco style, and is probably unique in the world in terms of the unity of design throughout the city. The 'bay city', as locals know it, has smartened itself up in recent years to capitalise on its architectural heritage, and is now reaping the rewards in the form of a tourist boom.

At the centre of a thriving horticultural district, Hastings lies inland 20km south of Napier in the middle of the Heretaunga Plains. Whilst not perhaps as attractive as its sister city, it is the main departure point for visits to the massive gannet colony at nearby Cape Kidnappers.

Art Deco architecture in Napier, at the centre of the Hawke's Bay wine-growing region

► Gisborne 108C3

Cook made his first landfall here in 1769, an event which is commemorated in the **Cook National Historic Reserve** at the end of Kaiti Beach, where there is a memorial to the explorer. Above the reserve, a statue of Cook gazes out from the top of **Kaiti Hill**, from where there is a terrific view of the city and harbour. Other landmarks celebrating this historic landing include a statue of **Young Nick** (the surgeon's boy on the *Endeavour* who first spotted land) on the north side of the rivermouth at Waikanae Beach, and a **totem pole** presented by Canada to mark the bicentenary of the landings (in Alfred Cox Park, just off Grey Street).

Beneath Kaiti Hill, the **Poho-o-Rawiri Meeting House►** is one of the largest and most decorative in the country, with elaborately carved gable boards inside (*Open* daily but ask permission before entering). A considerable number of Maori artefacts, as well as exhibits on the natural history of the area, are displayed in the **Museum and Arts Centre►** (18–20 Stout Street. *Open* Mon–Fri 10–4, weekends 1.30–4. *Admission charge* inexpensive). Local and touring exhibitions of arts and crafts are also staged here, while the grounds contain a number of historic cottages and other buildings; on the riverbank is a small maritime museum housed inside the remains of the *Star of Canada*, wrecked on a reef off-shore in 1912.

Hawke's Bay Wines
Hawke's Bay is the oldest established wine-growing region in New Zealand and has an unusually warm and balmy climate. Since its vineyards are planted on a range of soil types, there is scope for all the classic grape varieties. The growing season continues right through to April, which is ideal for late-maturing varieties such as Cabernet Sauvignon and Riesling. The region's Chardonnay and Cabernet Sauvignon blends are often considered the best in New Zealand, with its Sauvignon Blanc and Riesling also commanding recognition.

Gannet trips
Most tours to the gannet colony at Cape Kidnappers depart from Te Awanga, 20 minutes south of Hastings. The long-established Gannet Beach Adventures (tel: 06 875 0898) have been running tours by tractor-trailer (four hours) for over 40 years. Gannet Safaris (tel: 06 875 0511) run a three-hour trip in 4WD vehicles. Another option is a tour in a Mercedes Benz Unimog, which has the advantage of much higher seats; contact Unimog Adventure Tours (tel: 06 835 4446). Finally, you can have a lot of fun driving there yourself on a four-wheel motorbike with Quadventures (tel: 025 482 989). All tour times are dependent on tide tables.

Up to 15,000 gannets crowd the rocks at Cape Kidnappers during the nesting season

▶ Hastings *108B2*

The Maori knew this area as *Heretaunga Haukunui Ararua*, poetically translated as 'Heretaunga of life-giving dews and arcadian pathways'. Today, the countryside is clothed with rows of fruit trees and vines, and fruit-processing and wine-making are the major industries.

Like Napier, Hastings was devastated by the 1931 earthquake; more buildings survived here, but many lost their masonry façades, so the rebuilt town looked almost completely new. The town centre has numerous interesting architectural embellishments, shopfronts and other Spanish Mission style features to discover described in *Take a Walk through Historic Hastings*, available from the Visitor Information Centre (Russell St North, tel: 06 878 0510. *Open* Mon–Fri 8.30–5; weekends 10–3).

In the town centre, the **Hawke's Bay Exhibition Centre▶** (Civic Square. *Open* Mon–Fri 10–4.30; weekends 12–4.30. *Admission charge* variable) is the region's major venue for touring exhibitions. A few minutes' walk from Civic Square, you can sample local beers on a tour of the **Hawke's Bay Brewery** (304–8 Ellison Rd. *Open* tours Mon, Wed, Fri 10.30am. *Admission charge* donation).

As well as the town's fine parks, children will also enjoy a visit to **Fantasyland▶** (Grove Road. *Open* 10–6 daily. *Admission charge* inexpensive/children free), with its numerous rides, boat trips and other amusements.

Hastings is the main access point for the **Cape Kidnappers Gannet Sanctuary▶▶▶**, situated on a dramatic promontory at the southern end of Hawke Bay. In Maori legend the cape was the hook with which Maui fished the North Island from the sea, but it was renamed by Captain Cook after the local Maori tried to kidnap a Tahitian boy from the *Endeavour*. The gannets flock here in their thousands from July onwards, making this one of their biggest and most spectacular mainland nesting sites in the world. The best time to visit is between November and late February.

Drive East Cape Road

The wharf at Tolaga Bay behind a crimson-flowered pohutukawa bush

See map on page 108.

This magnificent drive, starting in Opotiki and finishing in Gisborne, follows the East Cape Road past rocky coves and sandy beaches backed by jagged bush-clad ranges. The 342km road is at its most spectacular during the summer, when flowering pohutukawa trees add vivid splashes of crimson to the seashore.

From Opotiki, the road passes several small beaches and bays and crosses the Motu River before leading to **Te Kaha**▶, set in a picturesque cove. A whaling centre until the 1930s, the town is now a popular holiday resort. The **Tukaki Meeting House**▶ on the *marae* has an elaborately carved lintel, said to be the finest example of Maori carving in the region.

Beyond, the Bay of Plenty ends at **Cape Runaway**. The beach at **Whangaparaoa** played a prominent part in Maori history as the arrival point for the first great canoes from Hawaiki. **Hicks Bay** (153km from Opotiki) is the site of the **Tuwhakairiora Meeting House**▶▶▶, one of the grandest in Eastland, with carvings dating from the 1870s.

Te Araroa boasts a 600-year-old pohutukawa tree; turn off here to the **East Cape Lighthouse**▶, the most easterly in New Zealand, with fine views to East Island off the coast.

From Te Araroa the road passes inland to reach **Tikitiki**, which has an elaborately carved Anglican Church, **St Mary's**▶, built in 1924 as a memorial to local Maori who died in World War I. Further south, overlooked by the sacred mountain of Hikurangi, is **Ruatoria,** the main settlement of the Ngati Porou. **Waipiro Bay**▶ and **Tokomaru Bay**▶ are the next two beaches, with the hot springs of **Te Puia** between the two. Tokomaru Bay is a stronghold of Maori culture with four active *marae*. **Tolaga Bay** boasts the longest wharf in New Zealand and a good surfing beach; to the south is **Cooks Cove**▶▶▶ which is reached via a 4km walkway across private land.

The coast road ends at **Gisborne**.

One of Napier's splendid Art Deco buildings

Below and inset: the devastation after the earthquake

 **Napier** *108B2*

Napier – which was named after the British General Sir Charles Napier – developed from a whaling and trading station established in the 1840s. The Maori had for many years grown kumara crops on the flatlands in the bay, and gradually the settlers extended the area under cultivation; soon Napier was a thriving commercial centre with a busy port servicing a wide area.

But at 10.47am on 3 February 1931, the town's neat, orderly streets of brick buildings were reduced to a heap of rubble by a massive earthquake measuring 7.8 on the Richter scale. There was also widespread damage in neighbouring Hastings and as far afield as Wairoa and the northern Wairarapa, but Napier was a scene of devastation, as fires destroyed those buildings which had managed to survive the tremor. On that day, 256 people died. Rescue work was hampered by subsequent tremors, and by the destruction of road and rail links.

The town was completely rebuilt in the Art Deco style, then at the height of its popularity, a wholehearted choice which symbolised the burying of the tragedies of the past and the anticipation of a new age of optimism. Unique as an example of a planned townscape in a single, coherent style, Napier undoubtedly possesses the most significant collection of Art Deco buildings in the world.

A good starting point for exploring this rich architectural heritage is the **Art Deco Shop** at the headquarters of the Art Deco Trust (Desco Centre, 163 Tennyson Street, tel: 06 835 0022. *Open* daily 9–5). As well as showing a half-hour video (*Open* on demand. *Admission free*) on the

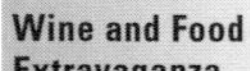

city's well-preserved buildings, they also conduct **guided walks** (26 Dec–19 Feb Sat, Sun, Wed 2pm. *Admission charge* moderate). If you want to wander on your own, pick up a copy of their leaflet, *Take a Walk through Art Deco Napier*. Numerous events designed to relive the glamour of the 1920s and 1930s are staged during Napier's annual Art Deco Weekend, held in February (details from the Art Deco Trust).

The story of the earthquake and its aftermath is told in the superb **Hawke's Bay Museum▶▶▶** (Marine Parade. *Open* daily 10–4.30. *Admission charge* inexpensive), with additional displays on Art Deco around the world and 20th-century interior design. The first gallery you pass through, however, entitled *Nga Tukemata* ('the awakening'), focuses on Maori history, presenting a visually exciting display of the art, carvings and other treasures of the Ngati Kahungunu people who dominated much of the eastern North Island.

The museum's newest section is part of the recently established New Zealand Dinosaur Centre, and includes the country's first robotic, animated dinosaur, as well as a display featuring the ground-breaking discoveries of local amateur palaeontologist Joan Wiffen.

Also on Marine Parade is the **Kiwi House▶▶▶** (*Open* daily 11–3. *Admission charge* inexpensive), which is the only place in the country (apart from in the wild) where you can see a live kiwi not enclosed behind glass (this may not sound very dramatic, but it is often hard to see these shy creatures in nocturnal kiwi houses). At 1pm daily 'Jeremy' (who is thought to be about 20 years old) is

Wine and Food Extravaganza
The Hawke's Bay Wine and Food Extravaganza is a three-day event held each February, with food and wine tastings, art exhibitions, live music, banquets and even a horse race through the vineyards. There is also a gourmet dinner (to raise funds for a local hospice), followed by an auction of wine by the barrel – the only wine auction of its kind in New Zealand. Details from Harvest Hawke's Bay Weekend, P O Box 7095, Taradale, tel: 06 844 2053; fax: 06 844 3378.

Wine trails and restaurants
A Guide to Hawke's Bay Wineries (available in either Napier or Hastings) lists around two dozen wineries which you can visit for tastings and purchases direct from the producer. Organised tours are also offered by Eastland Tours (tel: 06 836 6705) and Bay Tours Midi Coachlines (tel: 06 843 6953). Wineries in the Hawke's Bay area now sometimes have restaurants attached to them, where you can enjoy good food while sampling the often extensive range of wines from the vineyard. Those recommended for winery lunches include Brookfields Vineyards (tel: 06 834 4615), Clearview Estate (tel: 06 875 0150), Sacred Hill Winery (tel: 06 844 2576), St George Estate (tel: 06 877 5356) and Vidal Winery (tel: 06 876 8105).

Te Mata Peak
From the top of Te Mata Peak there are superb views of the Heretaunga Plains and Hawke's Bay, with Hastings laid out neatly in the foreground and Napier sparkling in the middle of the bay. Beyond, the panorama extends as far as the Mahia Peninsula and the Kaimanawa Ranges, with even Mount Ruapehu in the Tongariro National Park said to be visible on an exceptionally clear day. The 399m-high peak is popular for hang-gliding and paragliding, and there is a road all the way to the top (11km from Hastings via Havelock North).

brought out into the dimmed light of a small amphitheatre, where he grubs around for worms while staff deliver a highly informative talk about the kiwi and its habits. An exhibition area contains other kiwi (also more visible than elsewhere), as well as morepork, geckos, carnivorous snails and other fascinating creatures.

Further along Marine Parade, **Marineland▶▶** (*Open* daily 10–4.30. *Admission charge* moderate) features seals, penguins, sea lions and dolphins. Dolphin shows (*Open* daily 10.30 and 2) may be frowned upon nowadays, but Marineland has tried to keep abreast of the times with 'Behind the Scenes' tours (*Open* daily 9am. *Admission charge* moderate) and swimming with the dolphins (four times daily. *Admission charge* expensive; advanced booking required, tel: 06 835 7579).

Further down still, the **Aquarium▶** (*Open* daily 9–5. *Admission charge* moderate) is housed in a circular building with a giant fish tank at its centre holding up to 30 different species (including some massive rays and a seven-gill shark); again, you can take a 'Behind the Scenes' tour (*Open* daily 2.30pm. *Admission charge* moderate), and visiting divers can even swim in the main tank (*Open* by arrangement, tel: 06 835 7579 for bookings. *Admission charge* expensive).

Along the coast road is **Opossum World▶▶▶** (8 Normanby Street, signposted off SH2. *Open* daily 9.30–4. *Admission charge* inexpensive), which, though relatively small, is the only one of its kind in New Zealand and very imaginatively presented. Part of a working tannery for possum hides, it includes an extremely graphic display on the possum's life cycle.

Just outside Napier itself, the Otatara *Pā* Historic Reserve▶▶▶ (Springfield Road, signposted after the Taradale Shopping Centre 10km from the city centre. Open site. *Admission free*), is well worth a detour, not only because of its impressive size (some 33ha), but also because a large number of the original earthworks are still visible. They have been greatly enhanced by a conservation programme, completed in 1993, which included re-creating the palisades and the ancestral figures (*powhenua*) surrounding the *pā*, in order to create an impression of the true appearance of a fortified encampment all those hundreds of years ago. There are two separate *pā* (Otatara and above it Hikurangi), and a one-hour loop track around the site is dotted with panels indicating the various defensive systems, *rua* (food pits), gardens and *whare* (houses).

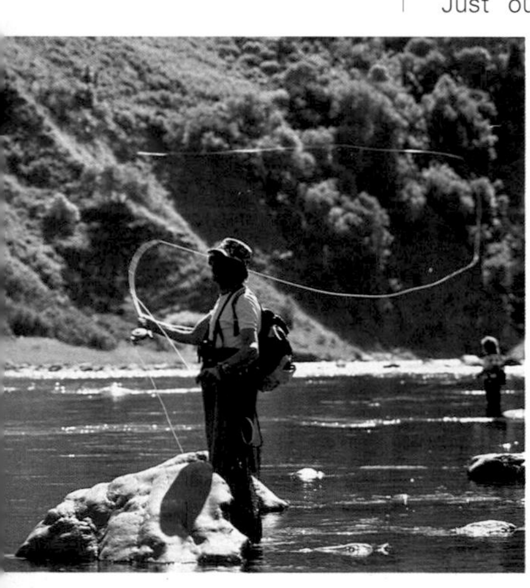

Fishing in the fast-flowing streams of the Urewera National Park, to the north of Hawke Bay

▶▶ Urewera National Park *108B3*

Urewera National Park is popular for tramping (with numerous walks, ranging from short strolls to the 51km-long Lake Track), fishing, bird-watching, canoeing and hunting (red deer and wild pig are widespread, and it is considered one of the best hunting grounds in the North Island). Covering 55 sq km at the southern edge of the park is **Lake Waikaremoana▶▶** ('the sea of rippling waters'), fed by waterfalls and streams from the dense forests which surround it.

According to mythology a local chief, Mahu, asked his daughter to fetch water from a well. She refused, and in his anger he drowned her. She turned into a *taniwha* (water monster), and in her desperate attempts to escape, filled the nearby valleys with water and created the lake. It is her spirit which is said still to agitate the lake waters, hence the name 'sea of rippling waters'. Later, Mahu also threw his other children into the lake, and they turned into stone and became the islands known today as Te Whanau-a-Mahu ('Mahu's children').

At **Aniwaniwa,** on the eastern shore of the lake, is the main DoC Visitor Centre (*Open* 8–12, 1–5) which has a number of informative displays on the park's natural and human history. As well as providing information on tramping, huts, fishing licences and so on, they produce a booklet, *Local Tracks,* which describes 23 short walks within the park. There is a motor camping ground here, and this is also a busy boating and fishing area.

The Lake Track embraces superb views of the lake from the surrounding beech forests, and there are plenty of opportunities for swimming from isolated beaches, fishing and bird-watching; one of the most popular walks in the North Island, the 51km track takes between three and four days to complete.

Eastland carvings
Eastland is noted for its vigorous and elaborate Maori carvings, examples of which can be seen at Te Kaha, Hicks Bay and Tikitiki. But many of the finest pieces are now elsewhere, notably the meeting house *Te Hau ki Turanga* (now in the Museum of New Zealand Te Papa Tongarewa in Wellington) and the war canoe *Te Toki a Tapiri* (now in the Auckland Museum).

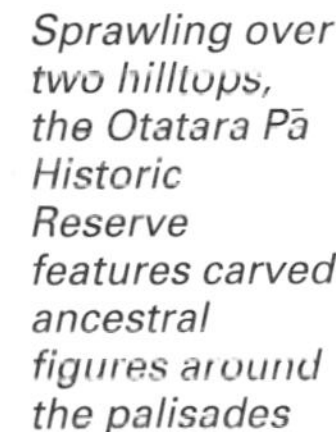

Sprawling over two hilltops, the Otatara Pā Historic Reserve features carved ancestral figures around the palisades

Cook's landings

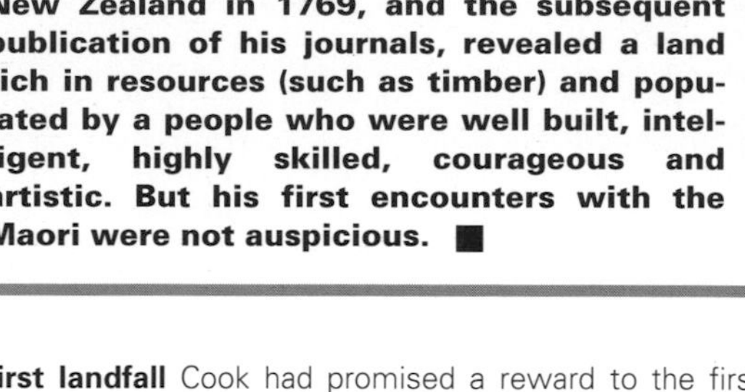

■ Captain James Cook's 'rediscovery' of New Zealand in 1769, and the subsequent publication of his journals, revealed a land rich in resources (such as timber) and populated by a people who were well built, intelligent, highly skilled, courageous and artistic. But his first encounters with the Maori were not auspicious. ■

The explorer Captain James Cook

First landfall Cook had promised a reward to the first crew member to spot land, and it was at 2pm on 6 October 1769 that a ship's boy, Nicholas Young, sighted the east coast of the North Island. As promised, the headland (off Gisborne) was named Young Nick's Head. Two days later Cook led a landing party ashore, hoping to establish friendly relations with the Maori, but their visit ended badly when they killed a Maori whom they believed to be attacking one of the ship's boats. Next day five more Maori were killed in a canoe which might (or might not) have been about to attack the ship.

Cook left the bay on 11 October, naming it Poverty Bay because 'it afforded us no one thing which we wanted'. He sailed north to Tolaga Bay (56km north of Gisborne), where the crew rested for six days, collecting wood, water and plant specimens and trading with the local Maori. At one end of the cove a natural rock arch (which still stands today) caught the eye of the naturalist Joseph Banks, who claimed it was 'certainly the most magnificent surprise I have ever met with'.

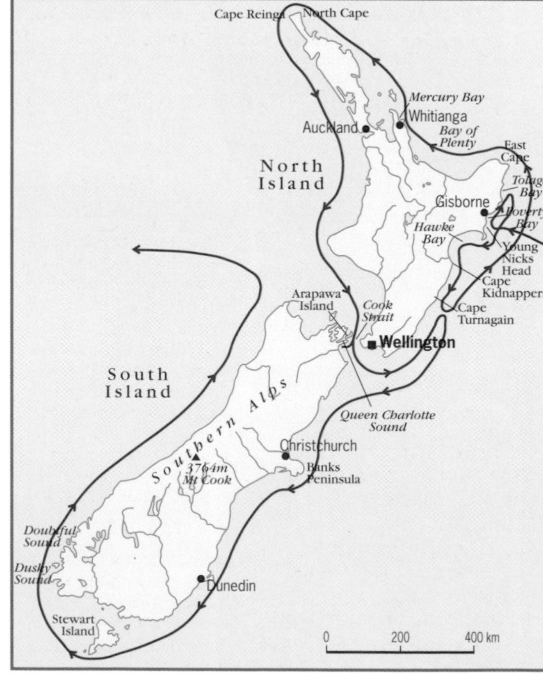

From Tolaga Bay, Cook then turned south again towards Hawke Bay, anchoring off the cape at its southern end. Here, while bartering with Cook from their canoes, local Maori seized a Tahitian boy and dragged him overboard. The crew opened fire, killing several Maori in the canoe. Cook named the promontory Cape Kidnappers, then continued on as far south as Cape Turnagain before doubling back around the East Cape.

His Majesty's name Crossing the Bay of Plenty, he then anchored off Whitianga in what is now the Coromandel. Here he stayed for eleven days, during which time he observed the transit of

the planet Mercury, after which he named the bay. He made friendly contact with the local tribes, then raised the Union Jack, and 'took formal possession of the place in the name of His Majesty'.

From Mercury Bay, Cook sailed around the North Cape following the western coastline of the North Island and then anchored off the South Island, having previously entered 'a very deep and broad inlet' which he named Queen Charlotte Sound. He spent three weeks here in an anchorage he named Ship Cove, while the ship's naturalists, Joseph Banks and Daniel Solander, made detailed studies of the local flora and fauna. Cook also climbed a hill on Arapawa Island and spotted open sea to the east, thus discovering the strait now named after him. He was to return to Ship Cove five times on this and subsequent voyages. On his second voyage, in 1773, he let loose the first sheep in New Zealand here and witnessed his first cannibal feast. Cook then sailed north to Cape Turnagain to prove to his sceptical officers that the North Island was indeed an island.

The South Island As he circumnavigated the South Island, Cook was four times blown out of sight of land – which accounts for his major errors in mapping the new land (he represented Banks Peninsula as an island and Stewart Island as a peninsula). Cook thought it too risky to enter Doubtful Sound, much to the disappointment of the naturalists on board. On his second voyage he spent several weeks in Dusky Sound, resting his crew, setting up workshops on shore and brewing spruce beer to counter scurvy.

Cook's expeditions collected plants, birds and insects previously unknown to Europeans

A near miss
At the same time as Cook was making his first landfall in New Zealand, the French explorer de Surville was somewhere off the North Island on board the *Saint Jean Baptiste*, desperately seeking an anchorage in order to rest his sick crew, but prevented from doing so by a storm. As Cook travelled anti-clockwise around the North Island, he sailed around Cape Reinga in the same storm. The ships passed each other unawares – thus narrowly avoiding a remarkable coincidence in the history of exploration.

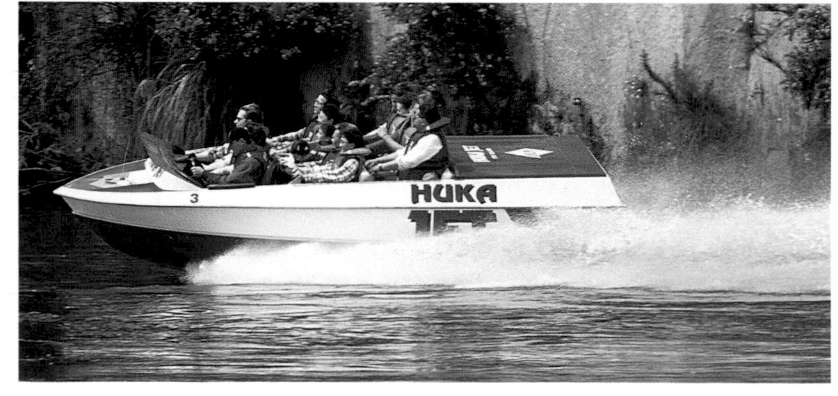
3
HUKA

CENTRAL NORTH ISLAND AND THE WEST COAST

Lake Taupo, in the centre of North Island south of Rotorua, is the largest inland lake in New Zealand and feeds the Waikato River. Famous for its trout fishing, the township of **Taupo** also has its own thermal attractions and a host of other activities geared towards tourism.

Active volcanic craters, lava flows, hot springs, lakes, forest and alpine herbfields are just a few of the natural attractions in the **Tongariro National Park**, at the heart of the North Island. As well as its three active volcanoes – Tongariro (1,967m), Ngauruhoe (2,287m) and Ruapehu (2,797m) – it also has the only permanent snow and commercial skifield in the North Island, and so draws skiers from the big cities throughout the winter. Summertime activities include day walks, tramping, rock and ice-climbing, mountain-biking, and flightseeing. Around a million people visit the park annually.

Pages 118–19 top: The Northerner crosses the Makatote Viaduct

Page 118 below: A jet boat on Lake Taupo

Mount Taranaki, a classically symmetrical volcanic cone, is the most striking feature of the West Coast. Captain Cook spotted it on 10 January 1770, noting that it was 'a very high mountain and in appearance greatly resembling the peak of Teneriffe'. He named it Egmont in honour of the Earl of Egmont, then First Lord of the Admiralty, but the Maori continued to know it as Taranaki. The matter was settled in 1986, when the Government ruled that both Mount Egmont and Taranaki may officially be used. The surrounding 33,000ha of parkland is still called the **Egmont National Park** (the second-oldest national park in the country, created in 1900). The mountain slopes are popular for skiing in winter, and in summer the numerous tracks are busy with day walkers and trampers. It is also possible to climb the summit in a day.

Sheltering beneath Taranaki's bulk is **New Plymouth**, a

Open tussock lands around Mount Taranaki

convenient touring base which is also well known for its parks and gardens and nearby surfing beaches.

Wanganui and the Whanganui River To the south-east of Taranaki, at the mouth of the **Whanganui River** is **Wanganui** (somehow it lost its 'h'), one of the oldest towns in New Zealand. Legend has it that a Taranaki chief spent several days here waiting for transport to cross the river mouth, from which the river became known as Whanganui (*whanga* = to wait, *nui* = long).

The first missionaries ventured up the river valley in 1840, collecting signatures for the Treaty of Waitangi. As settlers followed, the river developed into a major artery, and by the mid-1860s the first steamer service had reached **Pipiriki**. By 1891, this had become a regular service between Wanganui and Taumarunui, a journey which took three days with overnight stops at Pipiriki and a houseboat moored at Maraekowhai.

The wonders of the scenery soon attracted a thriving tourist trade, and by 1905 no fewer than 12,000 tourists had made the journey. The houseboat *Makere* was a model of elegance, with its own dining room complete with chandeliers (it even had electricity) and silverware. A hotel was built at Pipiriki in 1899, but burnt down in 1909. Rebuilt as one of the most luxurious hotels in the country, it was again destroyed by fire in 1959.

Today a network of tracks throughout the **Whanganui National Park** offers access to large tracts of wilderness. The Whanganui is the most canoed river in the country, and, despite some 239 rapids between Taumarunui and the sea, it is classed as a beginner's river. It can also be explored by a trip on a paddle-steamer or jet-boat, and there is an excellent scenic drive (see pages 138–9) along the valley.

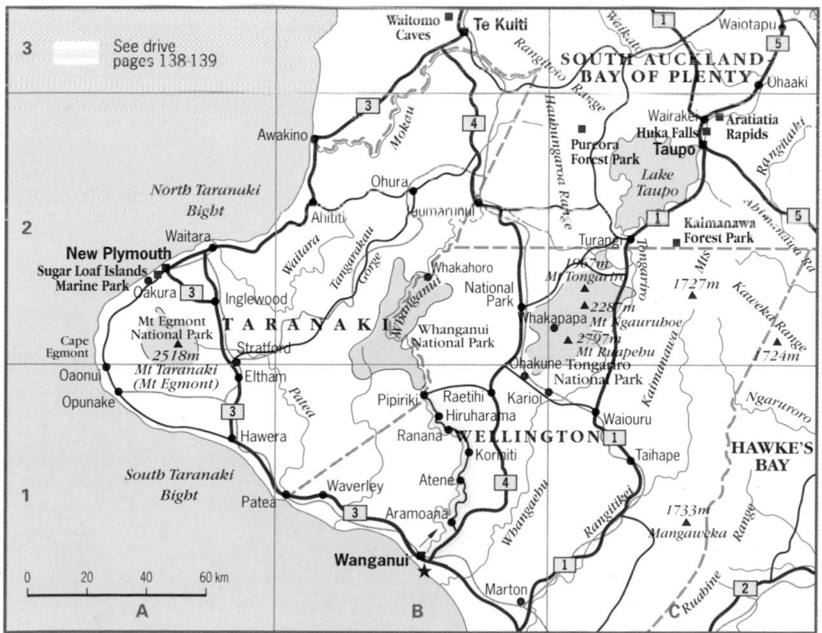

Walks around Taupo
There are a number of enjoyable short walks in the environs of Taupo that are suitable for the whole family; it takes around an hour, for instance, to walk along the river bank to Huka Falls, or you could walk from Huka Falls to the Aratiatia Rapids (two hours one way). There are also walks around the lakeshore to Acacia Bay, through nearby forests or to historic sites. Around 30 walks (including longer tramps) are listed in the *Walking Trails* booklet available from the Information Centre.

Central North Island

▶▶ Lake Taupo *121C2*

This famous trout-fishing mecca covers 606 sq km and lies some 359m above sea level. The lake is fed by a dozen or more streams and rivers flowing down into the ancient volcanic crater in which it lies; its only outlet is the Waikato River, which runs down alongside the township of Taupo through a series of rapids before beginning its long journey to the sea just south of Auckland.

The surrounding streams and river estuaries, and the lake itself, present almost unlimited opportunities for anglers. The fishery is tightly controlled, but there is always good fishing to be had somewhere: trout from the lake average about 1.5kg, although catches of twice this size are not unusual. The DoC operates an acoustic monitoring system to estimate the numbers of fish in the lake, and in the 1995 fishing season there were reckoned to be around 200,000 of these monsters out there waiting to be caught – about twice the number that there were when monitoring first started in the late 1980s. Nearly 900 tonnes of trout are caught in the lake each year.

Apart from fishing, Taupo offers a number of family-oriented attractions and a wide range of adventure activities, including river rafting, helicopter sightseeing, tandem skydiving from 2,700m and mountain-biking. There are also a number of rides which you might not find elsewhere, such as driving racing cars on the Taupo Raceway Circuit, setting off on a four-wheel motorbike into the bush, or going for a ton-up on the back of a Harley Davidson.

The township of Taupo is on Tapuaeharuru Bay, on the north-east corner of the lake. Laid out in a hard-to-get-lost grid pattern, it has the usual selection of resort shops, restaurants and take-aways. The Taupo Information Centre (Tongariro Street, tel: 07 378 9000. *Open* daily 8.30–5), at the front of the Great Lake Centre, can book any activity as well as supply information on fishing guides, licences and so on.

Across from the Great Lake Centre is the small **Taupo Museum** (*Open* Mon–Sat 10.30–4.30. *Admission free*), featuring colonial and natural history exhibits.

Most of Taupo's attractions (apart from those which are lake-based) are spread out along the west and east banks of the Waikato Riverdown as far as the Aratiatia Rapids: you can easily make a loop, setting off from town down SH1 (towards Auckland), and then returning via the Aratiatia Road, which will encompass all the sightseeing spots in a day. If you want to add on a river trip or jet-boat ride, the sights on the west bank would take a day.

The 'African Queen' (or MV Waireka*) cruises the Waikato River downstream to the awesome Aratiatia Rapids (right)*

Drive West and east of the Waikato River

Wairakei Park
Spread across a vast area of the west bank of the Waikato River, this combines rolling farmland with forests, geothermal areas (including power stations) and recreation facilities. New attractions (such as the Honey Hive and Prawn Farm) have recently sprung up, whilst others (such as the mock-colonial Huka Village) have closed down.

Following SH1, turn down the Huka Falls Road to reach the **Huka Falls Viewpoint▶**; known as *hukanui* ('great body of spray') to the Maori, the falls plunge down just over 10m, with the water flowing through at peak times at the rate of 62,000 gallons a second. A footbridge across the top leads to another viewpoint on the east bank. A short distance further on is the Helistar Centre, with a café and helipad, and then comes the **Honey Hive▶** (*Open* daily 9–5. *Admission free*), which has glass hives which enable visitors to see the bees busily at work, as well as videos about bees, and honey for tasting and for sale.

Next is the **Taupo Observatory▶▶** (*Open* Mon–Fri 9–5; Sat–Sun 10–4. *Admission free*), in which the Taupo Volcanic Zone can be explored through a series of audio-visual shows, active models and other displays. The observatory is part of the Wairakei Research Centre, run by the Institute of Geological and Nuclear Sciences, which studies and monitors the volcanoes and geothermal fields in this volatile zone.

At the end of the road is a jetty where the Huka Jet and *African Queen* riverboat share a berth: the *African Queen* (originally the MV *Waireka*, built in 1908) offers sightseeing tours along this section of the river at a leisurely speed (*Tours* daily 10am and 2pm. *Admission charge* expensive), or you can opt for a somewhat faster pace on board the Huka Jet (*Tour* every half hour. *Admission charge* expensive): both vessels visit exactly the same section of river, since neither can go further than the Huka Falls at one end or the Aratiatia Rapids at the other.

Beside the dock is the **Prawn Park▶** (*Tours* on the hour 11–4. *Admission charge* inexpensive), the world's only geothermally heated facility devoted to raising prawns; the 20-minute tour covers the complete life-cycle of the giant Malaysian river prawns bred here. You can buy the raw prawns or sample them barbecued or cooked in a dozen different ways at their Prawn Works Bar 'n' Grill (*Open* Thu–Sun 9–9; Mon–Wed 9–5; booking recommended).

Heading back up to the main road, double back briefly towards the **Craters of the Moon▶** thermal area (*Open* dawn till dusk. *Admission free*) administered by the Department of Conservation, which has walkways between the steam vents, mud pools and other geothermal phenomena.

Further down the main road are the unmistakable stainless steel pipes, wreathed in steam, of the **Wairakei Geothermal Power Station▶▶**: along with the nearby Ohaaki station, this produces around eight per cent of the country's electricity. The Visitor Centre (*Open* daily 9–4.30. *Admission free*) has detailed displays and videos on all aspects of geothermal power, and it is also possible to follow the massive pipes down through the steamfield itself (*Open* 24 hours. *Admission free*) to a look-out point.

Just past the road bridge over the steam pipes, a sign points to the **Wairakei Natural Thermal Valley** (*Open* summer 9–7.30; winter 9–5.30. *Admission charge* moderate) where there

are tea-rooms and walks through the bush either side of the Wairakei stream; the geysers and mudpools are no longer as interesting as they once were, since the neighbouring power project has taken the heat (literally) out of the ground.

Finally, branching off down SH5 and then turning right down the Aratiatia Road you will reach the **Aratiatia Rapids►**. These rapids were once a significant natural attraction, but since the building of a dam and the Aratiatia Power Station the spectacle can only be enjoyed at set times of day (summer 10am, 12 noon, 2pm, 4pm; winter 10am, 12 noon, 2pm. *Admission free*). A warning siren sounds just before the radial dam gates open, with the water thundering down the rapids for about half an hour before subsiding once more.

Heading out from the town centre on the south side of the Waikato River, Cherry Island is not far. Small children might enjoy **Cherry Island Park** (*Open* daily 9–5. *Admission charge* moderate), a small island roamed by peacocks, goats, ducks, angora rabbits and a few other tame animals, but they will probably be more thrilled by the new **Dinosaur Valley►►** (*Open* daily 10–4. *Admission charge* inexpensive) which is much better value, with a dozen or so life-size dinosaur models given added credibility by the hissing steam vents surrounding them. If you have not watched the madness of bungee-jumping before, stop off at **Taupo Bungee** (*Open* daily 9–5) to see people hurling themselves off the huge cantilever projecting out from the cliff face 45m above the Waikato. Finally, the **A C Thermal Baths** (*Open* daily 8–9. *Admission charge* inexpensive) contain a number of private hot mineral pools, sauna house, and giant swimming pool with water slide.

Lake cruises around the north shore of the lake are popular, with several sailings daily on different kinds of boat. Most visit Mine Bay, where there is a contemporary Maori rock carving depicting the arrival of the Tuwharetoa tribe in the Taupo area (on private land, it can be viewed only from the lake). Options for cruises include sailing on a 13m ketch, the *Spirit of Musick* (tel: 07 378 3444), on a 15m yacht once owned by Errol Flynn, the *Barbary* (tel: 07 378 3444), or on a replica 1920s steamboat, the *Ernest Kemp* (tel: 07 378 6136).

Walkways lead through the steaming fumaroles at the Craters of the Moon thermal area

An historic gift
Most of the land around Tongariro belonged to the Tuwharetoa, to whom the peaks were *tapu* (sacred), but this did not stop early Europeans attempting to climb them. Concerned about the fate of their sacred mountains, the paramount chief of the Tuwharetoa, Te Heuheu Tukino, took a visionary step and gifted the mountains to all of New Zealand's inhabitants on 23 September 1887. It was the first national park in the country, and only the fourth in the world. The original area of 2,640ha has since been expanded to 76,000ha; in 1991 it was declared a World Heritage site.

▶▶ Tongariro National Park *121C1*

Dominating the Tongariro National Park is **Mount Ruapehu**, the highest peak in the North Island, with a beautiful crater lake at its summit. Mount Ruapehu is still active: in 1945 it erupted over a nine-month period, showering fine volcanic ash over much of the central North Island; in 1969 and 1975 eruptions of ash and water caused volcanic mudflows (*lahars*) which damaged ski facilities and led to the installation of a *lahar* warning system in the park. In 1995 a giant mushroom cloud signalled its biggest eruption for 50 years, which continued in 1996 disrupting air traffic in the region and shooting boulders as large as cars into the air. **Mount Ngauruhoe** is the youngest of the volcanoes, and still occassionally bubbles and spits lava and ash in a menacing fashion. **Mount Tongariro** last erupted in 1926 and its truncated peaks conceal a number of spectacular craters and lakes.

The Park Headquarters is located in **Whakapapa Village**, which has a population of just 200 people and (at 1,127m) is the highest settlement in the country with permanent residents. The DoC Visitor Centre (*Open* daily 8–5) has interesting displays on volcanoes and the natural history of the park, as well as providing the usual information on tramping (there is a fine range of walks from here), huts, skiing and weather conditions. At the entrance stands a bust of Te Heuheu Tukino (see panel). Just below the Visitor Centre is the Grand Château, a splendid old hotel (built in 1929) which is worth a visit for tea.

Bust of Te Heuheu Tukino, Tongariro National Park

Above Whakapapa, ski lifts rise from Iwikau Village to the Whakapapa skifields, the biggest ski area within the park. Since 1995, these ski lifts have been kept open all year round to give sightseers and trampers easier access to the upper mountains.

Back down at the junction with SH4, **National Park** is a small settlement offering summer activities as well as skiing in winter. It has a railway station, and shuttle buses operate from here to either end of the Tongariro Crossing (see panel) and up to Whakapapa and the skifields.

On the southern side of the mountain is **Ohakune,** the biggest resort in the area, and the Turoa Skifield which was opened in 1978 to relieve pressure on Whakapapa; the Ohakune Visitor Centre (54 Clyde Street. *Open* Jun–Oct Mon–Fri 8–5.30, Sat 9–4, Sun 9–2; Nov–May

Mon–Fri 9–4.30, Sat 9–12, Sun 9–11) has details of the many activities available.

From Ohakune, an excellent scenic drive leads up the **Ohakune Mountain Road** to the Turoa Skifield. The road winds gradually up through majestic stands of rimu, matai and miro and then traverses the higher-altitude beech forest, tussock and alpine fields before emerging on to the bare volcanic reaches further up Mount Ruapehu. From the ski station (1,600m), there are fabulous views back across farmlands to the Mount Egmont National Park. The 17km drive takes about one hour, and there are several walking tracks off the road if you have more time.

Turangi *121C2*

On the south side of Lake Taupo, the town of Turangi was developed in the 1960s to meet the needs of the nearby Tongariro hydroelectric project and has since expanded into a resort – principally for fishing, but it also makes a good base for exploring the Tongariro National Park or the adjacent Kaimanawa Forest Park.

Turangi is sited on the banks of the Tongariro River, which is world-renowned for its rainbow and brown trout fishing. The Visitor Information Centre (Ngawaka Place, P O Box 34, Turangi, tel: 07 386 8999. *Open* daily 9–5) can provide details on fly-fishing guides, licences and other fishing services. To find out more about trout, visit the nearby Tongariro National Trout Centre▶ (*Open* daily 9–4. *Admission free*/donation), 4km south along SH1.

Around 270,000 visitors a year flock to the Whakapapa skifields

The Tongariro Crossing

The Tongariro Crossing is a seven to eight-hour tramp which skirts several of the crater lakes around the summit of Mount Tongariro, with fabulous views across the central North Island. Considered to be one of the finest one-day tracks (albeit an exhausting one) in the country, it is walked by around 40,000 people every year. In summer, DoC staff run guided walks along the track, taking up to 80 people at a time.

Drive Tongariro circuit

Allow a full day for this 170km round trip circling the volcanoes of Tongariro National Park, which also embraces forest and desert scenery, the Army Museum, and a historic *pā* site.

Starting in **Ohakune**, head east along SH49. The road passes the Rangataua and Karioi forests and the Karioi pulp mill before reaching a **memorial** (on the left) in front of the Whangaehu River Bridge at Tangiwai: this was the site of the country's worst-ever rail disaster, on Christmas Eve 1953, when a volcanic mudflow (*lahar*) from Mount Ruapehu swept an express train into the river.

Continue to **Waiouru**, turning right at the junction to reach the **Queen Elizabeth II Army Memorial Museum▶▶** (*Open* daily 9–4.30. *Admission charge* moderate). Mock-ups of the NZ Army in action, from the New Zealand Wars through to Vietnam, are accompanied by a 23-minute audio-visual presentation (9.15, then every 45 minutes from 9.45–3.45) on its history. A new pavilion, opened in 1995, houses a massive greenstone sculpture, *Tears on Greenstone*, commissioned to commemorate soldiers killed overseas in active service.

Return to the junction and continue north on SH1 along the **Desert Road▶▶**. Most of the original forest cover here has been destroyed by fire, and the harsh winds and free-draining volcanic soil have prevented trees from re-establishing themselves. The volcanic gravelfields and tussock plateaus create an eerie, empty landscape with an unearthly appeal. To the west rise the snow-clad peaks of Mount Ruapehu, with the North Island's only glaciers visible during summer.

After passing the summit (1,074m, signposted), the Desert Road cuts through a series of eroded banks of richly coloured desert ash, twisting and dipping over several streams. The regenerating bushlands of the **Kaimanawa Forest Park** now take over from the desert landscapes. As the road emerges from the Poutu Forest, the rounded form of the extinct volcano **Mount Pihanga** appears straight ahead.

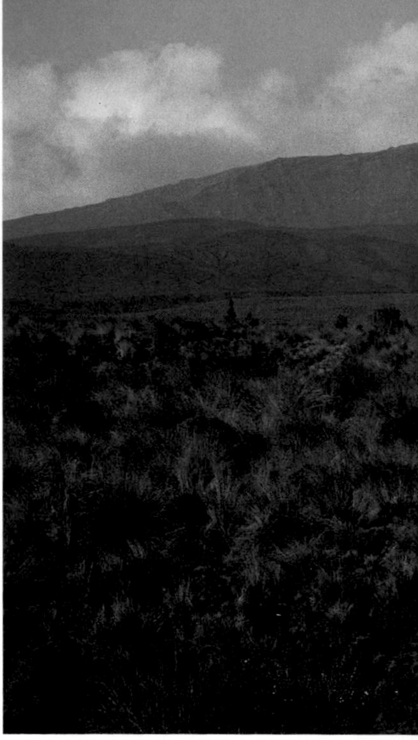

Tussock lands on the aptly named Desert Road to the east of Mount Ruapehu

Turn left at **Rangipo** along the road to National Park cutting behind Mount Pihanga and passing along the shore of **Lake Rotoaira▶▶**; beyond, steam rises from the Ketetahi Hot Springs beneath the cone of **Mount Tongariro's** north crater.

At the junction, turn left on to SH47. Another 1.5km further on, a signpost marks the car park for **Te Porere Historic Place▶▶**. The two sets of earthworks here are the remains of fortified *pās* built by the Maori warrior and prophet Te Kooti Rikiranga te Turuki. This was the site of one of the last battles of the New Zealand Wars, in October 1869, when Te Kooti and his people made a determined stand against Government troops. Thirty-seven of Te Kooti's men were killed but he himself escaped through the bush with his remaining forces.

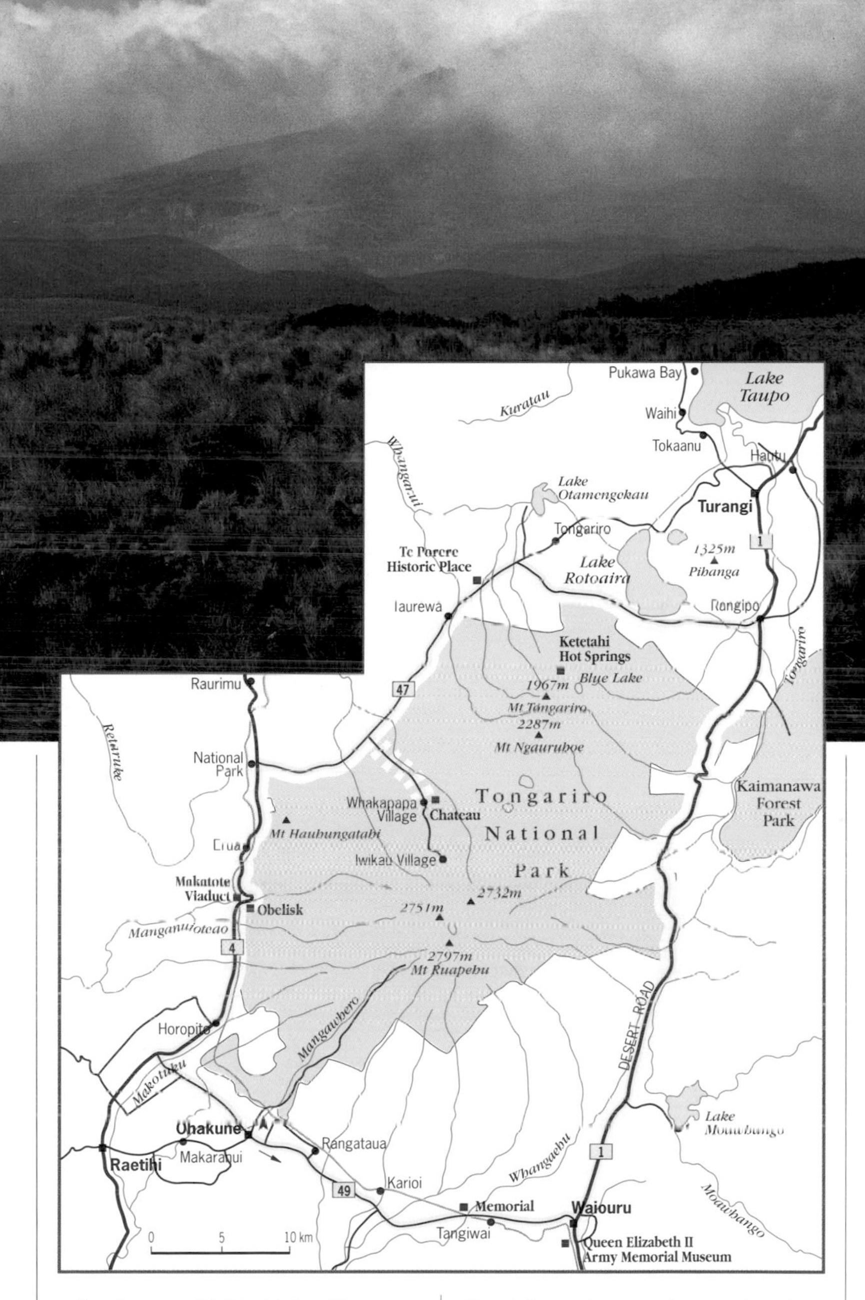

Continue on SH47, skirting **Mount Ngauruhoe** before reaching the turning for **Whakapapa**. Make a detour up here or continue on to **National Park** and turn left onto SH4. On your left is the bulky mass of **Mount Hauhungatahi**, now a nature reserve.

Running alongside the road is the last section of the North Island Main Trunk line to be completed: after the impressive **Makatote Viaduct▶**, an **obelisk** on the left-hand side of the road marks the spot where the north and south railheads met in 1908, completing the railway between Wellington and Auckland.

Just past Horopito turn left on SH49 to return to Ohakune.

The West Coast

Hawera *121A1*

Should you be passing through this small coastal town 74km south of New Plymouth, it is worth making a detour 4km to the north to visit the **Tawhiti Museum▶** (47 Ohangai Rd. *Open* Fri–Mon 10–4; Jun–Aug, Sun 10–4 only. *Admission charge* moderate), an extensive collection of life-size displays and dioramas depicting the heritage of south Taranaki. In addition, a bush railway runs through logging areas to an 'interpretation centre' set in an old sawmill.

New Plymouth *121A2*

Dominated by the towering peak of Mount Taranaki to the south, New Plymouth is the main focus of a rich dairy region (thanks in part to the fertile volcanic soil bequeathed by Taranaki's past explosions), as well as being a major energy production centre, with oil and gas flowing from several off-shore fields.

The early settlement was named after Plymouth, England, the hometown of many of the first colonists. One of the few remaining buildings from the earliest days is **Richmond Cottage▶** (corner of Ariki and Brougham Streets. *Open* Nov–May, Mon, Wed, Fri 2–4, weekends 1–4: Jun–Oct, Fri 2–4, weekends 1–4. *Admission charge* inexpensive). Built in 1853 from beach stones, it was moved to its present site in the 1960s, and has been furnished in period style with items from the neighbouring Taranaki Museum.

Similarly built from beach stones is **St Mary's Church▶** (Vivian Street), completed in 1846 and New Zealand's oldest surviving stone church. During the Taranaki wars it

Early troubles
The Plymouth Company sent six ships from Devon, the first of which arrived in March 1841. As the local Te Atiawa peoples had been driven away by the Waikato tribes, the early settlers snapped up large tracts of land – only to find themselves involved in a war lasting a decade or more when the Te Atiawa returned from exile on Kapiti Island. Despite this unpromising start, a new wave of immigrants in the 1870s led to the establishment of New Plymouth's major source of wealth, the dairy industry.

Charming Pukekura Park is in the heart of New Plymouth

was used as an ammunition dump and military post, and the graveyard contains the tombstones of soldiers who died in the wars as well as those of early settlers.

Also worth visiting is the **Taranaki Museum▶** (Ariki Street. *Open* Tue–Fri 10.30–5, weekends 1–5. *Admission free*), which has an extensive collection of Maori artefacts (including Te Atiawa woodcarvings) as well as displays on natural history and the colonial era.

In the city centre, the **Govett-Brewster Gallery▶** (Queen Street. *Open* Mon–Fri 10.30–5, weekends 1–5. *Admission free*) enjoys a good reputation for innovative contemporary art exhibitions featuring both national and international artists.

The city is famous for its parks and gardens, most notably **Pukekura Park▶▶** (main entrance on Fillis Street, three blocks south of the Visitor Centre. *Open* 9–5. *Admission free*), some 20ha of woodland, lawns and gardens, which also contains a fernery with begonias, orchids and fuchsias (*Open* daily 10–12, 1–4) and two lakes; the tea kiosk next to the main lake affords a lovely view of Taranaki framed by trees.

Separated from Pukekura by the 'Bowl of Brooklands' sound-shell and amphitheatre is **Brooklands Park▶▶,** equally delightful with its rhododendron dell, English-style gardens and woodlands. Within the grounds is **The Gables** (Sat–Tue 1–5, Wed and Fri 10.30–5, Thu 10.30–4), once a cottage hospital and now a medical museum and art gallery.

New Plymouth is something of a mecca for surfers, with good surfing and windsurfing at nearby beaches such as Fitzroy, Strandon, Back Beach and Oakura. The small rocky islets of Whareumu (Lion Rock) and Moturoa, just past the western end of New Plymouth's port, are part of the **Sugar Loaf Islands Marine Park** (see panel), and are home to a variety of marine life, including fur seals.

Seal watching
Trips to the Sugar Loaf Islands Marine Park depart from the main harbour regularly throughout the summer, organised by either Happy Chaddy's Charters (tel: 06 758 9113) or Peak Charters (tel: 06 751 0211). Happy Chaddy uses a former English lifeboat, and for a small extra fee you can start your harbour trip by being launched down the rails from the lifeboat shed.

New Plymouth environs

Following Carrington Road south from New Plymouth, it is a short drive (8km) to **Hurworth Cottage▶▶** (827 Carrington Road. *Open* Wed–Sun 10–4. *Admission charge* inexpensive), one of the earliest homesteads in the region. It is the sole survivor of six pioneer cottages built in a cluster here in the mid-1850s by members of two families from Devon, England. one of whom was Harry Atkinson, later to become four times premier of New Zealand. Hurworth Cottage's main claim to fame is that it was built by Harry Atkinson.

Surf's up

A further 20km down the same road is the **Pukeiti Rhododendron Trust▶▶** (*Open* daily 9–5. *Admission charge* moderate), which has superb displays of rhododendrons and azaleas amidst 400ha of native bushland. The best season is September to November.

Heritage Trail
The 150km Heritage Trail leads north-eastwards across from Stratford to Taumarunui, to the north of the Whanganui National Park. This interesting back country road passes through the scenic Tangarakau Gorge and touches the upper reaches of the Whanganui River; along the way, over 30 points of interest (from *pā* sites to historic graves) are marked by Heritage Trail plaques. A free booklet on the Heritage Trail is available from DoC offices in New Plymouth, Stratford and Taumarunui.

► Stratford *121A2*

The access point for the eastern slopes of Mount Taranaki, this market town was named in honour of Shakespeare's birthplace. The Patea River runs through the town, which was originally named 'Stratford-upon-Patea'. The town hosts an annual Shakespeare Festival.

South of the town centre (1 km along SH3) is the **Taranaki Pioneer Village►** (*Open* daily 10–4. *Admission charge* moderate), an outdoor museum with displays relating to local and provincial history.

►► Taranaki Egmont National Park *121A2*

The 2,518m high volcano at the centre of this national park dominates the lush farmlands of the surrounding Taranaki district.

Maori settlements on the lower slopes of Taranaki and the coastline were established soon after the first arrivals in New Zealand. The Maori considered higher slopes *tapu*, although they ventured up the valleys to collect red ochre for pigment, and to take the bones of their chiefs and *tohunga* to secret caves on the mountain.

According to one of the most enduring legends of the North Island, at one time Taranaki lived with the other volcanoes in the centre of the island. Once, however, when Tongariro was away, Taranaki seduced his beautiful wife, Pihanga. When Tongariro returned he exploded (literally) with jealousy. Taranaki beat a hasty retreat, gouging out the Whanganui River as he withdrew towards the coast, where he still weeps for his lost love.

Taranaki is part of a chain of three volcanoes running from New Plymouth southwards. The two other volcanoes (Pouakai and Kaitake) are older; Taranaki probably appeared approximately 70,000 years ago and last erupted in about 1755. Just to the south of the main crater is a secondary cone called Fantham's Peak, named after the first woman to climb it, Frances Fantham, in 1885.

The first climbers to reach the summit of Taranaki were Ernst Dieffenbach, a naturalist with the New Zealand Company, and James Heberly, a whaler, who made the ascent in December 1839. Summertime ascents became fashionable in the 1860s and 1870s, and today it is the 'most climbed mountain' in New Zealand.

Needless to say there are fabulous views from the summit, from the peaks of the South Island across to the Tongariro National Park, and northwards to Mount Pirongia in the Waikato – if it's not raining, that is. Taranaki also has one of the highest rainfall records in the country, with an average 7,000mm annually. Despite the relatively small size of the park there are some 140km of tracks, and if you do not feel like tackling the summit or the 55km round-the-mountain track, there are plenty of shorter walks. In winter skiing is popular.

The main point of access to the park is at **North Egmont**, 28km from New Plymouth, where there is an excellent DoC Visitor Centre (*Open* Nov–Easter 9–5; Easter–Nov 9.30–4.30 except Fri). On the south side of the mountain there is another DoC Visitor Centre at **Dawson Falls** (*Open* Mon, Thu, Fri, Sat, Sun 9–5.30). It is imperative to check with one of these centres before setting off up the mountain, since weather conditions can change rapidly.

Right: Lake Mangamahoe and the classic volcanic cone of Mount Taranaki

The pleasant city of Wanganui

 Wanganui 121B1

One of the oldest towns in the country, Wanganui was settled in the 1840s, when the New Zealand Company found itself running out of land at Wellington and had to relocate the constant flow of migrants somewhere else: Wanganui was an obvious choice (as the Maori had earlier discovered) thanks to its rich arable lands and the broad, navigable river. Colonel William Wakefield conducted dubious and hurried negotiations over the land in 1840, handing over blankets, tobacco and trinkets on the site of the present day Moutoa Gardens in return for the 'sale' of 16,000 hectares of land.

Several years of strife followed, but in 1848 an agreement was finally reached (again in Moutoa Gardens), and during the New Zealand Wars the Wanganui Maori even helped to prevent the destruction of the settlement by the Taranaki tribes.

To get an overview of the city and the broad Whanganui River estuary, head first for the **Durie Hill Elevator▶** (*Open* Mon–Fri 7.30–7, Sat 9–8, Sun 1–6. *Admission charge* inexpensive) on the other side of the Wanganui City Bridge. This unusual lift was built in 1919 to provide a commuter service to the city for residents of the suburbs of Durie Hill: a 213m tunnel leads into the hillside, from where the elevator rises 66m to the summit. Fit visitors can then walk up a further 176 steps to the top of the **Durie Hill Memorial Tower▶** (*Open* daily 8–6. *Admission free*); the view on a good day encompasses Mount Taranaki, Mount Ruapehu and the South Island coast.

The central thoroughfare of the city is Victoria Avenue, a semi-pedestrianised shopping street which in summer is ablaze with flowers that cascade down from over 600 hanging baskets. Halfway down Victoria Avenue and one block east is **Queen's Park**. To the right of the broad steps here is the **Memorial Hall**, and to the left the **Wanganui Regional Museum▶▶** (*Open* Mon–Sat 10–4.30, Sun 1–4.30. *Admission*

Durie Hill residents can commute by the tunnel and elevator inside the hill

charge inexpensive). The museum is renowned for its Maori collection, which includes the 23m war canoe *Te Mata O Hotorua*.

The domed building at the top of the steps houses a library and the **Sarjeant Gallery▶** (*Open* Mon–Fri 10.30–4.30, weekends 1–4.30. *Admission free* /donation), which hosts touring exhibitions as well as mounting displays from its permanent collection of British and New Zealand paintings.

Behind Queen's Park lie **Moutoa Gardens▶**, which have played a pivotal role in Wanganui's history. Originally a market where Maori from upriver traded their fruit and vegetables, they became the site of controversial negotiations over land sales in 1840 and 1848. In 1995, they were once more in the spotlight as Maori and Pakeha supporters from all over the country converged here to stage an occupation protesting at the Government's current offer to settle outstanding land claims.

Across from Moutoa Gardens on the quayside at Taupo Quay is the embryonic **Wanganui Riverboat Centre▶**, with the old paddle steamer *Waimarie* moored alongside. Built in 1900, this 34m steamer plied the river until 1952, when she sank at her moorings. Salvaged in 1993, she is gradually being restored.

River trips
One of the best trips from Wanganui upriver is aboard the paddle-steamer *Otunui*, built in 1907 and restored in 1984. The interior has been re-created as a Victorian salon, and there is ample deck space. There are twice-daily sailings (10am and 1pm) from the city marina to the Holly Lodge winery and the Edwardian mansion on Waireka Estate. Contact Captain Jack Dodd, P O Box 763 Wanganui, tel: 06 345 0344 or 025 432 997.

A Maori carving in the Wanganui Regional Museum

The Whanganui River

■ The longest navigable waterway in New Zealand, the Whanganui River flows for 239km from Taumarunui down to the sea and is steeped in legend and history. It lies at the heart of the Whanganui National Park, whose magnificent scenery was attracting tourists over a century ago. ■

Tramping in the National Park
The two main tracks in the Whanganui National Park (the Maungapurua and the Matemateonga) are accessible only by canoe or jetboat. For more details contact: DoC Wanganui District Office, P O Box 4065, Wanganui, tel: 06 345 2402, or DoC Taumarunui, Cherry Grove, Taumarunui, tel: 07 895 8201.

The environment The Whanganui River has its origins as an alpine stream on Mount Tongariro, winding its way down through the central volcanic plateau and sweeping in a huge arc northwards towards Taumarunui before turning southwards towards Wanganui and the Tasman Sea. In the central and lower reaches it wends its way through large tracts of lowland forest.

The landforms in the valley are only about a million years old: sandstone and mudstone (*papa*) from the ocean bed have been eroded by the water into deep gorges, sharp ridges and sheer *papa* cliffs. Cloaking this distinctive landscape is a broad-leaf podocarp forest consisting of species such as northern rata, rewarewa, rimu, tawa, kamahi and kowhai, with black beech dotted along the ridge tops. Distinctive tree ferns, sedges and herbaceous plants thrive on the steep river banks and in the gorges. This is one of the largest areas of untouched broad-leaf forest in the North Island, and it forms the heart of the Whanganui National Park.

The forested gorge of the Whanganui

Bird life commonly seen includes native pigeons, fantails, tuis, grey warblers, North Island robins and long-tailed and shining cuckoos. The distinctive call of the brown kiwi can often be heard at night.

The river legend When the mighty mountains of Taranaki and Tongariro came into conflict over Pihanga (see page 132), the defeated Taranaki tore himself free from his homeland. Wild with grief and anger, he ripped a deep gash through the earth as he left on his journey to the coast. Soon a clear stream sprang from the side of Tongariro, nourishing green forests throughout the valley, which filled and healed this wound. Thus was the Whanganui River born.

Maori habitation The legendary explorer Kupe is said to have sailed 22km up the Wanganui on his voyage to New Zealand in about AD 950. By 1100 Maori had begun to settle the river valley, and the river became an important canoe route linking the interior with the coast. Food was abundant within the forest, and *kāinga* (villages) sprang up on almost every bend of the river. The inhabitants cultivated the sheltered terraces and built elaborate weirs to trap eels and lamprey in the river channels; the sheer bluffs and sharp ridges along the river valley moreover provided ideal *pā* sites to which to retreat when war threatened. By about 1700 there were three *hapū* (sub-tribes) along the river: the Hinengakau occupied the upper sections, the Tamaupoko the middle reaches of the river, and the Tupoho the area stretching downstream to the sea. Collectively they were known as Te Atihau Nui a Papa Rangi.

Unpromising farmlands From the beginning of the century settlers had cleared sections of the river bank for farming, principally from Pipiriki downstream. Wheat was grown on the undulating lands around Pipiriki.

After World War I tracts of the rugged terrain above Pipiriki were offered to the returning servicemen as rehabilitation settlements, but the problems of access, erosion, and fighting an unequal battle against the ever-encroaching bush ensured that most of these farms were eventually abandoned.

Once an important canoe route, the Whanganui is New Zealand's longest navigable river

Canoeing the Whanganui
The 145km journey from Taumarunui to Pipiriki takes five to six days; a shorter, three to four-day journey from Whakahoro to Pipiriki is also feasible, or you can take a one-day 'picnic trip'. Independent canoeists should consult the *Guide to the Whanganui River* (New Zealand Canoe Association), available from local DoC offices. Adventure operators include: Plateau Outdoor Adventure Guides, P O Box 29, National Park, tel/fax: 07 892 2740; Wades Landing Outdoors, RD2, Owhango, tel: 07 895 5995; Yeti Tours, P O Box 140 Ohakune, tel: 06 385 8197; fax: 06 385 8492.

Drive The Whanganui River

See map on page 121.

This drive follows the Whanganui River for nearly 80km through isolated farmlands and forest-clad hillsides up to Pipiriki, passing many historic sites along the way. Black posts with red tops mark places of interest.

Leave Wanganui on SH4 to Raetihi, passing through Upokongaro (last chance for petrol) and then turning left along River Road. The road climbs steeply up to the summit of **Aramoana**, from where a view of the lower reaches of the river unfolds in front of you; on a clear day you can see Mount Ruapehu.

Descending to the valley floor, you pass the settlement of Parikino before reaching **Oyster Shell Bluffs**. These white cliffs rising sheer beside the road, embedded with clearly visible giant oyster shell deposits, are a reminder that this area once lay beneath the sea.

One of the curiosities of this route is the number of place names of classical or biblical origin, adapted to Maori pronunciation. With the arrival of the missionaries in the 1840s warfare between the tribes along the river ceased, and many villages moved from the *pā* sites down to the valley,

The Whanganui River seen from Elevator Hill

where farming was easier. The mission station suggested new names, which were then transliterated into Maori equivalents: Atene for Athens, Koriniti (Corinth), Hiruharama (Jerusalem) and so on.

Some 8km past Oyster Shell Bluff you reach the first of these settlements, **Atene**; the meeting house here is notable for its curved roof, a peculiarity of the region.

The next stop is at **Koriniti**, where you should turn left down a track to visit the *marae*, which has two well-maintained traditional **Wharenui▶▶**; the right-hand one, *Te Waiherehere,* is the original building, while *Poutama* was brought here from the old village of Karatia and was built in 1888. In front of the *marae* is the bow-piece of a large canoe, *Te Aomarua*, which once plied the river. To the south stands a small **Mission Church** (built in the 1920s); a memorial cairn of river stones in front of it was erected in memory of Sister Elsie Smith, a missionary who travelled the length of the river ministering to the local communities; awarded the MBE for her work, she died in 1968.

Just outside the village on the left-hand side of the road is **Operiki** ***Pā*▶** which, though it witnessed many attacks and skirmishes, was never taken in battle. Now obscured by trees and vegetation, its earthworks are nevertheless in good condition.

The next stopping point is the old **Kawana Flour Mill▶▶**, the longest-operating and most successful of many flour mills which existed in the valley at the turn of the century. Walk down a short track to peer through the windows of a reconstructed two-room **Miller's Cottage** and enter the **Mill** (Open site. *Admission free*), where displays amid the restored machinery on the first floor trace the history of the mill.

A few kilometres after passing through **Ranana** (London), you will see the picturesque settlement of **Hiruharama** (Jerusalem) on a bend in the river. This is still home to a Roman Catholic mission and convent, whose steepled **church▶** is a distinctive landmark; built in the 1890s, it has an elaborately carved Maori altar.

After Ranana there are several good viewpoints. The best are at the **River View Picnic Site**, the highest point on the river road, where you can look down on the Whanganui rushing through the steep, bush-clad gorges below, and at the **Omoehu Waterfall Lookout**, with the waterfall on the opposite bank.

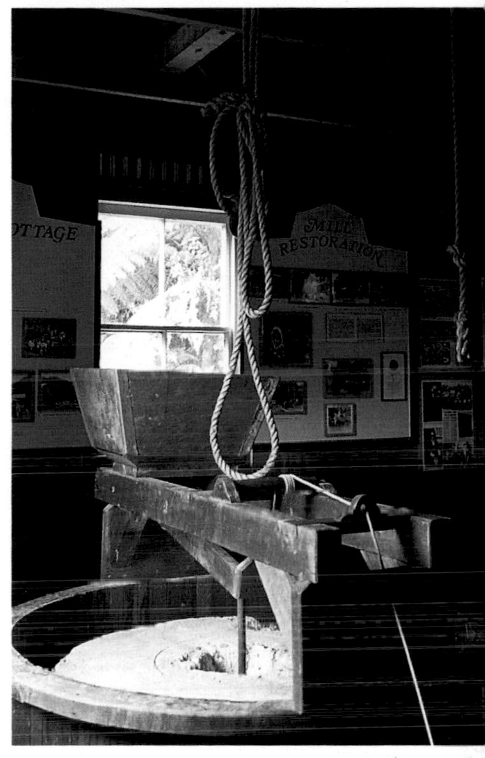

The mill-stone at Kawana Flour Mill

Finally you reach **Pipiriki**. This is the end of the road and the beginning of the wilderness. On the riverbank is an old riverboat, the *Ongarue*, and near by is the **Colonial House Information Centre and Museum▶▶** (*Open* Nov–Apr 11–4. *Admission charge* inexpensive), in a building dating from the 1880s. It has some interesting displays on early tourism on the river, the ecology of the Whanganui National Park, and the early inhabitants of the house itself.

Take the road to Raetihi and either return to Wanganui on SH4 or continue on to the Tongariro National Park.

ELLINGTON

SOUTHERN NORTH ISLAND

The first sheep stations Although Cook had landed sheep in the South Island in 1773, none survived. The first flocks in the country date from 1843 when a certain Charles Bidwill brought 1,600 sheep with him from Sydney to Nelson, and then on to Wellington, from where he drove them around the coast to the Wairarapa. Together with several partners, Bidwill leased grazing land from the Maori, and although his partners eventually gave up he persisted in his efforts and the country's first true sheep station was thus established near Martinborough in 1844.

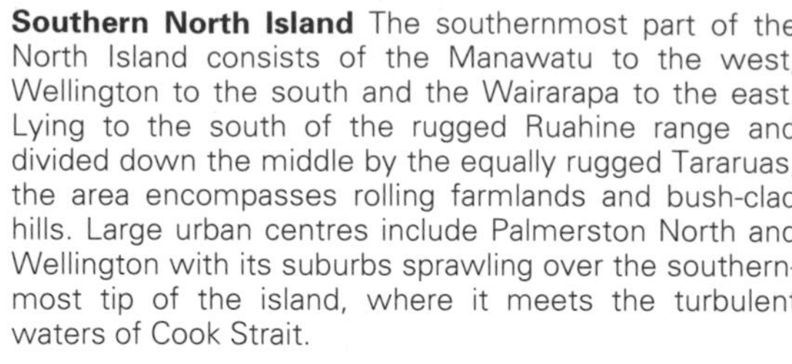

Southern North Island The southernmost part of the North Island consists of the Manawatu to the west, Wellington to the south and the Wairarapa to the east. Lying to the south of the rugged Ruahine range and divided down the middle by the equally rugged Tararuas, the area encompasses rolling farmlands and bush-clad hills. Large urban centres include Palmerston North and Wellington with its suburbs sprawling over the southernmost tip of the island, where it meets the turbulent waters of Cook Strait.

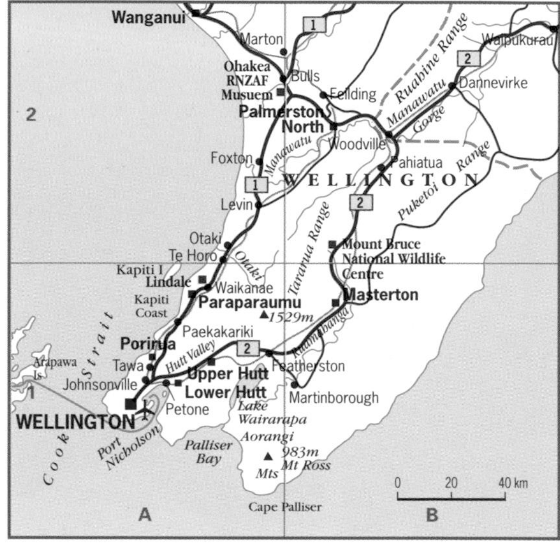

South to Wellington The Manawatu, lying on the western side of the ranges which divide the southern North Island, consists mostly of flat, tree-studded plains devoted to sheep and cattle-farming. The main commercial centre is Palmerston North, a university town well known for its agricultural and biochemical research.

Cutting through between the Ruahine and Tararua Ranges, the Manawatu Gorge is one of the few road routes through the mountains and a gateway to the Wairarapa. Reaching down to the rugged Pacific coastline, the Wairarapa was one of the first sheep-grazing regions in the country (see panel). International sheep-shearing competitions are an annual fixture in the main town, Masterton. Some of New Zealand's rarest birds are bred and studied at the Mount Bruce National Wildlife Centre to the north of Masterton; a major feature of the centre is that many of the species you can see here are otherwise found only in inaccessible or remote parts of the mainland or on off-shore islands.

Greater Wellington The Kapiti Coast stretches northwards from the suburbs of Wellington to the fruit-growing areas around Otaki, some 35km along the coastline. A popular weekend retreat for Wellingtonians, with an abundance of sandy beaches, seaside attractions and watersports, it is easily accessible for day trips from the capital.

Pages 140–1: Wellington and the cable car

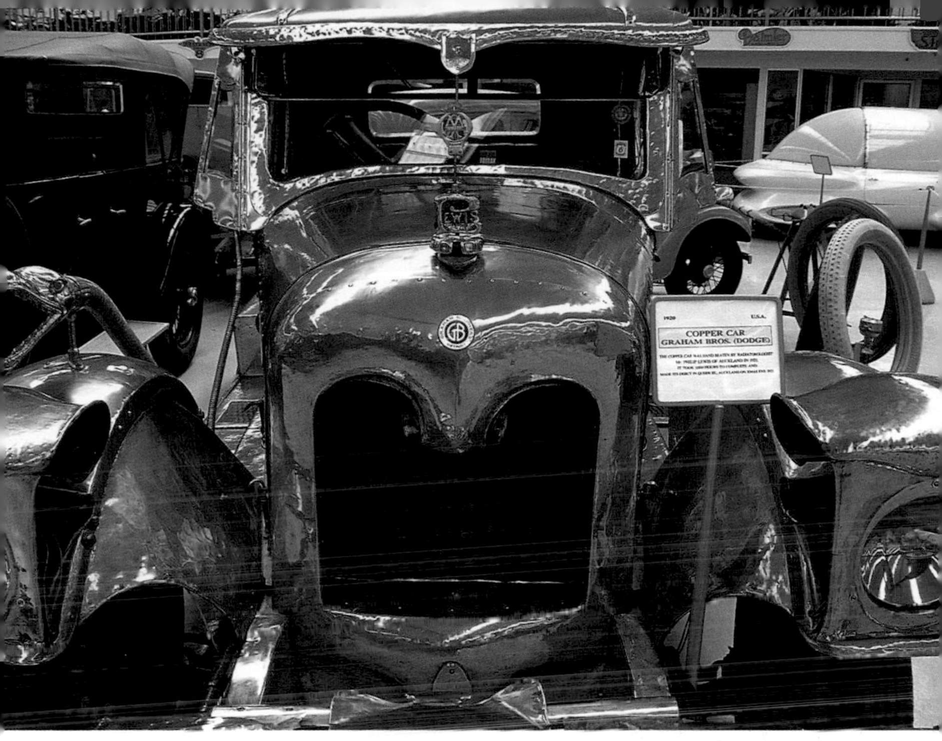

A copper car: one of the many unusual exhibits in the Southward Car Museum

▶▶ Kapiti Coast *142A1*

The Kapiti Coast starts at the dormitory town of **Paekakariki**. Here the **Engine Shed** (*Open* Sat only 10–4.30. *Admission charge* inexpensive) has old steam locos on display, and the Wellington **Tramway Museum** (*Open* weekends and holidays 11–5. *Admission charge* inexpensive) in Queen Elizabeth Park 5km north of the town features rides down to the beach.

Paraparaumu, 50km north of the capital, is the biggest resort along the coast, with a fun park and a wide sandy beach. Just 2km to the north is **Lindale▶** (*Open* daily 9–5) a big, tourist-oriented farm park with craft and souvenir shops, farm shows (Sat and Sun at 2pm. *Admission charge* inexpensive) and a restaurant. Off-shore is Kapiti Island, which was a Maori stonghold and is now a nature reserve (see panel).

Further down the main road, the **Southward Car Museum▶▶▶** (*Open* daily 9–4.30. *Admission charge* inexpensive) is the largest and most varied collection of its kind in the southern hemisphere .

The next halt is at Te Horo, where the grandly named **Hyde Park Museum▶** (*Open* daily 10–5, closed Mon. *Admission charge* inexpensive) features an enjoyable and quirky collection of Kiwiana, including a grocery shop with over 3,000 items (complete with their 1937 price tags), as well as craft shops, a garden centre and a café.

Otaki, marking the end of the Kapiti Coast, is predominantly a Maori community. Until recently, they were able to boast one of the grandest Maori churches in the country, the **Rangiatea Maori Church**. Known as the Maori cathedral, it was built in 1850 and elaborately decorated. Sadly, this magnificent wooden building was burned to the ground by arsonists in 1995.

Kapiti Island

Off-shore from Paraparaumu looms the bulk of Kapiti Island – forested on the shore facing the mainland and with dramatic cliffs on the far side – which has a long history as the power base of one of the great Maori leaders, Te Rauparaha, and later as the site of seven whaling stations and a farming community. Almost a century ago the 1,760 ha island was declared a nature reserve, and access is now strictly limited. Of the several tracks on the island, two lead to the summit of Tuteremoana (521m). Permits to visit Kapiti can be obtained from DoC, Wellington Conservancy (58 Bowen Street, Wellington, tel: 04 472 5821).

Rare birds
The Mount Bruce National Wildlife Centre had its beginnings in 1958 when a captive rearing programme was set up for four takahe chicks brought here from the South Island: this rare bird, once thought to be extinct, had been rediscovered in Fiordland in 1948. Today the centre plays an important role in ensuring the survival of some of the country's most vulnerable species. Work is currently focused on the Campbell Island and Auckland Island teals, the New Zealand pigeon, the shore plover, the saddleback, the stitchbird and the kokako.

►► Mount Bruce National Wildlife Centre *142B2*

30km north of Masterton
Open: daily 10–4. Admission charge: moderate.
Well worth a stop if you are travelling on SH2 between Wellington and Hawke's Bay, the National Wildlife Centre (see panel) lies by the side of the main road. As most of the birds here are strongly territorial, only a few can be held in each aviary, so you need some patience in order to spot them in their bush surroundings. There is a large nocturnal house for watching kiwi and tuatara.

► Ohakea RNZAF Museum *142A2*

Ohakea RNZAF base, 3km south of Bulls
Open: Mon–Sat 9.30–4.30; Sun 10–4.30. Admission charge: inexpensive.
This small but interesting museum features a number of hands-on displays (flight simulators and so on), and tells the story of the people and planes of Ohakea from the time of its establishment during World War II. A good café overlooks the runway, giving a tremendous view of fighter planes, air-trainers and other operational aircraft taking off and landing.

► Palmerston North *142B2*

On the banks of the Manawatu River, this provincial city is a major junction for road, rail and air links in the North Island and the main focal point of the Manawatu district.

Gardens in the Square, at the heart of Palmerston North

Palmerston North styles itself 'the Knowledge City', a tag which is justified by the presence of Massey University (the second largest university in the country), a polytechnic, a college of education, and the private International Pacific College. 'Knowledge industries' (including a number of agricultural research companies) contribute some $500m annually to the local economy, and it is estimated that at least 40 per cent of the population either attends or teaches at one of the 70 local educational establishments. Not surprisingly, it has a high proportion of young people, with around a quarter of the population aged 15–24.

The original settlers (who bought the land from the Rangitane in 1866) destroyed the surrounding bushland to create pastures, but set aside a vast green space in the centre of their township, and the tree-lined **Square** is still the main focal point of the city. Surrounded by shops, it contains the Civic Centre and Visitor Information Centre (*Open* Mon–Fri 8.30–5, Sat 10–2) and is a pleasant place to stroll.

A short distance from the Square is the city's top attraction, the excellent **Science Centre and Manawatu Museum▶▶** (Main Street. *Open* daily 10–5, Tue 10–8. *Admission free*). Opened in 1994, the new complex has brought the Science Centre and the 22-year-old museum together under one roof, providing a huge amount of space for the museum's extensive collections. The Maori galleries are outstanding, with skilfully lit and well-presented exhibits from the Manawatu, Rangitikei and Horowhenua areas, including elaborate carvings and rare *taonga* (treasures). The 'Slices of Lives' gallery takes the history of the Manawatu through colonial times up to the present day through the eyes (and voices) of local people. The Science Centre (*Admission charge* moderate) features interactive exhibits and changing displays geared towards young people.

Next door to this complex is the **Manawatu Art Gallery▶** (*Open* Mon–Fri 10–4.30, weekends 11.30–4.30. *Admission free*), which has five galleries with an ever-changing programme of touring exhibitions and others from the permanent collection.

Back at the Square, the **Square Edge Creative Centre▶** is the local community arts centre, with some 17 craft shops under one roof (*Open* Mon–Fri 9.30–5.30, Sat 9.30–4, Sun 10–3).

Claiming to have the most comprehensive collection of rugby memorabilia anywhere in the world, the **New Zealand Rugby Museum▶** (87 Cuba Street. *Open* Mon–Sat 10–12, 1.30–4.30, Sun 1.30–4. *Admission charge* inexpensive) houses displays on New Zealand international rugby, with videos of famous international games.

A load of bulls

The small farming community of Bulls (at the junction of SH3 and SH1 around 30km from Palmerston North) has put itself on the map by erecting signs outside almost every shop and business in town (about 50 altogether) with word plays on their names such as 'const-a-bull' (police station), 'indispens-a-bull' (pharmacy), 'bank-a-bull' (bank) and 'relieve-a-bull' (public toilets).

Sporting heroes

■ New Zealanders' addiction to sport is legendary, with over a third of the population belonging to a sporting club of some kind. In a land where sport is almost a religion, sports heroes are probably better known than many elected politicians. ■

Sporting heroines
Although perhaps not as well known internationally as some of the great sportsmen, sportswomen in New Zealand have shown a vast improvement in international competitions within the last decade. Some of those who have excelled include Sandra Edge in netball, Susan Devoy in squash, Brenda Lawson and Philippa Baker in rowing, Lynette Brooky in golf, Barbara Kendall in windsurfing, Annelise Coberger in skiing, Alison Rose, Lorraine Moller and Anne Audian in athletics, Madonna Harris in cycling, Tinks Pottinger in equestrian events and Sarah Harrow and Erin Baker in triathlons.

Mountaineering
Probably one of the most internationally famous New Zealanders, **Sir Edmund Hillary** was born in Auckland on 20 July 1919. As a member of John Hunt's Everest Expedition he attained the summit of Everest with Sherpa Tensing Norgay in 1953, an achievement for which he recieved a knighthood. Not content with that, he then completed a journey to the South Pole as leader of the New Zealand Transantarctic Expedition in 1958, and then in the 1960s took up jet-boating, leading several expeditions up Himalayan rivers (which included the first ascent of the 290km Sun Kosi River by jet–boat in 1968). A prolific writer and lecturer, he has been showered with awards from around the world, and was responsible for setting up a charity to provide hospitals and schools for Sherpas as well as the Hillary Commission, which promotes sports in New Zealand.

Cricket
The man responsible for putting Kiwi cricketers on the map was **Sir Richard Hadlee**, who was born in Christchurch and started his career with Canterbury in the early 1970s. In 1973 he made his Test debut, and over the following 17 years, before his retirement in 1990, went on to break several Test records. A great all-rounder, he was an aggressive left-hand batsman and right-arm fast bowler; he also played for Nottinghamshire and Tasmania. In 1985 he became the first New Zealand player to complete the 2,000 runs/200 wickets Test double during a match-saving innings against the West Indies; in 1988 he took his 374th Test wicket (against India at Bangalore), surpassing the previous Test record held by Ian Botham. On his 80th Test appearance at Lancaster Park in Christchurch, he bowled out Indian Sanjay Manjrekar to become the first player from any country to take 400 Test wickets. At 38 years old, he was knighted for his services to cricket.

Yachting
New Zealanders have always loved messing about in boats, and keen competition in off-shore waters (particularly around the northern half of the North Island) combined with a burgeoning yacht-building industry was bound to produce results sooner rather than later. In 1990 *Steinlager II* came first in the prestigious Whitbread Around-the-World race, an achievement repeated by *New Zealander Endeavour* in 1994. But it was not until 1995 that the ultimate prize, the Americas Cup, fell to the Kiwis. During May work seemed to grind to a halt as the nation was glued to coverage of the race, with the

legendary **Peter Blake** and skipper **Russell Coutts** in New Zealand's *Black Magic I* trouncing Dennis Conner's *Young America* in the first five races of a best-of-nine series by an average of three minutes per race. With his famous lucky red socks, Blake had played a canny game, even spreading rumours in Auckland waterfront bars that their boat was no good. The day they won was proclaimed 'New Zealand's proudest day since Everest' by Dame Catherine Tizard, Governor-General of New Zealand.

Champagne flows after New Zealand's victory in the 1995 America's Cup

Rugby Possibly the game which excites the most passion and commitment amongst New Zealanders is rugby, with the nation's self-esteem seeming to rise and fall according to the fortunes of the **All Blacks**, the national team. In 1995 they came within reach of winning the World Cup, with the hero of the team undoubtedly being the Maori winger **Jonah Lomu**. Against Japan, New Zealand broke all records by putting 145 points on the board, including 21 tries, but it was against more evenly matched teams that the myth of Lomu escalated: he may well have weighed 18 stones and stood 6ft 5in tall, but for all the fear his massive bulk engendered he could have been bigger still. In the semi-final, Lomu got the credit for the All Blacks' demolition of England, and although the Kiwis were favourites for the Johannesburg final, the Cup eventually went to the South Africans.

Jonah Lomu (below) has joined the ranks of New Zealand's sporting heroes, which includes cricketer Sir Richard Hadlee (left)

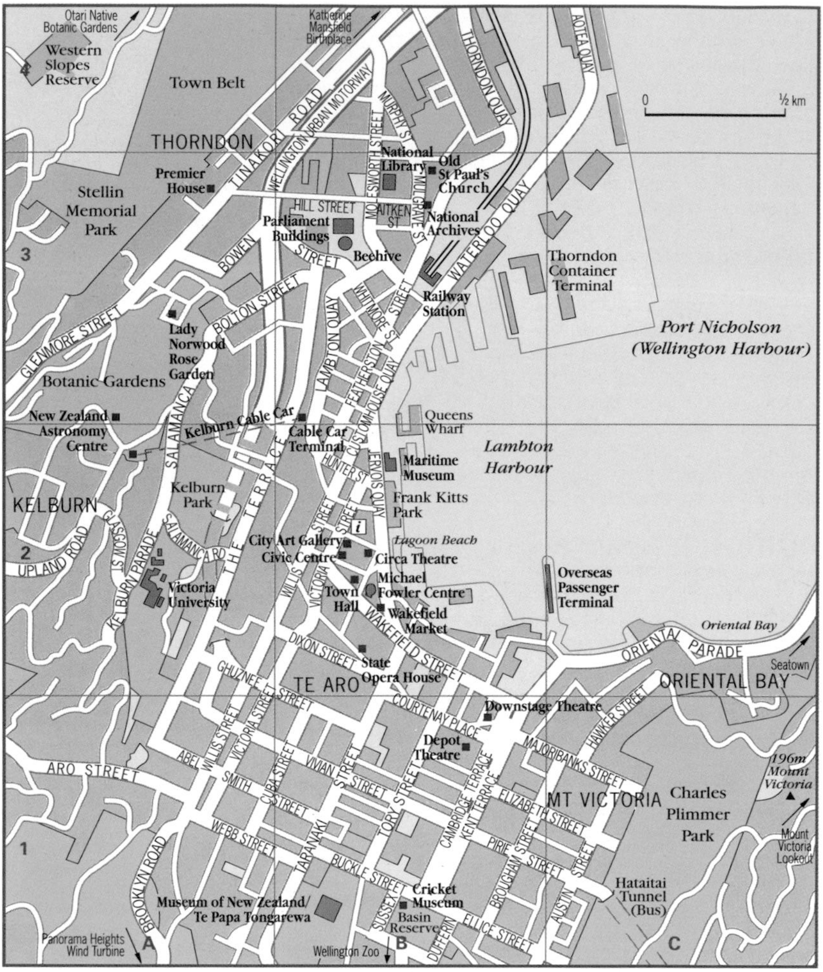

Wellington

A huge harbour, steep hills and ferocious winds are the three defining physical characteristics of the nation's capital. It was probably its strategic position in relation to the South Island which prompted the New Zealand Company to choose Wellington as the site of its first settlement in 1840. In so doing, it successfully anticipated the colonial administration – which 25 years later moved the capital from Auckland to Wellington for that very reason, fearful that the inhabitants of the South Island might try to form a separate colony. Previously, the land had been occupied by the Ngati Tara tribe, and the New Zealand Company's dubious and premature 'purchase' of land blocks later led to bitter fighting. None the less, this was the most successful of their settlements, and with the arrival of the diplomats and Government officials in 1865 the future of the city was assured.

Today the 'harbour city' lies partly on reclaimed land, with the original waterfront streets (such as Thorndon

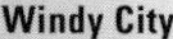

Windy City
The Venturi effect caused by the channelling of air flows through Cook Strait can produce winds of 90kph whistling through the capital – not for nothing is it known as 'Windy Wellington'. Most prevalent in the spring and autumn, these ferocious winds are further funnelled by high-rise buildings in the downtown area to create some distinctly bracing conditions.

Quay and Lambton Quay) now high and dry in the middle of the central business district. Most of the compact downtown area is flat, but the rest of the city climbs across the surrounding hillsides, with high-rise developments and old houses clinging to their steep slopes. Many city centre buildings are still being rebuilt or renovated to meet stricter earthquake-resistance laws.

As well as being a major transport centre and the departure point for ferries to the South Island, Wellington has plenty of attractions in its own right, and is well worth exploring for a day or two – preferably on a weekend, since many of the best hotels offer weekend deals to compensate for the massive outflow of their city clientele on Fridays. There is always plenty going on, with a lively programme of performances, festivals and entertainment right through the year. Wellington is home to the Royal New Zealand Ballet and the New Zealand Symphony Orchestra, as well as four professional theatre groups. This cultural vibrancy is complemented by excellent shopping and a cosmopolitan range of cafés, bars and restaurants.

►► Botanic Gardens 148A3

Sprawling down the hillside behind Wellington's commercial district, these extensive gardens are the city's green heart. They feature a range of native and exotic plantings with separate areas for succulents, herbs, ferns, rhododendrons, threatened and Australian species, begonias, fuchsias and roses.

The top entrance to the gardens is just next to the cable-car terminal (see map), and once you have wandered downhill through the gardens you can leave either through the exit on the north side to explore around Tinakori Road and visit Katherine Mansfield's birthplace, or through the rose gardens to walk back to the Parliament Buildings.

Also at the top end of the gardens is the **New Zealand Astronomy Centre►** (*Open* daily 10–5. *Admission charge* inexpensive), which has astronomy displays, video shows, hands-on computer programmes and a planetarium

Dockside developments Wellington's wonderful setting on Lambton Harbour is likely to be further enhanced by the current redevelopment of the waterfront zone. A huge shopping mall on Queen's Wharf, a new marina, Events Centre, dockside seafood restaurants and wine bars and recreation areas (such as Frank Kitts Park, opposite Civic Square) are just some of the developments already completed. A casino, hotels and residential developments are also in the pipeline. But for most visitors, the highlight will undoubtedly be the imaginative new Museum of New Zealand Te Papa Tongarewa, scheduled to open in 1998.

The lights of Wellington sparkle across the harbour

Earthquake-proof
Delegates at an earthquake conference in Wellington recently expressed surprise that the massive new Museum of New Zealand was being built in what is effectively an earthquake zone. In fact, the new museum is planned to be one of the safest public buildings in the country: it sits on a series of base isolators, huge shock absorbers which are designed to minimise the effects of any tremors.

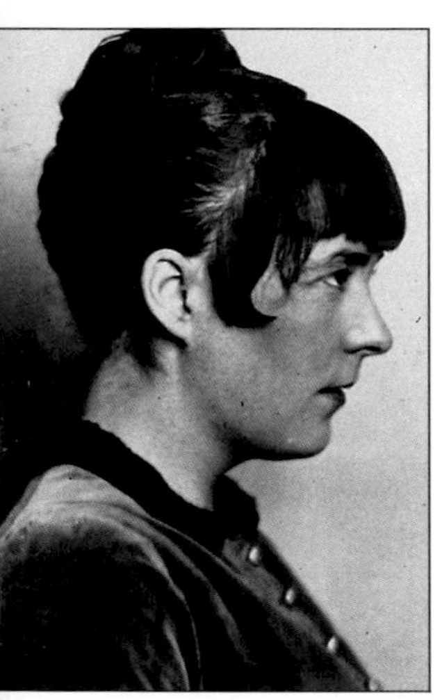

The novelist Katherine Mansfield was born in Wellington

(continuous shows 10.15–4.15 on weekends and public holidays. *Admission charge* inexpensive).

▶ Cable car *148A2*

Open: Mon–Fri 7am–10pm, Sat 9am–10pm, Sun 10.30am–10pm. Admission charge: inexpensive.
A good start to any visit to Wellington is to jump on the cable car for the five-minute ride from Lambton Quay up to Kelburn, from where there are good views of the city and harbour. Built in 1902 to link the suburb of Kelburn with the city centre, it still carries commuters along with tourists – although the historic wooden cable cars were replaced in 1979 by Swiss-built carriages.

▶▶ City Art Gallery *148B2*

Open: summer 10–6, winter 11–5, until 8pm every Thu. Admission charge: donation.
Also on Civic Square, the city art gallery is housed in the former public library building. It covers a broad spectrum of art, architecture, design and the moving image, with several first-rate exhibitions at any one time. There are also guided tours of the exhibitions (Tue 12.30 and 1.30, Sat and Sun 1 and 2. *Admission free*).

Cricket Museum *148B1*

Cambridge Terrace
Open: daily in summer 10.30–3.30, weekends only in winter 10.30–3.30; all day on match days. Admission charge: inexpensive.
Cricketing memorabilia from the earliest days to present times are housed in this small museum. It is situated beneath the old grandstand at the city's top cricket ground, Basin Reserve, at the end of Cambridge Terrace.

▶▶▶ Katherine Mansfield's Birthplace *148B4*

25 Tinakori Road
Open: daily 10–4, closed Mon. Admission charge: inexpensive.
The birthplace and childhood home of Katherine Mansfield, New Zealand's most famous author, was built in 1888 for her father, Harold Beauchamp, a merchant who later became a successful businessman. Although the young writer left for Europe at the age of 19, she drew directly on her memories and experiences of this house in some of her best-known short stories (including *Prelude, The Aloe*, and *A Birthday*).

The house has been lovingly restored and features permanent and changing exhibitions, including photographs and excerpts from Mansfield's writings, an exhibition on the restoration itself, and a biographical video. The garden has also been faithfully restored to its appearance in 1880–1900.

▶ Maritime Museum *148B2*

Quayside
Open: Mon–Fri 9.30–4, Sat, Sun and public holidays 1–4. Admission charge: donation.
Wellington's long association with seafarers and its history as a harbour are well documented in this two-storey museum housed inside the old Harbour Board building on the quayside. It includes over 80 ship models

as well as figureheads, ships' paraphernalia, video displays, an oil-spill computer game – the aim is to save the coastline – and a beautiful old teak cabin from an 1879 steamship. The ground floor has a display on the tragedy of the *Wahine*, an inter-island ferry which was blown off course and sank in the harbour in 1968 with the loss of 51 lives – one of the country's worst maritime disasters.

► Mount Victoria Lookout *148C1*

The wind whistles around the top of Mount Victoria (196m), but the trip up here is worth it for the panoramic views of the city, the harbour and surrounding hills. Early Maori appreciated the strategic advantage of this spot, which they called Matai-rangi ('to watch the sky'). The road to the lookout is signposted from Oriental Bay and Courtenay Place, or you can take a bus (No.20 from the railway station).

►►► Museum of New Zealand Te Papa Tongarewa *148B1*

Open: 9–5. Admission charge: donation.

The new Museum of New Zealand, which will open in 1998, aims to reflect the bicultural heritage and identity of the country, setting out to celebrate the diversity of Tangata Whenua ('those who belong to the land by right of discovery') and Tangata Tiriti ('those who belong by right of treaty') within the context of the natural environment.

Three times the size of the old Museum of New Zealand and covering the area of three football fields, it is one of the largest new museums in the world. The innovative design makes full use of the harbourside setting, with a landscaped outdoor area incorporating exhibitions and performance space amongst gardens, waterways and bridges.

On entering the building you encounter a dramatic 20m-high lobby with stairs and bridges passing through its upper levels, which will afford views outwards to the city and inwards to the exhibitions. Projected exhibition spaces include one devoted to the natural environment, a children's learning centre, a canoe gallery (with windows overlooking the harbour), a human cultures gallery, a gallery of the future and a host of other attractions.

This exciting museum is expected to attract over 500,000 visitors annually, thus becoming Wellington's top attraction. With all that there is to see, one visit may not be enough to do it justice.

National Archives *148B3*

10 Mulgrave Street

Open: Mon–Fri 9–5, Sat 9–1pm. Admission free.

Archives may not usually feature highly on sightseeing tours, but it is certainly worth looking in here to see the original Treaty of Waitangi. Other displays include the 1893 Women's Suffrage petition, and many other interesting if less well-known documents.

Wellington walks

The harbourside is one of the city's pleasantest places to stroll; other good walks include the Red Rocks Coastal Walk (where fur seals 'haul out' between April and September) and the Eastern Walkway (see pages 154–5). The Information Centre can also provide leaflets on longer walks, and the Historic Places Trust produces a booklet, *Historic Wellington*, which describes a walk encompassing some 30 historic buildings. The Wellington City Information Centre is on Civic Square (tel: 801 4000. *Open* daily 9–5). Bush walks, pub crawls and other walks are organised by Wellington Walkies (tel: 04 388 7025).

Artist's impression of the new Museum of New Zealand

City tours
Several companies offer minibus tours of the city's highlights, including City Scenic Tours (tel: 04 499 1282); Wally Hammond's Tours (tel: 04 472 0869); Harbour Capital Tours (tel: 04 499 1282); and Heritage Highlights Tours (tel: 04 478 8315).

▶▶▶ Old St Paul's

148B3

Mulgrave Street
Open: Mon–Sat 10.30–4.30, Sun 1–4.30pm. Admission free.

Consecrated on 6 June 1866, this lovely church has a wonderful interior designed in Early English Gothic revival style and built exclusively with native timbers, including rimu for the framing and trusses, matai and totara for the flooring and rimu and kauri for the pews. The subtly lit roof vaults and dark timbers combine with the brilliance of the stained-glass windows to create a warm, peaceful atmosphere. The church served as the city's cathedral for 98 years until this function was transferred to the new St Paul's Cathedral; the old building was then purchased for the nation and underwent extensive renovation. Weddings, funerals and other services

The glowing interior of Old St Paul's

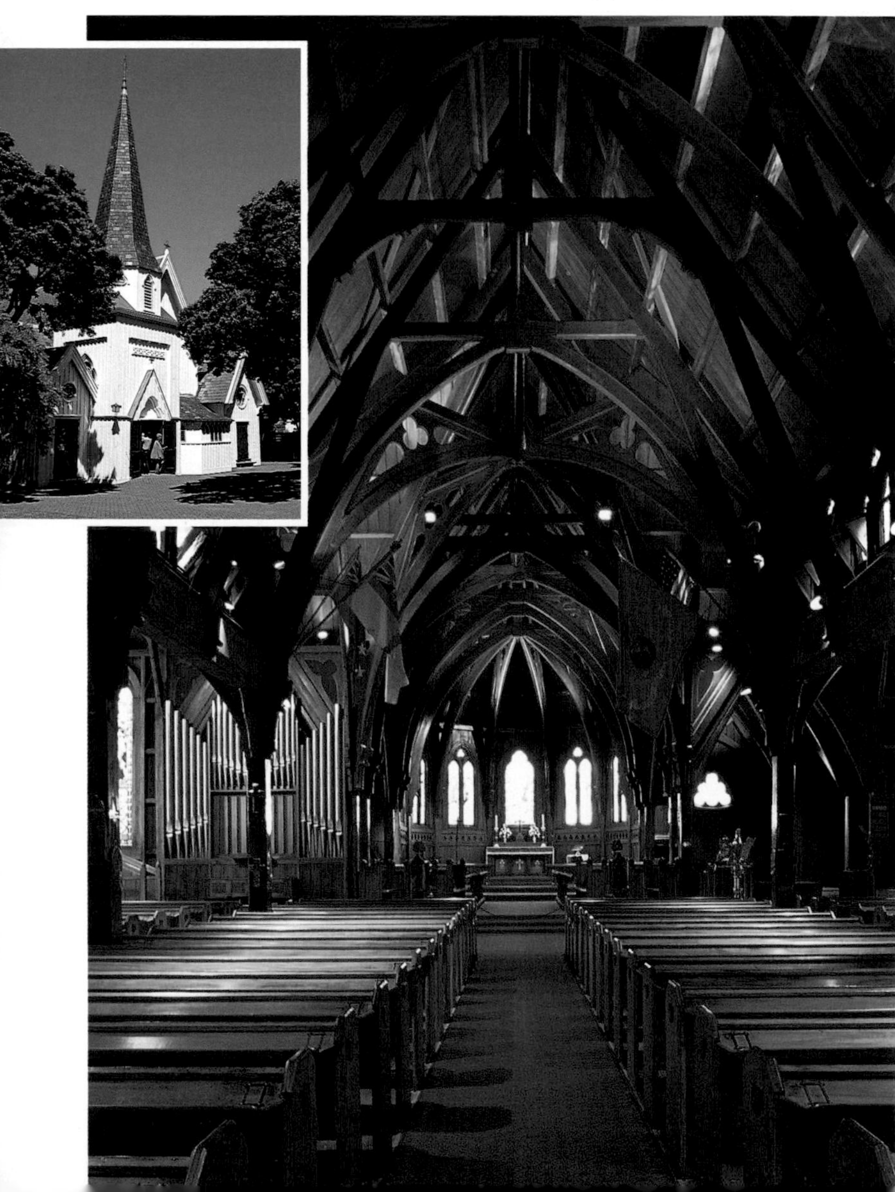

are still held here, and it is also used for musical and cultural events.

►► Parliament Buildings *148B3*

An unmistakable landmark in the downtown area at the end of Lambton Quay is the Beehive, part of the Parliament Buildings complex. Old photographs show that this really was the end of the original quay, with the recently restored first Government Buildings, on the opposite side of Lambton Quay and one of the largest wooden structures in the world, built in 1876, surrounded on two sides by the sea. The site of the Beehive was the home of the New Zealand Company's first resident, Colonel William Wakefield, and later of the country's first Government House.

The oldest building in the complex is the Gothic-style General Assembly Library, completed in 1897. In the middle is Parliament House (1922) which contains the legislative chamber and has recently been re-opened after extensive earthquake-proofing. The circular Beehive is the third building in this disparate trio, designed by British architect Sir Basil Spence, and opened in 1980.

Designed by British architect Sir Basil Spence, the Beehive contains the executive offices of Parliament

► Panorama Heights Wind Turbine *148A1*

Signposted from Brooklyn Road
Open: in summer 8–8; in winter 8–5.
Admission free.

If you have your own transport, it is well worth driving up to this aptly named viewpoint, with its comprehensive vista of Wellington and its surroundings laid out at your feet. Towering 30m above the hilltop site is a Danish wind turbine, commissioned by the Electricity Corporation (ECNZ) as part of a continuing study into the feasibility of wind power in New Zealand. At Panorama Heights the wind averages 32 km per hour, generating a maximum output from the turbine's slender blades of 225 kilowatts – a read-out on the display boards shows how much energy is being generated at the time.

► Wellington Zoo *148B1*

Manchester Street, Newtown, 4km from the city centre
Open: daily 9.30–5. Admission charge: moderate.

The Wellington Zoo began life in 1906 when a visiting circus presented the city with a tame young lion, King Dick. The council set aside part of Newtown Park to house the beast, so initiating the first zoo in the country. Today it houses a wide range of animals, including chimps, tigers, lions, meerkats, golden lion tamarins, reptiles and birds. Native species include kiwi in a nocturnal house (*Open* daily 10–4), tuatara and weta. Like most modern zoos, it is gradually moving away from small caged exhibits towards more naturalistic ways of housing the animals, with open enclosures wherever possible. The Zoo has an active conservation and breeding programme for several threatened and endangered species.

Beaches
No one expects beach life in Wellington, but surfers and windsurfers will find plenty of good locations (such as Island Bay and Houghton Bay) within easy reach of the city centre. The nearest resort beaches are on the Kapiti Coast. One of the best swimming beaches within easy reach is Days Bay, on the east side of the harbour; behind it, the native bush of Williams Park is a popular picnic area, and Eastbourne village has restaurants, cafés, craft and antique shops. The Trust Bank Ferry (tel: 04 499 1282) runs from Queen's Wharf, with up to eight departures daily for the 30-minute crossing.

Walk Eastern Walkway

An inter-island ferry passes the Barrett Reef

This pleasant coastal walk makes a welcome change from the city streets. Starting from Tarakena Bay, it follows 4.5km of the southern coast of the Miramar Peninsula, and can easily be walked in 1½ hours.

To reach the starting point, follow signs from the city centre for Seatoun and the airport, forking left at the airport junction. In Seatoun, turn right at Inglis Street, just past the shops, continue round the coastal bays and park in Tarakena Bay.

The Eastern Walkway path is clearly signposted up the hill, a brief ascent which brings you to Palmer Head, the site of the **Kemal Ataturk Memorial**. Erected in 1990, this monument to the founder of the modern Turkish state also honours the New Zealand troops who died at the battle of Gallipoli in World War I; a container of soil from Anzac Cove, Gallipoli, is buried within it.

Out at sea the inter-island ferries ply back and forth, and on a clear day you can see the Kaikoura Ranges in the South Island. To the right is a small headland on which there lies Wellington's only untouched *pā* site:

although they are not easily discernible, there are traces of terraces and ditches dating back to the earliest Maori occupation, when this area was known as Te Whanganui a Tara ('the great harbour of Tara'). In the 17th century it became the stronghold of Tutere Moana, chief of the Ngati Tara.

The track now traverses the saddle below Palmer Head, with views of the Wellington Harbour Heads to the right. Below, the small inlets of Palmer Bay, Reef Bay and Eve Bay lead round to the sweeping beach at Breaker Bay. Directly off-shore is the notorious Barrett Reef, the site of many shipwrecks since the last century (including the ill-fated *Wahine*: see page 151). Canoeists now paddle happily around these treacherous rocks, while yachts returning through the Heads give them a wide berth.

Passing behind a residential area, the track dips up and down through an area of typical coastal vegetation; although gorse and other introduced plants dominate the eastern hills, some native plants (such as flax, cabbage tree and *kapuka*) are being reintroduced here.

Make a brief detour at a sign reading 'Exit to Beacon Hill Road' to reach the Beacon Hill lookout, from where there is virtually a 360-degree panorama of the eastern suburbs and airport on one side, with Cook Strait and Baring and Pencarrow Heads on the other. Return to the track to pass beneath the Beacon Hill Signal Station, which has been in operation since 1864 and still maintains a round-the-clock, 365-day-a-year look-out for shipping in the Harbour Heads.

The track now winds gently round the hillside until it starts to descend through a pine forest. Opening out to the right are views of Point Dorset, with an observation point and gun battery (manned in both world wars) visible on the top of the headland.

Leave the track at the Pass of Branda to walk back around the coast to Tarakena Bay, passing many unusual and interesting little seaside dwellings on the way: note the 'Slow Down! Penguins Crossing' signs.

SOUTH ISLAND
MARLBOROUGH AND NELSON

North South Island Straddling the northernmost section of the South Island, the provinces of Marlborough on the east and Nelson on the west embrace a diversity of attractions, ranging from wine tours to whale watching, and craft trails to country hiking. Glorious beaches and a sunny, warm climate contribute to the region's popularity as a holiday destination.

Marlborough The small port of Picton is the point at which visitors arrive by ferry from the North Island, and and it is also the gateway to the extensive **Marlborough Sounds**, a fascinating maze of inlets, beautiful islands, bays and peninsulas with plenty of opportunities for walking, fishing, camping, yachting, kayaking or simply enjoying the scenery. The islands and inlets are mostly thick with vegetation and largely unspoilt – roads are unsealed and often tortuous, and boats are the principal means of transport. The two main sounds are Queen Charlotte and Pelorus, two of the hundred or so scenic and nature reserves which make up the Marlborough Sounds Maritime and Historic Park.

The province of Marlborough is protected to the south by the Kaikoura Ranges and to the west by the Richmond Ranges, with the Wairau Plain stretching between them. The sheltered climate has led to the establishment of numerous vineyards, most of them dotted around the region's main town, **Blenheim**.

Pages 156–7 top: Marlborough Sound. Below: sperm whales

To the east of the Kaikoura Ranges the coastal highway hugs the coast for 60km on the way to **Kaikoura**, 130km south of Blenheim. This small seaside town is riding on the crest of an eco-tourism wave, with up to 50,000 visitors coming here annually for just one activity – whale-watching. Since its beginnings in 1987, whale-watching has taken off in a big way, and there are now numerous operators offering trips by air or sea to view sperm whales. More than 40 new businesses have been created in order to cater for the tourists – ironically, the town has

Below: Dial-a-ride to explore the Marlborough Sounds by seaplane

not enjoyed such prosperity since the days when it was a major whaling port.

Nelson Set at the head of Tasman Bay with views over the Tasman Range to the west, Nelson is the northernmost city in the South Island, lying on the same latitude as Wellington – although the climate here is far more equable, and it claims the second highest sunshine records (averaging 2,500 hours per annum) in the country.

Nelson was one of the first European settlements in New Zealand, and its early days were dogged by problems. The land had been bought by Colonel William Wakefield on behalf of the New Zealand Company, but even after the first ships full of settlers had set sail from England, there were disputes as to where they were going to create their new town: Governor Hobson wanted it near Auckland and the Company wanted it at Lyttelton, but eventually Wakefield had no option but to head for Tasman Bay.

After discovering Nelson Haven (a sheltered anchorage which still protects the present-day harbour), Wakefield landed in December 1841; the first migrant ships arrived the following February. By May 1842 some 2,000 migrants had landed; very few had any capital, however, and economic depression soon set in. With the collapse of the New Zealand Company in 1844, many families were reduced to near-starvation.

But Nelson struggled through, and in 1858 Queen Victoria signed a charter granting it city status – the second in the country, even though the population was still only 2,700 people. Today it has a population of 47,000 and is a prosperous centre for horticulture (particularly fruit), forestry and fishing.

In the **Richmond Ranges** to the south of Nelson there are opportunities for tramping, fishing, hunting or just taking it easy in the extensive **Nelson Lakes National Park**, centred around two scenic glacial lakes.

Beyond Nelson to the west is the **Abel Tasman National Park**. Embracing a glorious stretch of coastline in the sheltered north-western corner of the South Island, Abel Tasman is the smallest national park in New Zealand (covering just over 200 sq km), yet its scenic attractions and remarkably mild and sunny climate have turned it into one of the most popular in the country.

Adjoining Abel Tasman National Park to the south, and protected from the open ocean by Farewell Spit to the north, are the superb sandy beaches of **Golden Bay**, popular for family holidays. **Farewell Spit**, which curves around the top of Golden Bay and extends some 26km out into the sea, is a bird sanctuary of international importance, with over 90 recorded species. South-west of Farewell Spit is the Kahurangi National Park (see pages 186–7).

Whale-watching has brought new life to the small seaside town of Kaikoura

Tasman's landfall
Abel Tasman anchored in what is now Golden Bay on 18 December 1642. That evening, two Maori canoes pulled out to inspect his ships, then departed. The next morning they returned, just as a small boat was crossing between the two Dutch vessels. The Maori attacked the boat, killing four sailors. Tasman named the bay Murderers' Bay because of this 'detestable deed', and never set foot here or anywhere else in the country he named Staten Landt.

Coastal walk
The Abel Tasman Coastal Track, which takes walkers round the coastal bays and along the magnificent beaches, is one of the easiest in the country, with hardly any steep hills to climb. If you want to do just one walk in New Zealand, this is a good choice. Altogether, it is 51km long and takes between three and five days, though you can of course walk shorter sections (see pages 174–5).

Setting off from Marahau at the start of the Abel Tasman Coastal Track

Marlborough

▶▶▶ Abel Tasman National Park *158B2*

It is not difficult to understand the popularity of this park, which boasts a succession of beautiful sandy beaches gently curving round wooded inlets and bays, with wildlife including seals, blue penguins and dolphins in the off-shore waters, and shags, gannets and other sea-birds nesting on the rocky headlands. Oyster catchers, herons and stilts feed in the park's many large estuaries. There is great variety in its vegetation too; the coast is cloaked in fertile rainforest, rich with perching plants, vines and tree ferns, while further inland beech forests are the predominant feature.

For many visitors, the Abel Tasman National Park combines much of what is best about New Zealand – sun, sea, wildlife, beaches and bush – in one convenient, handy package. And it *is* both convenient and accessible: you do not need to be a hardened hiker to reach the best parts, and there is the additional bonus of frequent water taxis and other boats hopping between the beaches. If you were feeling really lazy, you could just stay on the boat and see it all without having to walk anywhere. In fact, experiencing the park from the sea is now an increasingly popular option, with plenty of opportunities for kayaking along the coast.

The main point of access to the park from the south is Marahau, to the north of Motueka (see page 169), while the northern half can be reached via either Wainui Bay or Totaranui, both accessible from Takaka in Golden Bay (see page 162).

Panoramic walk
The Wither Hills Walkway, just outside Blenheim, has a network of trails with extensive panoramas over Blenheim and the Wairau Valley. This once-barren area has been replanted to create a nature reserve, and several short circular walks are now signposted; a complete circuit takes about two or three hours. The entrance is off Taylor Pass Road (7km from Blenheim town centre).

► Blenheim *158C2*

Famous for the wineries which surround it, Blenheim is the capital of the Marlborough region. Set on the Wairau Plains, it was originally the centre of a sheep rearing district, but has now been given a new lease of life thanks to the Marlborough vineyards. The high annual sunshine rate (one of the best in the country), long summers and low autumn rainfall led to the planting of the first vines in the 1970s. Many fine wines are now produced here, and grapes are also 'exported' to North Island wineries from this region.

Within a 15km radius of Blenheim there are over 20 wineries, ranging from the country's biggest producers to the small 'boutique' vineyards, which can be visited for tastings. The Information Centre (The Forum, Queen Street. *Open* daily 8.30–6.30) has details of a 'Scenic Wine Tour', or alternatively you can pick up a copy of their *Wine Trail Guide* and set off on your own.

The countryside around Blenheim, which enjoys one of the best annual sunshine rates in South Island

Blenheim now also has a growing reputation for gourmet food, with an abundance of fine products available, ranging from award-winning cheeses to venison from local deer farms. Green-lipped mussels, crayfish and salmon come from the nearby Sounds, and hazelnuts, olives, garlic, cherries and berry fruits from the plains. The twin pleasures of eating and drinking are highlighted by the increasingly popular **Marlborough Wine & Food Festival**, held in early February every year at the Montana Estate wineries.

Blenheim's modern, compact town centre holds few notable attractions, but there are several pleasant gardens for relaxation: in the heart of the town is **Seymour Square** (*Open* daylight hours. *Admission free*) which features floral displays and lawns surrounding a clock tower and a multi-coloured fountain. On the other side of the Taylor River (reached via a footbridge) is **Pollard Park** (*Open* daylight hours. *Admission free*) with water gardens, rose gardens, rhododendrons and a native rock garden.

About 2km from the town centre is **Brayshaw Historic Museum Park** (*Open* daylight hours. *Admission charge* inexpensive), featuring old farming equipment, a mock colonial village and a miniature railway.

Farewell Spit tours
The oldest operator of tours to Farewell Spit is Collingwood Safari Tours, who have been carrying mail out to the lighthouse at the end of the spit since 1946; several tours are available, depending on the tides and other factors (booking essential, tel: 03 524 8257). Trips to the lighthouse are run by Collingwood Bus Services (tel: 03 524 8188), and you can also join them in the Mail Bus for the daily mail run (departing at 9.30am Mon–Fri) for a scenic five-hour trip around outlying farms and communities.

►► Golden Bay *158B3*

In early Maori times, Golden Bay (then known as Mohua) was fairly heavily populated, owing to the presence of resources such as quartzite (quarried for knives), valuable red and black pigments, flints, and the rare aromatic herb *kakara taramea* (karamea). The bay was also strategically placed on the supply routes to Westland, as a result of which there are signs of early habitation to be found on almost every promontory and headland. It was at the hands of the local Tumatakori tribe that Abel Tasman lost four of his sailors when he anchored in the bay in 1642. In the 19th century coal and timber were exploited here, and there was a mini gold rush in 1857. Dairy farming is now the main activity, and this tranquil area has also attracted a number of craftspeople and artists.

The principal township in Golden Bay is **Takaka►**, with a number of good beaches within striking distance. Most of the town's facilities are on Commercial Street, where there is also a **Museum and Gallery** (*Open* daily 10–1. *Admission charge* inexpensive) with venerable artefacts and relics of the colonial era alongside paintings, arts and crafts in the converted post office next door. At the southern entrance to the town you will also find the Visitor Centre (*Open* daily 9–5) and the DoC office (*Open* Mon–Fri 8.30–12, 1–4); if you want to visit craft workshops in town or in the outlying areas, pick up a leaflet, *Golden Bay Craft Trail*, from the Visitor Centre for details.

Other attractions in the vicinity include the massive **Rawhiti Cave►** the entrance of which, some 50m wide, is adorned with hundreds of stalactites; a guided tour takes about three hours (*Open* on demand. *Admission charge* expensive; booking essential, tel: 03 525 9061). One of the most popular places to visit is **Pupu Springs►►**, the largest freshwater spring in New Zealand. The name is an abbreviation of Waikoropupu ('bubbling waters') the water flows up from underground at a rate of up to 21 cu m per second. Its chief source is the Takaka River, which sometimes disappears underground in the summer, flowing through a network of caves and sinkholes before bursting through the eroded sandstone at this point. There are also vents a few kilometres off-shore in the bay, so that sea water is sucked back into the system only to re-emerge at Pupu Springs, making the water slightly salty. Walkways through the Pupu Springs Reserve (5km from Takaka, signposted off SH60) also encompass old gold workings in the bush.

Continuing from Takaka, after 28km you reach the tiny settlement of **Collingwood▶** at the mouth of the Aorere River. In 1842 a surveyor came across three Europeans living here and building trading ships; later, it boomed briefly during the 1850s gold rush (with no fewer than seven hotels) and was named Gibbstown, after a pioneer settler, William Gibbs. In those heady days there was even a proposal to site the capital here, but once the miners had drifted away it reverted to being the quiet backwater that it remains today. It boasts an old church (St Cuthbert's, built in 1873), a courthouse, a dairy/café, and two adventure-tour operators.

Collingwood is the jumping-off point for the northern end of the Heaphy Track, but the focus for most of the activities here is **Farewell Spit▶▶▶**. Bird species seen here range from kea to gannets and spoonbills, but the most notable are the waders. Each year hundreds of thousands of migratory waders arrive here to feed in the intertidal zones, the best-known of the many regular species being the bar-tailed godwit and the knot.

The spit was considerably over-grazed in earlier years, and much of it is now bare, unstable sand, with frequent high winds (80kph is not unusual) whipping the tops off the shifting dunes and sending curtains of stinging sand along the wide open beaches. Farewell Spit was declared a nature reserve in 1938, and access is limited to licensed operators (see panel).

Beached whales
Farewell Spit has always been a navigational hazard for ships (it has claimed around a dozen vessels), and also, it would seem, for whales, who often get stranded on the innermost curve of the spit, near Puponga Point. On at least four occasions (in 1937, 1948, 1977 and 1991) pods of over one hundred pilot whales have been stranded *en masse*, and others found beached up here have included sperm, minke and fin whales. Dolphins have also been stranded, and seals (who usually prefer rocky sites) often come ashore on the ocean-side beach.

The crystal clear waters of Pupu Springs, near Takaka

The tranquil township of Kaikoura nestling in the bay beneath the Kaikoura Ranges

Scenic mail run
The Scenic Mail Run departs from Havelock on Tuesdays, Wednesdays and Thursdays at 9.30am. Booking is essential; contact: Beachcomber Cruises, The Waterfront, Picton, tel: 03 573 6175; fax: 03 573 6176.

Maori enterprise
The first whale-watching operation was set up in Kaikoura in 1987, eventually evolving into Whale Watch Kaikoura with the help of funding from the local Ngai Tahu tribe. Since then the company has expanded rapidly. Wholly Maori-owned, it has given a massive boost to the local economy, funded schemes to improve community education and health and above all given the local Maori community a sense of self-esteem and pride.

▶ Havelock *158C2*

It is hard to believe that this tiny little port once had 23 hotels, but just over a century ago it was indeed a boom town, thanks to the nearby Cullen Creek and Wakamarina gold fields. When gold fever subsided, Havelock reverted to its former life as a sleepy fishing village, relying then (as it does now) on the famous green-lipped mussels which are grown in the Sounds and exported from here. Situated at the only point where the main road (SH6) joins the shoreline of Pelorus Sound, it is a charming little spot that invites you to linger.

You can explore the superb scenery of the Sounds from Havelock by joining the Pelorus or Scenic Mail Run, which visits isolated homesteads in the many quiet, secluded bays, dropping off supplies and mail as it has done for decades (see panel).

▶▶▶ Kaikoura *158B1*

One of New Zealand's best known 'eco-tourism' destinations, Kaikoura has become famous for whale-watching, thanks to the deep trenches in the sea bed which start less than a kilometre from the shore: cold, north-moving currents are met here by warm, southward-moving currents, creating a constant upwelling of nutrients which supports a complex food web – an 'all you can eat' banquet for seals, dolphins, birds, shellfish, sharks, and of course whales. In some places these canyons exceed 1,600m in depth, and contain many of the deepwater fish and squid which make up much of the sperm whale diet.

The sperm whales are present throughout the year, although at some seasons there are more of them, such as between April and August when they come in-shore to feed on spawning groper. Conditions in the open sea mean that it is not always possible to reach them, so if you are looking forward to a whale-watching trip, be prepared and allow an extra day or two if necessary. Do not plan to go whale-watching if you have a flight to catch!

Sperm whales are not the only cetaceans to take advantage of these rich feeding grounds. In the summer, orca (killer whales) pass through every three weeks or so, usually in pods of between 6 and 18 individuals, and their territory is thought to extend from Cook Strait down as far as Christchurch. Longfin pilot whales, sometimes in groups of up to 300 individuals, have also been spotted. Humpbacks pass through on their annual migration (during June and July) from Tonga to the Antarctic, although they are now few in number.

Dusky dolphins are another highlight of Kaikoura, and these charming, playful creatures appear in their hundreds between October and April. The endangered Hector's dolphin (of which there are only 2,000–3,000 left in the world) is also seen here, with two populations living near Kaikoura throughout the year. Fur seals are also plentiful.

Kaikoura was a major pre-European Maori stronghold, since the peninsula was easily defendable and food was plentiful; there are numerous *pā* sites scattered across the peninsula. In the 19th century, sealers and whalers reaped the harvest from the off-shore waters, with the first whaling station being established here in 1842 by Robert Fyffe. He was later joined by his cousin George, and between them they pioneered sheep farming around Kaikoura.

The only surviving building from the whaling days is the **Fyffe House▶▶** (*Open* daily 10–6. *Admission charge* inexpensive) at Avoca Point, 2km south of the town centre. Originally a cooper's cottage built some time between 1842 and 1852, it was constructed on whalebone piles which can still be seen. George Fyffe and his wife Catherine moved in and extended it in the early 1860s, and it has changed little since then; the house was renovated (using traditional techniques) in 1993 by the Historic Places Trust, and the garden around it was re-created as a cottage garden of the time.

Whaling relics are a prominent feature in the small **Museum** (*Open* weekends 2–4. *Admission charge* inexpensive) on Ludstone Road, which also has Maori artefacts and a replica of the largest moa egg shell ever found, discovered by George Fyffe near his house.

The other main attraction in the vicinity is the **Maori Leap Cave** behind the Caves Restaurant, 3km south of Kaikoura. The origin of the name of this cave is obscure, but it has no basis in Maori mythology – the cave was only discovered during a lime-crushing operation in 1958. Thought to be around two million years old, the cave is 90m long and features numerous delicate limestone formations (tours depart from the Caves Restaurant six times daily. *Admission charge* moderate).

Whale-watching
Trips leave Kaikoura for the two-and-a-half-hour whale-watching excursion four times daily between 6.30am and 2pm. The cost is $85 (adults), $50 (children). Booking (preferably three to four days in advance) is essential. Contact: Whale Watch Kaikoura, the Whaleway Station, Kaikoura, tel: 03 319 5045; freephone: 0800 655 121; fax: 03 319 6545). You can fly over the whales by plane or helicopter (the DoC licences specify that they remain a certain distance away so that their noise footprint does not disturb the whales). Contact: Whale Watch Air, tel: 03 319 6580; Kaikoura Helicopters, tel: 03 319 6609; Air Tours Kaikoura, tel: 03 319 5986.

The sea has been the mainstay of Kaikoura since the earliest Maori settlement

Whale-Watching

■ There are some 76 species of whales and dolphins in the world, and of these 34 have been sighted in the waters around New Zealand: 15 different species have been identified off Kaikoura alone, and the regularity of their appearances has turned this small town into the main centre for the country's whale-watchers. ■

Hydrophones are used to locate the whales

First sightings Dawn spreads an orange glow over Kaikoura Bay as the first whale-watching trip of the day sets out. The rigid-hulled inflatable Naiad slips out of the harbour, past a seal colony at the end of the rocky peninsula, and in 20 minutes it has reached the edge of the continental shelf and the search for whales begins. The crew dip a hydrophone (underwater microphone) into the water, sweeping it round in search of the tell-tale clicks, amplified for all to hear, which betray the presence of sperm whales. Passengers soon discern the slow click of a whale about to surface, and the boat moves closer to the source of the sound. All eyes are on the look-out for the tell-tale jets of spray, and sure enough up comes a massive, 15m-long sperm whale, to gasps of appreciation. It rests on the surface for about 10 minutes, then, having absorbed enough oxygen for its next dive, takes one last breath and lifts its mighty tail flukes in the air before sliding down into the depths again. Those who are lucky might experience several such sightings on a two-hour trip.

Sperm whales When it is resting on the surface most of the sperm whale is invisible, its bulk really only becoming apparent when it performs spectacular leaps (known as 'breaches') out of the water. The sperm whale can dive down as far as 2,000m, using echo-location (sound beams emanating from its oil-filled jawbone) to pinpoint squid and other prey. The average dive usually lasts about 40–45 minutes.

An adult male can weigh up to 35–50 tonnes, the smaller females up to 22 tonnes, and they are believed to have a life span of between 50 and 70 years. The females breed every four to six years and nurse their young for two years; at between 4 and 15 years of age, the young whales form groups with others of the same age but remain in the same areas as the females. As they reach sexual maturity (at between 14 and 20 years of age), they leave the 'family' and set out on their own. The dilemma for the young male is that the acceptable breeding age is 25 – so for the next five or ten years they simply 'hang out' in groups with other bachelors, staying in the feeding areas all year round instead of migrating to the breeding grounds in winter. It is thought that most of the whales seen off Kaikoura are young males between 15 and 25 years old.

Sperm whales have a distinctive scalloped pattern on their tail flukes, and photo-identification has enabled researchers here to identify at least 40 individuals (all of whom have been given names) within the range of the whale-watching operation, which covers around 25 sq km. Another 20 or 30 whales move in and out of this area, and sometimes female sperm whales are also spotted.

Seals and dolphins
Usually aggressively territorial on land, fur seals are far more approachable in the water, and you can go snorkelling with these friendly, playful creatures; for guided snorkelling tours (including wetsuits and snorkelling equipment) contact Graeme Chambers, tel: 03 319 6182. Trips to swim with dolphins are also popular, with all equipment (snorkels etc.) supplied; you can also just view the dolphins. Contact Dolphin Mary Charters, tel: 03 319 6777 or NZ Sea Adventures, tel: 03 319 6622.

A sperm whale prepares to dive

The Murchison earthquake Probably the worst earthquake to hit South Island after European occupation, the Murchison earthquake on 17 June 1929 measured 7.8 on the Richter scale and was felt across the whole island. The epicentre was at White Creek to the west of the town, where the upthrust forced the land up by 4.5m. Nelson, Westport and Greymouth were all affected, and Murchison was almost totally obliterated;17 people were killed, and the town had to be evacuated. Two years later came the Hawke's Bay earthquake, the second biggest the country has ever experienced.

Wonderful views of the Marlborough Sounds unfold along the length of Queen Charlotte Drive

▶▶ Marlborough Sounds *158C2*

Crossing Cook Strait by ferry from the North Island, your first view of the South Island will be of the convoluted waterways of the Marlborough Sounds (see panel page 172). Regrettably, many visitors get off the ferry at Picton and head straight on down the highway to points further south, missing out on this wonderful area.

The Sounds were formed by the sea drowning an intricate system of branching river valleys, and were first explored by Captain Cook, who visited them five times between 1770 and 1777. On each occasion he anchored at Ship Cove (where there is now a memorial to him) to replenish supplies and rest his crew. The French explorer Dumont d'Urville followed in 1827, discovering the passage now known as French Pass.

The two main inlets are **Pelorus Sound** and **Queen Charlotte Sound**, while **Havelock** (see page 164) and **Picton** (see page 173) are respectively the main port and service centre.

One of the most spectacular walks in the region is the 67km-long Queen Charlotte Walkway, which passes through lush coastal forests and skirts historic bays with superb views over both Queen Charlotte Sound and Kenepuru Sound (off Pelorus Sound). There are frequent boat services from Picton, so you can either walk it in day sections or make a two to five-day journey of it.

Equally enjoyable (and not quite as strenuous) is the Queen Charlotte Drive, a superb route which winds around the hills from Picton with magnificent views of the wooded sounds, beaches and bays, ending up in Havelock. It is just over 100km long as a round trip, or you can make it part of your onward journey and continue from Havelock through to Nelson and points west and south.

► Motueka 158B2

Surrounded by a patchwork of orchards and fields producing crops as diverse as hops, kiwifruit and green tea, Motueka is a busy agricultural centre set on the fertile plains behind the Tasman Bay, 51km north-west of Nelson. As the nearest sizeable town to the Abel Tasman National Park it is also a service centre for trampers and day-trippers; the Kahurangi National Park (including the former North West Nelson Forest Park – see pages 186–7) is also accessible from here.

Motueka's long main street has all the usual facilities, including a DoC Centre (corner of King Edward and High Street, tel: 03 528 9117. *Open* 8–12, 1–4.30) for track information and a Visitor Centre (236 High Street, tel: 03 528 6543. *Open* weekdays 8.30–7, weekends 9.30–7) where you can book local activities such as Abel Tasman trips, kayaking and so on. If you are interested in visiting local craft workshops, the Visitor Centre can provide a *Craft Trail* leaflet which describes a 70km tour around a dozen or so in the vicinity.

Although the superb beaches of the Abel Tasman National Park are not far away, there are others nearer town, such as **Kaiteriteri Beach►**, a long strip of golden sand 14km to the north.

Rapid rivers
One of the most popular activites around Murchison is white-water rafting down the turbulent Buller River, with several options ranging from family-friendly trips on Grade 2 ('slight excitement') sections to non-stop rapids on Grade 4 ('very exciting') parts of the river; contact Go West Rafting, P O Box 99, Murchison, tel: 03 523 9315.

The wharf at Motueka, the base town for both the Abel Tasman National Park and the Kahurangi National Park

► Murchison 158A1

Surrounded by rugged mountains, Murchison lies on a small plain at the confluence of the Buller and Matakitaki Rivers. Because of its strategic position between Nelson and Westland on the Buller Gorge Heritage Highway (SH6), it is often treated as no more than a refreshment stop by travellers passing in either direction. However, the town has developed an enormous range of adventure activities and is ideally placed for exploring the surrounding bush-clad ranges, fast-flowing rivers and unspoiled lakes.

The Information Centre (Waller Street, tel: 03 523 9350. *Open* daily 10–5) can provide details on gold-panning, mountain-biking, hunting, fishing, 4WD safaris, caving, horseriding and much else besides.

Just off the main street is the **Murchison Museum►** (*Open* daily 10–4. *Admission charge* donation) with a large collection of antique telephones and a section devoted to the Murchison earthquake (see panel opposite).

The shoreline at Nelson, one of the oldest towns in New Zealand

Arts and crafts
The enormous range of arts and crafts being produced in and around Nelson is detailed in the *Arts Trail and Gallery Guide* from the Visitor Centre. Some of those near the city centre include: Art of Living (ceramics, glass, silk, original art; 20 Nile Street), Nelson Arts and Crafts (pottery, jewellery, jade, hand-painted clothes, woodwork; 105B Bridge Street), South Street Pottery Gallery (10 Nile Street West), and the Bead Gallery (18 Parere Street). Out of town, the long-established Craft Habitat (10 minutes south on SH6) contains half a dozen or more workshops.

Nelson

▶▶ Nelson *158B2*

One of the oldest settlements in the country, Nelson can also claim a number of 'firsts' for New Zealand, including the first Rugby Club in the country, formed on 14 May 1870, with the first match being played the same day in the grounds of the Botanic Gardens. The first commercial brewery in New Zealand (Paolo and Pelham) opened here in 1842, and the first recognised race course in the country was built at Stoke in 1845. The first commercial thoroughbred horse-breeding stud was opened in 1852, and the country's oldest state secondary school, Nelson College, was opened in 1856.

Leading up from the seafront is the central axis of the city, **Trafalgar Street**, where you will find most of the shops and the helpful Visitor Centre (corner of Trafalgar and Halifax streets, tel: 03 548 2304. *Open* weekdays 8.15–5.30, Sat 9–5, Sun 10–4). Near by is **Montgomery Square**, where there is a good weekend market with crafts, plants, bric-à-brac and fresh produce stalls.

Dominating Trafalgar Street at its southern end is **Christ Church Cathedral** (*Open* 7am–8pm), an unmissable monolith built on top of a small hill. Local people tend to stress the 'beautiful gardens' which surround it, thereby sidestepping a description of the building itself. Started in Takaka marble (a promising beginning) but finished in concrete blocks, the cathedral took nealy 40 years to complete (it was begun in 1925, completed in 1967 but not consecrated until 1972), and it looks as though it was designed by a committee. The politest thing you can say about it is that it has some nice stained glass – and, of course, some lovely gardens.

But in general Nelson is not a city lacking in artistic achievement – on the contrary, it is noted for its arts, music and crafts (particularly pottery), and there are plenty of outlets for browsing or buying around town. The city's best showcase is the Suter Art Gallery (Queens Gardens, Bridge Street. *Open* daily 10.30–4.30. *Admission charge* inexpensive), which houses a permanent collection (with works by Wollaston, Lindauer, Van der Velden and others), and also features touring and local exhibitions covering everything from sculpture to fibre crafts.

Nelson is home to a unique event, the Wearable Art Awards. Started by sculptor Suzie Moncrieff in 1987 as a publicity stunt when she opened a gallery, this has since grown into an international event which is now staged in the sports stadium in the last week of September every year. It is an explosion of creativity and anarchic design, and the concept is still evolving, with recently created categories including a Visual Arts section. Some of the winning garments can be seen at the **Wearable Art Gallery** (Spring Grove, between Brightwater and Wakefield on the main road south. *Open* weekends only 10–5. *Admission free*).

Nelson also has its fair share of historic buildings, albeit scattered quite widely across the city and neighbouring suburbs. One of the most interesting streets within the city centre is **South Street▶** (off Nile Street West, just behind the cathedral), which consists of 16 working-class cottages built between 1863 and 1867; most are private dwellings, but some house small galleries or craft shops. Many of the older historic buildings have been re-erected (or re-created) in **Founder's Park▶** (87 Atawhai Drive, five minutes' walk from the centre. *Open* daily 10–4.30. *Admission charge* moderate), where there is also a three-dimensional maze, train rides and an audio-visual exhibition on Port Nelson.

One of Nelson's most beautiful historic homes is **Isel House▶▶** (Marsden Road, Stoke. *Open* weekends 2–4 in summer only. *Admission charge* inexpensive), a two-storey homestead containing a collection of porcelain and furniture. Opposite Isel House is the **Nelson Provincial Museum▶** (Tue–Fri 10–4, weekends 2–5. *Admission charge* inexpensive) which has some interesting Maori artefacts as well as an extensive collection of historic photographs. Both buildings are within the grounds of the 6ha **Isel Park▶▶** which has extensive plantations of exotic trees. Also near by in Stoke is **Broadgreen House▶▶** (Nayland Road. *Open* Tue–Fri 10–30–4.30, weekends 1.30–4.30. *Admission charge* inexpensive), a good example of an early cob house, built in 1855 and recently restored with careful attention to period detail.

Ernest Rutherford
Ernest Rutherford, the 'father of nuclear physics', was born at Brightwater (20km to the south of Nelson) in 1871, and was educated at Nelson College before moving on to Canterbury University College in Christchurch and then Cambridge University, England. His main achievement was in discovering how to split the atom, but he also made many other outstanding discoveries in over 40 years of experimentation with atomic physics. He took the title Baron Rutherford of Nelson on his elevation to the peerage in 1931, and on his death (1937) was buried in Westminster Abbey in London.

On the Sounds
There are numerous ways to explore the Marlborough Sounds from Picton, including by sailing yacht (Marlborough Sounds Charters, tel: 03 573 7726; Paradise Sailing Charters, tel: 03 578 8236), on a three hour cruise to Endeavour Inlet (Cougar Line, tel: 03 573 7925); by kayak (Marlborough Sounds Adventure Co, tel: 03 573 6078; Sea Kayaking Adventure Tours, tel: 03 574 2765); or on a special cruise to look for dolphins and other marine life (Dolphin Watch Marlborough, tel: 03 573 8040).

Picton, port for the North Island – South Island ferry

▶▶ Nelson Lakes National Park *158B1*

This lovely park is easily reached from Nelson, or can conveniently be visited by making a detour off SH6 on routes to Westland. In 1859, the explorer von Haast exclaimed, 'I had no idea such a jewel in point of landscape existed so near to Nelson, and I am sure that the time is not far distant when this spot will become the favourite abode of those whose means and leisure will permit them to admire picturesque scenery.' And so it is, with fishing, tramping, mountain-biking, hunting and skiing also popular.

Covering 102,000ha of rugged terrain, the park features a diverse range of habitats, ranging from tranquil lakeside beech forests to open tussock lands beneath craggy peaks. The most popular area is around beautiful **Lake Rotoiti**▶▶, where you can swim from the lakeside picnic areas with the forested hills as a backdrop. The main gateway to the park and the centre for activities is the alpine village of **St Arnaud** (120km from Nelson) on the shores of the lake, where accommodation, camping, shops, and a DoC Visitor Centre at the lakeside (*Open* daily 8–5, closed weekends May–Aug) are all available.

The park has 270km of tracks and 21 huts, with the longest tramp being the 80km Travers-Sabine Circuit (four to seven days). For day visitors there are plenty of short walks around the shores of the lake, most of them well signposted and graded. You can also take a water taxi to the far shore and walk back from there.

Lake Rotoroa▶ is slightly harder to reach (down an 11km gravel road), and has fewer facilities; it is more popular with those who want to go hunting or trout-fishing. There are also short walks around Rotoroa, but the lakeshore has a tendency to be plagued by sandflies.

In winter there is skiing at the Rainbow field (36km from St Arnaud) and at the Mount Robert field (8km from St Arnaud).

▶ Picton 158C2

Primarily a transit point for ferry passengers crossing to or from the North Island, Picton sits near the head of Queen Charlotte Sound, and is often bypassed in favour of more exciting destinations. In fact it is a pleasant little port which makes a good base for visiting the Marlborough Sounds.

While catamarans, yachts and speedboats ply the harbour, one of the world's oldest ships still floats in its berth by the quayside. The ***Edwin Fox*▶▶▶** (*Open* summer 8.45–7, winter 8.45–5. *Admission charge* inexpensive) was built in 1853, and carried tea from the colonies, troops to the Indian Mutiny, convicts to Australia, immigrants to New Zealand, and frozen meat back to Britain before ending up as a coal hulk in Picton harbour. There is a superb new interpretation centre alongside the ship. On the other side of the harbour, the scow ***Echo*▶** a 90-year old coastal trader, is now a café/bar (*Open* summer 10–10, winter 10–5).

Overlooking the harbour is the **Picton Museum▶** (*Open* daily 10–4. *Admission charge* inexpensive), with whaling relics and equipment and a small but unusual Maori collection.

Walking tracks
Around Picton there are plenty of short to moderate walks which take you through scenic bush areas or up to vantage points over the Sounds. If you are short of time, one of the easiest is the 1km shoreline track to Bob's Bay, around the eastern side of the harbour. The Visitor Centre has a detailed leaflet on *Walkways and Mountain Bike Tracks*.

The oldest merchant ship still afloat, the Edwin Fox

Walk Abel Tasman Coastal Track

This easy walk follows the popular coastal track around one of the most scenic sections of the Abel Tasman National Park. Allow four hours for the walk back to Marahau from The Anchorage.

The Anchorage

After stepping ashore in The Anchorage, turn right past the DoC Camping area and continue until you see a track heading inland. After a short climb you reach a ridge from where there are terrific views back across The Anchorage and Torrent Bay, with the headlands, beaches and coastal inlets of the park stretching northwards. In front of you, the view encompasses the Astrolabe Roadstead and Adele Island, with the Richmond Mountains visible across Tasman Bay in the distance.

From here the track crosses one of the most arid sections of the park, a testament to the many fires (dating back to pre-European times) which have destroyed the original vegetation. In the poor soil even gorse and the hardy manuka struggle to survive.

Although the park is named after Abel Tasman, it was the French explorer Dumont d'Urville who was the true European discoverer of this coast, which he charted and explored in January 1827 while his corvette *Astrolabe* was anchored between Adele Island and the mainland. In contrast to Tasman, d'Urville established good relations with the Maori.

Take the track down to **Watering**

Coastal scenery in Abel Tasman National Park

Cove►►, another delightful beach with a stream running down behind it. D'Urville replenished the ship's water supplies here, and an engraving of the time shows the *Astrolabe's* sailors relaxing and doing their washing in the 'charming stream of very clear water'.

There is evidence of fire everywhere in the park,with blackened tree trunks and scorched scrub, but after the junction branching off up to Holyoake Clearing (which leads to the inland section of the track) the vegetation becomes greener, with a variety of broad-leaved species, rimu and kamahi shading the track, and treeferns spreading their fronds over the moist gullies on the hillsides.

This is one of the prettiest sections of the track as it follows round the hillside, crossing tumbling brooks with glimpses of a succession of sandy coves on the seaward side. Just before Yellow Point, turn down towards **Akersten Bay**►►, another beautiful beach where you can cool off with a swim or a paddle in the warm waters of the Astrolabe Roadstead. An early surveyor, Frederick Carrington, understandably fell in love with this superb coastline in 1841: 'Certain it is that if I ever settle for life in New Zealand, Astrolabe Roads would be the place I give preference to.' It is easy to agree with him as you relax on the sand

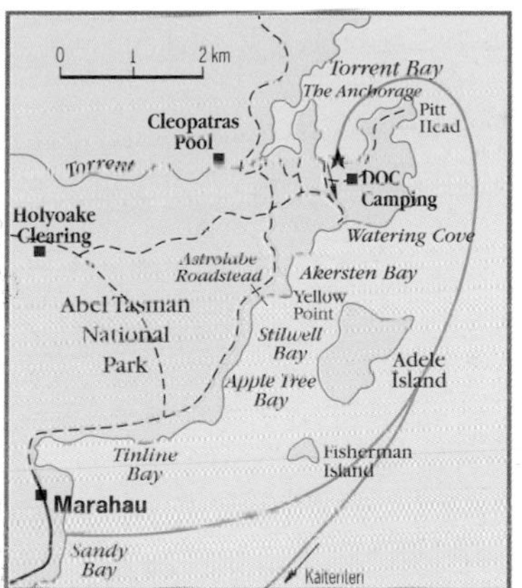

admiring this magnificent environment.

Past Yellow Point another track leads down alongside the stream bed of Lesson Creek to **Stilwell Bay**►►, also a gorgeous beach. Finally you come to **Apple Tree Bay**►►, which d'Urville described as 'the pleasantest spot on the whole coast...a narrow sandy belt, covered with nothing but herbaceous plants, runs along the edge of the sea....a magnificent stream crosses it from one end to the other, dashing its plenteous waters over a bed formed of enormous blocks of granite'. It is little changed today, apart from a strand of trees on the foreshore, and it is the last in this succession of splendid beaches.

Beyond here the track continues to **Tinline Bay**, surrounded by hillsides of bracken and gorse, until finally you emerge in the estuary of **Sandy Bay**, where a causeway leads across the tidal flats to the Park Café and bus stop at **Marahau**.

Cut off by the towering mass of the Southern Alps (above), the West Coast has numerous historic gold workings – in some, you can try your hand at panning.

SOUTH ISLAND
THE WEST COAST

The West Coast A narrow strip of land hemmed in on one side by the Tasman Sea and on the other by the Southern Alps, the West Coast is characterised by wild, magnificent scenery, and has several national parks. The coastal flats are scattered with the remnants of the gold rush era of the 1860s, with walking tracks around many of the old workings. Visitors can still sometimes have a try at gold-panning here themselves.

The weather is a perennial topic of conversation on the West Coast, which has a reputation for almost continuous rain. The high rainfall is caused by westerly winds coming off the sea and rising up to the mountains, where they condense to dump their watery cargo on the narrow coastal belt – thus encouraging the region's lush vegetation. Nevertheless, most of the rain tends to fall at night with the clouds parting during the day to reveal the peaks of the Southern Alps sparkling in the clear light. But don't forget your gumboots – just in case.

New Zealand's most recently established national park is the **Kahurangi**, which was designated as a park in 1995. Covering some 5,000 sq km of diverse and largely untouched terrain in the north-west corner of the South Island, it stretches from Murchison all the way up to Farewell Spit in Nelson, and contains a greater variety of plant and animal life, geology and landforms than any other national park in the country. The coastline encompasses everything from palm-fringed beaches north of Karamea to the rugged cliffs beyond the Heaphy River, while inland lie countless caves, river canyons and jagged peaks reaching up to 1,875m.

The main point of access for the Kahurangi, and a good base for a variety of activities, is **Karamea** (98km north of Westport) at the end of the road in the far north of the West Coast region.

The Paparoa National Park, 47km north of the town of Greymouth, is one of the most popular areas on the West Coast. Extending from the coast to the crest of the Paparoa Range, the park is fairly compact (covering just 300 sq km), but has a wide variety of features including delightful beaches, numerous limestone caves and cave systems, awesome gorges bordered by towering cliffs, and forested valleys. Sheltered by the mountains and warmed by ocean currents from the Coral Sea, it has a mild, moist micro-climate which favours luxuriant subtropical vegetation featuring masses of perching plants, tangled vines and nikau palms. In combination with the dramatic 300m-high coastal cliffs, this gives the park tremendous appeal.

Other natural attractions on the West Coast include seal colonies at **Cape Foulwind** and **Gillespies Beach**, a black petrel colony in Paparoa National Park, and a white heron colony near **Whataroa**.

To the south-west of Greymouth is **Arthur's Pass National Park**, straddling the Southern Alps and equally accessible from both the West Coast and Canterbury, either by car or on the famous TranzAlpine Express.

About half-way down the coast, the Fox and Franz Josef Glaciers form part of the **Westland National Park**, which offers guided ice walks or helicopter sightseeing.

The Haast, at the southern end of the West Coast, is a beautiful area which is all too often neglected as people speed through on their way to Otago and Fiordland. Only connected by a through route to the rest of the country in 1965, this rugged, unspoiled wilderness has a spectacular coastline backed by the towering peaks of the Southern Alps, with foaming glacial rivers and a series of forest-fringed lakes inland.

See drive pages 192-193
D'Urville Island
Farewell Spit
Cape Farewell
Golden Bay
Separation Point
Abel Tasman National Park
Tasman Bay
Collingwood
Mt Stevens 1213m
Takaka
Motueka
NELSON
Richmond
Kahurangi Point
HEAPHY TRACK
Brightwater
1760m Mt Richmond
Tasman Mts
Honeycomb Caves
Motupiko
Oparara Limestone Arches
Kahurangi National Park
Karamea
1875m Mt Owen
Wairau
St Arnaud
Karamea Bight
NELSON
Lake Rotoroa
Murchison
Nelson Lakes National Park
Granity
Buller
Gorge
Victoria
Westport
Victoria Forest Park
Charleston
Mitchells Gully Goldmine
Reefton
Lewis Pass
Pancake Rocks
Paparoa Nat Park
Punakaiki
Dolomite Point
1834m Mt Ajax
Grey
Greymouth
Lake Brunner
Arthur's Pass Nat Park
1987m Mt Crossley
Shantytown
Arthur's Pass
TranzAlpine Express
Hokitika
2400m Mt Murchison
Ross
WESTLAND
Lake Coleridge
0 20 40 60 km
CANTERBURY
2795m Mt Arrowsmith
Harihari
Arrowsmith Range
White Heron Sanctuary
Whataroa
2545m
Franz Josef
Mount Cook Nat Park
Franz Josef Glacier
Mt Tasman
Lake Matheson
Fox
3764m Mt Cook
Lake Tekapo
Gillespies Beach
Fox Glacier
Westland Nat. Park
Tasman Glacier
Mount Cook
Fairlie
Opuha
Tekapo
Ben Ohau Range
Lake Pukaki
Kirkliston Range
Roaring Billy Falls
Landsborough
Alps
Twizel
Lake Benmore
Haast
Gates of Haast
Lake Ohau
Waitaki
Haast Pass
Omarama
Otematata
Jackson Bay
Makarora
Hawkdun Range
Jackson Port
Mount Aspiring National Park
Southern
Lake Hawea
Cascade Point
2087m
St Bathans
Lake Wanaka
Hawea
3027m Mt Aspiring
Olivine Range
Wanaka
Dunstan Mts
Awarua Point
Shotover
2819m
OTAGO
Arrowtown
Cromwell

The TranzAlpine Express
One of the great railway adventures of the world, the TranzAlpine Express connects the east and west coasts via mountain passes, tunnels and impressive viaducts. The 233km narrow-gauge single-track line climbs via six viaducts and 16 tunnels to the station at Arthur's Pass, then descends through the 8.5km-long Otira Tunnel to Greymouth. The TranzAlpine departs from Christchurch daily at 9.00am, arriving at 1.25pm; from Greymouth it departs at 2.25pm, returning to Christchurch at 6.35pm. Bookings through Tranz Scenic agents or Central Reservations (tel: 0800 802 802 toll-free).

▶▶ Arthur's Pass National Park *179B3*

Straddling the mountainous spine of the Southern Alps, Arthur's Pass National Park covers 992 sq km and is one of the most popular walking areas in the South Island. With numerous peaks rising above 2,000m it is a dramatic and beautiful region, yet there are plenty of easy walks to waterfalls, scenic lookout points and mountain tarns. The beech forests provide a haven for birds such as the tui, bellbird and shining cuckoo, while the cheeky alpine parrot, the kea, can be seen at higher altitudes. The park has a good network of huts for longer tramps.

The small alpine community of **Arthur's Pass** offers basic accommodation, a couple of café/restaurants, and the National Park Visitor Centre (*Open* daily 8–5). Between June and September it becomes a skiing centre.

Arthur's Pass is 153km from Christchurch and 98km from Greymouth, with the spectacular Arthur's Pass Road, one of New Zealand's most dramatic mountain routes, running in between.

▶ Cape Foulwind *179A4*

Unjustly named by Cook, the Cape shelters Westport from westerly winds and was known to the Maori as Tauranga, 'a sheltered anchorage'. **Tauranga Bay▶** (15km from Westport) has a seal colony at its northern end, and pups are born here in late November and early December. The path above the cliffs forms part of the **Cape Foulwind Walkway**.

►►► Fox and Franz Josef Glaciers *179A2*

Among the highlights of the West Coast, the Fox and Franz Josef Glaciers are unusual, since nowhere else in the world do glaciers descend this far down into temperate zones, crunching their way down the valleys from the peaks of the Southern Alps until they are a mere 12km from the sea.

The reason for this is their unusual position: a huge tract of land at the head of both glaciers tapers down to two narrow valleys, so channelling the snow and ice down towards the sea. They are a spectacular sight, particularly since both glaciers are now advancing at a rapid pace (for glaciers), with huge blocks of ice breaking off at the terminal face and floating off downstream during floods.

The Franz Josef Glacier was named in 1864 by the explorer Julius Von Haast after the emperor of his native Hungary; it plunges 2,700m from the alpine peaks to just 300m above sea level at the terminal face. The township of **Franz Josef** offers a wide range of services and accommodation. The Westland National Park Visitor Centre (*Open* daily 8–5) features displays on the glaciers and details on local walks. From the town it is 6km to the car park at the **Glacier Terminal►►**, along a road which passes through overhanging rainforests along the way. The township of **Fox** has similar facilities to its twin at Franz Josef, including a Visitor Centre (*Open* summer 8.30–7, winter 8.30–12, 1–4.30). From Fox it is 7km to the **Glacier Terminal►►**.

Glacial trips
Guided ice walks leave from both Fox and Franz Josef twice daily, with a range of options depending on your level of fitness: the shorter trips (suitable for most people) take around three hours, with some 30 minutes on the glacier itself. More adventurous options include day-long glacier walks and heli-hikes to higher levels. Alpine Guides have bases in both townships (tel: 03 751 0825). Helicopter flights are also popular and reasonably priced: contact Glacier Helicopters, tel: 03 752 0755; 03 751 0803; Fox and Franz Josef Heliservices, tel: 03 751 0825; 03 752 0793; or Westair, tel: 03 752 0716.

Fox Glacier, named after politician Sir William Fox who painted it in 1872, starts slightly above the Franz Josef

Glaciers

■ Whether global warming is a reality or not, both the Fox and Franz Josef Glaciers are bucking the trend and advancing at an unprecedented rate. In fact, they have followed a pattern of advance and retreat for centuries. ■

Beware icefalls
The current hazardous state of the glacial terminals means that visitors should pay particular attention to the warning signs and barriers erected by park officials. Do not be tempted to step over the boundary ropes to pose for pictures: the terminus may look solid but in fact it is extremely fragile, and towering blocks of ice (seracs) have been crashing down with increasing regularity.

Crevasses on the Fox Glacier

On the move Glaciers are very sensitive to the balance between the volume of snow and ice accumulating on the upper slopes and the amount of ice melting at the terminus: only when both factors remain constant over a number of years will the terminus remain stationary.

During the last great ice age, some 18,000 years ago, both the Fox and Franz Josef Glaciers reached down as far as the present-day coastline and beyond. About 1,000 years ago they were reduced to mere pockets of ice on their névés (upper slopes), but then a deterioration in the climate caused them to advance once more. Since the beginning of the latest period of 'global warming' they have been gradually receding, with minor advances at roughly 20-year intervals.

During the last decade the terminal face of Franz Josef has advanced 1.7km down the valley, reaching a point it last occupied some 30 years ago, while the Fox Glacier has advanced almost a kilometre in the same period.

Measuring change The movement of the glaciers can be measured by following the progress of markers or debris on the glacial surface. In 1943, for instance, an aircraft crashed about 4km up from the terminus of the Franz Josef Glacier; six years later parts of the wreckage appeared at the glacier front.

Because glaciers are so sensitive to climate change, they are used by scientists as indicators of climatic conditions. Both the Fox and Franz Josef are particularly useful indicators because their large catchment areas feed into narrow valleys, so that small changes in the accumulation of snow and ice at the head can result in dramatic increases at the snout. But the response to climate change is not instantaneous: Fox Glacier takes about seven years to translate increased snowfalls into an advance at the terminus, whilst Franz Josef has a response time of around five years.

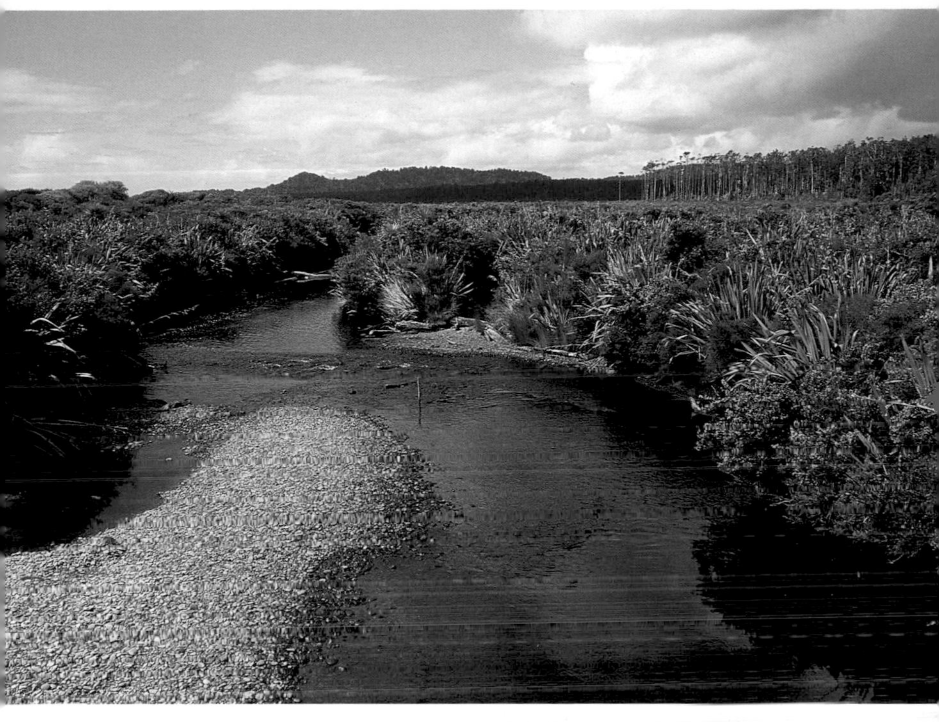

▶ Gillespies Beach *179A2*

The area surrounding Gillespies Beach, a short 20km drive to the coast from Fox Glacier, was mostly formed from the moraine dumped by the glacier some 18,000 years ago. The rimu forests which fringe the shore here are one of the best examples of their kind in the country, and the forest, lagoon and shoreline are rich in birdlife.

The Gillespies Beach **fur seal colony**▶ is a resting place for many different seal species during the non-breeding winter season, and can contain up to 1,500 seals. During the summer, it is home to around 30 immature bull seals. There is an excellent walk from the small settlement at Gillespies Beach to the seal colony; the return trip from the car park in front of Gillespies Lagoon takes around three hours, with spectacular views of the coast, mountains, glaciers and rimu forests from Trig Point HU on Waikowhai Bluff. It is only possible two hours either side of low tide: check tide tables at the Fox DoC Centre.

Greymouth *179B3*

As well as being the West Coast terminus for the TranzAlpine Express, the port of Greymouth is the region's main centre for coal, timber and a number of other industries including brewing: tours of the **DB Westland Brewery** (tel: 03 768 5101. Tours Mon–Fri 10.30 and 1.30. *Admission charge* inexpensive) are one of the few things to do in town. **Jade Boulder Gallery** (corner of Tainui and Guinness streets. *Open* Mon–Fri 8.30am–9pm, to 5pm in winter; Sat–Sun 9am–9pm, to 5pm in winter) has a wide range of knitwear alongside its jade displays.

The lagoons at Gillespies Beach are backed by rimu forests, home to a wealth of birds

Beware of trains
It may come as something of a shock to see a train coming towards you over road bridges on the West Coast highway, but there are combined road-rail bridges along this part of the coastline: across the Taramakau, 14km south of Greymouth, and across the Arahura, 8km north of Hokitika. Until recently these bridges had gates to stop road traffic while trains crossed, but these have now been removed – so watch out!

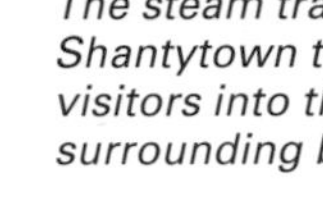

The steam train at Shantytown takes visitors into the surrounding bush

Some 13km south of Greymouth is **Shantytown►►**, a large open-air complex (*Open* daily 8.30–5. *Admission charge* moderate) which includes steam train rides, a stamper battery, a working sawmill, gold panning and horse-drawn vehicle rides. The star attraction is a re-construction of a gold rush town of the 1880s, complete with shops, livery stables, gaol, post office, hotel and church (which originally came from the genuine gold rush settlement of Notown).

►►► Haast *179A1*

The Haast has the most extensive wetlands in New Zealand, with coastal lagoons and swamps dominated by giant kahikatea and rimu forests, where native grey and paradise duck, bittern and shag can be spotted. The silver and mountain beech lowland forests are home to the largest population of kaka (bush parrots) in the country, as well as to fantails, tui, bellbird, morepork, falcon, warbler, and kiwi. Trout and quinnat salmon abound in the Okuru, Turnbull, Arawata and Jackson Rivers, with trout-fishing available year round. The area is famous for its whitebait, and fur seals, blue penguins and Fiordland crested penguins inhabit the rocky sections of the coast.

At **Haast Junction**, where the coast road (SH6) crosses the Haast River and becomes the trans-alpine road to Otago, is the **South West New Zealand World Heritage Visitor Centre** (*Open* 8–5.30), with imaginative displays and regular screenings of a film on the human and natural history of the area (*Admission charge* inexpensive). The Centre can also provide a leaflet detailing a dozen or so short, easy walks in the vicinity and take bookings for Haast Marine Safaris (tel: 03 750 0809) to view penguins, seals, dolphins and other marine wildlife along the coast.

Canoeing on the Moeraki River, which runs from Lake Moeraki to the coast just north of Haast

Greenstone (Jade)

■ **Intricately carved into elaborate ornaments, pendants and sculptures, greenstone or jade is a beautiful material which was traditionally revered by the Maori, who travelled great distances to seek it out on the wild West Coast.** ■

Jade nephrite True jade nephrite is a rare mineral, known to the Maori as *pounamu*. Jade is found only in the South Island, which they called Te Wai Pounamu ('the waters in which pounamu dwell'). *Pounamu* is also a Maori word for the colour green, and when the Europeans arrived they used the terms 'green talc' and 'greenstone' for both jade and bowenite (a softer stone found mostly around Milford Sound).

Modern carvers follow the tradition of Maori greenstone ornaments

A prized commodity The Maori had always prized greenstone, partly because of its usefulness in a culture which possessed no hard metals. It could be carved into tools (such as adzes, fish-hooks, axe-heads and chisels) and weapons of war (such as the impressive *mere* or fighting clubs), as well as being used extensively for personal adornment, in the form either of ear ornaments or of pendants such as the celebrated *heitiki*.

The Maori even endowed *pounamu* with life itself, tracing its origins back to the creation. They valued it more highly than gold, and the great importance attached to it is reflected in the number of names that they used for different types of jade, with 18 different expressions to cover the numerous subtle variations in its delicate shades.

Hard to find The difficulties of obtaining and transporting greenstone from the remote Westland sites where it was found only added to its allure. Expeditions to recover it were fraught with danger: few tracks penetrated the forests, and the unpredictable Tasman Sea made arrival by canoe hazardous. A *tohunga* (ritual expert) was often taken along to help in the search for jade boulders (*papa pounamu*), for it takes a discerning eye to detect the heightened colour of a boulder containing jade among the many similar looking rocks and stones in the river bed.

No trade
Prized jade possessions were never traded. Captain Cook tried, unsuccessfuly, to barter for *pounamu*, reflecting ruefully: 'These green talc axes that are whole and good they set much value upon, and never would part with them for anything we could offer.'

A tricky harbour
During the 1860s it was a major spectator sport in Hokitika to stand on the shoreline and watch sailing ships attempt to 'run the blockade' across the treacherous sand bar. The north/south orientation of the river estuary forced ships to enter almost broadside to the sea, and unless there was a good breeze they often had insufficient steerage to negotiate the sand bar. Between 1865 and 1867 a ship was beached on average once every ten days, and of these no fewer than 42 were wrecked completely. Craft which were beached undamaged were raised by screwjacks and dragged across to the river in an operation known as 'making the overland trip'.

Kahurangi flora and fauna
Kahurangi National Park is a rich storehouse of plant and animal life. Effectively isolated during the last ice age, the region became a major refuge in which new species and varieties evolved. At least half of New Zealand's native plant species can be found here, with nearly 70 endemic species. Amongst the hundred native bird species are several which are threatened, including the great spotted kiwi, South Island kaka, kereru, blue duck and rock wren. New Zealand's only two native land mammals, the long-tailed and short-tailed bat, have both been recorded in the area. There are also three seal colonies along the coast.

►► Hokitika *179B3*

Built on the back of the 1860s gold rush, Hokitika was once one of the busiest ports in New Zealand. On one fine Spring day in 1865 no fewer than 19 ships either entered or left the port. The Quayside often bristled with the masts of up to 40 ships at any one time, but as well as being one of the busiest, it was also one of the most notorious (see panel). One of the earliest ships wrecked here was the schooner *Tambo*, which has now been re-created as a **Shipwreck Memorial** at the northern tip of the Hokitika spit (five minutes' walk from the town centre). The quayside itself is also being refurbished, with the old **Custom House** standing at the centre of the Heritage Area. Hokitika's heritage is traced in the **West Coast Historical Museum►►** (Tancred Street. *Open* daily 9.30–5. *Admission charge* inexpensive). You can try gold panning here or at the **Phelps' Goldmine►** 2km to the south of town (*Open* daily 9–5. *Admission charge* inexpensive).

Try to stay until after dark in order to visit the magical **Glow-worm Dell►** (beside the main road on the northern outskirts of the town), said to be the largest outdoor colony of glow-worms in the country.

►► Kahurangi National Park *179B5*

The second largest park in the country after Fiordland, Kahurangi National Park has virtually no roads through it, but is criss-crossed with 600km of walking tracks, the best-known of which is the 77km-long Heaphy Track; others include the Wangapeka and Leslie Tracks. But you do not have to be a hardened hiker to enjoy this wonderful park since some of the most scenic parts can easily be reached from the West Coast village of Karamea.

►► Karamea *179A5*

Situated literally at the end of the road, this remote coastal settlement is 98km north of Westport on the northern continuation of road SH67. Until recently, most of its visitors were trampers emerging from the wilderness at the southern end of the Heaphy Track, but the creation of the Kahurangi National Park has set it firmly on the map.

Until now, Karamea has had a rough ride. The first settlers arrived here in 1874, but after three years of toil clearing the bush they discovered the land was useless. They moved further up the river valley, only to have their first crops destroyed by floods. Until the building of a road to Westport in 1915, the local inhabitants' only link with the outside world was an erratic steamer service. In 1929 the Murchison earthquake destroyed the harbour and cut the community's road link for a couple of years.

Flanked by bush-clad mountains, this tranquil backwater with its particularly mild climate now offers an expanding range of activities for the visitor, including canoeing, white-water rafting, fishing, and some enjoyable day walks. The area's unusual geology also provides some interesting excursions to nearby limestone caves and arches. The most spectacular of these are the **Oparara Limestone Arches►►**, which are reached by driving to the very end of the road and then following an unmetalled logging track (16km from the North Beach turn-off in Karamea); it is then a 20-minute walk from the car park.

Another essential sight is the **Honeycomb Caves▶▶**, which contain a remarkable assortment of sub-fossil remains including moa, the giant New Zealand eagle, the giant flightless goose and the flightless rail. The caves are also home to a cave-dwelling spider and giant carnivorous snails. Access is restricted to guided tours (contact the Last Resort in Karamea, tel: 03 782 6617).

If time is limited, one of the best ways to experience the Kahurangi is to walk the first part of the Heaphy Track north of Karamea. From the town, drive 13km north to the Kohaihai River car park. Cross the swing-bridge to start a pleasant 40-minute loop walk through nikau palm groves; beyond the Nikau Grove Track the path continues up and over the hill through the forest, opening out on to a magnificent section of the coastline to reach Scott Beach (90 minutes return).

▶ Lake Matheson 179A2

One of the most photographed panoramas in the vicinity of Fox Glacier is the reflection of the peaks of the Southern Alps in the waters of Lake Matheson, a 'kettle' lake formed from the melting of glacial ice. Make a detour off the road to Gillespies Beach, 5.5km west of Fox, and follow the path to the jetty (one hour return). You can also keep going to reach the 'View of Views' (two hours return) on the far side of the lake. The reflections are at their best in the still of early morning.

Jade workshops
Jade is a difficult material to work, but the results can be fabulous. You can watch jade carvers in several workshops in Hokitika, and prices for finished pieces are often far lower than they are elsewhere in the country. The best jade shops are: Mountain Jade Co (Weld Street, tel: 03 755 8007) and Westland Greenstone (34 Tancred Street, tel: 03 755 8713).

Below: moa bones in the Honeycomb Caves. Bottom: the Southern Alps reflected in Lake Matheson

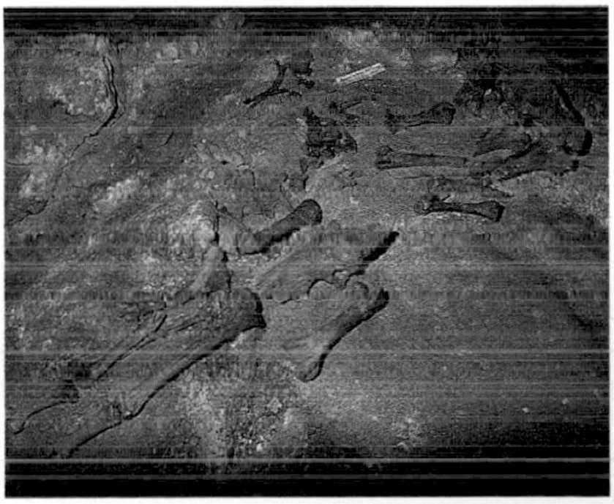

►►► Paparoa National Park *179B4*

Paparoa National Park, embracing one of the most scenic sections of this coastline, is best known for the Pancake Rocks at Punakaiki, but there is much else here besides this popular attraction, and it is well worth lingering a day or two to explore the area.

The main focal point of the park is **Punakaiki** (47km north of Greymouth), which has a limited range of accommodation, tea rooms and the Visitor Centre (*Open* daily 8.30–6, later in summer); as well as providing leaflets on local walks and activities, the centre also screens a short audio-visual presentation (on demand) about the park.

Just across the road from the Visitor Centre, a track (suitable for wheelchairs) leads to the **Pancake Rocks and Blowholes►►►** at Dolomite Point. These spectacular formations of stratified limestone were formed on the seabed millions of years ago by a chemical process known as stylobedding. Since being uplifted they have also been eroded by the waves, so that they are now undercut with arches and underwater caverns with blowholes. The blowholes are at their most spectacular during a stormy high tide, particularly when rough south-westerly storms combine with a high spring tide.

The bridge over the Fox River in the Paparoa National Park

It requires a little more effort to visit the **Fox River Caves►**, which were first opened to the public in 1906 and became a tourist attraction long before the Pancake Rocks. It is a scenic walk of about an hour and a half to reach them, and you can explore about 100m into the upper cave, which is decorated with intriguing calcite formations.

Other interesting walks include the **Truman Track** (signposted 3km north of Punakaiki), which leads down through subtropical forest to a lovely beach with sea caves, an islet and limestone overhangs. You can also meander up a delightful forested gorge along the **Pororari River Track** (singposted 1km north of Punakaiki); the Pororari River is also popular for canoeing.

Paparoa is home to a huge colony of Westland petrels, which spend most of the year soaring across the southern seas. They come here to breed between April and November, and can be seen in the greatest numbers between April and June, when they congregate offshore every evening at dusk, ready to return to the colony. You can observe them from beside the road at the Nikau Scenic Reserve 4km south of Punakaiki, or take a tour of the colony itself (contact Paparoa Nature Tours, tel: 03 731 1826).

In 1995 Paparoa was the scene of one of the worst disasters in New Zealand for two decades. According to police reports, 18 people were standing on a 3m square cliffside viewing platform when it collapsed, sending 14 of them – students on a geology trip to Cave Creek and a ranger – to their deaths on the rocks 30m below.

Sea views
Home to a variety of wildlife, some sections of the Paparoa coastline are inaccessible from land and are best seen from a boat. Kiwa Sea Adventures operate two purpose-built Naiad inflatables from Punakaiki, with two-hour trips to view a breeding colony of spotted shags at Perpendicular Point and a seal colony on Seal Island. If you are lucky you may also see rare Hector's dolphins riding the bow waves of the boat. Book at the Punakaiki Visitor Centre (tel: 03 731 1895).

Reefton *179B4*

Reefton is one of the few inland towns in Westland (everywhere else the only flat land is the narrow coastal strip, so settlements inevitably grew up on the coast), set in forested hills beside the Inangahau River. The town boomed in 1870, when rich gold-bearing quartz reefs were discovered in the surrounding hills. By 1872 it had been dubbed Quartzopolis, and even had its own stock exchange (one of only a handful in the country); by 1888 it had the first electric street-lighting in New Zealand (only six years later than New York), powered by a small hydro-electric plant.

But New York went one way and Reefton another, and now it is little more than a whistle-stop on the routes from Greymouth and Westport over to Canterbury via the Lewis Pass. There are plenty of service facilities in town, and if you were tempted to stay longer there is tramping, hunting and fishing in the nearby Victoria Forest Park, as well as walks to old gold-mining sites in the vicinity.

The spectacular stratified limestone columns of the Pancake Rocks at Dolomite Point

The Honourable Roddy
In 1907, on the banks of Jones Creek near Ross town centre, two gold-diggers unearthed the largest nugget ever recorded in New Zealand. Weighing 2.83kg, it was paraded from bar to bar and christened 'the Honourable Roddy' after the then Minister of Mines, the Hon Roderick McKenzie. It was later given away as the first prize in a raffle to raise funds for a local hospital, and then bought by the Government, who presented it to George V as a coronation gift. Buckingham Palace melted it down to create tableware.

▶ **Ross** *179B3*

This historic gold-mining town sits on some of the richest alluvial deposits of gold in New Zealand, and in 1907 it yielded the largest gold nugget ever found in the country (see panel). Unlike other gold-mining towns, such as Arrowtown, there is no tourist razzmatazz here, and the quiet main street has just one store, one café and one pub. A fork off the main highway leads after 100m to the gold-mining areas, where the old Bank of New South Wales building (1870) now houses a Visitor Information Centre (*Open* daily 9–4). Just up from here is a **Miner's Cottage▶** (*Open* daily 9–4), built in 1885 by a Belgian couple who had profited handsomely from the gold strikes: theirs was the most solid house in the old township, and the only one which survives today. Within the same area is the old town gaol and **St Patrick's Church▶**, a little cross-shaped chapel built in 1866 and ranked amongst the oldest buildings on the West Coast.

Two interesting short walks lead off from here through the goldfields. The **Jones Flat Walkway** and the **Water Race Walkway** each make a circuit of about an hour and a half, passing by dams, sluices, mining machinery and other relics from Ross's heady heyday.

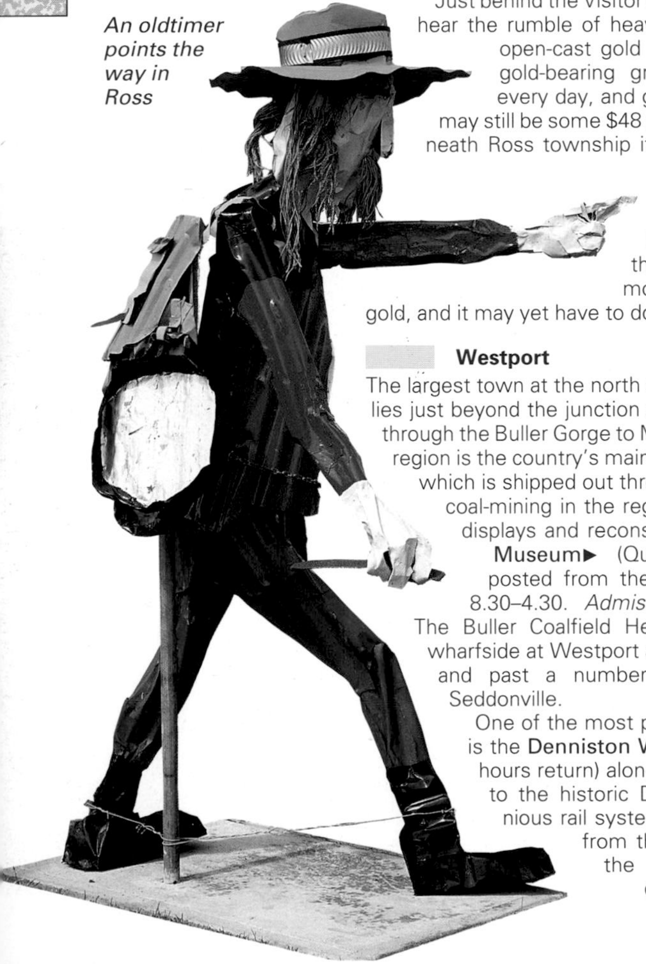

An oldtimer points the way in Ross

Just behind the Visitor Information Centre you can hear the rumble of heavy machinery from a large open-cast gold mine; around 800cu m of gold-bearing gravel are processed here every day, and geologists report that there may still be some $48 million worth of gold underneath Ross township itself. If it is decided to go ahead and dig the gold out, the town will have to be demolished. But locals are stoical about their fate – Ross has already moved once for the sake of gold, and it may yet have to do so again.

Westport *179A4*

The largest town at the north end of Westland, Westport lies just beyond the junction at which SH6 heads inland through the Buller Gorge to Murchison. The surrounding region is the country's main source of bituminous coal, which is shipped out through Lyttelton; the story of coal-mining in the region is told through various displays and reconstructions at the **Coaltown Museum▶** (Queen Street South, signposted from the town centre. *Open* daily 8.30–4.30. *Admission charge* inexpensive). The Buller Coalfield Heritage Trail starts on the wharfside at Westport and leads through the bush and past a number of coal settlements to Seddonville.

One of the most popular walks in the vicinity is the **Denniston Walkway**, a bush walk (five hours return) along an old bridle track leading to the historic Denniston Incline, an ingenious rail system used to bring coal down from the mines to the bottom of the plateau. Surrounded by dense bush and forest, the track crosses several tumbling watercourses, with views out to the coast on a clear day. A leaflet is available from the Visitor Centre in Westport (Brougham Street. *Open* daily 9–5).

To the west of Westport are the **Cape Foulwind Walkway** and seal colony (see page 180), while inland there is white-water rafting and jet-boating on the Buller River (contact Buller Adventure Tours, tel: 03 789 7286), as well as horse-trekking, fishing and caving trips in the surrounding hills.

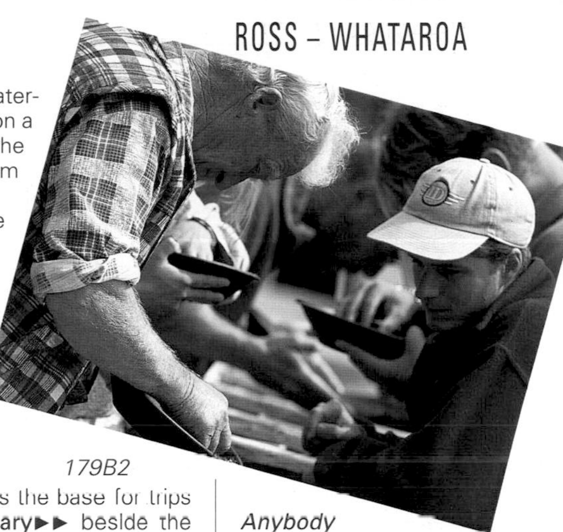

Anybody could strike lucky

Whataroa *179B2*

Whataroa (114km south of Hokitika) is the base for trips to the nearby **White Heron Sanctuary▶▶** beside the Waitangi Taona River. This is the only breeding site in New Zealand for these elegant birds (known to the Maori as *kōtuku*), which nest here from November to February. On average around 50 chicks are fledged in the colony each year, with 70 or more in a good season. In late February the herons fan out to their winter feeding grounds in estuaries elsewhere in Westland and all over New Zealand. The sanctuary is also a nesting ground for royal spoonbills and little shags.

Access to the colony is via a jet-boat ride followed by a short walk through native bush along a boardwalk to the colony itself. The return trip from Whataroa takes about two hours (contact White Heron Sanctuary Tours, Box 19, Whataroa, tel: 03 753 4120).

Open-cast gold mining behind the township of Ross

Drive

The Haast Pass Highway

See map on page 179.

This trans-alpine route is the only crossing between Otago and Westland, a superb drive past numerous spectacular waterfalls, with lake views and panoramas of the surrounding peaks. From the World Heritage Centre at the Haast river bridge it is about 150km to Wanaka.

Heading inland from Haast the road traverses dense rainforest before snaking alongside the wide silt and gravel bed of the **Haast River**. At **Depot Creek**, a set of waterfalls tumbles down the steep sides of the Haast Valley within a minute's walk of the road. About 5km further on, a track (30 minutes return) leads through silver beech and podocarp forest to the **Roaring Billy Falls►.** The Roaring Billy River tumbles over a jumble of boulders before dissipating itself in the gravel beds of the Haast River.

After several twists and turns the road now reaches **Pleasant Flat** (48km from the bridge), where there is a picnic and camping area with good views of Mount Hooker. From here a short bush walk makes a loop beside a bubbling mountain stream. Another 4km further on are the impressive **Thunder Creek Falls►►**, which drop 28m from the bluff down to the Haast River bed; a track leads to the falls (100m from the road) through stands of kamahi and silver beech. At the **Gates of Haast►** (54km from the bridge) the river drops down dramatically into a gorge. A short way (6km) further on are the **Fantail Falls►►**, which spread out in a fan shape at the foot of Fantail Creek; the Haast River itself is already much reduced in volume here.

The main divide between the western and eastern sides of the Alps comes at **Haast Pass►►** (562m), where a plaque honours the first explorers to cross the pass. In 1836, a northern chief, Te Puoho, used it to conduct a raiding party on the southern Kai Tahu and Kati Mamoe tribes,

and a gold prospector named Charles Cameron is credited with being the first European to traverse the pass, in 1863. Just a few weeks later Julius von Haast led a party of four all the way across to the coast, and by 1876 a narrow pack track linked the two sides. Work on upgrading the track to a road began in the 1880s, but was not completed until 1965.

Beyond Davis Flat is **Cameron Flat,** another pleasant spot for a picnic, with a short walk leading up through silver beech forest to a platform overlooking the surrounding peaks and the Makarora Valley to the east. Just beyond this, at the outlet of the Blue River, is a car park from which an easy track (30 minutes return) leads through more silver beech to a viewing platform over the **Blue Pools►►** at the mouth of the river. Large rainbow and brown trout can be seen feeding in these pools.

The road now opens out into the flat expanses of the **Makarora Valley**►, where the small hamlet of Makarora (population 30) boasts a grocery store, café and petrol station. Makarora was one of several places where Maori would camp on their hazardous journey across the pass to the West Coast (the other main camps were around the shores of Lakes Hawea and Wanaka), and its Maori name, Kaika Paekai, means 'the place of abundant food'. The forests which once carpeted the valley floor were extensively logged from the 1860s onwards, but a few remnants survive in the **Makarora Bush**►, where an easy track leads from the car park in Makarora through podocarp and silver beech forest; a pitsaw display on the track shows how the forest giants were dealt with before being floated down Lake Wanaka to the sawmills.

Glorious mountain and lake scenery on the road between the Haast Pass and Wanaka

The Makarora River flows out into **Lake Wanaka**►►► at the end of the valley. This is one of the most scenic sections of the road, traversing the bluffs high above the lake waters with the peaks of Mount Aspiring National Park rising up on the far shore. Turning south-east from Lake Wanaka, the road cuts across **The Neck**, a narrow valley which leads through to **Lake Hawea**►►►, another expanse of shimmering water stretching across to the steep glaciated slopes opposite. Most of the remainder of the route from The Neck to Wanaka (43km) follows along the picturesque lake shores. Past the settlement of Lake Hawea, the road crosses farmland before descending again to the shores of Lake Wanaka.

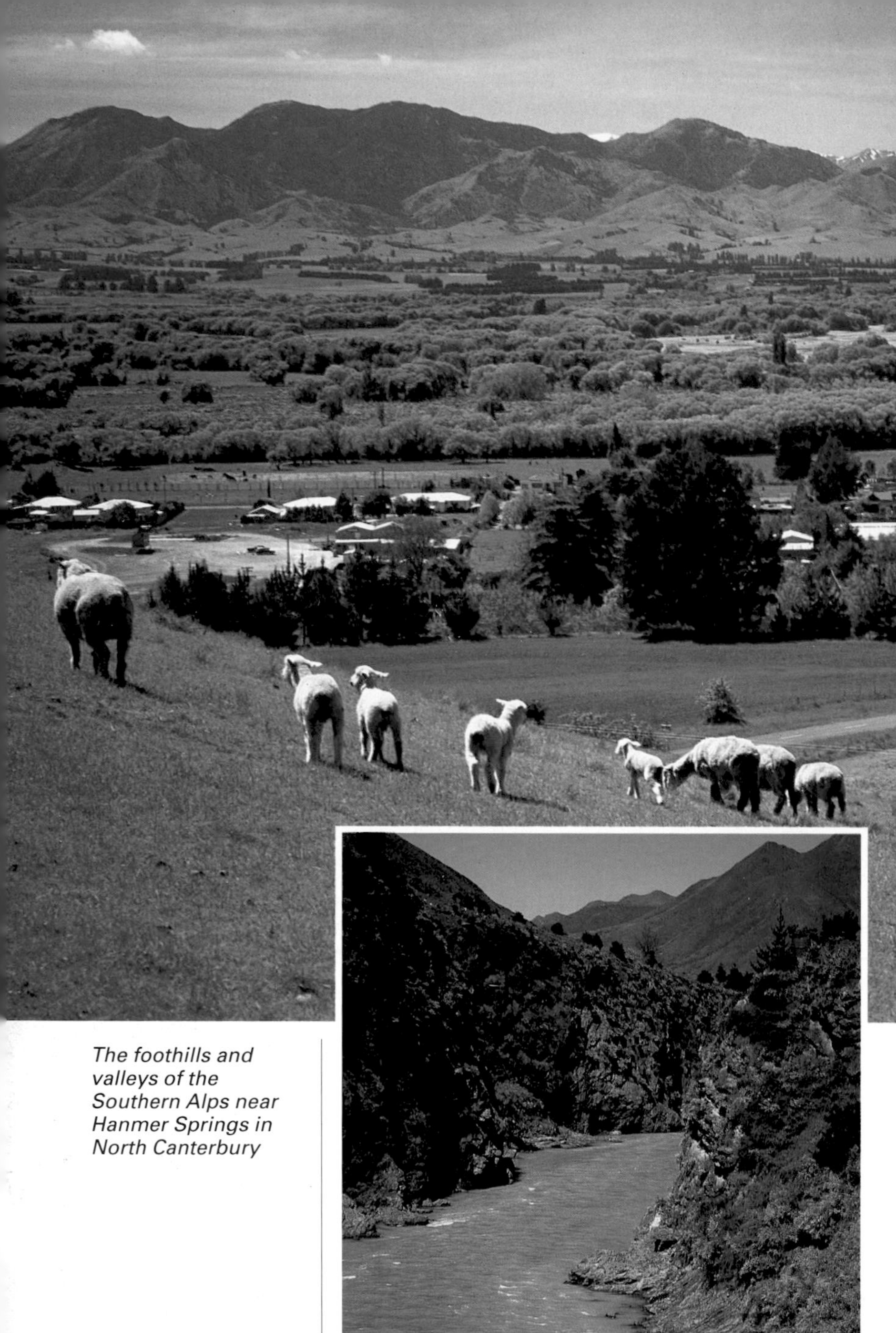

The foothills and valleys of the Southern Alps near Hanmer Springs in North Canterbury

Canterbury offers a host of adventure activities amongst its mountains and rivers – jet boating was invented here

SOUTH ISLAND CANTERBURY

Canterbury Stretching from the heights of the Southern Alps across the wide open expanses of the Canterbury Plains to the Pacific Ocean, the Canterbury region is a vast rectangular block encompassing both the flattest and the steepest landforms in the country. At its heart are the extensive farmlands of the Canterbury Plains, a rolling patchwork of fertile fields where sheep and racehorses are raised alongside extensive grain crops.

Threading through the plains are a number of wide, braided rivers, with numerous shallow channels and shingle banks which support trout and salmon-fishing: these meandering rivers were virtually unnavigable until the jet-boat, invented by a Canterbury engineer (see pages 210–11), opened them up to adventure activities. Beyond the plains, the alpine foothills offer a number of well-known skifields (such as **Mount Hutt**), while horse-trekking, hiking, rafting, and mountain biking are popular around areas such as **Hanmer Springs**, a delightful thermal resort in North Canterbury.

Horses and Harleys
For a sedate view of Christchurch's attractions you can take a tour round the city centre in an eight-seater open carriage pulled by Clydesdales (Carriage & Co, tel: 025 331 651). Another option is a 30-minute or one-hour tour in an open-top vintage car (Vintage Car Tours, tel: 03 323 8132). If something a little more speedy appeals, how about a ride on the back of a Harley Davidson? Short trips around the city can be combined with visits to wineries or other locations outside the city centre. Leather jackets, helmets, gloves and sunglasses are all provided (V-Twin Motorcycle Tours, tel: 025 358 975).

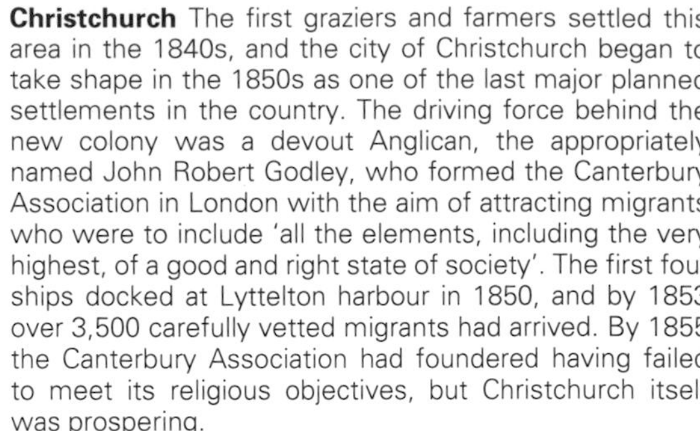

Christchurch The first graziers and farmers settled this area in the 1840s, and the city of Christchurch began to take shape in the 1850s as one of the last major planned settlements in the country. The driving force behind the new colony was a devout Anglican, the appropriately named John Robert Godley, who formed the Canterbury Association in London with the aim of attracting migrants who were to include 'all the elements, including the very highest, of a good and right state of society'. The first four ships docked at Lyttelton harbour in 1850, and by 1853 over 3,500 carefully vetted migrants had arrived. By 1855 the Canterbury Association had foundered having failed to meet its religious objectives, but Christchurch itself was prospering.

Banks Peninsula, a distinctive knobby peninsula jutting out to sea to the south of Christchurch, is the South Island's only notable volcanic area, and the two massive craters which form the peninsula now shelter two main harbour areas – Lyttelton (the port for Christchurch), and Akaroa, almost a former French colony. The peninsula itself has a rugged, dramatic coastline indented with small bays, with wonderful views from the crater rims. It makes an interesting day trip from Christchurch or, even better, a weekend excursion (there are plenty of places to stay in Akaroa) with a bit of walking or sea-kayaking thrown in.

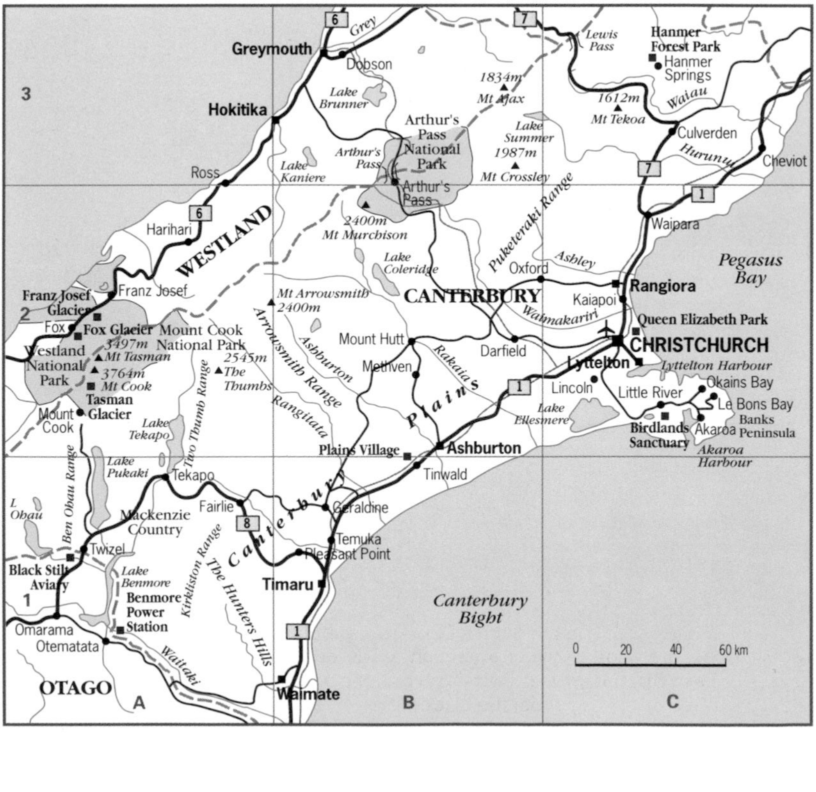

Mount Cook National Park This vast alpine wilderness covers some 70,000ha on the east side of the Southern Alps, and boasts some of the most dramatic mountain

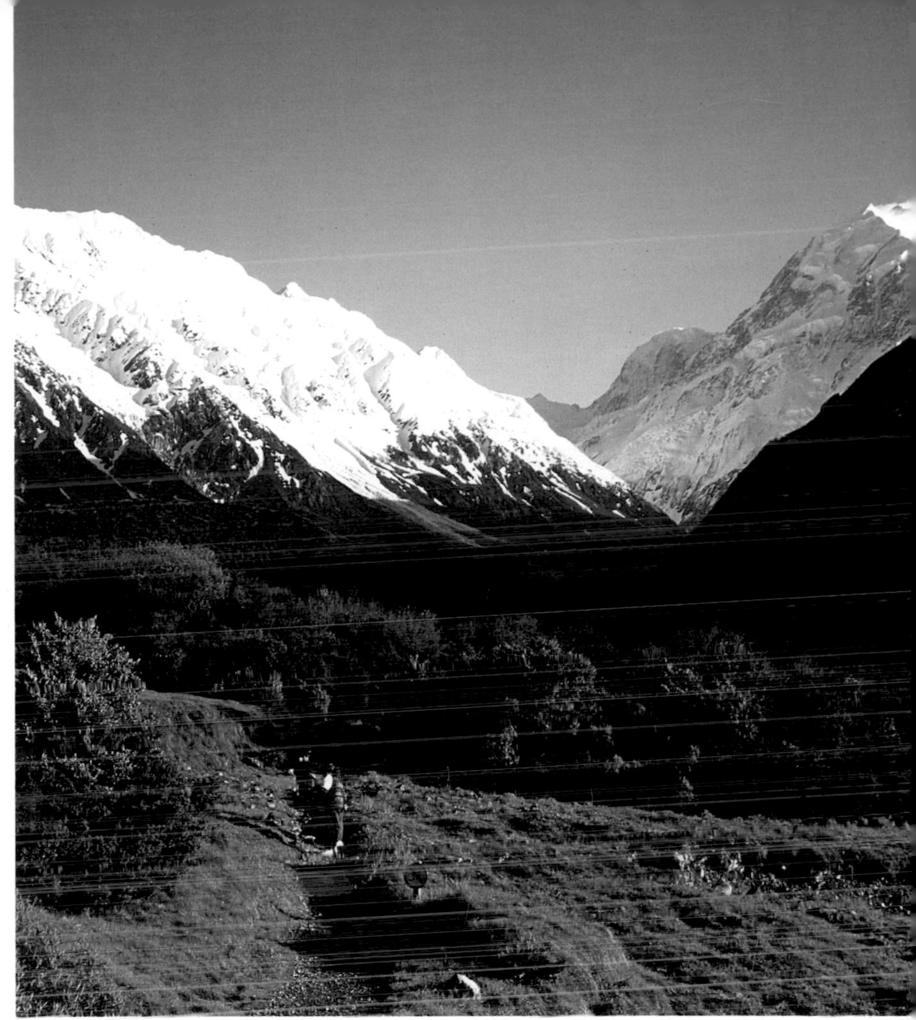

scenery in the country. All except one of New Zealand's peaks over 3,000m are found here, including mighty Mount Cook itself, at 3,764m the highest in New Zealand. More than a third of the park is permanently covered in snow and ice, while the Tasman Glacier, stretching some 29km down the south face of Mount Cook and estimated to be approximately 600m thick, is one of the largest glaciers outside of the Himalayas.

The first mention of Mount Cook by a European was made by the explorer Charles Heaphy, who sketched it in 1846. In 1851 the survey ship HMS *Acheron* named the peak after Cook, and its neighbour Mount Tasman (3,497m) was named after the Dutch explorer in 1862 by Julius Von Haast – although paradoxically neither Cook nor Tasman had glimpsed these mighty mountains from the sea.

Mount Cook is one of the unmissable sights and it is essential to book accommodation well in advance.

The beautiful glacial lakes of **South Canterbury**, below Mount Cook, are another major attraction, while on the shores of **Lake Ruataniwha** at Twizel you can see one of the world's rarest wading birds, the black stilt.

Hikers set off up the Hooker Valley track in the Mount Cook National Park

Making tracks
Christchurch was one of the first cities in New Zealand to have a horse tramway system, and electric trams began operating here in 1905. The system was shut down in 1954, but the elegant green and cream trams have now been painstakingly restored and new track has been laid in a 2.5km loop around the city centre. The tramway provides a convenient 'hop on, hop off' service for visitors operating 7am–11pm continuously.

The modern tram system (right) harks back to the time of Queen Victoria, who presides over Victoria Park in the heart of the city

Christchurch

New Zealand's third largest city (after Auckland and Wellington), Christchurch is the capital of Canterbury and the main international gateway to the South Island. Whether or not it is your first port of call, it is well worth setting aside a few days to explore this lovely city packed with things to see and do.

The Canterbury Association brought over 3,500 carefully chosen migrants to Christchurch in its early years. But all did not go according to plan: land intended for crops did not sell and drought in Australia brought many sheep farmers to the area. They were not popular (the Association was accused of giving the land over to 'squatting and barbarism') but the injection of capital saved the settlement from economic ruin.

New Zealand's English heritage is perhaps more evident in Christchurch than it is almost anywhere else in the country. The first Pilgrims had not forgotten to pack their cricket bats, and ever since the establishment of the Christchurch Cricket Club the city has been the country's headquarters for the game. A rowing club had been set up by 1864, and an archery club established by 1873. The first lawn tennis courts were built in Cranmer Square in 1881. The solid, Gothic–style stone buildings, the uniformed schoolboys at the famous Christ's College school, and above all the punts gliding down the sinuous River Avon, in the heart of the city, between overhanging willows and sycamores – all evoke images of traditional English university towns.

Christchurch is also renowned as a garden city, with over a third of its central area devoted to beautiful parks and gardens. Combined with the compactness of the city centre, this makes it a pleasurable place to explore on foot (see pages 202–3), or you can hop on and off the new tramway between sightseeing.

The city has a lively arts and cultural scene, with several theatres, frequent concerts and musical festivals, and probably the greatest concentration of arts and craft talent in the country. It also has excellent shopping, numerous restaurants, cafés and wine bars, and plenty of good quality accommodation. The country's first casino opened here in 1995 (see panel page 205).

CITY LOOP
152
Munns
SALE NOW ON
MUNNS
CHRISTCHURCH 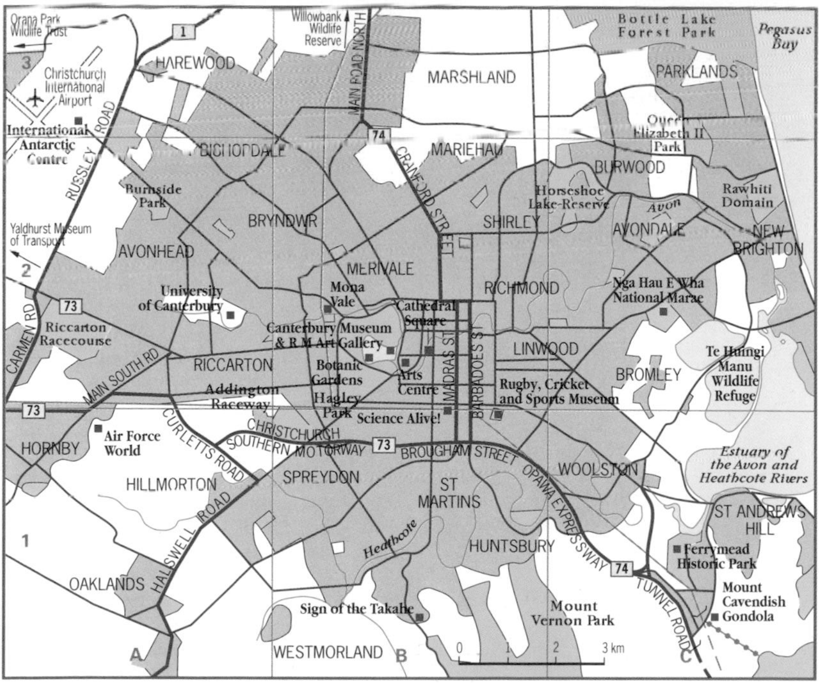
TRAMWAYS
Orana Park Wildlife Trust
Willowbank Wildlife Reserve
Bottle Lake Forest Park
Pegasus Bay
HAREWOOD
MARSHLAND
PARKLANDS
Christchurch International Airport
International Antarctic Centre
RUSSLEY ROAD
MAIN ROAD NORTH
Queen Elizabeth II Park
MARIEHAU
BURWOOD
CRANFORD STREET
Burnside Park
Horseshoe Lake Reserve
Rawhiti Domain
Avon
BRYNDWR
SHIRLEY
AVONDALE
NEW BRIGHTON
Yaldhurst Museum of Transport
AVONHEAD
MERIVALE
RICHMOND
Nga Hau E Wha National Marae
Mona Vale
University of Canterbury
Cathedral Square
Riccarton Racecourse
Canterbury Museum & R M Art Gallery
CARMEN RD
LINWOOD
Te Huingi Manu Wildlife Refuge
RICCARTON
Botanic Gardens
Arts Centre
MADRAS ST
BARBADOES ST
BROMLEY
MAIN SOUTH RD
Addington Raceway
Rugby, Cricket and Sports Museum
Hagley Park
Science Alive!
Air Force World
CHRISTCHURCH SOUTHERN MOTORWAY
HORNBY
CURLETTS ROAD
BROUGHAM STREET
WOOLSTON
Estuary of the Avon and Heathcote Rivers
HILLMORTON
SPREYDON
ST MARTINS
OPAWA EXPRESSWAY
ST ANDREWS HILL
HALSWELL ROAD
Heathcote
HUNTSBURY
Ferrymead Historic Park
OAKLANDS
TUNNEL ROAD
Mount Cavendish Gondola
Sign of the Takahe
Mount Vernon Park
WESTMORLAND
0 1 2 3 km
1
73
74
A
B
C
1
2
3

Arts Centre events
The Arts Centre is home to the Court Theatre (New Zealand's most successful professional theatre group), the Christchurch School of Music and the Southern Ballet. In the summer months, jazz, classical music, exhibitions and theatre performances spill out through the cloisters and courtyards during the Summertime Festival; Friday lunchtime concerts take place in the Great Hall, the grandest building in the Arts Centre, throughout the year. Details of events are available from the Information Centre (tel: 03 366 0989. *Open* daily 8.30–5).

► Air Force World 199A1

Wigram Aerodrome
Open: daily 10–5. Admission charge: moderate.
Located 15 minutes' drive outside the city centre, Air Force World is worth a stop if you are heading south on Highway 1. The museum covers the history of military aviation in New Zealand from the earliest days, and enthusiasts can also go aloft in an open cockpit Tiger Moth biplane with the Wigram Barnstormers (tel: 03 343 9460; $155 for a 20-minute flight including aerobatics).

►►► Arts Centre 199B2

One of the main focal points of the city, the Arts Centre is housed in the old University of Canterbury buildings which were completed in 1929; the university had outgrown the premises by the 1950s, and this rambling, neo-Gothic complex has taken on a new lease of life as the biggest and busiest cultural centre in New Zealand (see panel).

Nobel Prize-winner Ernest Rutherford studied here in the 1890s, and his 'den' in the North Quadrangle has been preserved, complete with authentic laboratory equipment, as a tribute to the man who split the atom. Now some of the country's leading painters and sculptors work in the galleries and studios, alongside musicians, actors, dancers and craftspeople. Here you will find specialists in stained glass, Maori carvings, ceramics, embroidery, leatherwork, hand-made clothing of all kinds, wooden toys, caneware and jade, bone and silver jewellery and much more. There is also a weekend market and food fair (*Open* 10–4) with more than a hundred outdoor stalls selling everything from antiques to Asian foods.

►►► Botanic Gardens 199B2

Open: daily 7am–one hr before sunset. Admission free.
These magnificent gardens covering 30ha, mostly within a loop of the Avon River on the west side of the city centre, contain many fine old trees – including the Albert Edward Oak, the first tree planted here, to commemorate the marriage of Prince Albert Edward to Princess Alexandra of Denmark in July 1863.

Claiming the finest collection of indigenous and exotic plants found anywhere in the country, the gardens are divided into a number of different planting areas, with sections devoted to roses, herbs, rock plants, and New Zealand native plants. The lovely conservatories (*Open* daily 10.15–4. *Admission free*) are also well worth a visit, with numerous varieties of ferns, palms, flowering plants, cacti and alpines. There is also an Information Centre (opposite the Rolleston Ave car park, tel: 03 366 8379. *Open* daily 10.15–4).

Canterbury tales
Te Puna Ora storytelling and water ceremony tours recount the history and mythology of Canterbury during a leisurely stroll through the Botanic Gardens (*Open* Mon–Fri 11–3. *Admission charge* moderate; book at the Information Centre or tel: 03 377 2025). There are also free 'mini-train' tours of the gardens (daily 11am; except Jun and Jul).

▶▶▶ Canterbury Museum
199B2

Open: daily 9–5 in winter, 9–6 in summer, free guided tours four times daily. Admission free.
Backing on to the Botanic Gardens, this museum is the most comprehensive in the South Island, and has recently undergone extensive redevelopment to update many of its displays. The excellent Hall of the Moa and Moa Hunters has several graphic dioramas depicting the lifestyles of the early Maori, and the Hall of Asian Decorative Arts has Chinese and Japanese artefacts from many different periods. There is a new Whalespace exhibition, and the award-winning and eternally fascinating Hall of Antarctic Discovery has recently been refurbished. A new Maori gallery is also planned.

▶▶▶ Cathedral Square
199B2

At the heart of the city, Cathedral Square is an attractive open space which can always be relied upon to provide entertainment, from buskers to breakdancers, or open-air preachers to eccentrics, hecklers, and anyone else who cares to mount a soapbox (see panel). Among the fine old buildings apart from the Cathedral itself is the **Four Ships Court** (next to the old Post Office) with the names of all the pilgrims who arrived on the 'first four ships' engraved on marble slabs on its walls.

It's all happening in Cathedral Square; leafy Hagley Park (left) is a more tranquil spot

▶▶ Christchurch Cathedral
199B2

Cathedral Square
Open: daily 8.30–4. Admission charge: inexpensive
The copper-sheathed spire of the cathedral dominates the east side of Cathedral Square, and from the viewing platform 30m (and 133 narrow steps) up you get a good view of the city. The cathedral itself was planned shortly after the arrival of the 'first four ships' and construction began in 1864; work was then halted owing to lack of funds, and the building was not finally consecrated until 1904. There are daily guided tours (11 and 2. *Admission charge* inexpensive).

▶ Ferrymead Historic Park
199C1

269 Bridle Path Road
Open: daily 10–4.30. Admission charge: moderate.
A re-created 19th-century township, Ferrymead Historic Park has a long main street containing livery stables, a blacksmith's forge and a gaol among other premises, with small museums on transport, sound, printing, rural history and phonographs. Admission includes a steam train or tram ride.

The Inimitable Wizard
He is a Christchurch institution, a flamboyant figure in black velvet robes and pointed wizard's hat who mounts his stepladder to poke fun and deflate pomposity amid the rhetoric of the Cathedral Square preachers. The wizard (alias Ian Brackenbury Channell) has been a thorn in the flesh of the authorities since his arrival in Christchurch in 1974; it was ten years before he was allowed to harangue the crowds in Cathedral Square, a freedom he now exploits with considerable glee on most days at about 1pm. A performance not to be missed.

Walk Christchurch

Sculptor Neil Dawson's Flying chairs *in the Botanic Gardens*

Christchurch is an enjoyable city for strolling, and there is plenty to see on this circular walk from Cathedral Square. Allow two to three hours, not counting visits to the Canterbury Museum, the Botanic Gardens or the Arts Centre.

Starting from Cathedral Square, head west down Worcester Boulevard. After one block you will come to the old **Municipal Chambers**, an elegant red-brick building of Queen Anne design which now houses the Visitor Information Centre. Opposite is a statue of **Captain Scott**, the Antarctic explorer, sculpted by his widow. Cross the Avon River over a bridge with wrought-iron balustrades and turn left to follow the Avon upstream.

Immediately on your right is the **Canterbury Club**; built in 1872, this long-established 'gentlemen's club' still has a gas lamp standard and a hitching post outside it. The next bridge along but one is the **Bridge of Remembrance**, a memorial to Kiwi troops who died in World War I.

On the opposite bank of a bend in the river you can now see the superb old church of **St Michael and All Angels►►**, built in 1872 with a detached belfry (1860) alongside, housing a bell from one of the 'first four ships'. Continuing on beneath the sycamores and willows which line the riverbank you reach the **Antigua Boatsheds►**, built in 1882 and the sole survivor of half a dozen or more similar boatsheds which once stood on the riverbank.

Carry on down Rolleston Avenue, with the entrance to the **Botanic Gardens** and the **Canterbury Museum** on your left, and the **Arts Centre** on the right. Just past the museum is the entrance to **Christ's College►**, the city's oldest school, with several attractive buildings

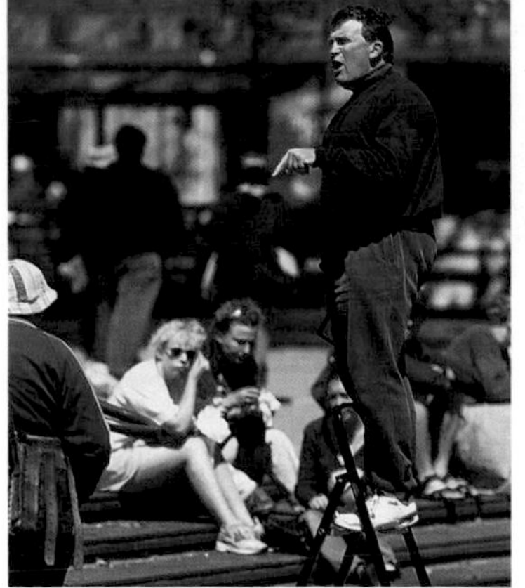

Beware: hecklers at work

grouped around a grassy quadrangle.

At the junction with Armagh Street another attractive old bridge leads over the Avon into **North Hagley Park**►, a huge area of sports grounds and playing fields. Continue down Armagh Street, crossing leafy **Cranmer Square,** with the Gothic edifice of the old **Christchurch Girls' High School,** into Chester Street West. Near the end of the street stands the city's oldest stone church, the **Durham Street Methodist Church**, with the new court buildings opposite.

Turning right down Durham Street you reach the **Provincial Council Buildings**►►►, a fine ensemble of Gothic architecture in stone and wood, surrounding a courtyard and dominated by a redstone tower (*Open* Mon–Fri 9–4. *Admission free*). Follow the riverbank round to the impressive new **Town Hall**► (*Open* Mon–Fri 9–5, Sat–Sun 10–5. *Admission free*), which has a fountain like a globe on the river's edge.

Cross another lovely old bridge to reach **Victoria Square**►►, a charming open space on the riverbank which was once the commercial heart of the city. Within the square are statues of **Queen Victoria** and **Captain Cook**, and by the riverbank itself you can also see an old stone ramp leading down to the Avon, formerly used for watering horses.

Follow the river along a gently winding stretch of Oxford Terrace, from where you can see on the opposite bank the fine Italianate **Edmonds Band Rotunda,** built in 1929 and now a restaurant. Past the Manchester Street bridge the Avon flows between a double row of stately poplars, with the **Centennial Pool** on the right-hand side. The **Oxford Terrace Baptist Church**►, on the corner of Chester and Madras Streets, has an imposing façade, and behind it in Chester Street itself there is an interesting row of two-storey wooden houses.

Walk down Madras Street to **Latimer Square**►, where you will find the stone-built **St John's Church** and the venerable **Occidental Hotel**►.

Follow Hereford Street to return to Cathedral Square.

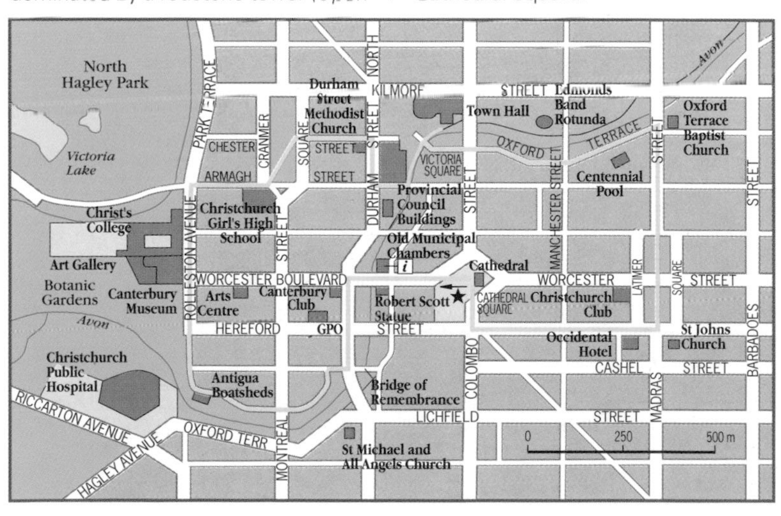

On a clear day the views from Mount Cavendish are unsurpassable

Homage to Dame Ngaio
Dame Ngaio Marsh, one of New Zealand's most prolific and successful authors, is best known throughout the world for her crime thrillers. On her home patch of Christchurch it was as a director of Shakespeare that she was celebrated. Many of her productions were staged at the Christchurch Arts Centre, which was the focus for celebrations in 1995 to commemorate her birth in 1899. The house in Christchurch's Cashmere Hills, where she penned most of her detective novels, has recently been converted into a museum, and at the time of going to press was scheduled to open imminently. Contact the Tourist Information Office for more details.

▶▶▶ International Antarctic Centre *199A3*

Orchard Rd, Christchurch Airport, tel: 03 358 9896
Open: daily 9.30–8.30 in summer, 9.30–5.30 in winter. Admission charge: expensive.

The award-winning Visitor Centre here contains one of the two most outstanding displays on Antarctica in New Zealand (the other being Kelly Tarlton's Antarctic Encounter in Auckland, see page 53), and gains added prestige from its position within the International Antarctic Centre, which serves as the supply and administration base for the New Zealand, American and Italian research programmes. Highlights include an 'Antarctic Experience' audio-visual presentation on the changing seasons of the frozen continent, a walk-through ice cave, a replica of the current Scott Base, an Antarctic aquarium and a stunning finale in the form of a 12-minute film entitled *The Great White South*. The Visitor Centre also has a good souvenir shop and a café/bar.

▶▶ Mount Cavendish Gondola *199C1*

Base station, 10 Bridle Path Road
Open: 10am–late. Admission charge: expensive.

Rising to the top of the Port Hills, 500m above sea level, the gondola terminates at the Mount Cavendish complex, from where there are unrivalled views across Lyttelton Harbour and Banks Peninsula to the south, with the sweep of Pegasus Bay and the Pacific Ocean leading to the distant Kaikoura Peninsula in the north – and Christchurch, of course, in the foreground.

There are nature walks through the alpine tussock of the Mount Cavendish Scenic Reserve around the complex, while inside, a multi-media **Time Tunnel▶▶**

(*Open* 10am–late. *Admission charge* inexpensive) has displays on the early history of the area and on volcanoes, and a first-rate replica of the interior of an early immigrant ship. The complex also contains a restaurant, café, shop and observation deck. To get there, take the shuttle from the Tourist Information Centre, Explorer Bus or No. 28 bus.

Another adrenaline rush
'The South Island's only dignified adrenaline rush' is how they like to describe the Christchurch Casino, opened in 1995 and the first in the country. The casino houses two restaurants, three bars, 30 gaming tables and 350 gaming machines (30 Victoria Street, tel: 03 365 9999. Open Mon–Wed 11am–3am, continuously 11am Thu to 3am Mon).

▶ Nga Hau E Wha National *Marae* 199C2

250 Pages Road, Aranui, tel: 03 388 7685.

The Nga Hau E Wha ('Four Winds') National *Marae* is said to be the largest *marae* in New Zealand, and features many fine carved buildings, such as the Wharenui ('meeting house') and Whare Wānanga ('house of learning'). It also has a splendid carved gateway which tells the story of the Maori and of European colonisation. This unusual *marae* is 6km from the city centre.

▶▶ Orana Park Wildlife Trust 199A3

McLeans Island Recreation Area, 18km north-west
Open: daily 10–4.30. Admission charge: expensive.

New Zealand's largest 'safari park', the Orana Park Wildlife Trust is known for the breeding of endangered and rare species, including both exotic animals and the more familiar native fauna. The New Zealand section consists of a nocturnal kiwi house, a native reptile house (with tuatara, skinks and geckos), and native bird aviaries. Elsewhere within the 80ha reserve are kangaroos, emus, pelicans and cockatoos from Australia; tigers and Himalayan thar from Asia; spider monkeys, llamas and wolves from the Americas; and lions, zebras, monkeys and rhinos from Africa. An unusual feature is a tall platform from which you can hand-feed giraffes, and there are regular 'cheetah chases', in which the cheetahs are exercised by racing at 100kph after a balted lure. The park also has barbecue areas and a restaurant.

▶▶▶ River Avon 199C2

The lovely River Avon, meandering at a leisurely pace through the centre of Christchurch, is perfect for exploring by canoe, punt or paddle-boat. You can either hire your own vessel from the Antigua Boatsheds (2 Cambridge Terrace, tel: 03 366 5885. *Open* daily 9.30–4. *Admission charge* moderate) or relax in an upholstered punt and glide along with a boatman in charge; there are several departure points, the main one being behind the Canterbury Information Centre on Oxford Terrace (trips operate daily 9–6 in summer, 10–4 in winter. In 1966 the cost was $10 per person for 30 minutes). The Canterbury Information Centre is on Worcester Boulevard (tel: 03 379 9629. *Open* Mon–Fri 8.30–5, Sat–Sun 9–4).

A good introduction to Christchurch is a leisurely punt along the River Avon

Out-of-town trips
Although most city centre sights are within walking distance, those on the outskirts require a bit more planning. If you have your own transport, you can make a circuit to the north-west (towards the airport), devoting a day to the International Antarctic Centre, Orana Park and Willowbank Wildlife Reserve. To the west, transport enthusiasts can combine the Yaldhurst Transport Museum with Air Force World. To the south-east, the Ferrymead Historic Park and Mount Cavendish Gondola are conveniently close together.

▶▶ Robert McDougall Art Gallery 199B2

Botanic Gardens
Open: 10–4.30. Admission free.
Housed in a lovely old building just behind the museum, this gallery is the foremost in the city, with exhibitions spanning everything from fine art to ceramics and photography. Many of the works come from the gallery's own collection of historical and contemporary works, but a number of touring exhibitions also visit from both within New Zealand and overseas. There are two guided tours daily (11 and 3. *Admission free*).

▶ Rugby, Cricket and Sports Museum 199B1

Lancaster Park
Open: daily 10–4. Admission charge: inexpensive.
A star feature of this museum is a room devoted to the country's greatest cricketer, Sir Richard Hadlee.

▶ Science Alive! 199B1

Moorhouse Ave
Open: daily 9–5. Admission charge: moderate.
A great one for the kids, with over 50 hands-on, fun exhibits – including a 3D Discovery Area. In addition to its permanent displays, the centre also features visiting exhibitions on the same 'learn through fun' theme.

▶▶ Willowbank Wildlife Reserve 199B3

Hussey Road, Harewood
Open: 10–10. Admission charge: moderate.
This compact wildlife park includes a zoo with exotic species, a farmyard with some interesting and rare breeds of 'colonial domestic animals' (such as kunae kunae pigs

Akaroa Harbour on Banks Peninsula

and Hokonui sheep), and a 'New Zealand Experience' section with endangered species. It is also open in the evening for a 'Wildlife by Night' guided tour, revealing kiwi and other nocturnal beasts foraging under the floodlights. Willowbank is around 20 minutes from the city centre.

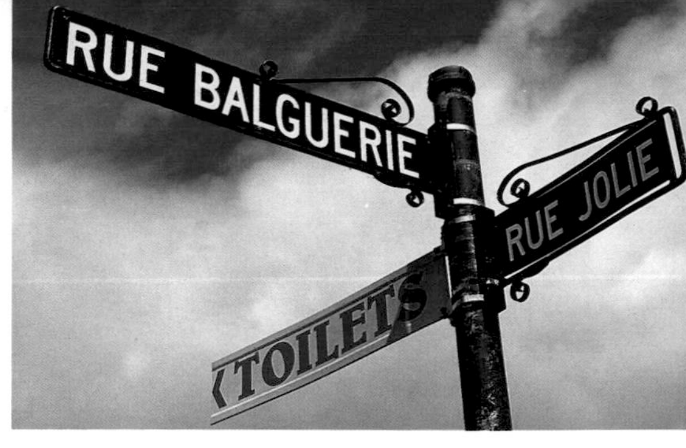

The French failed in their claim to New Zealand but their legacy lingers on in Akaroa

 **Yaldhurst Museum of Transport** *199A2*

School Road, Yaldhurst
Open: daily 10–5. Admission charge: moderate.
From being the proud possessor of just one 1910 two-cylinder Renault in the 1960s, this museum has grown to include hundreds of displays, from fire engines to motorbikes, carts, racing cars and more. It is 11km from the city centre, near the airport.

Canterbury

▶▶▶ **Banks Peninsula** *196C2*

When he circumnavigated New Zealand, Captain Cook mapped Banks Peninsula as an island, an understandable mistake as the spit connecting the peninsula to the mainland is very low-lying. This landbridge is bordered on its south side by **Lake Ellesmere**, a broad expanse of water rich in eels and flounders which, despite being one of New Zealand's largest lakes by area, is no more than two metres in depth at its deepest point.

The waters around the Banks Peninsula abound in marine life such as seals and penguins, with thousands of spotted shags nesting on the steep sea cliffs. The country's first marine mammal sanctuary (covering over 1100 sq km around the shoreline) was established here in 1988 to protect one of the world's rarest marine mammals, the Hector's dolphin.

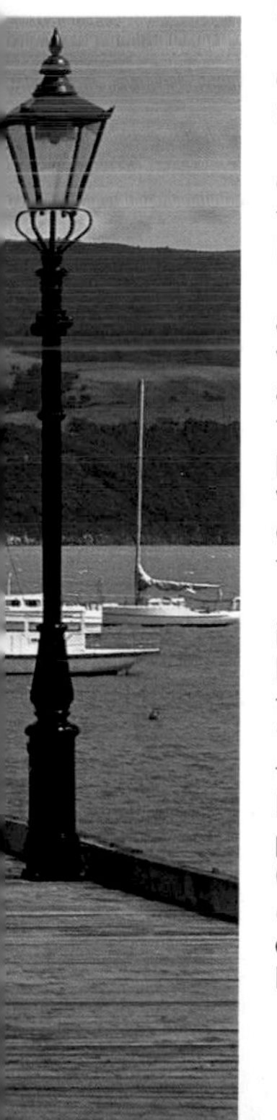

The first Maori to live here were assured of a plentiful food supply and easily defended villages, but a major feud in the 1820s virtually wiped out the local Ngai Tahu population. The numerous bays and inlets made perfect shelters for the early whalers, one of whom, Captain Jean Langlois, tried to establish French sovereignty by colonising the peninsula.

The French legacy lingers on in the charming port of **Akaroa▶▶▶**. There are only a handful of French-speakers here today but the French street names remain, as do the 'French' bakeries and restaurants. One of the early French settlers' cottages, the Langlois-Eteveneaux House, now forms part of the excellent **Akaroa Museum▶▶▶** (*Open* 10.30–4.30, to 4 in winter. *Admission charge* inexpensive) near the seafront. The old court house and the nearby Custom House are also part of the complex.

Harbour tours
Cruises around Akaroa Harbour on the *Canterbury Cat* are highly popular: the trip includes volcanic sea caves, a salmon farm, bird nesting sites and the chance of seeing Hector's dolphins riding the bow wave (usually from November to April). Tours depart 11.30 and 1.30 daily (bookings at the main wharf or tel: 03 304 7641). You can also take a day-long sea-kayak tour of the harbour with Banks Peninsula Sea Kayaks (tel: 03 304 8776).

Colonial style architecture graces the quiet streets of Akaroa

The French connection
In 1838, Jean Langlois bought a tract of land from the Ngai Tahu, before returning home to France and assembling a shipload of immigrants to colonise the peninsula. The French Government supported his venture, and even sent along a warship, *L'Aube*, to accompany him, but while Langlois was on the high seas the Treaty of Waitangi was signed, and he arrived to find British sovereignty a *fait accompli*. So concerned were the British at the impending arrival of the French that they immediately dispatched a ship to Akaroa, setting up a magistrate's court and hoisting the flag just five days before Langlois and his followers landed.

Akaroa is a lovely spot to wander around, with a handful of good cafés and restaurants, interesting craft shops (Rue Lavaud, in particular, has at least nine galleries) and many picturesque old houses and cottages lining its quiet streets. A *Historic Village Walk* leaflet gives details of over 40 historic buildings in the community (available from the Akaroa Information Centre, 80 Rue Lavaud and Rue Balguerie, tel: 03 304 8600. *Open* daily 9–5).

Elsewhere on the peninsula, **Le Bons Bay▶** is a good swimming spot (21km from Akaroa), as is **Okains Bay▶** (25km from Akaroa), home to the intriguing **Maori and Colonial Museum▶▶** (*Open* daily 10–5. *Admission charge* inexpensive). The Maori collection includes many *heitiki*, war clubs, flax cloaks, musical instruments and fishing implements, kumara gods (placed in the fields to ensure a good crop), and a rare 'god stick' which is thought to be over 500 years old. There is also a war canoe dating back to 1867, a carved meeting house (one of the few in the South Island), a 'slab cottage' built from totara wood, and other old colonial buildings. It is a fair drive over the twisting summit road from Akaroa to Okains Bay, but well worth it if you have the time.

Banks Peninsula was one of the first regions in the country to export cheese, and at the turn of the century there were at least eight cheese factories here. Traditional cheesemaking continues today at the dairy in **Barrys Bay** where they produce and sell a wide range of tasty cheeses. From October to April you can watch the cheesemakers at work. **Barrys Bay Cheese** (*Open* Mon–Fri 8–5, Sat–Sun 9.30–5) is 12km outside Akaroa.

Back in the direction of Christchurch, the **Birdlands Sanctuary▶** (*Open* daily 8–6. *Admission charge* inexpensive) covers around 10ha at Little River, with several aviaries and a native bush area with boardwalks (accessible to wheelchairs).

Geraldine *196B1*

Between Mount Cook and Christchurch, the SH79 passes through Geraldine, a small town where you can stretch your legs and find refreshments. The **Vintage Car & Machinery Museum▶** (178 Talbot Street. *Open* daily in summer 10–12, 1.30–4, Sat–Sun only in winter.

Admission charge inexpensive) has several curiosities, including a Harley Davidson with a coffin-carrying sidecar (once used by the Geraldine undertaker), one of the oldest working tractors in the country, an early Mount Cook Line charabanc, and a 1928 biplane which is the sole survivor of its kind in the world.

►► Hanmer Springs *196C3*

This delightful thermal resort is set in a beautiful wooded area on the edge of the Hanmer Plain, with the mountains rising up behind. The regal Hanmer Lodge Hotel, built in 1897, was used as a convalescent home for soldiers returning from World War I; the Queen Mary Hospital (1916) served the same purpose, later becoming a treatment centre for alcoholics.

Nowadays the focal point of the resort is the recently redeveloped **Thermal Reserve►►** (*Open* Sun–Thu 10–8, Fri–Sat 10–10. *Admission charge* inexpensive), which has several attractively landscaped hot pools, an outdoor café, a health and fitness centre and aqua therapy rooms. Across the road, the comfortable old Lodge is gradually being restored. Otherwise, this peaceful village has a scattering of discreet motels and a few bars and restaurants: there are plenty of activities available (including horse-trekking, mountain-biking, canoeing, jet-boating, rafting, kayaking, hunting and fishing), but since they all take place outside Hanmer the place is remarkably quiet. Less demanding activities include safari tours of the nearby **Molesworth Station**, New Zealand's largest upcountry farm station (covering 182,000ha), or walks in the beech and pine forests of the **Hanmer Forest Park►►**. Details on walks and activities are available from the Information Centre next to the Thermal Reserve (tel: 03 315 7128).

Fire from the sky
Legend has it that the Hanmer Springs were formed by fire which fell from the sky as Mount Ngauruhoe erupted, and early Maori gave them the name Waitapu ('Sacred Waters'). A local farmer, William Jones, rediscovered the springs in 1859, when seeking out the source of 'a remarkable fog'.

The geothermal waters of Hanmer Springs are used to treat a variety of conditions – or simply for a relaxing soak

Jet-boats

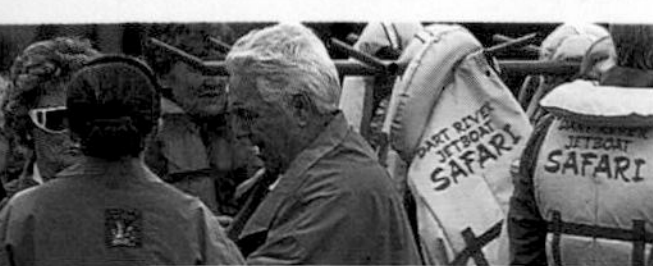

■ No one should visit New Zealand without at least once taking a ride in a jet-boat, a fast, shallow-draught craft which was perfected by Kiwis to navigate the country's extensive river system. ■

A thrilling ride Almost anywhere in the country where there is a navigable river you will find jet-boat operations. The beauty of the design is that jet-boats can go into much shallower waters than any other type of craft – they can navigate with ease the shallow, braided rivers of Canterbury, for instance, where conventional boats would not dare to venture. When planing, a jet-boat draws as little as 10cm of water.

Propelled at top speeds of up to 100kph, they slide around boulders, bounce their way down shallow rapids, skim across gravel banks and bank sharply to avoid floating logs and other hazards. The noise, the wind and the spray can seem overwhelming, but then suddenly you are on a tranquil stretch of the river and all is quiet – and you are aware of the fact that you are miles into the wilderness, with no one else around. It is this ability to go almost anywhere that makes jet-boats so special.

Not really a jet? Although they have always been known as 'jet-boats', in fact these craft are propelled by a jet of water, not a jet of air. Many are simply powered by old car engines which drive the 'jet unit': an internal propeller (impeller) which is little more than a sophisticated pump. Water is drawn in through an intake in the bottom of the hull and then driven out at high pressure through a nozzle at the back of the boat. Steering is accomplished simply by turning the nozzle laterally, with braking and reversing achieved by a deflector which drops down behind the nozzle. The boat is propelled along by the force of water, and has no rudder or propeller.

Kitted up for a jet-boat safari into the wilds of the Dart River Valley

Early beginnings Jet-boats are usually thought of as a Kiwi invention, but in fact the idea had been around for more than 200 years. In 1769, two British inventors designed a steam-driven pump which drew in water at the bow of a vessel and ejected it at the stern, and in Queen Victoria's time the Admiralty designed a gunboat fitted with a similar means of propulsion. In

1888, Britain's National Lifeboat Institution commissioned the world's first jet-lifeboat, which was built with a back-up jet system in case the main prop became fouled. By 1900, however, marine architects had decided the system was inefficient, and jet-boats fell out of favour.

It was left to a Canterbury sheep-farmer, Bill Hamilton, to perfect the system. A prolific inventor, from an early age he had played on the local rivers, but decided that he wanted to go upstream instead of just down-river. His first attempt at a boat to navigate shallow rivers (which had a retractable screw) were not successful, and it was not until the 1950s that he realised that the jet propulsion unit had to have the nozzle above the water-line to work efficiently. Following this breakthrough jet-boats capable of 80kph or more were soon developed using an axial flow design in the pump. The first boats had plywood hulls, but as these were easily damaged on shingle banks, fibreglass hulls soon became standard.

Masters of the river In just over 30 years since the jet-boat was invented, Kiwis have become the most skilled drivers in the world, conquering the most difficult rivers and winning international river marathons hands down. As you watch the skipper on your jet-boat trip it may look deceptively easy, but a jet-boat race over unfamiliar waters with hidden hazards is a different matter altogether. You can learn how to drive a jet-boat in five minutes, but 'reading a river' requires considerable skill and judgement: you have to anticipate at speed, looking for ripples which might indicate a sandbank, white-water crests which betray a hidden rock, and much else besides. It is a subtle, exacting sport.

The noise factor
Some people consider it incongruous that these noisy machines should be used to explore the country's wildest natural areas, but Sir Edmund Hillary, for one, gives them his wholehearted endorsement: 'Somehow the roar of the engine has never worried me. The jet-boat seems to fit into its environment. The constant change of direction, the struggle against steep rapids, the long, deep, fast stretches, the sharp corners – all seem to tune into the engine from a gentle hum to the scream of power in a difficult section. Rivers are exciting, noisy things anyway.' (Foreword to *The Jet Boat – the Making of a New Zealand Legend* by Les Bloxham and Anne Stark, Reed Books 1994.)

Manoeuvrability and speed are the key elements of jet-boating

Flying and climbing
One of the most popular activities around Mount Cook is to take a flight-seeing trip; the several available options include a glacier-landing on the Tasman, a Grand Circle flight (crossing the divide over to the Fox and Franz Josef Glaciers), or a short Tasman Glacier flight. Contact Mount Cook Airline (tel: 03 435 1849). Potential mountaineers can obtain information on routes, huts and weather conditions from the Visitor Centre, or contact Alpine Guides (tel: 03 435 1834), who rent equipment, supply guides and run courses.

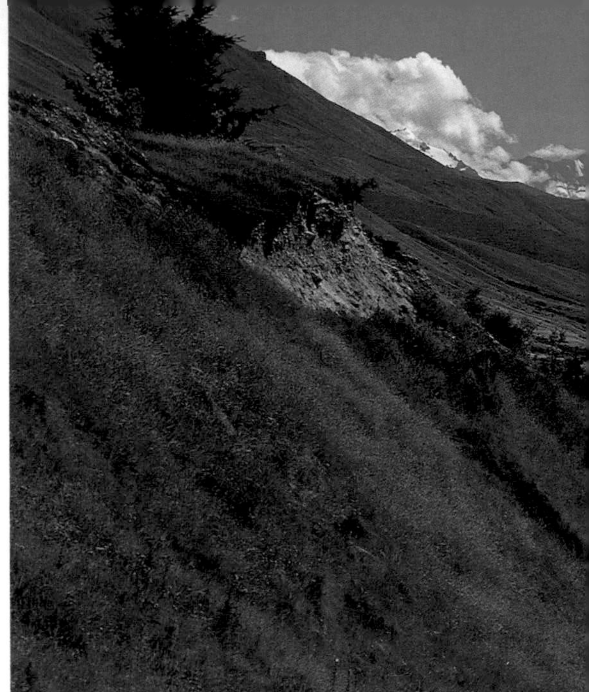

▶▶▶ Mount Cook National Park *196A2*

The first recorded attempt to scale Mount Cook was made in 1882 by the Reverend William Green, a young Irish clergyman. A storm prevented him from reaching the summit, but from that day the race to conquer the peak was on. In 1894 an English climber, Edward Fitzgerald, announced plans to make another attempt, but on hearing of his plans, three New Zealanders (Fyfe, Graham and Clarke) decided to beat him to the top. At 1.30pm on Christmas Day they finally made it, leaving Fitzgerald – who was fishing at the time – fuming. Since then, many famous climbers (including Sir Edmund Hillary) have trained on these awesome slopes.

Inevitably, Mount Cook National Park has become one of the great tourist honeypots of the South Island, exceeded in its tally of annual visitors only by the Fiordland National Park. Most of the 20,000 visitors drawn each year to this great amphitheatre of snow, rock and ice pass through **Mount Cook Village** – a rather haphazard scattering of buildings including the famous Hermitage Hotel, the Alpine Guides shop, a hostel, a motel and the DoC **Visitor Centre** (tel: 03 435 1818. *Open* daily 8–5).

This is primarily climbers' country, with few tramping tracks; there are nevertheless some lovely walks on the valley floor – particularly the famous **Hooker Valley Walk**, an easy three or four-hour round trip up to the terminal lake of the Hooker Glacier, with stunning views of Mount Cook and the surrounding ranges. Several other short walks are described in the *Walks in Mount Cook National Park* leaflet available from the

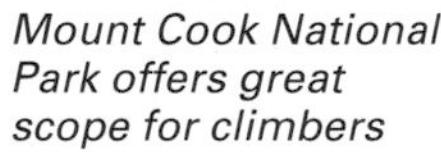
Mount Cook National Park offers great scope for climbers

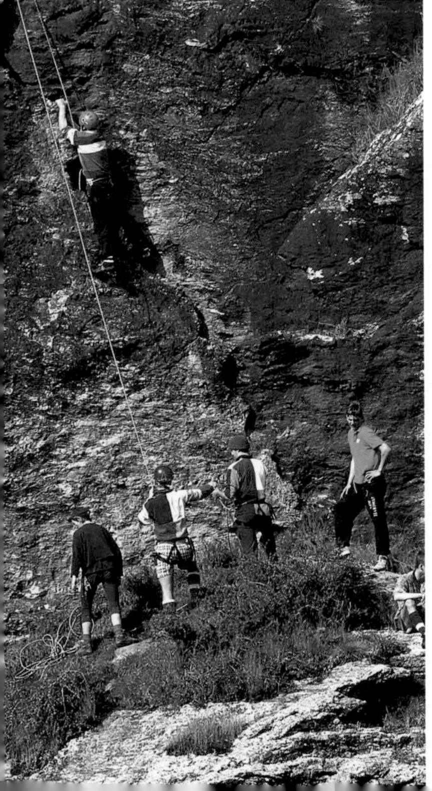

Visitor Centre. Other activities include 4WD safaris, horse-trekking, mountain-biking and hunting (the hunting of introduced animals such as deer, chamois and tahr – considered as pests – is encouraged).

The most notable of the park's flora is the famous Mount Cook lily (*Ranunculus lyallii*), while buttercups, snow gentians and mountain ribbonwood flower on the alpine slopes. Native birds include the kea, kereru (native pigeon), tomtit, rifleman and grey warbler.

At 20km, the **Tasman Glacier▶▶** is the longest glacier in the Southern Hemisphere. Its average width is 1.5km, and the terminal is in much the same place as it was when Julius von Haast first explored the area, although the 'ablation zone' (where the ice starts to melt) is much thinner and consists mostly of a jumble of rocks and debris at the terminal. The Tasman is notable for the numerous large sinkholes in the ablation zone, probably above glacial streams. Sightseeing trips (coach followed by a short walk) are organised by Alpine Guides (daily 10am and 2pm, Sep–May).

In the early days of tourism to Mount Cook, a simple cob building called the Hermitage sufficed to welcome visitors. Destroyed by floods in 1913, it was rebuilt as an elegant Edwardian building, which in turn was destroyed by fire in 1957 and replaced by the present hotel of the same name. In the face of the huge numbers now visiting the park, its facilities and infrastructure are no longer able to cope. But should any new facilities be in the Mount Cook village or further back down the valley in order to spread the impact? The debate treads a familiar fine line between development and conservation. A review is currently under way to try to find solutions to these problems and their effect on one of the country's most spectacular parks.

Beautiful Lake Pukaki, fed by the meltwaters of the Tasman Glacier

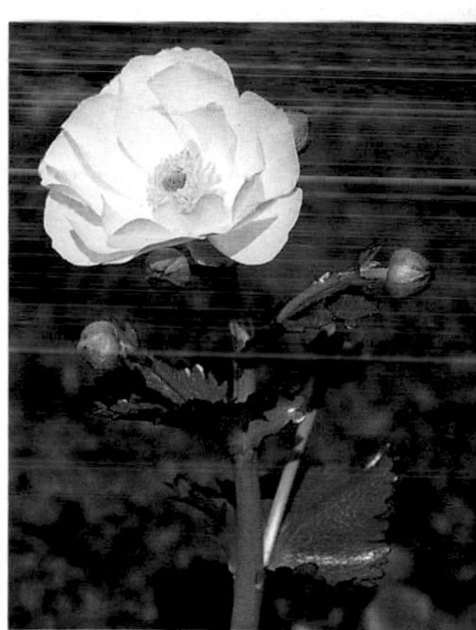

The Mount Cook lily

Rock drawings
Maori rock art, which is concentrated in the centre of the South Island, spans New Zealand history.
To help preserve this valuable heritage, a nine-year survey, begun in 1995, is intended to produce the first-ever definitive record of Maori rock art.

Methven *196B2*

Lying at the foot of the Southern Alps some 95km south-west of Christchurch, Methven is basically a farming centre during the summer months, but in winter it transforms itself into a busy resort in order to service the nearby Mount Hutt skifields. Outside of the skiing season, activities include fishing, hot air ballooning, riding and golf. Just outside Methven, at the **Mayfield Merino Show**, there is a twice-daily sheep-shearing demonstration (daily 10 and 2. *Admission charge* inexpensive).

Mount Hutt *196B2*

One of the most popular ski areas in the South Island, Mount Hutt overlooks the Canterbury Plains 25km north of Methven. It not only has an excellent range of runs suitable for all levels of ability, but also enjoys one of the longest seasons of any New Zealand skifield. Facilities include restaurants, café and equipment hire (tel: 03 302 8811 for more details).

▶ Tekapo *196A2*

To the east of the Mount Cook National Park lies the Mackenzie Country, a vast basin of tawny tussock grass with the glacier-fed **Lake Tekapo▶▶** at its north end. Finely ground rock in the outflows of the Macauley and Godley Rivers which feed the lake give it a luminescent turquoise hue, creating a stunning view from the lakehead village of Tekapo up towards the mountains.

The name Tekapo derives from the Maori Taka-po (*taka* = sleeping mat, *po* = night), recalling an incident when a group of Maori sleeping here awoke with a fright in the night, rolled up their mats and fled. They were

The remote Church of the Good Shepherd, built in the 1930s to commemorate the pioneer farmers of Mackenzie County

probably on a hunting expedition for moa, other birds and eels, which were then taken back to the coast to be traded. The first Europeans settled here in the 1850s, and a guest house was built in the 1880s: it was demolished in 1954 when the lake waters were raised for power generation.

On the east side of the lake outlet is the picturesque **Church of the Good Shepherd►►**, built in the 1930s to commemorate the pioneer farmers of Mackenzie Country. The view of the lake and the mountains through the east window of this simple chapel is sublime. Near by is a bronze statue of a sheepdog, sculpted in 1968 by a Mackenzie farmer's wife (see panel).

The lake waters are too cold for swimming, but you can fish for rainbow or brown trout; there are windsurfers, kayaks, and mountain bikes for hire, and in the winter months ski facilities are available for the nearby Round Hill and Mount Dobson skifields.

The control gates for the dam lie beneath the road bridge connecting the two halves of the village: the outflow travels from here down a series of canals to eight power stations, also fed by other nearby lakes. One of these, **Benmore Power Station**, is open for guided tours (Tue, Thu, Sun 11, 1 & 3. *Admission free*; booking essential, tel: 03 438 7848).

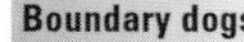

Temuka *196B1*

The 'pottery centre of the south', Temuka has a long history as a ceramics centre: early settlers noted the numerous earthenware ovens adjacent to the *pā* sites of the Nga Tahu and the name 'Temuka' is a contraction of *te umu kaha*, meaning 'fierce strong ovens'. The biggest local manufacturer, New Zealand Insulators, produce popular tableware as well as industrial components. Just off the main road is the **Temuka Domain►**, an attractive 74ha park with many stately old trees, rose gardens, fountains and statues.

The road to Hanging Rock Bridge (a popular picnic spot), passes the scene of Richard Pearce's first flight on Waitohi Main Road (13.5km from Temuka).

Boundary dogs
The bronze statue next to the Church of the Good Shepherd in Tekapo is a memorial to the faithful sheepdogs of Mackenzie Country, 'without the help of which the grazing of the mountainous country would have been impossible'. Many of them were 'boundary dogs', tethered at crucial points on the outskirts of unfenced farmland to keep the flocks from straying. Sometimes provided with a small kennel for shelter, they were often left for days on end to do their work. You can still sometimes see boundary dogs, posted at strategic points either side of the road next to a bridge, for instance, to stop the sheep from wandering into danger.

The bronze statue of a boundary dog

The unsung aviator
A South Canterbury farmer and inventor, Richard Pearce, may well have been the first person in the world to achieve powered flight. He is thought to have flown his home-built aircraft several months before Orville Wright made his historic flight in the USA in 1903: eye-witnesses recall Pearce making a hopping flight above Waitohi school lane in Easter 1903. After serving in World War I, he returned to live in Christchurch, and focused his ambitions on developing an aircraft capable of hovering. He built a prototype but it never flew. Having spent two years in a mental home, Pearce died in 1953, his place in history sadly unrecognised.

Timaru *196B1*

South Canterbury's largest town and port, Timaru is a busy industrial centre which has little in the way of visitor attractions; however, since it is about half-way between Christchurch and Dunedin on the main coast road, you might want to stop on the way through.

Originally named Te Maru ('place of shelter'), the harbour was used by Maori travelling by canoe along this otherwise shelterless coastline. A whaling station was established in the 1830s, but the difficulties of berthing – dozens of ships were wrecked here in subsequent years, and on one fateful day, 14 May 1882, no fewer than four sailing ships came to grief on the shore – led to the building of an artificial harbour in the 1870s. The sand which built up behind the harbour moles eventually became the beach of **Caroline Bay▶**, one of the few protected and safe swimming beaches on the east coast. Behind the beach are a park, a maze and a small aviary (*Open* daily 10–5. *Admission free*).

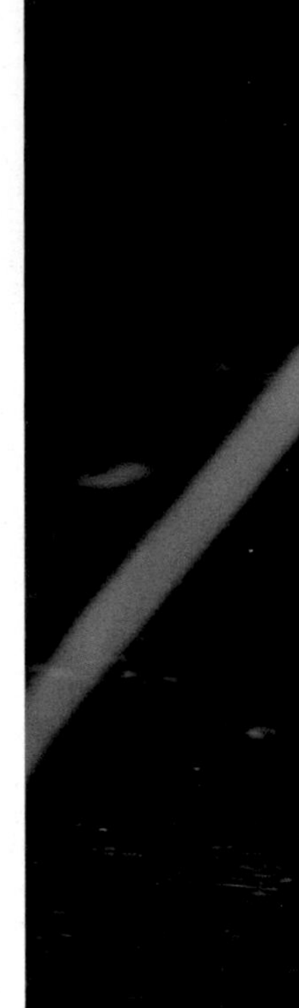

Mid-way between Christchurch and Dunedin, Timaru is South Canterbury's largest town and has a busy port

If you have got half an hour to spare it is worth looking in on the **South Canterbury Museum▶** (*Open* daily 10–4, Sun and holidays 1–4pm. *Admission free*), which has displays relating the story of South Canterbury from the early Maori onwards; it also has a replica of possibly the first aeroplane in the world ever to fly, built by Richard Pearce (see panel).

Several town walks are described in leaflets available free from the Tourist Information Centre, and you can also take a tour of the huge **DB Brewery** (Sheffield Street, Washdyke. *Tours* Mon–Thu 10.30 and 2. *Admission free*).

▶ Twizel *196A1*

Originally built to house workers constructing the Upper Waitaki hydroelectric scheme in the 1960s, Twizel is a rather featureless looking place which has recently developed as a holiday centre for the nearby lakes (Ruataniwha, Ohau and Benmore), with facilities for

The black stilt (or kaki), the world's rarest wading bird

camping, boating, fishing and the like. It is also a convenient base for visits to the Mount Cook National Park, which is just 40 minutes' drive around the shores of Lake Pukaki.

The chief attraction in the vicinity is the **Black Stilt Aviary►►** (see panel), on the shores of Lake Ruataniwha. Once common throughout New Zealand, the black stilt (or kaki) is now the world's rarest wading bird. A captive breeding programme was established in 1979 at the Mount Bruce National Wildlife Centre in order to try to halt the decline in numbers, and the Twizel aviaries were built in 1987 to continue this programme in an environment nearer to the birds' natural home. Viewing hides have been built and the guided tours (Mon–Fri 10.30 and 2, weekends and public holidays 3. *Admission charge* inexpensive; booking essential, tel: 03 435 0802) also include viewing of breeding pairs with binoculars, and a close look at captive (non-breeding) stilts.

Waimate *196B1*

This small town 45km south of Timaru is the centre for a flourishing soft fruit and flower-growing district, and has a huge white horse (a tribute to the Clydesdale horses which once ploughed these lands) outlined on the slopes of Mount John behind it. As well as an old wooden church, Waimate has an unusual mud-floored cottage, known as **The Cuddy►**, constructed using slabs from a single totara tree. Built in 1854, it was the first European dwelling in the area. (*Open* by arrangement. tel: 03 689 8737).

Black stilts
Found only in New Zealand, the black stilt was once widespread, but its numbers have been decimated by predation of eggs and chicks and the loss of its breeding habitat. Their last remaining natural home is amongst the braided rivers of South Canterbury's Mackenzie Country. There are currently only about 80 of these birds left in the wild, with a dozen pairs nesting each spring on the side channels of the rivers. Artificial incubation, as part of the black stilt recovery programme, has raised the survival rate of the fledglings from 1 per cent to 35 per cent, and numbers are now steadily increasing.

Gold fever

New Zealand was the third country (after Australia and the USA) to experience a gold rush in the late 19th century, an event which significantly affected the economic fortunes of the South Island.

The power of the press Australian miner, Gabriel Read claimed the reward for discovering gold offered by the Otago Provincial Council, and the news was published in July in the *Otago Witness*, precipitating a rush to Tuapeka. By the end of the month over 11,000 people were camping in the district, and gold fever had gripped the Otago capital, Dunedin.

First strike The Maori had long been aware that there was gold in New Zealand, but they valued jade more highly. The first gold rush was in the Coromandel in 1852, a time when settlers were being lured to the recently discovered goldfields of California and Australia. When rumours of gold near Thames first emerged, an Auckland committee was quick to offer a reward of £500 to anyone who could find a 'payable' goldfield in New Zealand. Within two days Charles Ring, a Coromandel sawmiller, raced to Auckland with some gold-bearing quartz to claim the reward. Land around Thames was immediately leased from the Maori by hopeful prospectors; unfortunately for them, expensive machinery proved necessary to extract the gold, and within a few months the excitement had fizzled out – so Charles Ring was denied his reward since the goldfields were not considered 'payable'.

Gold rush The Coromandel finds were followed by others in the South Island, notably in Golden Bay in 1856, when there were major strikes in the Aorere River. More than 2,000 miners and hangers-on flooded into the area, but by 1859 most of the gold had been worked out.

Prompted by these finds, the Otago Provincial Council also offered a reward to anyone who could find a payable field. An Australian miner, Gabriel Read, set off for the Tuapeka area (now Lawrence) where he had heard that a miner called Black Peter had found gold at Woolshed Creek. On 23 May 1861 he finally struck lucky, panning 200g of gold from a creek in what became known as Gabriels Gully.

The following year two prospectors, one Irish and one American, arrived in Dunedin with 87 pounds (40kg) of gold. A reward tempted them to reveal their source, the Clutha River near Dunstan (now Clyde), and the next great rush was on.

Fox-hunting Meanwhile, suspicions were aroused in Dunstan by the behaviour of a tight-lipped miner named William Fox, who would appear periodically to sell quantities of gold and then vanish into the bush again. When a group of miners followed him, he managed to give them the slip, and it was some time before he was discovered with some 40 companions working the rich deposits of the Arrow River. Then came the first finds in the Shotover River (later described as 'the richest river in the world'), and the rush was on again – this time the largest the country had seen. Queenstown, Arrowtown and several other settlements sprang up in the wake of the prospectors, and Dunedin became the richest and biggest settlement in the country.

Last strikes By 1863 it was almost over in Otago, and in 1865 reports of new finds in Westland led to swarms of miners crossing the Southern Alps via Arthur's Pass to try their luck there. Prospecting on the West Coast was hard work, hampered by thick bush, heavy rain and the ubiquitous sandflies, but Greymouth and Hokitika boomed nevertheless, with the latter's port becoming the busiest in the country as thousands more miners arrived from Australia.

The last major gold rush was in the Coromandel in 1867–8, but this time the quartz reefs were worked mostly by companies who could afford to invest in stamper batteries to beat out the gold.

In just under a decade the gold rush was over, with only isolated graves, battered shacks and heaps of tailings to show where thousands of hopeful prospectors had toiled. But short-lived though it was, it had a profound effect on the New Zealand economy, bringing instant wealth to many areas; in 1863, gold had accounted for 70 per cent of all overseas exports.

Population growth
The European population of the country was given an enormous boost by the influx of miners, many of whom stayed on – particularly in Otago, where they founded fruit farms and other businesses.

Miners camped close to rivers to pan for gold, but flash floods were always a danger

MILFORD HAVEN

THE DEEP SOUTH

The Deep South The southernmost region of the South Island embraces a wide diversity of landscapes, from semi-arid high-country basins to fertile plains and forested mountains. The range of fascinating things to see and do in the Deep South is no less varied, from the stunning scenery of Fiordland to historic gold-mining sites in Central Otago and wildlife-viewing on the Otago Peninsula. Adventure tourism is probably better represented here than almost anywhere else in New Zealand, with action-packed thrills available all year round.

Fiordland The glacial landscapes of Fiordland National Park are one of the major attractions of the South Island. Covering 1.2 million ha, this is one of the largest national parks in the world: parts of it are so mountainous they have yet to be fully explored. The famous **Milford Sound** is just one of 14 fiords along the coastline, while inland are numerous freshwater lakes (the biggest of which are **Manapouri** and **Te Anau**), tumbling waterfalls and virgin forests beneath the mountain peaks.

One way of exploring this untouched wilderness is by tramping (either independently or with a guide) along well-known walking tracks such as the Milford, Kepler, Routeburn, Greenstone or Hollyford; climbing, hunting and fishing are other possibilities, while flightseeing and cruising on the fiords and lakes are more relaxing ways to enjoy this splendid natural environment. The main gateway to the Fiordland National Park is the township of Te Anau, on the shores of Lake Te Anau.

Otago Central Otago was the scene of one of New Zealand's greatest gold rushes (see pages 218–19), and there are still remnants of those heady days scattered around the towns and countryside. Today fruit-growing is almost as lucrative, with peaches, apricots and other stonefruit thriving on the well-irrigated plains.

The busiest resort in the South Island, **Queenstown**, lies at the foot of the Remarkables Range, on the shores of glittering Lake Wakatipu. In winter skiing is the main attraction, but in the summer months there are almost endless opportunities for outdoor adventure and sports – name almost any thrill you can imagine, from bungee-jumping to surfing down rapids, and they do it here. The second main resort area is **Wanaka**, on the shores of Lake Wanaka, which offers almost as many adventure options as Queenstown, but has a much more laid-back atmosphere.

While Central Otago typically has hot summers and frosty winters, Coastal Otago has a somewhat milder climate. The coastal areas were settled by Scottish migrants in the 19th century, a heritage which is evident in the well-preserved architecture of the regional capital, **Dunedin**. On the city's doorstep is the **Otago Peninsula**, where royal albatross and rare penguins can be seen at remarkably close quarters.

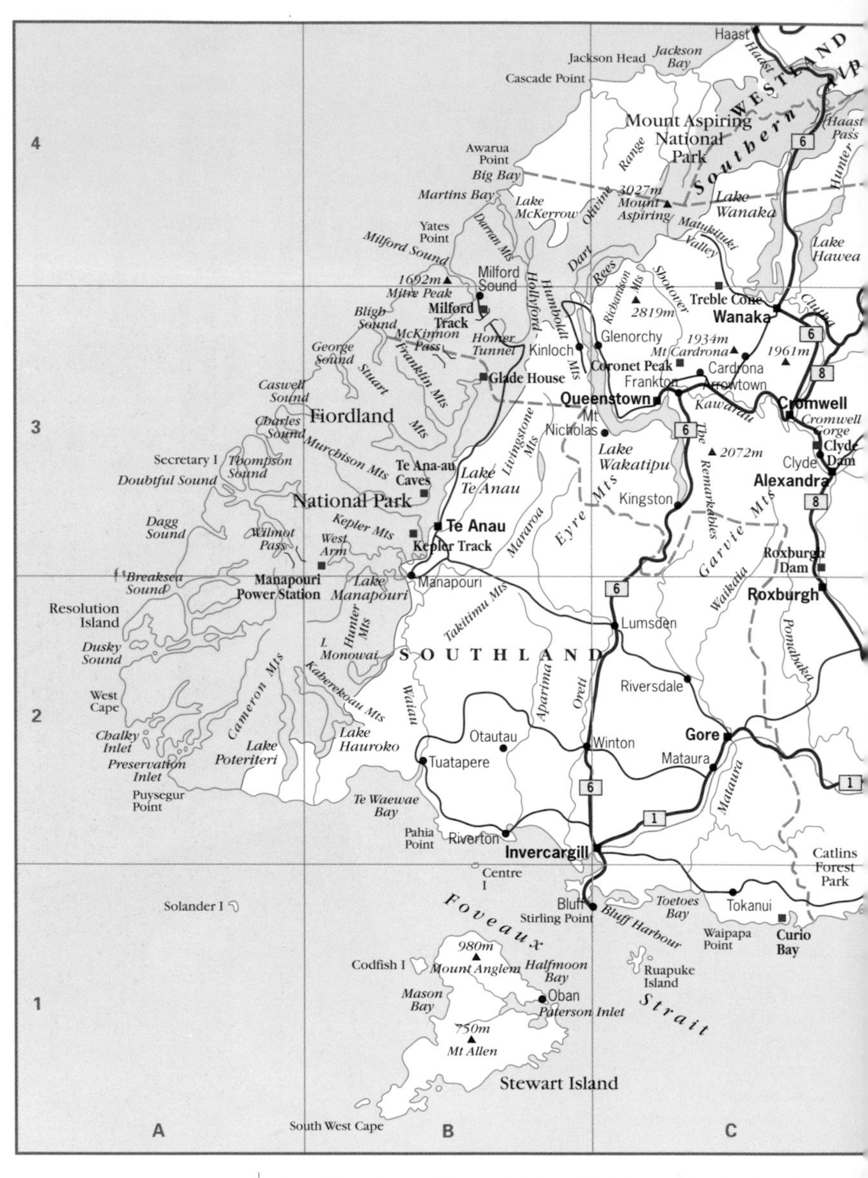

Page 220: Milford Sound. Page 221: canoeing the rapids

Southland and Stewart Island Adjoining Fiordland is the rest of the province of Southland, a triangular wedge of sheep farms and trout streams; like Dunedin, the region has strong Scottish connections: inhabitants still display traces of a Scots burr, and many place names are Gaelic in origin. At the bottom of this triangle is Invercargill, New Zealand's southernmost city and the jumping-off point for much-neglected Stewart Island, where rare birds outnumber people and trampers will find miles of deserted coastline and bush to explore. This is one of the few places in New Zealand where you can be almost sure of seeing kiwi in the wild, with regular excursions to view a beach colony of these elusive birds.

CANTERBURY
Ashburton
Tinwald
Canterbury Plains
Lake Tekapo
Lake Pukaki
Tekapo
Ben Ohau Range
Fairlie
Opuha
Mackenzie Country
Lake Ohau
Twizel
Temuka
Pleasant Point
Caroline Bay
Timaru
Canterbury Bight
Ahuriri
Lake Benmore
Benmore Power Station
Kirkliston Range
Hakataramea
The Hunters Hills
Omarama
Otematata
Lake Aviemore
Kurow
2087m
Hawkdun Range
Dunstan Mts
St Bathans
Waimate
Waitaki
Duntroon
45th Latitude
Naseby
Ranfurly
Kakanui Mts
Oamaru
OTAGO
Moeraki Boulders Scenic Reserve
Moeraki Point
Shag
Moeraki
Taieri
Palmerston
Shag Point
Middlemarch
Lammerlaw Range
Lake Mahinerangi
Port Chalmers
Taiaroa Head
Royal Albatross Centre
Portobello Aquarium
Otago Peninsula
Mosgiel
Dunedin
Larnach Castle
Lawrence
Clutha
Milton
Balclutha
Owaka
Nugget Point
0 20 40 60 80 100 km
D
E

Paua (abalone) shells

Take a night safari to spot kiwis on remote Stewart Island

Bluff oysters
These deep-water shellfish have a sweet, succulent flavour, and are much sought after; although supplies may be erratic elsewhere in the country, you can usually find oysters here during the season (1 March–31 August). You can also visit the dockside oyster sheds during this time, and oyster-opening and other competitions form part of the Bluff Oyster Festival (mid-April).

Coastal Otago and Southland

▶ Bluff *222B1*

The southernmost town on the South Island, Bluff is a major port and fishing centre, with the massive Tiwai aluminium smelter dominating the far side of the harbour. From the top of **Bluff Hill▶** (265m) there is a terrific panorama of the harbour, with Foveaux Strait and Stewart Island to the south, whilst nearby **Stirling Point** has a compulsory photo-stop at an 'international signpost' showing the distances from Bluff to major cities worldwide.

Bluff is well known for its seafood, principally Bluff oysters (see panel), but grouper, blue cod and crayfish are also fished locally. One Bluff couple have put mollusc shells to good use in their amazing **Paua Shell House▶** (corner of Marine Parade and Henderson. *Open* daily 9–5. *Admission charge* donation) which features an entire room lined with beautiful *paua* (abalone) shell, and an enormous collection of shells from around the world.

Stirling Point Lookout, the end of the road in South Island

▶▶▶ Dunedin 223D2

There is no mistaking the ancestry of Dunedin's founding fathers: with a statue of Robert Burns at its heart, the city also has the only whisky distillery in the country and the only kilt store, not to mention an architectural heritage whose Scottish roots are plain to see. You may even hear the strained notes of a bagpipe during a haggis ceremony here; it comes as no surprise to discover that 'Dunedin' is the old Gaelic name for Edinburgh.

The early settlement, founded in 1848, struggled along with just a few hundred people attempting to carve a living from this difficult terrain. Thirteen years later the town was galvanised by the Central Otago gold finds: although the goldfields were some 120km inland, Dunedin was the nearest port and its prosperity was soon assured. Between 1861 and 1865 the population leapt from some 2,000 to over 10,000, and it developed into New Zealand's wealthiest city. Great public buildings were erected, the country's first university (the University of Otago) was founded, and Dunedin became the proud possessor of the first cable tramway outside the USA (this ran for over 70 years until it was closed down in 1957).

Although the Scottish heritage predominates, Dunedin is now demographically much more cosmopolitan, with a population including descendants of Irish and Dutch settlers, a large Chinese community (many of them descendants of gold-diggers), third and fourth-generation Lebanese, and newly settled Cambodians and Vietnamese. Similarly, although the city may be most famous for its architecture, it also boasts a lively artistic and cultural life and fine museums. The city's large student population (around 14,000 of whom attend one of four higher education institutions) has helped to foster a vibrant entertainment and music scene, and Dunedin has produced a number of successful rock bands. The 'Dunedin Sound' gained international recognition in the 1980s, and numerous inventive bands are now based here.

Recently, Dunedin has also capitalised on the accessibility of the nearby Otago Peninsula (see pages 232–3) to become a major centre for eco-tourism based on the region's unique wildlife attractions.

An obvious place to start exploring Dunedin is the eight-sided **Octagon** at the heart of the city, where Robbie Burns gazes, 'with his back to the kirk and his face to the pub'. The kirk in question is **St Paul's Cathedral**, which has an impressive vaulted nave and a rather less impressive 1970s-chancel. On the north side of the Octagon, the Municipal Chambers contain the helpful and efficient Dunedin **Visitor Centre** (tel: 03 474 3300. *Open* daily

A wee dram
Wilson Distillers, New Zealand's only whisky distillery, offers a video and tour (George Street, tel: 03 474 3300, booking essential. *Open* Mon–Fri 2.45. *Admission free*), followed by a tasting. You can also tour one of New Zealand's oldest small traditional breweries at Speights (Rattray Street, tel: 03 477 9480, booking essential. *Open* Mon–Thu 10.30. *Admission charge* inexpensive).

Robbie Burns statue, Dunedin

8.30–5, weekends 9–5, longer hours in summer).

Opposite the Visitor Centre, an old department store has recently been imaginatively converted into the brilliant new **Dunedin Public Art Gallery►►►** (*Open* Sat–Wed 10–5, Thu–Fri 10–8). Opened in 1996, the gallery has a wonderful glass façade providing a window on to the interior displays from the street. It boasts one of the two best collections in the country (the other is at the Auckland City Art Gallery), a legacy which began with the early acquisition of Van der Vedlen's *Waterfall in the Otira Gorge*, considered to be the country's greatest 19th-century landscape painting. The gallery also has over 40 works by Frances Hodgkins (whose father was one of the gallery's founders), as well as paintings by Constable, Gainsborough, Reynolds, Monet, Lorrain and Landini. The decorative arts and modern works are also well represented in its collections.

Dunedin's railway station, with its magnificent interior (top), gave the nickname 'Gingerbread George' to its architect George Troup

Heading down Stuart Street from the Octagon, you pass the magisterial **Law Courts►** to reach the splendid **Railway Station►►**, reputedly 'one of the most photographed railway buildings in the world'. Completed in 1907 and faced with Oamaru stone, the station is dominated by a massive tower and embellished with rampant lions and stained-glass windows depicting steam locomotives, while the foyer features an impressive Royal Doulton mosaic floor.

A short distance south-west of the station is the **Otago Settlers Museum►►** (*Open* Mon–Fri 10–5, Sat–Sun 1–5. *Admission charge* moderate) which has recently undergone a major and successful revamp. At the entrance, the main Hall of Otago History encompasses the story of early Maori settlers as well as European immigrants and Chinese gold-diggers. Beyond, a fabulous Edwardian Hall houses temporary exhibits, while the atmospheric Portrait Gallery, lined with hundreds of nostalgic photographs of early settlers in Dunedin and Otago, also features Edwardian furniture and other antiques.

The museum's expansion is due largely to the acquisition of the Railways Bus Station next door, where the marvellous Art Deco booking hall now forms the centrepiece of a permanent exhibition on transport in Otago.

If you visit only one museum in Dunedin, it should be the main **Otago Museum▶▶▶** a few minutes' walk away on Great King Street (*Open* Mon–Fri 10–5, Sat–Sun 1–5. *Admission free*). Founded in 1868, this has outstanding collections on Maori and Pacific Island culture, displays on New Zealand's natural history, and exhibits of archaeological treasures from around the world – a legacy which reflects the wealth of the local community at the turn of the century.

The museum presently comprises a 'Discovery World' hands-on science exhibit on the ground floor, with the first floor devoted to cultural artefacts from all over Oceania, and a comprehensive southern Maori collection.

The top floor features the natural history collection, with a 'Survival and Extinction' section containing stuffed specimens of some of the 44 species and 32 genera of birds which have become extinct since humans first set foot in Aotearoa – ironically, many of these species vanished because they were over-zealously hunted by collectors for export to museums overseas. Also on this

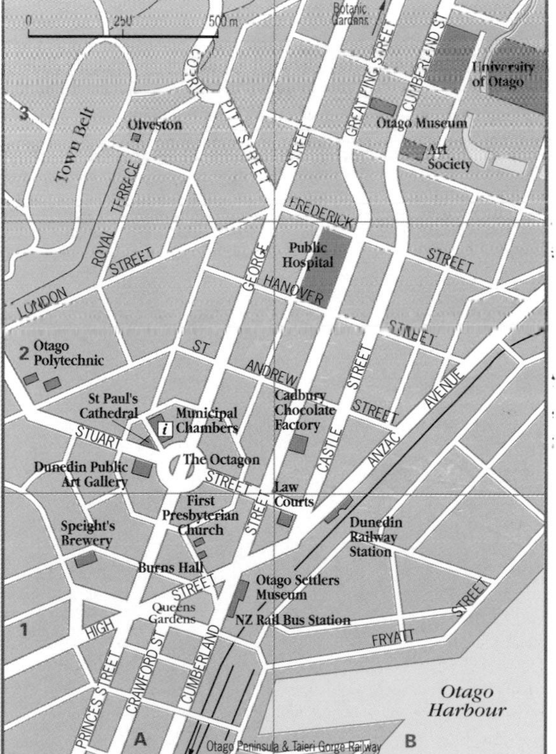

Tasty tours
In the middle of the last century an illiterate, penniless orphan made his way to New Zealand to seek his fortune in the Otago goldfields. However, it was biscuits, not gold, which made young Richard Hudson's name. He established a biscuit bakehouse in Dunedin, and later manufactured the first chocolate bars in the southern hemisphere in 1884. Now owned by Cadburys, the factory can be visited (280 Cumberland Street, tel: 03 467 7800. *Open* Mon–Fri 1.30 and 2.30. *Admission free*), but tours (complete with free samples) are so popular that booking is essential – one month in advance during school holidays.

The Otago Museum displays an outstanding collection of artefacts from Maori and Pacific Island cultures

floor are pottery, textiles and decorative arts, as well as a Maritime Hall with ship models, and a whale skeleton.

The museum is currently undergoing an extensive redevelopment programme which promises to transform it into one of the best in the country; among other changes, the plan features the opening up of the interior to reveal the three-storey Victorian gallery which originally formed the building's magnificent centrepiece.

One of the most popular historic buildings in Dunedin is **Olveston**▶▶, a Jacobean-style mansion built in 1906 by local businessman David Theomin. Bequeathed to the city by his daughter in 1966, it had been left virtually untouched since her father's death in 1933, and so shows the lifestyle of a prosperous Edwardian family. Complete with billiard room, library and an impressive oak gallery and stairway, this spacious and comfortable family home (42 Royal Terrace, tel: 03 477 3320. *Guided tours daily* 9:30, 10:45, 12, 1:30, 2:45, 4. *Admission charge* moderate) is furnished with artefacts collected by the Theomins in Asia, ranging from Chinese jade and ceramics to Persian carpets and weaponry and helmets from Japan. There are also French antiques, English silverware and early New Zealand paintings.

Gorge trip by rail
To the west of Dunedin, the Taieri River wends its way through a picturesque gorge which is for the most part accessible only aboard the Taieri Gorge Railway. Railway enthusiasts will also appreciate the many fine examples of Victorian stone bridges and iron latticework viaducts along the route. The four-hour return trip departs from Dunedin Railway Station daily in summer (tel: 03 477 4449 for times and bookings).

Though not something that its inhabitants like to advertise, Dunedin merits a place in the *Guinness Book of Records* as having the world's steepest street. A few minutes from the city centre, **Baldwin Street** climbs dramatically from the main road at a gradient of 1 in 2.7, only to come to a dead end halfway up the hillside. It remains a secret, however, because its residents are fed up with the sound of splintering fences and crumpling metal as cars career out of control down the hill. Leave the driving to the locals, and walk up the 270 steps to the top.

Turn-of-the-century furnishings in the historic family home of Olveston

Invercargill *222C2*

New Zealand's southernmost city, Invercargill sprawls across wide open plains almost at the tip of the South Island – only the port of Bluff lies closer to Foveaux Strait and nearby Stewart Island. The capital of Southland (or Murihiku, 'the tail end of the land', as it was known to the Maori), the city is flat as a pancake, having been mostly reclaimed from swampland, and is laid out on a spacious grid pattern. The main transport centre for Southland, it is the principal departure point for Stewart Island (see pages 234–5).

Invercargill's main attraction is the excellent **Southland Museum and Art Gallery▶▶** (*Open* weekdays 9–5, weekends 1–5. *Admission charge* donation) on the edge of Queens Park. Founded over a century ago, the museum was redeveloped in 1990, when it was roofed over with a gigantic pyramid. The complex includes displays on natural history, early colonial settlers and the Maori heritage featuring stone tool-making and jade-carving. The evocative 'Roaring Forties Experience' vividly brings to life the wild subantarctic territories administered by New Zealand. The unusual wildlife, giant alpine flowers, spectacular topography and appalling weather of these islands are convincingly conveyed in a 25-minute audio-visual show (Shows on the hour. *Admission charge* inexpensive) and a new display gallery.

The museum is also home to a successful captive breeding programme for tuatara, an ancient reptile which has survived only in New Zealand.

Southern Scenic Route
Part of the Southern Scenic Route traverses an almost-forgotten corner of the coastline between Invercargill and Balclutha, crossing ridges and valleys close to the coast, and passing through tracts of native forest in the Catlins with superb views of sandy bays, estuaries and rocky headlands. The numerous places of interest along the way include Nugget Point (see page 230) and Curio Bay, where the fossilised remains of an ancient forest can be seen embedded in the rocks along the foreshore. From Invercargill to Balcutha is 170km, with 55km of this along unsealed roads.

Brewing up
On his first visit, Cook noted the huge number of seal colonies on the Fiordland coast, and it was not long before sealers and whalers were setting up camp wherever they could along this inhospitable coastline. Whatever else Cook may have achieved of scientific value, his second voyage in 1773 is remembered for the fact that he brewed the first beer in New Zealand: made from rimu leaves and manuka, it was apparently 'esteemed by everyone on board'.

'Henry', one of 40 tuataras in the Southland Museum's Tuatara House

Boulder formation
There are about 50 boulders at Moeraki, the largest of which weighs over 7 tonnes and measures over 2m in diameter. Although their position on the beach and their shape would seem to suggest that the boulders were formed by surf action, in fact they emerged from the mudstone cliffs behind the beach, having been created by the chemical action of minerals crystallising at their core when they were formed in the sediment some 65 million years ago. An informative leaflet on this process, published by the Institute of Geological and Nuclear Sciences, is available from the café shop.

▶ Moeraki Boulders — *223E3*

These unusual spherical boulders strewn along the beach, in what is now the Moeraki Boulders Scenic Reserve, are the finest examples of their kind to be found anywhere in the world (see panel). According to Maori legend, they are the remains of food baskets washed overboard from a great canoe shipwrecked here on its way from Hawaiki. Geologists know them, more prosaically, as septarian concretions, and these are the last remaining ones on this coast; they were once plentiful on nearby Katiki Beach and around Shag Point, but all the smaller examples have long since been claimed as 'souvenirs'. Perhaps the main reason for people's curiosity is their almost perfect roundness, combined with the veined surfaces which give them the appearance of a turtle's back.

There is a good café/restaurant just above the boulders at the car park, and the nearby fishing village of Moeraki (78km from Dunedin, 38km from Oamaru) is also worth a brief visit.

▶▶ Nugget Point — *223D1*

Nugget Point rises some 130m above the beach with a series of sea stacks – one with a lighthouse – extending out into the ocean beyond the South Otago coastline. A popular spot for viewing wildlife, this remote promontory is the only place on the mainland where fur seals, elephant seals and Hooker's sea-lions are known to coexist. Yellow-eyed penguins and little blue penguins both breed here, and other penguins (Fiordland crested, Snares crested, and rockhopper penguins among them) are also sometimes seen. Birdlife includes spotted shags, gulls, and Australian gannets; the largest known mainland colony of sooty shearwaters is also located here.

The Moeraki Boulders are strewn across a beach close to the coast road

There is a viewing hide for the yellow-eyed penguins (which come ashore in the evenings) in Roaring Bay, and a viewing platform at the lighthouse (binoculars recommended). Nugget Point is 289km south-west of Balclutha.

►► Oamaru *223E3*

Oamaru would probably be just another declining coastal port, were it not for the timely discovery – soon after the town was founded – of large deposits of pure limestone in the surrounding area, which encouraged architects and stonemasons to design a magnificent series of buildings along its main street. Most of these still stand, earning Oamaru the title 'whitestone city', and a stroll along Thames Street will reveal a bewildering variety of architectural styles on historic buildings such as the National Bank and the court house.

Oamaru's port was dogged by early misadventures, but it nevertheless brought sufficient prosperity to lead to the development of the harbour area and, when it closed down in the 1970s, to bequeath a legacy of well-designed wool and grain stores, warehouses and other buildings. These now form the heart of the **Harbour-Tyne Street Historic Precinct►►**, which is being gradually and sympathetically redeveloped as a Victorian town.

Creamy limestone adds allure to Oamaru architecture

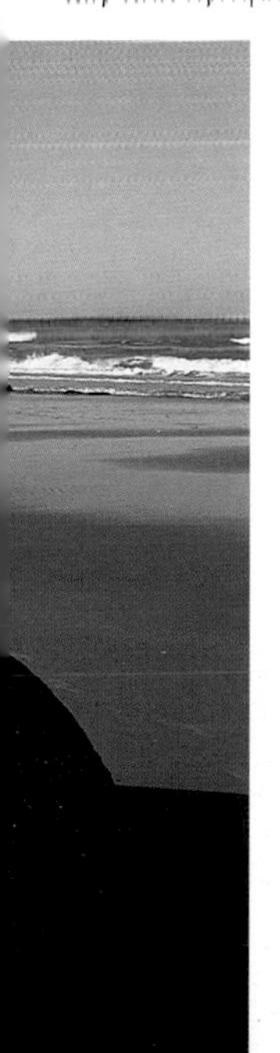

The Oamaru Information Centre (*Open* daily 9–5) has recently moved into the old Colonial Bank Building in this area, close to the Oamaru Display Centre in the old Wool Store (*Open* daily 9.30–4.30; architectural tours of the district by arrangement, tel: 03 434 5685).

The mild, sheltered climate has benefited the lovely **Public Gardens** (Severn Street. *Open* daylight hours. *Admission free*), founded in 1876, with an oriental garden, Japanese bridge, rhododendron dell and wallaby park.

The penguin nesting colony on the harbour edge is probably the only one in the world in such close proximity to a town centre – sometimes, indeed, the penguins get confused on their way home at night and wander downtown. A penguin refuge has been created in an old quarry at the end of Waterfront Road, with two viewing platforms for watching them as they waddle inland to their nests after a day's fishing out at sea, usually about half an hour after dark (Visitor Centre/viewing platforms *Open* 7pm–10pm. *Admission charge* inexpensive).

Sheep and rain
Invercargill shares its Scottish origins with Dunedin, but while the latter rose to prosperity thanks to the goldfields, Invercargill has gained its wealth largely through the rich grasslands which surround it, providing grazing for millions of sheep. The lushness of the grasslands is partly due to a higher than average annual rainfall, and while this may be good news for the sheep, it is not so much of an incentive for visitors – particularly given the fact that Invercargill also holds the national record for the lowest mean average temperatures and the lowest annual average for hours of sunshine.

Royal albatross breed on Taiaroa Head near Dunedin

The royal albatross
One of the largest of all seabirds, the royal albatross glides across the oceans on its enormous wings, sometimes staying aloft for days on end. Adults arrive at Taiaroa late in September, building their nests ready for egg-laying in November. The parents share incubation duties over eleven weeks – one of the longest incubation periods of any bird. The chicks hatch during January and early February, but are not ready to fly until eight months later.

Disappearing Gun
Guided tours at Taiaroa Head include a visit to an underground military complex inside Fort Taiaroa, which was built to counter the (imagined) Tsarist threat in the 1880s. Inside is the world's only working example of an Armstrong Disappearing Gun.

▶▶▶ The Otago Peninsula 223E2

'Seals for breakfast, albatross for lunch, penguins for dinner' as they say in Dunedin – not to be found on local menus, of course, but rather to be observed at close quarters on the adjoining Otago Peninsula. The concentration of wildlife here is even more remarkable because of its proximity to the city (it is in fact within the city limits), and it is with ample justification that Dunedin proclaims itself 'the wildlife capital of New Zealand'.

The volcanic hills of the peninsula terminate in steep headlands on the ocean side, and with the edge of the continental shelf close to shore, wildlife such as seals and sea-birds have a plentiful source of food as well as sheltered breeding and resting sites on the cliffs. Fur seals breed in several locations, as do Hooker's sea-lions, which are twice the size of seals and amongst the world's rarest sea-lions.

The most spectacular resident is the royal albatross, which breeds on the grassy slopes at Taiaroa Head at the tip of the peninsula, the only place in the world where these magnificent birds nest on a mainland site. The nesting areas can be viewed from an observation post which is part of the **Royal Albatross Centre▶▶▶** (*Open* summer 9–dusk, winter 10–dusk; tours on the hour and half-hour in summer, restricted hours during winter, closed mid-Sep to late Nov. *Admission charge* expensive. Booking recommended, tel: 03 478 0499). Allow at least a couple of hours to visit the reserve and the Centre, which also houses displays on the wildlife and history of the area (*Open* same hours. *Admission free*).

The other main wildlife attraction on the peninsula is penguins: blue penguins breed at Taiaroa Head and elsewhere around the coast, and rare yellow-eyed penguins breed on just about every beach on the peninsula. There are two main viewing areas for the latter: the first is at the **Southlight Wildlife Reserve▶**, the entrance to which is just past Taiaroa Head. The penguins nest on a sandy bank some distance below the viewing area, but you can spend as much time as you want here (there are fixed binoculars, but bringing your own would be better), and there are also fur seals and a spotted shag colony just down the beach (collect the key from Southlight Wildlife, Harington Point before arriving at Taiaroa Head. *Open* dawn–dusk. *Admission charge* inexpensive).

For a really close-up view of the penguins, take one of the tours at the award-winning **Yellow-Eyed Penguin Conservation Reserve▶▶▶** (*Open* daily 9–dusk. *Admission charge* moderate; booking essential, tel: 03 478 0286). After an introductory talk, a short ride brings you to the reserve, on the opposite coast of the peninsula, where a viewing platform allows you to watch the penguins as they waddle ashore. A series of covered sunken paths and viewing hides then leads to the nesting areas, giving an intimate insight into nesting activity.

Further back down the north coast, the **Trust Bank Aquarium▶** has a series of tanks with plants, invertebrates and fish from the waters around this region, as well as a touch tank (*Open* daily 12–4.30 in summer, weekends only 12–4.30 in winter. *Admission charge* inexpensive). Near by, **Glenfalloch Woodland Gardens▶** (*Open* daily 9–dusk. *Admission charge* donation) have a wonderful collection of fuchsias, roses, azaleas and rhododendrons, including some species not found elsewhere in the country.

The peninsula's main historical attraction is the impressive **Larnach Castle▶▶▶**, built in 1871 in the Scottish baronial style, with some fine craftsmanship and antique furniture inside (*Open* daily 9–5. *Admission charge* moderate). The ballroom now houses a café, and from the attractive grounds there are extensive views over the peninsula and out to sea.

Sea-borne viewing
Seals, albatross, penguins and birdlife on the peninsula can also be viewed on sea-borne cruises such as those run by Monarch Wildlife Adventures (tel: 03 477 4276); naturalists Colleen and Fiona Black operate these highly recommended tours aboard the MV *Monarch*, with several options around the harbour and peninsula. A more adventurous option is surf-rafting, with an exciting ride through the surf on fully equipped Zodiacs followed by a tour around the cliffs and nesting sites of the peninsula. Surf Rafting NZ (tel: 03 478 0046) operate daily in summer.

Larnach Castle features elaborate plasterwork ceilings and early New Zealand furniture

Getting there
Stewart Island can be reached in an hour aboard the Foveaux Express from Bluff (tel: 03 212 7660), or in 20 minutes on board the frequent flights from Invercargill operated by Southern Air (tel: 03 218 9129); accommodation, water taxis and excursions can be booked through either Stewart Island Travel (tel: 03 219 1269) or Stewart Island Adventure Centre (tel: 03 219 1134).

Below: yellow-eyed penguin. Bottom: Halfmoon Bay, Stewart Island

▶▶ Stewart Island *222B1*

Some 30km across Foveaux Strait from Bluff, Stewart Island is largely uninhabited by humans. Some 65km long and 40km at its widest point, it covers 172,000 ha and has a local population of just 400 souls – most of whom live in and around the one township, Oban, on the shores of Halfmoon Bay.

Captain Cook made his second major mistake in mapping the coastline in 1770 when he drew the island as a peninsula (conversely, his other error was to assume that Banks Peninsula was an island). Whalers and sealers later sought the shelter of Paterson Inlet, and timber mills were established, with most settlements developing on the north side of the island.

Today there are only 20km of roads on the entire island, so if you want to explore beyond the immediate vicinity of Oban then hiking (or a boat) is the only way to go. Most of the island has a dense cover of native bush and rainforest, with bush walks and tramping tracks spreading out from Halfmoon Bay around the coastline and into the interior. Tramping huts are strategically placed on the main hiking routes, which include the arduous North-West Circuit (a ten-day trip) and the Rakiura Track (three days). Launches can also be chartered to reach the more remote areas for hunting, track drop-offs, fishing, or simply fossicking in isolated bays.

Nearly 90 per cent of the island is protected, with the native birdlife including kaka, tui, bellbirds, robin, fantail, longtail and shining cuckoo. Numerous sea-birds breed around the shoreline and on surrounding islands, and yellow-eyed, little blue and Fiordland crested penguins are also found here. Most of the islanders live from fishing, with crayfish, abalone, blue cod and salmon exported overseas.

The pace of life on Stewart Island is relaxed, and the islanders are friendly. Oban has plenty of accommodation (from motels to homestays), a general store and the venerable South Sea Hotel. Within the township there is also a small **Museum** on Ayr Street (*Open* Mon–Sat 10–noon, Sun noon–2. *Admission charge* inexpensive), with displays on whaling, Maori history, fishing, timber-milling and so on. The natural history of the island is explored at the nearby Department of Conservation Centre (Main Road, tel: 03 219 1130. *Open* daily 9–5), which can also provide leaflets on tramping tracks and short walks around Halfmoon Bay.

Other activities include kayaking in Paterson Inlet (which has over 100 sq km of sheltered waterways and 20 islands), visiting the nearby bird sanctuary on Ulva Island, and one-hour trips by minibus around (most) of the island's 20km of roads.

One of the highlights of a stay here, however, is the rare chance to see kiwi in their natural environment. The southern tokoeka, the species found on Stewart Island, is unusual in that it forages both by day and by night: trampers may well spot them nosing out sand hoppers under washed-up kelp on the beaches (particularly in Mason Bay). Boat trips from Oban cross Paterson Inlet to Ocean Beach, where a handful of kiwis can usually be seen – an opportunity not to be missed (departures are every other day and numbers are limited, so booking is essential. Bravo Adventure Cruises, tel: 03 219 1144).

Mutton birds
If you fly into Stewart Island you will notice a small cluster of islands to the east of the flight path on approaching the coast. These are the northern Muttonbird islands, so named after the fledglings of the sooty shearwaters which migrate here from the North Pacific during the summer months. The Maori know them as titi and prize them as a gastronomic delicacy; most Pakeha find them too rich and oily, which is perhaps why they were also called muttonbirds. Hundreds and thousands nest in burrows here, and the fledglings are collected from April onwards only by Maori who have inherited the ancestral right to do so.

► Waitaki Valley *223E3*

Straddling the boundary between Canterbury and North Otago, the Waitaki River drains down from the Southern Alps and flows out to sea just north of Oamaru. A major source of hydroelectric power, it has three lakes created by dams along its length (Benmore, Aviemore and Waitaki), which are now stocked with trout and salmon.

At the head of the valley is **Omarama**, popular with anglers and famous as a gliding centre. Near by (10km north west, off SH8) are the **Clay Cliffs►►**, a spectacular natural example of 'badland' erosion, with a series of elegant pinnacles, columns, ravines and ridges.

Further downstream, the **Benmore Power Station** is the first of three hydroelectric plants; the community of **Otematata** provides service facilities for all three. At the junction of the Waitaki and Hakataramea Rivers, **Kurow** has some interesting old limestone buildings from the 1890s. Finally comes **Duntroon,** a farming centre with some fine fishing in the vicinity. Just outside the township is a remarkable set of Maori **rock drawings►** (see panel page 214) on the walls of a limestone shelter (signposted 2½km west of town on SH83).

Stewart Island is just one of the places in South Island to watch sea lions

Kiwi

■ New Zealand's national symbol, the amiable kiwi is a one-off evolutionary design, a bird which holds all sorts of biological records. But now the unthinkable might be about to happen, and its very survival is threatened. ■

Where to see kiwi
Auckland Zoo; Kiwi and Birdlife Park, Queenstown; Kiwi House, Napier; Kiwi House and Native Bird Park, Otorohanga; National Wildlife Centre, Mount Bruce; Orana Park Wildlife Trust, Christchurch; Rainbow and Fairy Springs, Rotorua; Willowbank Wildlife Reserve, Christchurch

A great spotted kiwi

A truly curious bird The flightless, nocturnal kiwi evolved some 70 million years ago, at about the time when the New Zealand landmass drifted away from Gondwanaland. A relation of Australia's emus and cassowaries, the kiwi thrived at ground level where there were then no mammals to hunt it. Its only predators at the time were New Zealand goshawks and the gigantic Haast's eagle (both now extinct), and it may have been this threat which turned it into a creature of the night.

The kiwi is one of the few birds with a highly developed sense of smell, and is the only known bird with external nostrils at the end of its bill, with which it literally sniffs out its food below the surface of the ground. Its diet consists mostly of earthworms, spiders, seeds, fallen fruit and insect larvae. It lays simply enormous eggs, with a mature example averaging 20 per cent of the female body weight. Once laid, they take up to 80 days to hatch, and in some varieties the male does most of the incubating. Kiwi form monogamous pairs and bond until death; the females are bigger than the males, and tend to dominate them. As they forage for food during the night they call to each other, performing a duet that may last for hours on end, with the female giving a lower, hoarser call than the male. Kiwi are highly territorial, and protect their patch (which can be as big as 40ha) by calling or, if that fails, attacking the intruder. Generally considered gentle creatures, they are in fact often bad-tempered, and are capable of inflicting nasty wounds with their razor-sharp claws.

Types of kiwi There are six identified varieties of kiwi, the rarest of which is the **little spotted kiwi**, of which just 1,000 remain. The **great spotted kiwi** lives mainly in mountainous regions in north-west Nelson, central Westland and east Canterbury. One of the most bad-tempered is the **North Island brown kiwi**, which is found only in the upper two-thirds of the North Island. The **Okarito brown kiwi** is one of the most recent to be identified (in 1993), and lives in lowland forest just north of Franz Josef. Squat and round, the **southern tokoeka** are found in Fiordland and Stewart Island. Finally, the **Haast tokoeka** was also identified (thanks to DNA testing) as a new species in 1993.

Under threat Forests all over the country, which once rang at night to the sound of kiwi calls, are now ominously silent. The little spotted kiwi is now extinct on mainland New Zealand and survives only on Kapiti Island. Other species are also at risk, partly because of the loss of their forest habitat, and extinction looms if effective action is not taken quickly.

The kiwi's main predators today are possums, stoats, ferrets and feral cats, which steal eggs and kill the young. Larger predators include pigs and dogs. In a single incident in 1987 a dog went on the rampage for six weeks in Waitangi State Forest; by the time it was found (and shot) it had killed as many as 500 to 1,000 kiwi.

The Kiwi Recovery Plan Started in 1991, the Kiwi Recovery Plan is a joint initiative by the Department of Conservation and the Royal Forest and Bird Protection Society, funded by the Bank of New Zealand. In an attempt to halt the kiwi's slide towards extinction, the programme carries out research (surprisingly little is known about these birds, owing largely to their nocturnal habits), funds captive breeding programmes and transfers of endangered populations to predator-free off-shore islands, and provides educational material to every school in the country, as well as to farmers, foresters – and dog owners. With luck, the unthinkable can be prevented and the kiwi saved.

Kiwi feather cloaks
According to Maori legend, the kiwi is the oldest of Tanemahuta's bird family; as it was Tane who created most of the natural world, kiwi are in effect our elder siblings, and patrol the forest nightly to protect us. The *kahukiwi* (kiwi feather cloak) is donned as a symbol of high birth and chieftainship at important ceremonies relating to death, marriage and so on. The cloaks, which are nearly always named, are great *tohunga* (treasures), which carry the *wairua* (spirit) of the birds themselves. Nowadays *kahukiwi* are made only from feathers of kiwi which have died naturally or accidentally.

Central Otago and Fiordland

Alexandra 222C3

Like so many other Otago towns, Alexandra was founded in the gold rush days; more recently it has prospered on the surrounding fruit orchards – originally planted to feed the miners. This comfortable, conservative and little-visited town is attempting to put itself on the map with a series of events such as the annual Blossom Festival and the increasingly popular Easter Bunny Shoot. You can also visit wineries and the country's first freshwater crayfish farm; canoeing and other outdoor adventures are centred on the nearby Roxburgh Gorge.

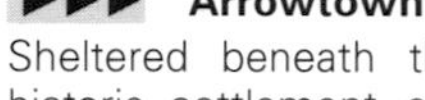

►►► Arrowtown 222C3

Sheltered beneath the towering Crown Range, the historic settlement of Arrowtown is just 20km from Queenstown.

The displays of the spacious and well-laid out **Lakes District Museum►►** (*Open* daily 9–5. *Admission charge* inexpensive) give a good impression of life during the pioneering and gold-rush days when Arrowtown was founded. The town has numerous historic buildings, amongst which are. many picturesque gold-miners' cottages. A pamphlet on *Historic Arrowtown* (available from the Information Centre at the Museum) details some 50 or so listed buildings, which must be a record for a township as small as this one.

A Chinese miner's hut at the Chinese Settlement reconstructed after excavation

The **Chinese Settlement►►** near Bush Creek is an evocative collection of rudimentary huts (reconstructed following an excavation in 1983) which speak volumes about the hardships endured by the Chinese gold seekers. In front of Ah Lum's store stands Ah Wak's lavatory – almost certainly the only 'dunny' in New Zealand to sport a Historic Places plaque!

Chinese miners
Arrowtown's boom years were relatively brief, lasting only from 1861 to 1865, when many gold-diggers left for richer fields in Westland. To bolster the goldfields' economy, Chinese miners were invited over from Australia, and within two years there were 1,200 Chinese in Otago. The Chinese made their living by sifting through the tailings, extracting the finer gold which others had left behind. The fascinating story of the Arrowtown community is told in *The Arrowtown Chinese Settlement*, available from the Museum.

► Cromwell 222C3

A major fruit-growing centre, Cromwell was redeveloped in the 1980s to house the workers on the nearby Clyde Dam, which was completed in 1989. The town lost some of its older streets to the flood waters but gained Lake Dunstan. The story of the dam, and of Cromwell's early days as a gold mining town, is told in the well-presented displays at the **Information Centre and Museum►►** (*Open* daily 10–4. *Admission charge* donation) which is in the middle of the pedestrianised town centre.

Before the lake waters rose, many historic buildings were salvaged, and a dozen or more have been reconstructed on the lakeshore as **Old Cromwell Town►►**: several craft workers have taken up residence and you can also take a **guided tour** (tel: 03 4450 633. *Admission free*) around the old buildings.

▶▶▶ Fiordland National Park *222B3*

New Zealand's largest national park, covering some 12,000 sq km in the remote south-western corner of the South Island, Fiordland is a rugged wilderness where dramatic coastal fiords allow the Tasman Sea to penetrate deep into the bush-clad hills and mountains. The majestic glacial lakes of **Te Anau▶▶▶** and **Manapouri▶▶** are the largest of scores of inland lakes.

The most accessible of the 14 fiords in the park is **Milford Sound▶▶▶**, which is surrounded by steep, forest-clad cliffs riven with waterfalls dropping vertically into the sea. Milford Sound has the highest average rainfall in the country, and it is after heavy rains that these falls are at their most spectacular. Rising sheer from the sea on the south side of the sound, dominating the inlet, is the 1,683m high pinnacle of Mitre Peak.

There are three ways to reach Milford Sound: on foot, by road, or by plane. The **Milford Track** from Lake Te Anau is one of the most popular in the country, and needs to be booked months in advance at peak times. The road route (119 km from Te Anau) is a spectacular drive. Flights operate from Te Anau and Queenstown, landing at the tiny Milford Sound airstrip. From Milford, launch cruises depart regularly for tours with commentary.

The next most frequently visited fiord is **Doubtful Sound▶▶▶** (see pages 246–7). **Dusky Sound** and **Preservation Inlet** both require a five to seven-day cruise.

Tour times
Doubtful Sound tours depart from Manapouri wharf daily at 9.30am for the Long Trip, which lasts eight hours. Connecting coaches leave Te Anau at 8.45am and Queenstown at 7.15am (from Queenstown the tour makes a very long day, returning at around 8pm). You can also take a Short Trip, which cuts short the cruise down Doubtful Sound and just visits Hall Arm within the fiord. Contact: Fiordland Travel, Lakefront, Te Anau (tel: 03 249 7419); Steamer Wharf, Queenstown (tel: 03 442 7500).

The magnificent glaciated landscape of Doubtful Sound in the Fiordland National Park

Steamer Wharf Village on the edge of Lake Wakatipu

▶▶▶ Queenstown *222C3*

The South Island's liveliest tourist centre, Queenstown is a year-round resort, with skiing in the nearby Coronet Peak and Remarkables ranges during the winter months, and a whole host of summer activities focusing on the mountains, lakes and rivers of Central Otago.

The first Maori settled here over 1,000 years ago, but once the moa they hunted were gone, so too were the Maori, who moved back to coastal encampments. Later Maori passed through in search of greenstone in Westland, following the ancient 'greenstone route' from the head of Lake Wakatipu across the Hollyford Valley to the sea. When the explorer Nathaniel Chambers sighted the lake from the heights of the Remarkables in 1853, the area was deserted. In 1859, William Gilbert Rees explored the lake and laid his claim to a run on its eastern shores, thus deciding the future site of Queenstown.

During the 1860s, gold strikes in nearby Arrowtown opened up the area to a huge influx of prospectors. Queenstown quickly became a major supply depot for the miners, with sailing boats and paddle-steamers plying the lake to bring in supplies, and to ship the gold out via Kingston, at the south end of Lake Wakatipu. It was the biggest gold rush the country had ever seen (one pair of prospectors, trying to rescue their dog from the river, found over 11kg of gold in rock crevices in a single day), and the Shotover River became known as 'the richest river in the world'.

By the turn of the century the gold had started to peter out, and a new influx of visitors started. The paddle-steamers were put to good use ferrying sightseers around the lake, and buggy rides to Skippers Canyon to see the miners at work were a popular attraction. A Scotsman, Donald Sutherland, built the first hotel in

Lake cruises
The TSS *Earnslaw* departs for up to six cruises daily (9am, 12.30pm, 2pm, 5.30pm, 7.30pm and 9.30pm), bookings through agencies or Fiordland Travel, tel: 03 442 7500. You can also cruise the lake on board the *City of Dunedin* (which was one of the few competitors to complete the course in the 1982 Round the World Race), helping crew or taking the helm if you wish (sailings four times daily, tel: 03 442 7390). For a bird's eye view 76m above the surface, you can parafly behind a boat, taking off from a floating flight deck so that you don't get wet (Paraflights NZ, tel: 03 442 8507).

Milford Sound, and travellers journeyed by boat and overland to see the remarkable Sutherland Falls and the awe-inspiring fiord itself. Now Queenstown is a tourist honeypot, receiving just under half a million visitors annually.

At the heart of the town are the pedestrianised streets of the Mall and Church Street, running down to the lake's edge and parallel to Shotover Street, where you will find the Visitor Information Centre, Department of Conservation Visitor Centre and booking offices for many of the activity operators. At the end of Shotover Street is the new Steamer Wharf Village, with up-market boutiques, wine bars and restaurants.

Steamer Wharf is the departure point for lake trips aboard the historic TSS *Earnslaw*, a vintage steamship which was built in Dunedin and then completely dismantled before being taken to Kingston by rail and reassembled. Launched in 1912, it is the last of the many steamships which once plied the lake, and still chugs across the waters at a rate of 13 knots, burning a ton of coal every hour. Its destination is **Walter Peak Farm,** founded in the 1860s, and one of the oldest sheep and cattle stations in the country, where sheep-shearing and other agricultural demonstrations are given before morning or afternoon tea in the old homestead.

For a view of what happens beneath the lake's waters, the **Underwater World Aquarium** on the main jetty (*Open* daily 9–5.30. *Admission charge* inexpensive) has large viewing windows five metres down where rainbow and brown trout and long-finned eels come close to the glass to be fed – with the country's only diving duck, the scaup duck, popping down amongst them.

The **Skyline Gondola▶▶▶** (*Open* daily 10–10. *Admission charge* moderate) rides up 450m from the base station at the end of Brecon Street to a viewing complex at the top, with a restaurant, café, viewing platform and a small cinema (screening daily on the hour 10am–8pm. *Admission charge* moderate). From here there are magnificent views of the town and the lake, set against a splendid backdrop of the Remarkables.

Also on Brecon Street is a **Motor Museum▶** (*Open* daily 9–5.30. *Admission charge* moderate), packed with

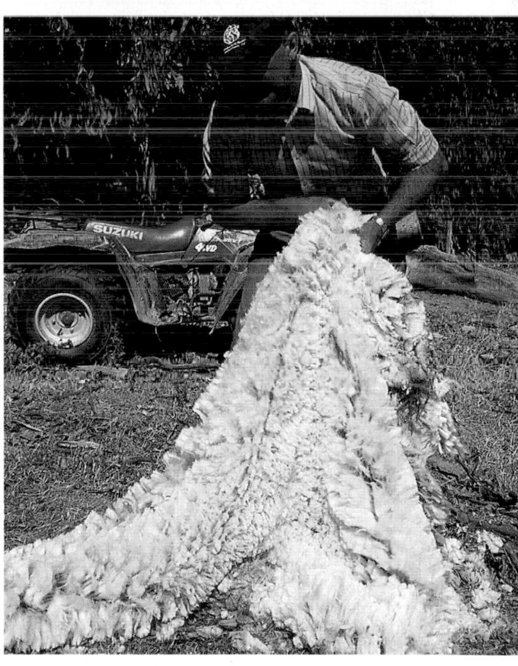

The TSS Earnslaw *(top) steams across to Walter Peak Farm for sheep-shearing demonstrations (above)*

'marvellous machines and motoring memorabilia'. Behind it, the **Kiwi and Birdlife Park**►► (*Open* 9–late in summer, 9–5 in winter. *Admission charge* moderate) has several aviaries with endangered species, waterfowl, a native bush area and a nocturnal kiwi house.

One of the most peaceful areas on the lakeside is the **Queenstown Gardens**, founded in 1867 on a small promontory jutting out into the lake. At the entrance to the gardens, look out for the **Williams Cottage**, one of the last remaining early buildings in Queenstown. Built in 1866–7 and currently undergoing restoration, it will eventually open as a cottage museum. Look out too for **Eichardt's Tavern** (The Mall) which has a long and colourful history and is still one of the town's most popular watering holes. The **Old Stone Library** on Ballarat Street dates back to the 1870s, and has two giant sequoia trees outside. Opposite is a pleasant park with a stream crossed by a stone humpback bridge.

Horseriding amidst the glorious scenery of Lake Wakatipu

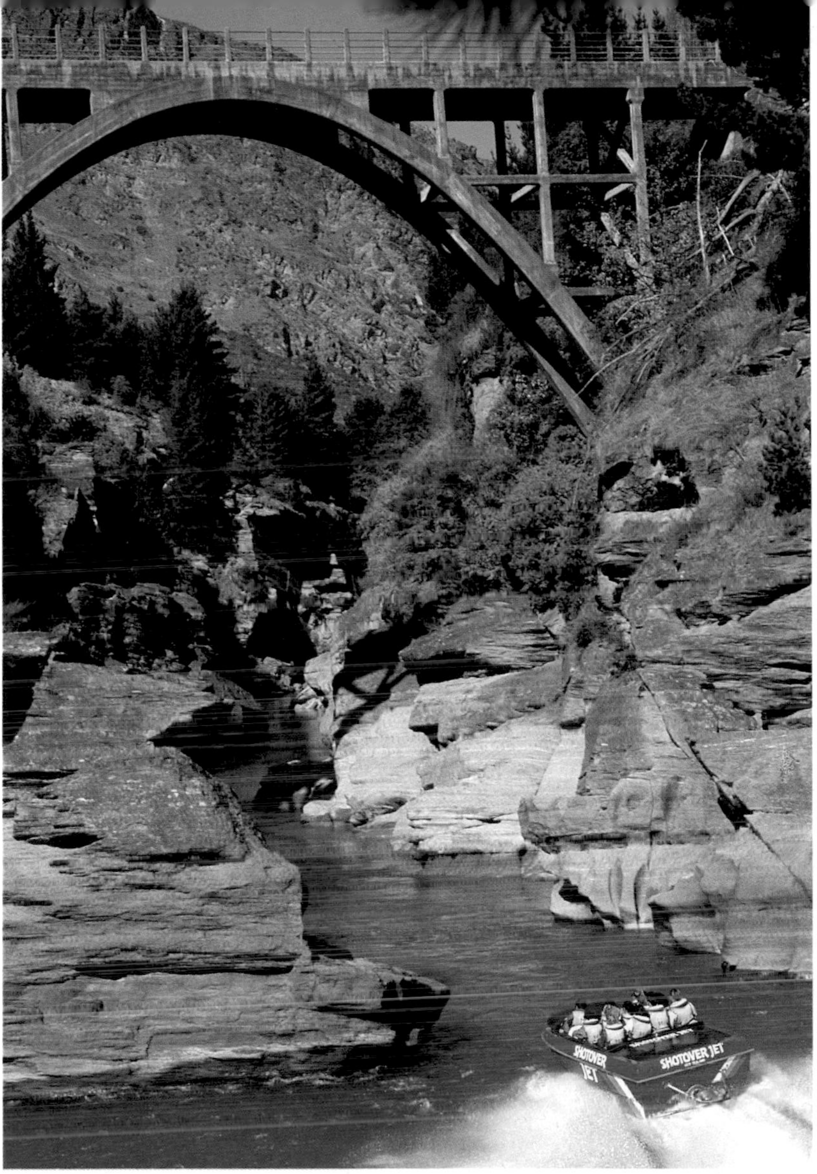

The Shotover jet powers up and down the river canyon to the north of Queenstown

Queenstown environs

The number of adventure activities on offer in Queenstown is phenomenal, with fierce competition to provide yet more thrills and spills on the surrounding lakes, rivers and mountains. Many of these activities are perfectly well suited to anyone of whatever age, however unfit they might be. One of the most popular is **jet-boating** with around ten operators offering a choice of different trips. The narrow chasms and shallow rapids on the lower reaches of the **Shotover River** provide an exciting ride, as does the **Kawarau River** – both within a short minibus ride of Queenstown. But to experience the true potential of a jet-boat (see pages 210–11), consider a half-day safari across the top of Lake Wakatipu and up the broad expanses of the

'Black singlet' literature
As well as producing outstanding contemporary fiction by writers such as Keri Hulme, Patricia Grace, Alan Duff and Witi Ihimaera, New Zealand also has a tradition of honest, down-to-earth fiction about bush life, known as 'black singlet' literature. Its champion exponent is Barry Crump, whose entertaining tales started in 1960 with *A Good Keen Man*. Other 'black singlet' writings are perhaps of more esoteric interest: *New Zealand Farm* and *Station Verse*, for instance, include poems with such alluring titles as 'Shorn Sheep', 'Wet Sheep' and 'Frozen Lamb'.

Dart River▶▶ – a longer trip but well worth it for the wilderness scenery of the Dart River Valley.

The Kawarau and Shotover Rivers are equally popular for rafting. All trips involve a pre-departure briefing, full safety gear and the services of qualified guides; thereafter, calm periods drifting down river are interspersed with the thrills of plunging over seething rapids. Other ways to get wet include kayaking, white-water sledging and river surfing.

Queenstown is the home of commercial bungee-jumping, and nearly all the bungee sites have observation platforms which give good vantage points for spectators. The original bungee jump is the 43m drop from the **Kawarau Suspension Bridge**, 23km east from Queenstown along SH6. The most recent area to open up is Skippers Canyon (see below), where there is a spectacular 72m drop from the Skippers Canyon Bridge above a narrow gorge, and an even more heart-stopping 102m drop from the Pipeline Bungee further downstream.

Alternative ways to take to the air above Queenstown include parapenting, tandem hang-gliding, glider flying, helicopter sightseeing, paragliding, tandem parachuting and biplane rides.

The historic and fascinating **Skippers Canyon▶▶▶**, upstream on the Shotover River, was one of the main gold rush areas in the last century. A levy on gold found here was used to build the tortuous road (it took eight years to complete) up through the canyon. Bumpy and pot-holed, with sheer drops of 120m down to the river below in some places, this road is definitely not recommended as a self-drive route (indeed, signs at the entrance advise that hire-car insurance is invalid here). Besides the dramatic scenery of the canyon itself, there are also many relics of goldmining days and, at the head of the canyon, the remains of the old Skippers township, with a restored schoolhouse, homestead and other dwellings. Options on these safaris include jet-boat or helicopter rides or mountain-biking back down the canyon to base.

Take a tour down dramatic Skippers Canyon but take turns to drive

In winter, skiing is the activity, with **Coronet Peak** considered one of the country's premier ski areas. Regular shuttle buses make the 18km journey from the town centre, with a series of chair-lifts and T-bars rising from the base station to the top of the runs at 1,585m and 1,620m. There is good skiing here for all levels of ability, with snowmaking equipment ensuring a long season (from mid-June to October). The **Remarkables** are also a top-rated ski area with runs for all abilities.

The art of bungee

■ It is a bizarre idea, jumping from a great height with nothing but a huge elastic band tied to your ankles... Welcome to the world of bungee-jumping, a typically Kiwi phenomenon. ■

Polynesian origins Bungee-jumping is not a new sport: for many centuries leaping from a tall tower has formed part of the initiation ceremonies to manhood in Vanuatu. Young men traditionally plunge headlong from rickety bamboo structures, only to be pulled up short – inches from the ground – by the stout vines attached firmly to their feet.

Inspired by this example, New Zealander Alan John Hackett set out to devise a safe, controlled method of jumping using the same principles. Experimenting with latex rubber and a parachute harness, he and his companions started leaping off New Zealand's bridges, including the Auckland Harbour Bridge. In 1987 Hackett captured the world's attention by leaping off the Eiffel Tower, and went on to set up a bungee empire with outposts in many parts of the globe.

Way to go – but don't forget to empty your pockets

The home of bungee The world's first professional bungee jump operation was opened by Hackett in 1988 on the Kawarau Bridge, 43m above the Kawarau River just to the east of Queenstown. Bungee-jumping has since become a Kiwi export to Australia, Indonesia, the UK, the USA and France.

Who can do it? All it takes is willpower. The oldest bungee-jumper so far was a 90-year-old in Normandy. Anyone from the age of 13 upwards is eligible (though 13 to 16 year olds require parental supervision), and anyone over 60 goes free. At one stage, Hackett offered free jumps to anyone who went nude: demand was so great that the offer had to be discontinued!

Tour Doubtful Sound

Tours to Doubtful Sound (pictured on page 239) first cross the vast expanse of Lake Manapouri

This boat and coach tour (see panel page 239) encompasses not only Doubtful Sound but also the island-studded waters of Lake Manapouri, the impressive Manapouri power station, and the rainforests of Wilmot Pass. An all-day trip, it departs from Queenstown, Te Anau or Manapouri.

From Manapouri wharf your first boat ride takes you out of the Pearl Harbour Inlet and past Stoney Point Light on to the broad expanses of **Lake Manapouri►►.** As you pass the Lake islands, you get a fine view of the Hunter Mountains rising up to 1,768m on the south bank, with the impressive peaks of the Kepler Range on the north shore. Halfway across, the boat skirts Pomona Island, the largest on the lake; the waters beneath the hull are at their deepest (444m) here.

Disembarking at the wharf at the end of West Arm, you transfer to a coach for the tour of the **Manapouri Power Station►►.** Even for people who are not technically minded, this visit is of great interest: above ground, only the transmission lines and a control centre are visible, but once you have descended the 2km spiral access tunnel the full extent of this engineering achievement becomes apparent. The machine hall and its seven humming turbine generators are a testament both to the dedication of the builders and to the power of the water, which flows through at a constant rate to generate around ten per cent of the country's electricity requirements.

Emerging into daylight once more, you continue over the **Wilmot Pass Road▶**. Constructed to provide access for heavy equipment to the power station, this 22km-long road took two and a half years to build and was at the time the most expensive road ever to be built in New Zealand. Today it serves as the only land access to Doubtful Sound, traversing a range of forest types with several spectacular waterfalls en route; there is a brief stop to admire the **Moss Gardens**, where some of the 500 varieties of moss and lichen found in Fiordland can be appreciated at close quarters.

The tour continues down one of the country's steepest roads (with a gradient of 1 in 5) to arrive at Deep Cove, where the tailrace, some 10km long and tunnelled through the heart of the mountains, emerges from the power station. Here, you embark on a catamaran for the trip down the magnificent **Doubtful Sound▶▶▶**.

Captain James Cook sighted the entrance to Doubtful Sound in 1770, but refused to enter it as he believed that he would only get out again with a (rare) east wind. It was left to a Spanish scientific expedition, led by Alessandro Malaspina, to explore the inlet fully in 1793. During the early 19th century the area was a favourite haunt of sealers and whalers, but once these animals had been depleted (which happened within the space of 20 years), Doubtful Sound was left in peace for a hundred years or more.

As you cruise down this superb fiord, various features become apparent: hanging valleys – the remnants of tributary glaciers – are one of the most obvious, and numerous waterfalls tumble down the sheer rock faces, with rainbows often adding to the enchantment of the magical scenery. The boat noses in close enough for passengers to capture a cup of pure drinking water from the mountain-fed falls, and to appreciate the extraordinarily tenacious hold of the moss, plants and trees which intertwine their roots on the sheer rock surfaces.

At Malaspina Reach, in the first section of the Sound, a resident pod of bottlenose dolphins frequently frolics on the bow wave; beyond, where the turbulent Tasman Sea rolls in towards the coast, fur seals – now returning after a long absence – bask on the rocks. At Shelter Island, at the limits of the Sound, the rare Fiordland crested penguin can be seen at close quarters in the summer months.

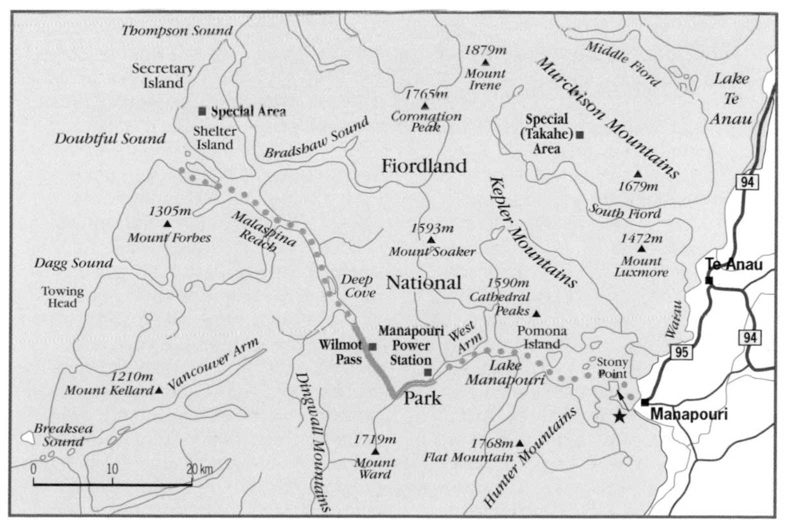

Te Anau

222B3

Spreading across the eastern shoreline of Lake Te Anau, the township of Te Anau is the main departure point for tours into the wilds of Fiordland: the dense rainforests which mark the boundary of New Zealand's largest national park cloak the western shores of the lake, rising up into the dramatic mountains beyond.

A floatplane on the shores of Lake Te Anau

Although for most people Te Anau is merely a transit stop, there are a number of activities locally, should you have a day or half day to spare. Top of the list of priorities should be a tour of the remarkable **Te Ana-au Caves▶▶▶** at the base of the Murchison Mountains, reached by boat across the lake (tours take two and a half hours and depart up to five times daily, depending on the season; tel: 03 249 7419. *Admission charge* moderate).

The Te Ana-au caves are relatively young on the geological time-scale, dating back a mere 15,000 years, and for this reason they lack the delicate limestone stalactites and stalagmites found in other cave systems. Instead they are a fine example of a 'living cave', where the stream that originally formed them (in this case the Tunnel Burn) is still actively eroding the rock, cascading through and chiselling away at a rate of around 1 cubic metre every 100 years.

The caves featured in Maori legends as Te-Ana-hinatore ('the cave of phosphorescence') and, later, as Te Ana-au ('the cave of rushing waters') but remained unknown to Europeans until rediscovered by local explorer Lawson

Tranquil Lake Wanaka, backed by the peaks of Mount Aspiring National Park

Burrows in 1948. Once inside the caves, walkways and two short boat journeys along the Tunnel Burn take you past whirlpools and underground waterfalls to the inner depths, where there is an enchanting glow-worm grotto, with the glow-worms' sticky threads twinkling in the silent darkness of the ledges and ceilings above.

There are several ways of exploring the lake itself (the country's second largest after Lake Taupo): by kayak, on a beautiful old handcrafted gaff ketch (the *Little Ship Manuska*), or by floatplane from the wharf. There are also a number of lakeside walks (ranging from 15 minutes to eight hours).

The Department of Conservation Visitor Centre (*Open* daily 8–6) on the southern edge of Te Anau has information on local walks and long-distance tracks; they also screen an audio-visual show (on the hour and half hour. *Admission charge* inexpensive) describing the formation of Fiordland and the flora and fauna of the area, and the first floor houses a small museum (*Admission free*) with displays on early mining and whaling along the coast. Relics of some of the many ships which have come to grief here include a cannon from New Zealand's first ever shipwreck, the *Endeavour*, which ran aground in Dusky Sound in 1795.

Continue 1km past the DoC Centre and you will come to the **Te Anau Wildlife Centre▶** (*Open* 24 hours. *Admission free*), one of the very few places in New Zealand where you can see the rare takahe (see panel page 250). Other enclosures house red deer, parrots, parakeets, morepork and lizards.

▶▶▶ Wanaka *222C3*

A peaceful township surrounded by mountains, Wanaka is tucked into the southern end of Lake Wanaka. It could be an embryonic Queenstown, but locals are keen to emphasise the differences: it is unspoiled, uncommercialised and not overcrowded, and there is no pressure to do anything more strenuous here than put your feet up and enjoy a good book for a few days. This relaxed,

Wings over Wanaka
Wanaka airport has developed into something of a focal point for aviation buffs, with the Fighter Pilots Museum now organising the biennial 'War Birds Over Wanaka' show with dozens of vintage, veteran and classic aircraft taking to the skies. At any time you can go flying in a number of unusual or old aircraft, such as a de Havilland Dominie biplane, an open-cockpit Tiger Moth biplane, or a Pitts Special stunt plane (loop the loop, barrel rolls and inverted flight obligatory). Contact: Biplane Adventures (tel: 03 443 1000).

An unusual island
Lake Wanaka has the unusual attribute of an island – Mou Waho – with a lake in the middle of it – or, as they put it here, a lake in the middle of an island in the middle of a lake in the middle of an island! The largest of the Wanaka islands, Mou Waho is 16km from the town. The spectacular Arethusa Pool lies in a rock cradle within walking distance of the landing point.

The takahe
Once thought to be extinct, the takahe (*Notornis mantelli*) was rediscovered in the Murchison Mountains in 1948 by a local doctor, Geoffrey Orbell; it had not been sighted since the previous century, and even then only rarely. Following this discovery, a huge tract covering 530 sq km of the mountains was declared a 'Special Area' to protect this flightless bird, about the size of a chicken, which lives for most of the year on alpine tussock grasslands. Currently there are only 120 takahe still in the wild, and ways are now being sought to prevent them from becoming extinct – including removing their eggs for artificial rearing.

pleasant resort remains very 'Kiwi' in character: the majority of visitors are summer campers who come to swim, fish and boat on the lake or walk in the nearby **Mount Aspiring National Park**, whose headquarters are here. In the winter, skiers head for the renowned **Cardrona** and **Treble Cone skifields**.

The lake is fringed by a broad, grassy park lined with poplars and willows, with barbecue areas beside the beach. Good day walks in the vicinity include the popular **Diamond Lake–Rocky Mountain walking track**, which takes about two and a half hours and is considered one of the South Island's most stunning half-day walks.

Lake Wanaka is the country's fourth largest lake, and the numerous ways of exploring it include trips on the country's only commercial hovercraft, or by kayak, jet-boat, catamaran or power boat.

On the outskirts of Wanaka, **Puzzling World▶▶** (*Open* 8.30–5.30. *Admission charge* inexpensive) was the originator of the 'maze craze' which saw many imitators all over New Zealand. As well as the 1.5km long, three-dimensional maze, it also has a hologram gallery and a new Tilted House which is truly disorientating. At Wanaka airfield the **NZ Fighter Pilots Museum** (*Open* daily 9.30–4. *Admission charge* moderate) features famous planes from both world wars, as well as a re-created briefing room (complete with authentic film footage) and biographical displays on the country's fighter aces.

The brilliantly hued takahe

TRAVEL FACTS

By air
The majority of overseas visitors arrive in New Zealand at **Auckland International Airport**, which handles more than 20 international airlines. The national airline, Air New Zealand, has an enviable reputation worldwide and flies direct from Los Angeles, Honolulu, Tokyo, Hong Kong, Singapore, Bangkok, Australia, Pacific Island, Taiwan and South Korea.

Christchurch airport has direct flights from Singapore, Tokyo, Brisbane, Sydney, Melbourne and Hobart. Because of restricted runway length, the only direct flights to **Wellington** are from Australia, Fiji and Pacific Island .

If you are flying from the USA or Europe, the long flight times (23 hours from London and 19 hours from New York, for instance) mean that it makes sense to break your journey along the way, either in South-East Asia or in the Pacific. Air New Zealand offers some enticing options under their Coral Route programme, with possible stopovers in Fiji, French Polynesia, the Cook Islands, Tonga, Western Samoa and Hawaii. Each additional stopover (with unlimited stay) costs around NZ$100.

Auckland Airport (AKL) has separate terminals for international, Ansett and Air New Zealand domestic flights, with a shuttle bus operating between the three. Banking and exchange facilities are available for all international arrivals and departures. There are direct line (free) telephones in the welcoming halls at both terminals for making hotel or motel reservations, and Information Centres in each terminal can help with bookings for accommodation, onward travel arrangements and other services. Luggage storage facilities are available. Both terminals are equipped with elevators and disabled toilet facilities.

The airport is 22km from downtown Auckland, with a taxi fare of around NZ$40 one way in 1996. Several private operators offer door-to-door shuttle services from both terminals to downtown hotels, motels or hostels: they operate on a regular circuit but will drop you off at any downtown address on request. The fare is NZ$10–12 per person one way.

Both Wellington and Christchurch airports have similar facilities, including currency exchange and information desks. Wellington airport is 8km from downtown, with a taxi fare of around NZ$15 and a shuttle bus fare of NZ$8. Christchurch airport is 10km from the city centre, with a taxi fare of around NZ$15–20 and a shuttle bus fare of NZ$5.

Customs Arriving passengers are entitled to bring in 200 cigarettes, 200g of tobacco or 50 cigars, or a mixture of all three weighing not more than 250g. Alcohol allowances are 4.5 litres of wine (equivalent to six 750ml bottles), and one 1125ml bottle of spirits or liqueur. Apart from personal effects, goods up to a total of NZ$700 in value may be imported free of tax.

Note that New Zealand airports all have duty-free arrivals shops, so that you do not have to haul your duty-free purchases halfway around the world from your departure point. Prices are competitive and they carry a wide range of stock.

There are restrictions on the import of certain animal and plant materials (including some foodstuffs), designed to keep the country free of animal and plant diseases. You will be asked to fill out a declaration on arrival stating whether you have any plant or animal materials or foodstuffs in your baggage. If you have recently visited a farm you might well benefit from a free shoe shine in order to avoid importing soil-borne diseases.

There are no exchange controls or restrictions on the import or export of currency. Hunting rifles may be imported, although you will need to obtain a firearms permit on arrival. The import of narcotics is prohibited.

Vaccinations No vaccination certificates are required.

Visas Many nationals can enter New Zealand for up to six months without requiring a visa. You will need to be in possession of a passport valid for at least three months beyond the date when you intend to leave the country, a fully paid onward or return ticket and sufficient funds to support yourself during your stay. Visas are required if you intend to work, study or seek medical treatment or if you are being sponsored by a friend, relative or business organisation during your stay. Details are available from the Immigration Service at your nearest diplomatic or consular office.

Insurance A comprehensive personal travel insurance policy is recommended, covering medical expenses, loss of luggage or money, cancellation of your holiday or flight, delayed departure and so forth. If you are planning to take part in any adventure sports (such as scuba-diving, skiing, white-water rafting or bungee-jumping) make sure that you are covered in case of accidents.

Departing There is an airport departure tax of NZ$20 payable on all international flights.

Shuttle buses run between the airport and central Auckland

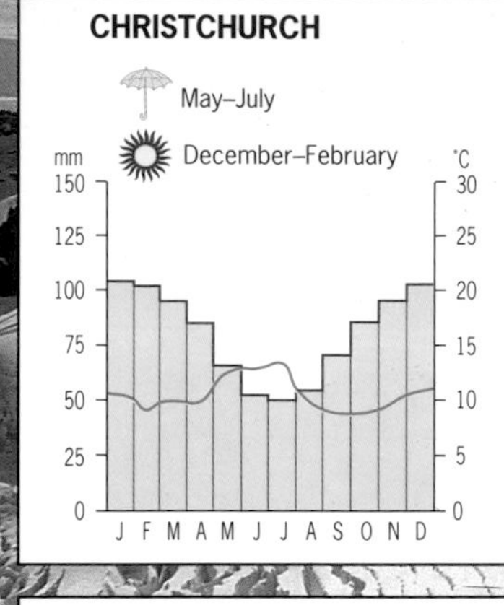

AUCKLAND

May–July

December–March

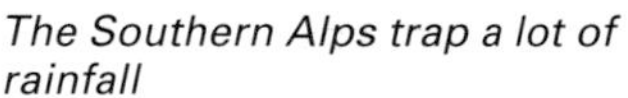
The Southern Alps trap a lot of rainfall

Climate and when to go
The seasons in New Zealand are the reverse of those in the northern hemisphere, with spring from September to November, summer from December to February/March, autumn from March to May, and winter from June to August.

Being nearer to the equator, the North Island has the warmer climate, often described as 'Mediterranean', with short, mild winters and long, warm, summers. Northland ('the winterless north') and the Bay of Islands experience some of the highest summer temperatures in the North Island, with Auckland not far behind. The climate in the South Island is more variable, with the coldest winters and hottest summers usually being found in Central Otago.

New Zealand lies across the 'Roaring Forties' latitudes, and prevailing winds are therefore from the west. In general, the western areas receive higher rainfall, and conversely many eastern areas can have drought conditions in the summer months; the most extensive vineyards and sheep stations are on the eastern sides of the islands.

In the South Island, the Southern Alps act as a natural barrier to the westerly winds, causing high rainfall on the West Coast. The variation in rainfall either side of this north–south mountainous spine is extreme, with annual averages of 6,000mm on the West Coast compared to just over 300mm in Central Otago.

In the North Island east–west variations are less marked, with the annual average rainfall of 1,300mm being fairly evenly spread across the island. Snow falls on the peaks of Mount Egmont and Tongariro National Parks in the winter months, but it is not nearly as reliable as the snowfalls in the Southern Alps, so if you are planning to ski in winter, head for the South Island.

The annual sunshine hours are higher in Central North Island (2,100) than in the north or south (1,900), and in the north of the South Island (2,400), averaging 1,700 elsewhere. Because of New Zealand's unpolluted atmosphere, ultra-violet radiation is high, and care must be taken to avoid sunburn (see page 263).

Holidays
Kiwis are great travellers (both at home and abroad), and many families visit resorts or explore the countryside during the school holidays. Pre-booking of accommodation during these periods is almost essential in the more popular resort areas, unless you are prepared to take pot luck or continue to somewhere less crowded. The worst period is during the summer holidays from mid-December to the end of January, which coincides with the peak tourist season. Other school holidays are in May, July and August. Accommodation can be hard to find in resort areas on national holidays.

Most businesses (apart from those related to tourism) and all banks are closed on public holidays, but increasing numbers of shops are open. Museums and tourist attractions are open on nearly all holidays except Christmas Day and Boxing Day.

- New Year's Holiday
  1 and 2 January
- Waitangi Day
  6 February
- Easter
  March/April
- Anzac Day
  25 April
- Queen's Birthday
  First Monday in June
- Labour Day
  Fourth Monday in October
- Christmas
  25 and 26 December

Time differences
With the International Date Line just 300km to the east of the Chatham Islands, New Zealand is one of the first countries in the world to witness the start of the new day. Local time is 12 hours ahead of Greenwich Mean Time (GMT), 2–4 hours ahead of Australia, 17–22 hours ahead of the USA, 15–20 hours ahead of Canada, and 4 hours ahead of Hong Kong. New Zealand Daylight Saving Time (summer time) runs from 2am on the first Sunday in October to 2am on the third Sunday in March: clocks are set an hour forward.

Money matters
The New Zealand dollar (NZ$) is divided into 100 cents, with notes in denominations of $5, $10, $20, $50 and $100, and coins of 5c, 10c, 20c, 50c, $1 and $2.

There are no restrictions on the import or export of foreign currency in any form. Travellers cheques can be changed at *bureaux de change*, banks and hotels, and in large stores in resorts and large cities. All international credit cards (American Express, Diners' Club, JCB, Visa and MasterCard) are generally accepted. Automatic Teller Machines (ATMs) are widely available and can be used to obtain cash on a card/PIN number system. EFTPOS (Electronic Funds Transfer at Point of Sale) is also increasingly common.

Driving
New Zealand is ideally suited to exploring by car, with a good road network offering safe, easy driving. Driving is on the left and the wearing of seatbelts is compulsory. Speed limits are generally 100kph on the open road and motorways, 50kph in urban areas, but other limits may be indicated. Motorways are usually only to be found on the approaches to larger cities.

Most rural roads are well maintained, although sometimes narrow – often narrowing further on the approach to river bridges, many of which are one-lane (with signs indicating priorities). Many back country roads are unsealed (metaled gravel), and indeed until recently there was a section of major highway through the Waipoua Kauri Forest which was also unsealed: this was finally sealed over in 1995, with considerable ingenuity being employed to avoid damaging the roots of the mighty kauri trees.

Unsealed roads have their own particular hazards (including large grading machines which seem to lurk around corners), and require care: restrictions may apply to some unsealed roads if you are hiring a car.

Driving documents
Drivers must have a current UK, USA, International or other approved overseas licence. No further documentation is necessary.

Car hire
There are numerous car-hire companies operating in major cities and resorts, with competition ensuring rental rates are reasonable, particularly for long-term rentals (one month or more). You must be over

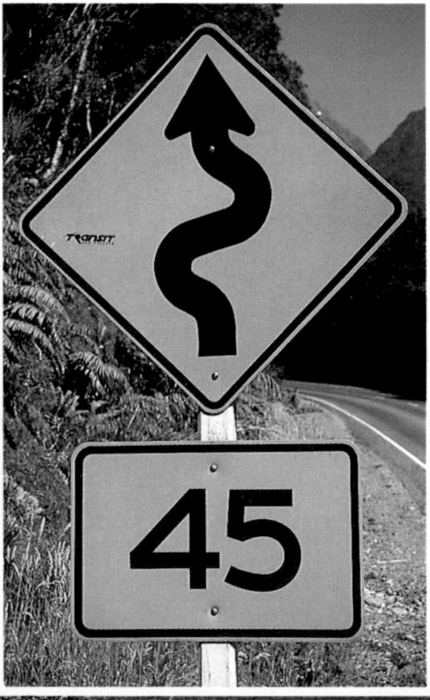

Driving in New Zealand is easy, even in a campervan

21 years of age to hire a car or campervan, and some companies insist on a minimum age of 25 unless the hire fee is pre-paid from overseas. Insurance is not compulsory, and is usually quoted on top of the hire cost.

Campervans are popular in New Zealand and represent an economical and flexible means of exploring the country. With a campervan you are by no means limited to camp grounds, although there are many excellent camp grounds for overnight stops.

All the major agencies are represented in New Zealand, and cars can also be booked through their offices overseas. Maui Tours are the biggest agency for campervans.

Many companies do not allow rental cars to travel between the North and South Islands, and in any case it can work out cheaper to turn your car in before crossing on the ferry, and then pick up another car at the depot on the other side. The rental companies can organise this, but you will have to carry all your luggage across with you. Most companies can also arrange one-way rentals if, for instance, you wanted to drive from Auckland southwards and then return by plane from Christchurch or elsewhere.

Car hire from the major firms costs from around NZ$90 per day. Some of the best deals are available through smaller independents such as Ace Tourist Rentals, Trusty Rentals and Pegasus Rentals: a small four-door saloon could be hired for as little as NZ$35 per day in 1996, with some firms offering even lower prices for hire periods over one month. These prices are inclusive of Goods and Services Tax (GST), insurance and unlimited mileage, and represent a real bargain.

Standard campervans cost from NZ$144 per day for a two-person van, rising to around NZ$230 per day for a four to six person van in high season. Again, there are bargains to be had with the smaller companies; in 1996 it was possible to hire a two-berth van from NZ$70 per day (low season) to NZ$99 (high season), inclusive of unlimited mileage, GST and insurance.

Ace Tourist Rentals, 39-43 The Strand, Parnell, Auckland tel: 09 303 3112; freephone: 0800 502 277; fax: 09 309 2258.
Avis, 666 Great South Road, Penrose, Auckland tel: 09 525 1982; fax: 09 525 0309
Budget, 83 Beach Road, Auckland tel: 09 309 6739; freephone: 0800 652 227
Hertz, 154 Victoria Street West, Auckland tel: 09 309 0989.
Maui Tours, Private Bag, Auckland tel: 09 275 3013; freephone: 0800 651 080; fax: 09 275 9690
Pegasus Rentals, corner Quay Street/Britomast Place, Auckland tel: 09 358 5757; fax: 09 373 5727.
Trusty Rentals, 205 Lichfield Street, Christchurch tel: 03 366 6329; fax: 03 366 6382.

Car breakdown

Most rental companies include a free breakdown service as part of the hire package. Automobile Association members receive free reciprocal membership of the New Zealand AA, including breakdown assistance, the provision of maps, touring advice and accommodation guides. Further details from the New Zealand Automobile Association, P O Box 5, Auckland, tel: 09 377 4660; fax: 09 309 4563.

Car-sharing

A concept usually associated with urban commuters elsewhere in the world, car-sharing in New Zealand also operates for country-wide rides. Mostly suited to young people with flexible itineraries, it is one way of cutting costs and sharing the enjoyment of the journey without the risks of hitch-hiking. Car-sharing is organised by Travelpool, PO Box47–292, Auckland, tel: 09 307 0001.

There are plenty of coach tours covering the country

Air travel
The domestic airlines are Air New Zealand and Ansett New Zealand, with an extensive network of reasonably economical scheduled services to and from most domestic destinations. The services of Air New Zealand National and Air New Zealand Link (Eagle Airways, Air Nelson, and Mount Cook Airline) are grouped together into one reservation system offering more than 460 flights a day to some 31 domestic destinations. There are also several smaller commuter services, and light planes and helicopters can be chartered.

Airpasses and discounts Alongside the standard Business Class and Economy fares, Air New Zealand offers various discounted fares, most of which involve booking restrictions; these include '10-OFF' fares, Thrifty Fares and Super Thrifty Fares. Overseas visitors can take advantage of the Explore New Zealand Airpass, which must be bought outside New Zealand and then used on a coupon basis (one flight sector per coupon, with prices starting from NZ$450 for three coupons) once in the country. Ansett New Zealand also have a G'day Pass, and Mount Cook Airline offers a Kiwi Air Pass.

Coach travel
All towns, cities and resorts are connected by an extensive coach network, which provides a comfortable and economical means of travelling the country. The main operators are InterCity, Newmans and Mount Cook Landline. InterCity have the most extensive network. For most destinations there are several daily departures, and except during holiday periods it is not usually necessary to book your seat more than a couple of days ahead.

All the operators offer various discounts or coach passes, which makes this an even more economical way to travel. InterCity's 3-in-1 Travelpass, for instance, in 1996 offered unlimited travel throughout the country by coach, ferry or rail for eight days of travel within a three week period at a cost of around NZ$470, 15 days of travel within a five week period for NZ$590, and 22 days over eight weeks for NZ$690. A 4-in-1 Pass, which includes one air sector, can only be purchased overseas. Other passes can either be bought overseas or when you arrive in the country.

Mount Cook Landline has a Kiwi Coach Pass which is valid for all their services plus selected routes of affiliated operators (such as Newmans, InterCity and Northliner), and which also includes a one-way flight sector on Air New Zealand Link across Cook Strait between Wellington and Blenheim or Nelson. The cost in 1996 was NZ$335 for seven days' travel within a 30-day period, rising to NZ$699 for 33 days' travel within 90 days (there are also options for 10, 15, and 25 days of travel). These passes can also be bought in advance from overseas travel agents or on arrival in New Zealand.

Newmans have a slightly different system, with a 14-day Auckland–Wellington (or vice versa) pass for NZ$99.

Other discounts available include the Youth Hostel Association Travel Card (NZ$24 for one year, with a 30 per cent discount on all InterCity services).

Inter-Island ferries
The North and South Islands are linked by ferries between Wellington and Picton, with up to five departures in each direction daily. Of the two conventional ferries *Arahura* takes 3 hours and *Aratika* 3 hours 20 minutes to make the crossing, but since 1994/5 a new high-speed catamaran, the *Lynx*, has been introduced in summer on this route. The *Lynx* makes the crossing in just under two hours. Foot passengers should make reservations for ferry services at peak times, and car drivers should also pre-book in peak periods (December to February and other school holidays, see page 255).

Rail travel
Trains are another great way to see the countryside, and there are eight main routes across the country.

In the North Island the main services are between Auckland and Wellington (The Overlander daytime service and The Northerner night time service); Auckland–Tauranga (The Kaimai Express); Auckland–Rotorua (The Geyserland, daily, twice daily on Fridays and Sundays); and Wellington–Napier (The Bay Express).

In the South Island, The Coastal Pacific runs between Christchurch and Picton, with The Southerner operating from Christchurch to Invercargill. In addition, there is the famous TranzAlpine Express across the Southern Alps from Christchurch to Greymouth, which offers fantastic views of the Southern Alps (see panel page 180). The Express leaves Christchurch in the morning, arrives in Greymouth early in the afternoon and returns to Christchurch the same day.

Discount fares are available within the country, and there are also the InterCity 3 in 1 and 4 in 1 Travelpasses (see above) which include rail as well as coach travel.

Internal transport ranges from helicopters to old lake steamers

The media

There is no national daily newspaper in New Zealand. The largest circulation dailies are the *New Zealand Herald* (published in Auckland), followed by the *Dominion* (published in Wellington) and the *Press* (published in Christchurch). There are also numerous local newspapers and two Sunday newspapers.

Magazines worth looking out for include *North and South* (monthly, with an emphasis on current affairs) and *Metro* (also monthly, covering mainly issues relating to Auckland).

New Zealand has three national free-to-air television channels, all of which carry commercials: TV One (news, sport and current affairs) and Channel Two (predominantly drama and light entertainment) are both Government-owned, while TV Three combines elements of both and is privately owned. Sky TV (with channels devoted to 24 hour news, sport and movies) is available in hotels and motels.

New Zealand's hilly terrain means that many radio stations have a fairly limited broadcasting range, and this combined with deregulation has led to a proliferation of radio stations. Government-owned radio stations include the AM National Radio (news, drama, light entertainment and talk programmes) and Concert FM (classical music). In addition, there are several Maori stations, Pacific Islands Radio, and non-profit-making religious broadcasters.

The BBC World Service can be picked up in Auckland. Tourist FM Radio broadcasts 24 hours a day in English (88.2MHz), Japanese (100.8MHz) and German (100.4MHz).

Post Offices

Most of the larger towns and cities have Post Shops (open Mon-Fri 9–5), which sell stationery, postcards and other items as well as stamps. Stamps can also be purchased in other outlets such as bookshops and supermarkets. The two different types of domestic mail delivery are Standard Post (next-day delivery within town and 2-3 day delivery nationwide) and Fast Post (next-day delivery between towns and cities within New Zealand). Postcards cost NZ$1 to anywhere in the world (do not forget a Fast Post sticker).

Telephone and fax

The majority of the 4,000 public telephones in New Zealand have now been converted to operate on pre-paid phone cards. Telecom PhoneCards (available in denominations of NZ$5, NZ$10, NZ$20 and NZ$50) can be bought at numerous outlets including Information Centres, hotels, newsagents, supermarkets and petrol stations. Coin phones accept 10c, 20c, 50c, $1 and $2 coins.

Call charges start from 20c per minute or part minute for local calls (although these are free from residential phones), and you can find out how much a call is going to cost simply by dialling the number you want without inserting the phonecard: the digital display will then tell you the cost per minute or part minute. Another option is the call-back service. Dial 013 instead of the initial 0 when making a call and an operator will ring back after you have finished to tell you how much the call has cost: the service adds an extra NZ$2.80 to the cost of the call but is useful if you need to pay a third party.

There are also credit card phones (indicated by a yellow phone symbol) which accept major international credit cards.

❑ A highly useful service if you want to keep in touch is the Travelphone system, which allows people to leave messages on your own personal voice mailbox (like an answering machine). You are given a personal telephone number for the duration of your stay, which allows you to access your messages or change your 'out-going' message – for instance, to leave the phone number of your next hotel. The service is easy to use and very cost effective. Further details: Travelsafe International, P O Box 13343, Tauranga, tel: 07 578 4777; fax: 07 578 9944. UK contact: tel: 01784 465294. ❑

❑ **Useful telephone numbers**
National Operator 010
International Operator 0170
Directory Enquiries 018
International Directory Enquiries 0172
Telecom Help Desk 123
International access code 00
International dialling code for New Zealand 64

International dialling codes
Australia 61
Canada 1
Germany 49
UK 44
USA 1. ❑

Language guide
The Maori language has lent many words and phrases to New Zealand English, including the greeting 'Kia Ora' which means 'your good health'; it is answered with the same words. Special programmes for language immersion have been started in some schools to try and halt the decline in usage of Maori, and 1995 was designated Maori Language Year. The most obvious manifestation of Maori for visitors is in place names, a large number of which are of Maori origin. Many derive from real or mythical stories in Maori history, as for instance Taumatawhakatangihanga-koauauotamateapokaiwhenuaki-tanatahu, which is in Hawke's Bay and records 'the place where Tamatea played his flute to his loved one'. Other place names refer to geographical features and may include these commonly used words:

Ara	path
Ao	cloud
Awa	river
Ma (manga)	stream
Maunga	mountain
Moana	sea
o	the place of
Puna	spring
Puke	hill
Rangi	sky
Roto	lake
Tomo	cave
Wai	water
Whanga	bay

'Kiwi' English also tends to have its own idiosyncratic expressions or phrases. Some of those which may leave you puzzled include:

bach	a holiday chalet in the North Island (pronounced 'batch')
bludge	scrounge, borrow
bush	the forest
chook	chicken
cocky	farmer (usually 'cow-cocky')
chilly bin	portable cooler box
crib	the South Island equivalent of a bach
crook	sick, ill
dag	a character, or entertaining person
dairy	corner store/convenience store; it usually sells a wide range of goods apart from the expected dairy products
gidday	good day (hello)
good as gold	fine, OK
handle	beer glass with a handle
jandals	flip-flops/thongs
judder bars	speed bumps in the road
morning tea	mid-morning tea or coffee break ('elevenses')
mozzie	mosquito
Pakeha	person of European descent
Pom	an English person (mildly derogatory)
smoko	tea or coffee break
togs	swimwear
wopwops	the back of beyond

Crime

New Zealand's reputation as a sane and generally safe society has been tarnished in recent years by a series of multiple killings (including the random murder of 13 people in Aramoana, near Dunedin, in 1990). Although these are considered isolated incidents they have been linked to the social upheaval experienced in the country since the economic restructuring of the 1980s. High unemployment rates have also led to an increase in muggings and thefts, and rape and assault are more common than they used to be.

Despite this, New Zealand still has a low crime rate by international standards, and statistically you are fairly unlikely to be the victim of a serious crime while on holiday. One area in which there has been a marked increase in crimes against tourists is in the theft of valuables from cars, however. It is highly likely that at some point you will leave your car parked in some remote spot to go for a walk, climb up to a viewpoint or whatever; be warned that thefts from cars parked near 'beauty spots' or similar places are very common. Take your cameras, camcorders or other valuables with you.

A common-sense rule to follow is always to either take your valuables with you, or leave them in the hotel safe

As in any overseas country, take common-sense precautions such as locking large amounts of money in the hotel safe and avoiding badly lit urban areas at night. Women should not hitch-hike alone.

Embassies and consulates
Wellington
Australian High Commission, 72–78 Hobson Street, tel: 04 473 6411
British High Commission, 44 Hill Street, tel: 04 472 6049
Canadian High Commission, 61 Molesworth Street, tel: 04 473 9577
German Embassy, 90–92 Hobson Street, tel: 04 473 6063
United States Embassy, 29 Fitzherbert Terrace, tel: 04 472 2068
Auckland
Australian Consulate ,Union House, 32–38 Quay Street, tel: 09 303 2429
British Consulate, Fay Richwhite Building, 151 Queen Street, tel: 09 303 2973
Canadian Consulate, Jetset Centre, 48 Emily Place, tel: 09 309 3690
German Consulate, 52 Symonds Street, tel: 09 377 3460
United States Consulate, General Building, Shortland Street, tel: 09 303 2724

Emergency services
Dial 111 for police, fire or ambulance.

Lost property
Lost property should be reported to the police; lost or stolen travellers cheques or credit cards should be reported within 24 hours to the issuing company.

Health
No vaccinations are required. New Zealand is a clean, healthy place and no unusual precautions are required while holidaying here. Tap water is safe to drink everywhere; city water supplies are chlorinated and most are also fluoridated. In some back-country rivers and lakes the parasite giardia is present, so if camping in remote areas make sure water is either boiled or otherwise treated before drinking it.

The most serious potential health risk in New Zealand is from the sun. Ultra-violet radiation over the country is particularly high, not only because of the clean, unpolluted air but also because of the increase in the hole in the ozone layer over nearby Antarctica. Take adequate precautions (even on overcast days – the sun can burn through clouds) such as wearing a sun-hat and sunglasses, covering up vulnerable areas and using sunblock.

There are no dangerous wild animals or poisonous snakes (although there is one very rare poisonous spider, the katipo). The most irritating insects are sandflies and mosquitoes, which can occur in relentless swarms in some areas – particularly western coastal areas in the South Island, such as Fiordland. The 'mozzies' do not carry diseases (such as malaria) but can none the less be a severe irritant. Make sure you are adequately protected with insect repellent, particularly at dusk and/or near water.

Private and public health care facilities are of a high standard. Doctors and other medical facilities are listed in the front of the telephone directory; your hotel may also have an arrangement with a local doctor.

If you have an accident you are entitled to make a claim for some medical or hospital expenses under the national Accident Compensation scheme for personal injury. Because of the existence of this scheme, actions for damages may not be brought in New Zealand courts, so it is best to ensure that your personal travel insurance covers such eventualities. The scheme does not cover illness.

Chemists
Chemists are usually open during normal shopping hours. Urgent dispensaries in cities are open later, and can be found listed in the 'Hospitals' section in the phone book – or ask your hotel receptionist. If you are on an unusual prescription take sufficient supplies with you, since there is no guarantee that it will be available locally. To avoid potential difficulties with customs, it is wise to take your prescription certificate.

❑ New Zealand lies on an earth quake zone (see pages 98–9) but the likelihood of an earthquake of any magnitude occuring during your stay is minimal. If you do start to feel the earth move, shelter under a strong table or in a doorway. ❑

Camping
New Zealand has an excellent network of well-equipped campsites in national parks, beach resorts and urban areas. Most camping grounds have facilities for campervans and caravans as well as tents, plus cabins, bunk rooms and self-contained, fully equipped 'tourist flats' (motel-type rooms). Facilities are usually communal, with on-site launderettes in many places. Costs average NZ$8 per person for tents, with slightly higher charges for sites with power hook-ups for campervans. Several federations of campsites, such as the Cabin and Camp Association (CCA) and Kiwi Camps of New Zealand, publish brochures with details of their members' camping grounds. The AA Accommodation Guide also lists camp grounds and motor camps.

The Department of Conservation (DoC) manages around 200 campsites in national parks and other areas, ranging from 'informal camping areas' with limited facilities to standard camping areas and well-appointed serviced camp grounds. A leaflet on *Conservation Campsites* is available from DoC offices or DoC Head Office, PO Box 10420, Wellington.

Guest houses can be found all over the country to suit all tastes and pockets

Self-catering
A wide range of self-catering accommodation is available, from basic 'tourist flats' in camping grounds to fully serviced motel units. Motels represent one of the best budget options for independent travellers, with clean, comfortable units at affordable prices (around NZ$50–70, rising to NZ$100 or more).

Most motel rooms have basic tea and coffee making facilities, fridge, toaster and usually an electric hob and basic cooking utensils. Not all motels have fully equipped kitchens; most have television, telephone and lounge facilities, and sometimes also a bar, restaurant or swimming pool. Reliable chains include Best Western, Budget Motels and Flag Hotels. Motor Inns tend to be slightly more upmarket, with prices in the range of NZ$75–200 per day.

Hotels and lodges
Smart hotels – from international chains such as Hyatt, Sheraton and Regent, and national chains such as Scenic Circle and Pacific Park – are found in all the major cities and resort areas, with room rates ranging from NZ$175 per night upwards.

Independent hotels offer a cheaper option to motels, with rooms from NZ$30–50 per night; facilities vary widely, and in many old-style hotels the rooms are merely an adjunct to the bar.

New Zealand also has a network of top-class sporting retreats and wilderness lodges, often set in beautiful countryside and offering the services of guides. A brochure on *New Zealand in Style: Exclusive Retreats and Sporting Lodges,* is available from the tourist board.

Bed and breakfast, guest houses and country pubs
Bed and breakfast establishments and guest houses all over the country provide a homely place to stay as well as the chance to meet local people. In 1996 prices started from around NZ$45 (single), NZ$70 (double). The NZ Federation of Bed & Breakfast Hotels is at 52 Armagh Street, Christchurch, tel: 03 366 1503; fax: 03 366 9796; the *New Zealand Bed &*

Breakfast Book (J. and J. Thomas, Moonshine Press) is also useful.

Some of the best bed and breakfast accommodation is in historic homesteads; nearly 30 of these are grouped together in the *Heritage Inns of New Zealand* brochure (available from Visitor Information Centres or the tourist board). Prices start from NZ$100 per night.

Country pubs often have similar facilities to the older urban hotels, at similar prices. A booklet on *Pub Beds* is available from P O Box 32-332, Auckland, tel: 09 445 4400; fax: 09 445 1010.

Farmstays and homestays

Staying on a farm for a night or two is a great way to find out about the rural way of life. Bookings can be arranged through Rural Holidays New Zealand (P O Box 2155, Christchurch, tel: 03 366 1919; fax: 03 379 3087) and New Zealand Farm Holidays Ltd (P O Box 256, Silverdale, Auckland, tel: 09 426 5430; fax: 09 426 8474). Charges in 1996 were from NZ$50 upwards per person per night.

Homestays overlap to some extent with bed and breakfast accommodation. Most Visitor Information Centres carry brochures or lists for local farmstays and homestays.

Hostels and backpackers

Budget hostel accommodation is available almost everywhere in the country. Beds in shared rooms start

One of the network of backpacker hostels

from around NZ$12–15 per night, and nearly all hostels have communal kitchens, dining areas, lounge and laundry room. The *YHA Accommodation Guide* provides details on member hostels (available from YHA, P O Box 436, Christchurch, tel: 03 379 9970; fax: 03 365 4476). There are also hundreds of privately run hostels, usually referred to as 'backpackers' or 'backpacker lodges': guides include the *Backpackers Guide to New Zealand* and the *New Zealand Budget Backpackers Accommodation Guide*.

❑ The Qualmark is a new classification system developed by the New Zealand Tourism Board and the New Zealand Automobile Association to encourage high standards of hospitality and service. Lists of Qualmark-rated properties are available from Visitor Information Centres and AA Travel Centres. Another quality symbol is the New Zealand fern. Products and services with this symbol have passed a strict set of criteria including quality of service, environmental responsibility and business achievement, all 'delivered with a uniquely New Zealand personality'. ❑

Disabled travellers
In general New Zealand has better provisions for the disabled than many holiday destinations. By law, all new or redeveloped buildings must be accessible to the disabled, although interpretation of the law varies widely. Ramps and disabled toilets are usually provided in museums, theatres and other public venues. Specialised equipment can be hired. With regard to transport, it is always best to phone ahead to ensure that your requirements can be met. Full details on local services can be obtained from regional Disability Resource Centres; a list of contacts is available from the head office: Disability Resource Centre, P O Box 24-042, Royal Oak, Auckland, tel: 09 625 8069.

Opening times
Most offices and businesses are open from 8.30am to 5pm Mondays to Fridays, with late-night shopping in the bigger towns, usually on Thursday or Friday until 8.30 or 9pm. Some shops close at lunchtime on Saturdays, whilst many others (particularly in tourist resorts and larger centres) are open all the weekend. Local convenience stores ('dairies') are usually open from 7am to 10pm seven days a week. Petrol (gas) stations may be open 24 hours in the larger centres, and many also have a small stock of basic necessities (such as bread and milk).

The Anglican Cathedral, Christchurch

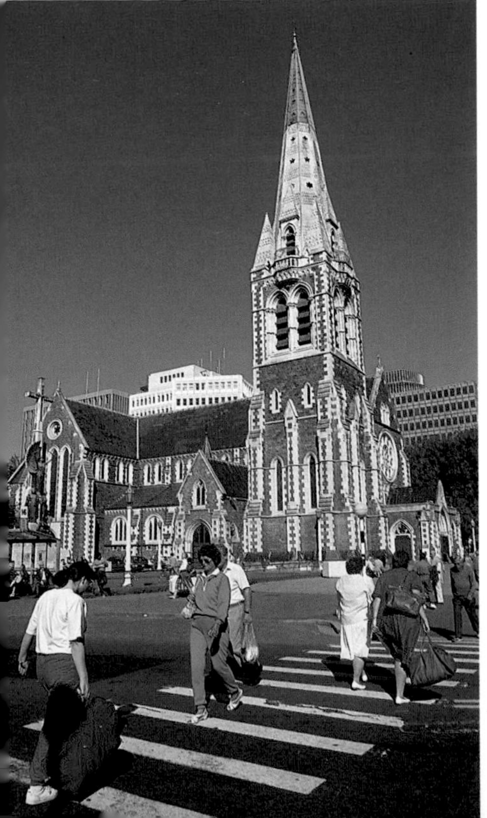

Places of worship
There are Anglican, Presbyterian, Baptist, Methodist and Catholic churches or chapels in most large urban centres, plus a handful of mosques and synagogues. Hotels should be able to advise on locations and times of services.

Toilets
Public conveniences can be found at major tourist attractions, some visitor centres, petrol (gas) stations, libraries, urban parks and of course in bars and restaurants.

Electricity
The AC electricity supply runs at 230-40 volts/50 hertz. Motels and hotels provide 110-volt/20 watt AC sockets for shavers only. Adaptors for other electrical equipment are readily available in hardware stores.

Consumer taxes
Goods and Services Tax (GST) applies to all goods and services bought within the country and currently stands at 12.5 per cent. Advertised prices usually include the GST.

Etiquette and local customs
New Zealanders are on the whole easygoing and friendly, and there are few strict rules on etiquette. Dress codes are almost universally casual, although under-dressing (singlets, beach wear, dirty bush clothes, flip flops and such like) may be frowned upon and in some cases banned in pubs and restaurants. Some of the smarter restaurants require ties for men. Tipping is not generally expected, although it will not be refused if you wish to reward exceptional service.

The most important aspects of etiquette relate to visiting Maori *marae*. It is particularly important to remove footwear on entering meeting houses (even those on display in museums), and you should always seek permission before looking around a meeting house or other building on the *marae*.

Books and films

New Zealand has a thriving literary scene and its film industry has also recently produced several international successes.

Perhaps the most acclaimed New Zealand-born writer is Katherine Mansfield, whose short stories can be found in several anthologies including *The Stories of Katherine Mansfield: Definitive Edition* (ed: A. Alpers, OUP Auckland 1984). One of the country's most distinguished living novelists is Janet Frame, whose autobiography *An Angel At My Table* (Hutchinson 1984) was turned into an acclaimed film. Other representative works by Janet Frame include *Owls Do Cry*, *A State of Siege*, and *Living in the Maniototo*. Maurice Shadbolt is a popular historical novelist whose best-known work is *The Season of the Jew* (Hodder and Stoughton 1986). There are several excellent compilations of poetry available, including *An Anthology of Twentieth Century New Zealand Poetry* edited by Vincent O'Sullivan (OUP 1987) and the more recent *Penguin Book of Contemporary New Zealand Poetry Nga Kupu Titohu o Aotearoa* edited by Miriama Evans, Harvey McQueen and Ian Wedde (Penguin Auckland 1989).

One of the country's most celebrated Maori writers is Keri Hulme, whose novel *The Bone People* (Picador London 1983) won the British Booker McConnell Prize for fiction in 1985. Another established Maori author is the prolific Witi Ihimaera, whose better-known writings include *Pounamu, Pounamu*, (Reed Publishing 1972) and *Tangi and Whanau: Two Classic Maori Novels* (Secker and Warburg 1994). Other Maori writers to watch out for include Apirana Taylor, Hone Tuwhare and Patricia Grace; the latter achieved prominence with her third novel, *Cousins* (Penguin Books) in 1992; her most recent collection of short stories is *The Sky People* (Penguin Books 1994).

The first novel of contemporary writer Alan Duff, *Once Were Warriors* (Tandem Press), a harrowing tale of a poor Maori family's struggle with despair, anger and alcohol in south Auckland, caused a sensation when it was published in 1990. More recent works include *One Night Out Stealing* (Tandem Press 1992) and *State Ward* (Vintage 1994).

New Zealand's film industry has also received international acclaim in recent years. Jane Campion's film about a mute immigrant, *The Piano*, was an award-winner at the 1993 Cannes Film Festival. Also outstanding are Peter Jackson's compelling *Heavenly Creatures*, the bizarre but true story of two schoolgirl killers in Christchurch in the 1950s, and Lee Tamahori's *Once Were Warriors*, the prize-winning film of Alan Duff's book. Other notable Kiwi films made in recent years include *An Angel At My Table*, *Smash Palace*, *Utu*, *Vigil* and the *Quiet Earth*.

CONVERSION CHART

FROM	TO	MULTIPLY BY
Inches	Centimetres	2.54
Centimetres	Inches	0.3937
Feet	Metres	0.3048
Metres	Feet	3.2810
Yards	Metres	0.9144
Metres	Yards	1.0940
Miles	Kilometres	1.6090
Kilometres	Miles	0.6214
Acres	Hectares	0.4047
Hectares	Acres	2.4710
Gallons	Litres	4.5460
Litres	Gallons	0.2200
Ounces	Grams	28.35
Grams	Ounces	0.0353
Pounds	Grams	453.6
Grams	Pounds	0.0022
Pounds	Kilograms	0.4536
Kilograms	Pounds	2.205
Tons	Tonnes	1.0160
Tonnes	Tons	0.9842

Overseas

Overseas branches of the New Zealand Tourism Board (NZTB) can supply a wide range of information, including maps, a comprehensive *Where to Stay Guide* and a lavish *Holiday Planner* (including a brochure-ordering service for tour operators, car-hire firms, hotels and other companies with contact addresses in your home country). Regional information can also be requested.

Australia: 8th floor, 35 Pitt Street, Sydney, NSW 2000 (tel: 02 247 5222; fax: 02 247 1136)
Canada: Suite 1200, 888 Dunsmuir Street, Vancouver BC V6C 3K4 (tel: 1 604 684 2117; fax: 1 604 684 1265)
UK: New Zealand House, Haymarket, London SW1Y 4QT (tel: 0171 930 1662; fax: 0171 839 8929; brochure-ordering service [premium rate line] 0839 300 900)
USA: 501 Santa Monica Boulevard #300, Santa Monica, CA90401 (tel: 1 310 396 7480; fax: 1 310 395 5453)

In New Zealand

Over 70 tourist offices throughout the country form the Visitor Information Network, co-ordinated by the NZTB. Their friendly, helpful staff provide impartial information on everything from local attractions to adventure activities, and many can also handle bookings for accommodation, transport and tour operators. They also distribute free maps and brochures.

Because they are linked in one network, Visitor Information Centres can also access information on areas other than their own. They provide an invaluable, up-to-date service and should be your first port of call.

For their addresses and telephone numbers see under the relevant entries in the A to Z section.

❑ As well as the Qualmark rating and the New Zealand Way fern symbol, another logo to look out for is the KiwiHost sign. This symbol means that staff in the business concerned have undergone customer-service training , and that you can expect 'a warm Kiwi welcome, friendly attention and good service'. In general it would be surprising if you did not receive this kind of reception anyway, so do not necessarily be put off if somewhere does *not* have the KiwiHost logo. ❑

Visitor Centre, Te Anau

HOTELS AND RESTAURANTS

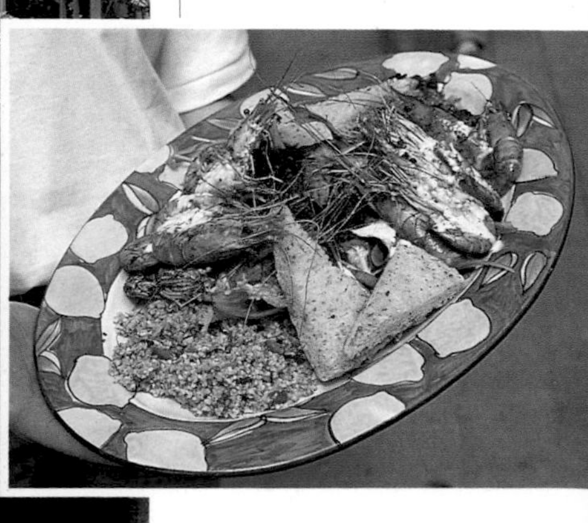

ACCOMMODATION

£ = under NZ$75
££ = NZ$75-150
£££ = NZ$150 plus

North Island

AUCKLAND

Aachen House (££) 39 Market Road, Remuera (tel: 09 520 2329; fax: 09 524 2898). A lovely Victorian-style house in Remuera, 4km from downtown. Comfortable and welcoming; recommended, but better with your own transport.
Albion Hotel (££) Corner of Wellesley and Hobson Street (tel: 09 379 4900; fax: 09 379 4901). Moderate-sized rooms (no views) but reasonable prices. Recently restored.

Ascot Parnell (££) 36 St Stephens Avenue, Parnell (tel: 09 309 9012; fax: 09 309 3729. A small historic house converted into an efficiently run and friendly B & B. Very comfortable rooms, all non-smoking. Within walking distance of Parnell Village. Recommended.
Aspen Lodge (£) 62 Emily Place (tel: 09 379 6698; fax: 09 377 7625). One of the closest B & Bs to the central downtown area (five minutes' walk away), comfortable and friendly.
Carlton (£££) (formerly Pan Pacific) cnr Mayoral Drive and Vincent St (tel: 09 366 3000; fax: 09 366 0121). Near the Aotea Centre, this smart hotel has spacious rooms all with floor to ceiling windows overlooking the city and harbour.
Centra (£££) 128 Albert Street (tel: 09 302 1111; fax: 09 302 3111). Primarily a hotel for business travellers but good value for the quality of rooms offered.
Devonport Villa (££) 46 Tainui Road, Devonport (tel: 09 445 2529; fax: 09 445 9766). Superb old colonial villa converted to a B&B with just three extremely comfortable guest rooms. Plenty of atmosphere, and huge breakfasts. Pool, and near the beach.
Hôtel du Vin (£££) Lyons Road, Mangatawhiri Valley (tel: 09 233 6314; fax: 09 233 6215). Sheer extravagance but worth every dollar if you have just got off a long flight, this superb hotel is 45 minutes from the airport or downtown Auckland. Set amidst the vineyards of the De Redcliffe Estate, the Hôtel du Vin has received many awards; palatial rooms, heated pool, tennis, gym.
Novotel Auckland (£££) Customs Street East (tel: 09 377 8920; freephone: 0800 444 422; fax: 09 302 0993). Good location near the quayside, but the rooms, although recently renovated, are on the small side.
Quality Hotel Anzac Avenue (£££) 150 Anzac Avenue (tel: 09 379 8509; free-phone: 0800 808 228 fax: 09 379 8582). Overlooking the harbour. Smallish but comfortable rooms.
Skyway Lodge (£–££) 30 Kirkbride Road, Mangere (tel: 09 275 4443; fax: 09 275 5012). One of numerous motels along Kirkbride Road and McKenzie Road which offer decent accommodation within easy reach (five minutes) of the airport. All offer free transfers if you are catching a flight. The Skyway has a range of rooms, from shared accommodation to self-contained family units. It also has a pool, sauna and spa.
Stamford Plaza (£££) Albert Street (tel: 09 309 8888; fax: 09 379 6445). Handy downtown location. Well-appointed rooms (ask for the harbour side) and first-class facilities and service have continued to earn the Stamford Plaza top ratings amongst Auckland's de luxe hotels.

NORTHLAND

DOUBTLESS BAY
Kaitaia

Kaitaia Hotel (£) Commerce Street (tel: 09 408 0360; fax: 09 408 0360). One of the oldest hotels (1837) in Northland, this local landmark is right in the town centre and has a licensed restaurant and four bars. Rooms are in need of refurbishing, but excellent value. The hotel has thermal and volcanic baths and a unique 'herbal sauna'.
The Northerner Motor Inn (£–££) North Road (tel: 09 408 2800; fax: 09 408 0306). On the main street, quiet with good quality rooms at reasonable prices. Pool, sauna, spa, gym.

Mangonui

Beach Lodge (££) Coopers Beach (tel: 09 406 0068). Great location on the lovely Coopers Beach, 2km from Mangonui. The five beach-front lodges all have sundecks and full facilities.
Mangonui Motel (£–££) Colonel Mould Drive (tel & fax: 09 406 0346). The hotel overlooks Mangonui Harbour, and all the fully self-contained units have sea views.
Old Oak Inn (£) 19 Waterfront Drive (tel: 09 406 0665). This historic hotel on the water's edge was built to accommodate whalers and sealers in the 1860s. Today it is a small, comfortable lodge with eight rooms (communal facilities) at budget prices.

Matakohe

Old Post Office Guest House (£) Paparoa (tel: 09 431 7453). Cosy little B&B in Paparoa's converted post office, shared facilities but a good budget choice and just 7 km from Matakohe Kauri Museum.

BAY OF ISLANDS
Paihia

Abel Tasman Lodge (£–££) Marsden Rd (tel: 09 402 7251; fax: 09 402 7576). One of several motels on the north side of Paihia, the Abel Tasman has 25 self-contained units and is right opposite a sandy beach.
Autolodge Hotel (££–£££). Marsden Road (tel: 09 402 7416; freephone: 0800 652 929; fax: 09 402 8348). Right

on the waterfront just 100m from the main wharf and shops. Pool, spa, sauna. All suites and rooms have kitchenettes, and guests have complimentary use of dinghies and bikes.

Bay of Islands Motel (££) 6 Tohitapu Rd (tel: 09 402 7348; freephone: 0800 402 402; fax: 09 402 8257). Set in 1ha of park-like grounds within easy reach of the town centre (1½ km) and close to a swimming beach. The individual cottages are all fully self-contained and good value for the area.

Bay of Islands Quality Resort Hotel (££–£££) Waitangi Road (tel: 09 402 7411; fax: 09 402 8200). This sprawling old hotel is right on the shore within the Waitangi National Trust Ground. It has a superb position, with landscaped gardens and a large heated pool. Popular with package tours, it suffered neglect under the previous management but is now owned by Quality Hotels.

Beachcomber Resort Hotel (£££) 1 Seaview Road (tel: 09 402 7434; freephone: 0800 732 786; fax: 09 402 8202). An unattractive-looking hotel but in a good position on the headland south of town, with sea views from all the rooms and its own private beach. Studios, family suites and luxury suites available.

Casa Bella Motel (££) MacMurray Rd (tel: 09 402 7387; freephone: 0800 800 810; fax: 09 402 7166). Spanish-style complex 200m from the beach, central but quiet. Units are well furnished with full kitchen facilities.

The Cedar Suite (££) 5 Sullivans Rd (tel: 09 402 8516; fax: 09 402 8555). Tucked away in woodlands south of the town, this modern complex includes self-contained apartments, B&B units and a cottage with sea views.

Paihia Pacific Resort Hotel (££–£££). 27 Kings Road (tel: 09 402 8221; fax: 09 402 8490). Lavish units set amidst tranquil, landscaped gardens within walking distance of the seafront.

Swiss Chalet Lodge Motel (££) 3 Bayview Road (tel: 09 402 7615; fax: 09 402 7609). Centrally located, this Swiss-owned chalet has 12 spacious self-contained units with balconies or patios, plus family and honeymoon suites. Well-run and comfortable.

Russell

Duke of Marlborough Hotel (££) The Strand (tel: 09 403 7829; fax: 09 403 7828). A historic landmark which has been a hotel since 1827, the Duke of Marlborough has a convivial atmosphere and its seaside terraces and bar are popular local watering holes. The cosy, wood-panelled rooms all have en suite facilities; front rooms can be noisy.

Kimberley Lodge (£££) Pitt Street (tel: 09 403 7090; fax: 09 403 7239). Superb white-timbered mansion perched on the hill above Pompallier House, with views over the bay. The immaculate rooms are furnished with antiques and the whole house exudes old-world charm. Very expensive, but well worth it if your wallet can take it. Heated pool, spa.

Motel Russell (£–££) Matauwhi Road (tel & fax: 09 403 7854; freephone: 0800 240 011). Set on a wooded hillside a few minutes' walk from the town centre, with a pool fed by a waterfall. The attractively decorated units are well equipped.

Russell Lodge (£–££) cnr Chapel and Beresford Streets (tel: 09 403 7640; fax: 09 403 7641). Surrounded by park-like gardens three minutes' walk from the town centre, Russell Lodge has very reasonably priced rooms and units (including family units, all en suite) as well as backpackers' beds.

Whangarei

Cheviot Park Motor Lodge (££) cnr Western Hills Drive and Cheviot Street (tel: 09 438 2341; fax: 09 438 0442). In a quiet location within walking distance of the town centre, this AA Host property has 15 comfortable self-contained units. Recommended.

Manor Inn Whangarei (££) 260 Kamo Road (tel: 09 437 5779; freephone 0800 806 688; fax: 09 437 5780). A few minutes outside of town. Friendly service and comfortable surroundings characterise this property, which is part of the Manor Inn chain.

Pembroke Park Motor Lodge (££–£££) cnr of Hatea Drive and Deveron Street (tel: 09 437 6426; fax: 09 437 6457). Just outside the town, luxurious accommodation (executive suites have spa baths).

FROM COROMANDEL TO THE WAIKATO

COROMANDEL

Coromandel town

Anglers Lodge and Motor Park (££) Amodeo Bay (tel: 07 866 8584). 18km north of town in a wonderful bush setting beside the sea. One- or two-bedrooms units all with cooking facilities. Pool, spa, tennis, boats for rent.

Coromandel Colonial Cottages (££) Rings Road (tel: 07 866 8857). In a rural setting on the outskirts of town. Spacious and well-appointed units (each with two bedrooms, sleeping up to six people) suitable for families, good value. Barbecue, playground, billiards, spa pool.

Karamana 1872 Homestead (££) Whangapoua Road (tel: 07 866 8138; fax: 07 866 7138). Lovely Victorian homestead 1km outside town in a tranquil valley. Just three rooms (only one with en suite facilities), all individually decorated in period style.

Pauanui

Puka Park Lodge (£££) Mount Avenue (tel: 07 864 8088; fax: 07 864 8112). This exclusive lodge has 50 superb 'tree hut' chalets built into the wooded hillside, each secluded enough from their neighbours but with balconies opening out into the treetops. It is worth splashing out to experience a night or two in one of these luxurious rooms. The main building is like a hunting lodge, with log fires and a sophisticated atmosphere.

Thames

Brian Boru Hotel (££) 200 Richmond Street (tel: 07 868 6523; fax: 07 868 9790). Established in 1868, this atmospheric old hotel is right in the centre of Thames and its snug bar is popular with locals. Request a room in the main hotel (rather than the new units alongside) if possible. The hotel is also well known for its award-winning 'murder & mystery' weekends.

Crescent Motel (£–££) cnr Jellicoe Crescent and Fenton Street (tel: 07 868 6506; freephone: 0800 474 700; fax: 07 868 8050). A Best Western hotel; large family units at reasonable prices.

Whitianga

Buffalo Beach Resort (£) Eyre Street (tel: 07 866 5854; fax: 07 866 5854). Centrally located, handy for shops and the ferry to Ferry Landing. Fully equipped units plus tent sites and campervan facilities.

Cosy Cat Cottage (££) 41 South Highway (tel: 07 866 4488). Comfortable little B & B which will be appreciated by cat lovers – the whole house is stuffed with cat statues and other feline memorabilia.

Mercury Bay Beachfront Resort (££) 111–13 Buffalo Beach Road (tel: 07 866 5637; freephone: 0800 222 344; fax: 07 866 4524). One of the few motels on Mercury Bay situated directly on the beach, with rooms opening out on to gardens (with spa pool) and the sea. Ten fully equipped units plus one luxury unit available. Boats, fishing rods, bikes free to guests. Super location, welcoming hosts. Recommended.

BAY OF PLENTY

Rotorua

Acacia Lodge Motel (£–££) 40 Victoria Street (tel: 07 348 7089; fax: 07 346 1104). In a quiet location within walking distance of the town centre, this friendly motel is a good budget choice. The 18 ground floor units all have kitchen facilities and there are some family units. Sauna, mineral pools.

Boulevard Motel (£–££) cnr Fenton and Seddon Streets (tel: 07 348 2074; freephone: 0800 331 177; fax: 07 348 2072). Centrally located and set in its own grounds (which include swimming pool, spa baths, putting green and games room) this is another good-value motel. The 33 units range from small studios to three-bedroom family suites.

Eaton Hall Guesthouse and Homestay (£–££) 39 Hinemaru Street (tel: 07 347 0366). Pleasant two-storey wooden building near the town centre, one of the handiest of Rotorua's B&Bs. The house has an interesting interior and a welcoming atmosphere.

Lake Plaza (£££) 6 Eruera Street (tel: 07 348 1174; fax: 07 346 0238). Near the Polynesian Pools and Government Gardens, very handily located for downtown attractions. The best rooms overlook the lake. Unfussy but well-appointed rooms. Recommended.

Princes Gate Hotel (££–£££) 1 Arawa Street (tel: 07 348 1179; fax: 07 348 6215). This award-winning hotel is just next to the Government Gardens in the central downtown area and is one of the leading 'boutique' hotels in New Zealand. The 22 luxurious, old-fashioned rooms are complemented by eight suites. Heated pool, spa, tennis, health complex , restaurant and bar.

Sheraton Rotorua (£££) Fenton Street (tel: 07 349 5200; fax: 07 349 5201). Within walking distance of the Whakarewarewa Thermal area on the fringes of the city, with all the facilities and standards of service you would expect from a Sheraton. 122 rooms with IDD, TV, mini-bar etc; eight suites with spa bath, separate lounge and private balcony. The best rooms overlook the golf course from the top two floors. On-site services include shops, health club, heated pool, sauna, two restaurants, bar.

Solitaire Lodge (£££) Lake Tarawera Road (tel: 07 362 8208; freephone: 0508 552 552 fax: 07 362 8445). In a spectacular setting on a wooded peninsula overlooking Lake Tarawera, Solitaire Lodge is a sophisticated hideaway catering for a maximum of 20 guests. All suites overlook the lake and feature king-size beds. The lounge and dining area have open fireplaces, with the restaurant emphasizing New Zealand game and fine wines. Private beach, spa pool. Free use of windsurfers, dinghies, fishing tackle and yachts.

Tauranga/Mount Maunganui

Ambassador 15th Avenue Motel (£–££) 9 15th Avenue (tel: 07 578 5665; fax: 07 578 5226). Small motel just outside town with eight comfortable units (some with spa baths). Attractive pool and spa complex.

Bayfair Motor Inn (££) Girven Road (tel: 07 575 5089; fax: 07 575 9768). First-class facilities and well-furnished, comfortable rooms. Heated pool, poolside bar. Just off Papamoa Beach.

Taipororo House (££) 11 5th Avenue (tel: 07 5779 607; fax: 07 577 9264). Lovely historic home in a quiet suburb not far from the town centre. Rooms (all with private facilities) are nicely furnished and there is a large, sunny guest lounge and conservatory. A good base from which to explore the area. Recommended.

Willow Park International Hotel (££) 9 Willow Street (tel: 07 578 9119; fax: 07 577 9198). Convenient downtown location with plenty of facilities (restaurants, heated pool). 79 rooms with satellite TV.

Whakatane

Camellia Court Motel (£–££) 11 Domain Road (tel & fax: 07 308 6213; freephone 0800 500 554). Handy location a few minutes' stroll from downtown, 12 well-maintained and spacious units with full facilities. Recommended.

Whakatane Caravan Park Motor Camp (£) McGarvey Road (tel: 07 308 8694). Just under 1km from town on the banks of the Whakatane River, with powered sites, tent sites, and basic cabin units. Swimming pool, spa.

THE WAIKATO

Hamilton

Glenview Motor Hotel (£) 200 Ohaupo Road (tel: 07 843 6049; fax: 07 843 3324). Between the city and the airport, well-appointed rooms (some with kitchens). Waterbed suite. Swimming pool.

Hotel Alcamo (££–£££) 290 Ulster Street (tel: 07 839 0200; freephone: 0800 802 468; fax: 07 838 3240). Stylish new hotel with 56 luxury suites (complete with spa baths) and a presidential suite. Pool, restaurant, conference facilities.

Le Grand Hôtel (££–£££) cnr Victoria and Collingwood Streets (tel: 07 839 1994; fax: 07 839 7994). Opened in 1995, this lavish development in old-world style has been built inside a former commercial building – rooms are consequently palatial in scale. 28 de luxe suites, three executive suites (even more spacious than the rest) and seven business suites.

The Monastery (££) Newell Road (tel: 07 856 9587). This historic house was built as a private home in 1906 and became a monastery in 1952. In 1990 it was moved to its present location on the edge of the Waikato River, and now has just four guest rooms. The house has stained-glass windows, antiques and pleasant verandas.

Tudor Motor Lodge (£–££) 24 Thackeray Street (tel: 07 838 2244; freephone: 0508 382 244; fax: 07 838 2243). One of the closest motels to the central business district, 24 serviced units with kitchen facilities. Quiet surroundings. AA Host property.

Waitomo

THC Waitomo Caves Hotel (£–£££) Waitomo (tel: 07 878 8227; fax: 07 878 8858). Characterful hotel built at the turn of the century which retains a country club atmosphere. Although old-fashioned, the guest rooms are comfortable and there are also good-value economy rooms, plus backpackers' accommodation in a separate unit. Public rooms are spacious and include a lounge, cocktail bar and restaurant.

Caves Motor Inn (£–££) SH3 Waitomo Junction (tel: 07 873 8109). Located at the main road junction, ten minutes from the caves, with 20 spacious and cosy units as well as cabins and backpackers' rooms.

EAST COAST

Gisborne

Green Gables Travel Hotel (£–££) 31 Rawiri Street (tel: 06 867 9872). A typically friendly B&B with 20 beds in an old house just a few minutes' walk from the city centre. The spacious rooms have no en suite facilities but are very good value.

Teal Motor Lodge (££) 479 Gladstone Road (tel: 06 868 4019; freephone: 0800 838 325; fax: 06 867 7157). Set in large, landscaped gardens with a salt-water pool 500m from the city centre. The tastefully decorated units have one or two bedrooms and kitchen facilities.

Hastings

Angus Inn Motor Hotel (££) Railway Road (tel: 06 878 8177; freephone: 0800 109 595; fax: 06 878 7496). The largest hotel in Hawke's Bay, with numerous facilities including a pool, spa and sauna. 61 hotel rooms and 12 motel units with self-catering facilities.

Ebbett Park Lodge Motel (£–££) 616 Gordon Road (tel: 06 878 9860; freephone: 0800 801 830; fax: 06 876 3888). Next door to an extensive park, this unassuming motel has quiet, well-maintained rooms at reasonable prices.

Napier

Anleigh Heights (££) 115 Chaucer Road (tel: 06 835 1188; fax: 06 835 1032). Situated high on Napier Hill with views over Hawke Bay, this restored Edwardian home has been converted to a splendid 'boutique' hotel with refined, old-fashioned service.

Blue Dolphin Motel (££) 371 Kennedy Road (tel: 06 843 9129; fax: 06 843 9227). Long-established and comfortable motel five minutes from the city centre. Self-contained units with kitchen facilities.

Edgewater Motor Lodge (££–£££) 359 Marine Parade (tel: 06 835 1148; fax: 06 835 6600). One of many hotels and motels along the seafront, with studio units and executive suites – all upstairs ones have balconies which overlook the sea.

Mon Logis (££–£££) 415 Marine Parade (tel & fax: 06 835 2125). Superb old hotel, built in 1915 and now renovated to offer the highest standards of French hospitality in the heart of Napier. Just four rooms, all en suite. No smoking, no children.

Napier Travel Inn (££) 311 Marine Parade (tel: 06 835 3237; freephone: 0800 404 800; fax: 06 835 6602). One of the better-class hotels along the seafront, popular with business travellers (conference facilities available). The 59 well-appointed rooms are spacious and comfortable with tea- and coffee-making facilities. Request a room overlooking the seafront.

CENTRAL NORTH ISLAND AND THE WEST COAST

New Plymouth

Amber Court Motel (££) 61 Eliot Street (tel: 06 758 0922; freephone: 0800 654 800; fax: 06 758 6559). A few minutes' walk from the city centre and close to Pukekura Park. Good-quality units sleeping from two to seven with kitchens, some with spa baths. Large heated pool.

Carrington Guesthouse (£) 32 Carrington Street (tel: 06 758 2375). Atmospheric old manor house near Pukekura Park and handy for the city centre. Comfortable and welcoming.

Ohakune

The Hobbit (££) cnr Goldfinch and Wye Streets (tel: 06 385 8248; fax: 06 385 8515). Handily located motel with a range of units from studios with kitchens to family units (sleeping six or seven), with or without kitchens. Spa pool, lounge with open fire, restaurant and bar.

Lahar Lodge (££) Matapuna Road, Horopito (tel: 06 385 4136). Delightful log cabin set amidst woodlands with views of Mount Ruapehu; two spacious, warm bedrooms (with shared balcony) and an open-plan lounge (with log fire), dining and kitchen area downstairs.

Powderhorn Château (££–£££) Mountain Road (tel: 06 385 8888; fax: 06 385 8925). The closest hotel accommodation to the Turoa skifield, this traditional-style ski chalet has 30 well-furnished rooms. The public areas feature open fires, bars and two restaurants. Lively après-ski atmosphere.

Taupo

Anchorage Resort Motel (££) Lake Terrace, Two Mile Bay (tel: 07 378 5542; fax: 07 378 7287). One of many motels strung along the Taupo lakefront, the Anchorage is fairly typical, with moderately luxurious units (some with their own spas) in a two-storey block surrounding a heated pool. It also has a sauna, gym, mineral pools, conference room and games room.

Cedar Park Motor Lodge (£–££) Two Mile Bay (tel: 07 378 6325; fax: 07 377 0641). An AA Host property almost on the lakefront, with 24 fully self-contained two-bedroom family units. Heated pool, spa pools, boat ramp.

Le Chalet Suisse (££) 3 Titiraupenga Street (tel: 07 378 1556; fax: 07 378 1577). Five minutes' walk from town centre. Sixteen modern units all with lake views (executive units have their own spa baths). Large heated pool, spa.

Gillies Lodge (££) 77 Gillies Avenue (tel & fax: 07 377 2377). Once popular with Government ministers and other visiting officials, this traditional-style hotel has eight rooms with private facilities, all recently refurbished. Lounge with open fire, bar and restaurant.

Huka Lodge (£££) Huka Falls Road (tel: 07 378 5791; fax: 07 378 0427). Originally developed as a fishing lodge in the 1920s and cut off by dense woodland from the rest of Taupo, Huka Lodge is now amongst the leading 'exclusive retreats' in the country. Guest accommodation consists of 17 individual lodges near the banks of the Waikato, each with spacious bedrooms and glass-ceilinged bathroom. Library, cocktail lounge with open fire, heated pool, all-weather tennis court.

Stillwater Lodge (££) 56 Kaka Street (tel: 07 377 6219). One block back from the lakefront and within easy reach of the town centre, this interesting B&B has a convivial lounge, sundeck, and en suite bedrooms with attractive furnishings and old bedsteads.

Wairakei Resort (£££) Wairakei Valley (tel: 07 374 8021; fax: 07 374 8485). Five minutes' drive north of Taupo in the Wairakei Thermal Valley and set in 60ha of woods and parkland, this is Taupo's best resort and has recently been extensively refurbished, with rooms tastefully furnished and equipped with IDD telephones and other facilities. There are two heated pools, tennis, golf, children's adventure playground, restaurants and bars. A very peaceful and well-run resort.

TONGARIRO

Whakapapa Village

The Grand Château (£££) Mount Ruapehu (tel: 07 892 3809; fax: 07 892 3704). This impressive local landmark is a grand old hotel which has recently been extensively refurbished. The elegant rooms are furnished in Victorian style but also have IDD phones, TV, fridge and other modern comforts. The hotel also has a pool, sauna, tennis, golf course and cinema.

Ruapehu Skotel (£–££) Mount Ruapehu (tel: 07 892 3719; fax: 07 892 3777). This attractive ski lodge claims to be the country's highest hotel, with spectacular views of the cone of Mount Ruapehu. The 57 well-appointed rooms include self-contained units and hostel beds.

Wanganui

Avenue Motor Inn (££) 379 Victoria Avenue (tel: 06 345 0907; fax: 06 345 3250). Smart new motel near the city centre. Very comfortable units with all the usual facilities; family units also available. Large swimming pool, restaurant.

Manor Inn Wanganui (££) 63 Dublin Street (tel: 06 345 2180; freephone: 0800 806 688; fax: 06 345 8711). Part of the Manor Inns group, 20 self-contained units with kitchens, eight luxury suites with spa baths, ten studio units. Pool, sauna, spa. Close to the city centre.

The Riverside Inn (£) 2 Plymouth Street (tel: 06 347 2529). Nicely decorated and furnished historic (1895) house near the river. Twin or double budget rooms and backpackers' bunks.

SOUTHERN NORTH ISLAND

Palmerston North

Aztec Lodge Motel (££) 109 Ruahine Street (tel: 06 356 7125; freephone: 0800 328 082; fax: 06 356 7123). 3km away from The Square, affordable units ranging from one-bedroom studios to family units with fully equipped kitchens. Large garden and pool.

Rose City Motel (££–£££) 120 Fitzherbert Avenue (tel: 06 356 5388; freephone 0800 356 538; fax: 06 356 5085). Close to the city centre, 26 modern and spacious units (sleep up to five), most with double spa baths. Waterbed and honeymoom suites also available. Squash court, spa, sauna, children's play area.

Wellington

Abel Tasman City Hotel (££) 169 Willis Street (tel: 04 385 1304; freephone: 0800 500 141; fax: 04 385 8416). Small hotel in the city centre offering no-nonsense rooms at very reasonable rates. Also studio units with kitchens.

Apollo Lodge Motel (££) 49 Majoribanks Street (tel: 04 385 1849; fax: 04 385 1849). Reasonably priced rooms in a convenient location.

Downtown Backpackers (£) cnr Waterloo Quay and Bunny Street (tel: 04 473 8482; fax: 04 471 1073). Very basic rooms at rock-bottom prices in the heart of the city.

Carillon Motor Inn (££) 33 Thompson Street (tel: 04 384 8795; fax: 04 385 7036). Large two-storey house halfway up a hillside, with great views of the harbour and city. 28 attractive rooms (some with waterbeds) with showers or shower and bath. Guest lounge, licensed restaurant.

Museum Hotel de Wheels (££) 90 Cable Street (tel: 04 385 2809; fax: 04 385 2483). Excellent location close to the harbour across from the site of the new Museum of New Zealand – the unusual name derives from the fact that it was put on wheels and moved to its present location after being threatened with demolition to make way for the Museum. The rooms (all recently refurbished) are of a high standard and very good value for the city.

Plaza International (£££) 148–76 Wakefield Street (tel: 04 473 3900; freephone: 0800 655 555; fax: 04 473 3929). Top-class hotel right in the centre of the downtown area with views over the harbour. Guest rooms have all the comforts you would expect; executive suites all with uninterrupted harbour views. Several bars and restaurants, gym, conference facilities, business services.

Richmond Guesthouse (££) 116 Brougham Street (tel: 04 385 8529; fax: 04 384 2146). Ten minutes' walk from the downtown area, 20 comfortable rooms on a B&B basis.

Tinakori Lodge (££) 182 Tinakori Road (tel: 04 473 3478; fax; 04 472 5554). Delightful old house with ten comfortably furnished rooms (most share bathrooms). Huge breakfasts served as a buffet. Complimentary tea, coffee and newspapers available in the conservatory overlooking a bushland reserve.

Trekkers Hotel (£) 213 Cuba Street (tel: 04 385 2153; fax: 04 382 8873). Mostly a backpackers' hostel, but also offers basic double or twin rooms (with or without en suite facilities) at a very moderate cost. Spa, sauna, restaurant, bar.

Wellington Parkroyal (£££) Grey Street (tel: 04 472 2722; fax: 04 472 4724). The city's top hotel, right in the heart of the central business district. 232 rooms, seven suites (with spa baths). Indoor heated pool, business centre, gym and health centre, spa, conference facilities, several restaurants and bars.

West Plaza Hotel (££–£££) 110–16 Wakefield Street (tel: 04 473 1440; fax: 04 473 1454). 102 rooms and seven suites all with en suite bathroom and shower, tea and coffee facilities, satellite TV, IDD phones and other facilities. Good location.

South Island

NELSON AND MARLBOROUGH

Abel Tasman National Park

Abel Tasman Marahau Lodge (££) Marahau Beach, RD 2, Motueka (tel: 03 527 8250; fax: 03 527 8258). Further down the hill from the Ocean View Chalets (see below) and lacking the views, the eight luxury units are nevertheless very comfortable and handy for the start of the Coastal Track (see pages 174–5).

The Awaroa Lodge and Café (£) P O Box 72, Takaka (tel & fax: 03 528 8758). Tucked away in Awaroa Bay on the Abel Tasman Coastal Track, this lovely lodge is just 300m from the shore and has twin/double rooms as well as backpackers' accommodation.

Ocean View Chalets (££) Marahau Beach, RD 2, Motueka (tel & fax: 03 527 8232). In a superb position overlooking Marahau Beach at the start of the Abel Tasman Coastal Track, these timber chalets have all the amenities, including TV, phones and balconies with wonderful views.

Blenheim

Blenheim Country Lodge (££–£££) cnr Alfred and Henry Streets (tel: 03 578 5079; freephone: 0800 507 077; fax: 03 578 0337). Very comfortable, family-run lodge just a few minutes' walk from downtown, 54 rooms. Licensed restaurant.

Chardonnay Lodge (££) Rapaura Road (tel & fax: 03 570 5194). In the heart of the Marlborough wineries, this modern lodge has a pool, tennis court and spa.

Self-contained units or rooms within the house.

Montana Lodge Motel (££) 71 Main Street (tel: 03 578 9259; fax: 03 578 9258). Peaceful atmosphere and yet centrally located. The 12 comfortable units sleep up to six people.

Peppertree Homestead (££) SH1, Riverlands (tel: 03 578 7009; fax: 04 577 9533). 5km outside Blenheim, this old homestead (1901) has five spacious bedrooms (some with en suite facilities and balconies) and a lovely farmhouse kitchen where breakfast is taken. Garden with pool, veranda.

Golden Bay

Kahurangi Lodge (££) RD2, Takaka (tel: 03 524 8312; fax: 03 524 8316). Decorated with paintings and hand-crafted furniture, this attractive lodge has an open fire, lounge and restaurant. Rooms have balconies with great views.

Sans Souci Inn (£) Richmond Road, Pohara Beach (tel: 03 525 8663). A couple of minutes' walk from Pohara Beach, this rustic-looking house (with thick clay walls and a grass roof) has six bedrooms and a shared kitchen; breakfast and dinner also available.

Kaikoura

Blue Seas Motel (£–££) 222 Esplanade (tel & fax: 03 319 5441; freephone: 0800 507 077). Standard motel-type units (sleeping up to six) all with kitchens. Handy location on the seafront.

The Clifftop (£££) 12 Cromer Street (tel: 03 319 6649). Modern luxury apartments with fabulous views across the bay and mountains.

The Old Convent (£–££) Mount Fyffe Road (tel: 03 319 6603). Good quality rooms (not all en suite) in a peaceful atmosphere 3km from town overlooking Kaikoura and the mountains. The lounge is in the former convent chapel.

White Morph Inn (££–£££) 92 Esplanade (tel: 03 319 5014; freephone: 0800 803 666; fax: 03 319 5015). A modern motel, with 19 high-quality units and four luxury suites (with spa baths) on the waterfront. Licensed restaurant.

Marlborough Sounds

Punga Cove Resort (£–£££) Punga Cove (tel: 03 579 8561; fax: 03 579 8080). Superb little hideaway resort tucked into the hill-side above Punga Cove, Endeavour Inlet (45 minutes by water taxi from Picton). Chalets all have balconies overlooking the Sounds; smaller chalets sleep two to three (with en suite facilities), family chalets are self-contained. Back-packers' accommodation and tent sites also available.

Nelson

Beachcomber Motor Inn (££) 23 Beach Road, Tahunanui (tel: 03 548 5985; fax: 03 547 6371). Five minutes from the airport and the city centre, this award-winning complex is close to the beach and golf and tennis facilities. The 36 spacious and comfortable units include 11 family units with kitchens. Bar, restaurant.

Biddle Cottage (££) 1 South Street (tel: 03 548 2575; fax: 03 546 8855). One of several historic cottages in South Street, within the city centre, this charming old cottage has just two bedrooms.

California House Inn (££–£££) 29 Collingwood Street (tel & fax: 03 548 4173). Gracious colonial villa (1893) with oak panelling, stained-glass windows, guest lounge with open fire, and verandas. The four guest rooms are furnished in period style and have en suite facilities. 'Californian breakfasts' a speciality.

Midcity Motor Lodge (££) 218 Trafalgar Street (tel: 03 546 9063; fax: 03 548 3595). In the heart of the city and yet with very quiet rooms. 15 self-contained units (sleeping one to four).

Picton

Ancient Mariner Motor Inn (££) cnr Waikawa Road and Wellington Street (tel: 03 573 7002; fax: 03 573 7727). Two minutes from the town centre, affordable but good-quality rooms. Executive rooms have circular beds and video screens. Pool, spa, sauna, gym.

Grandvue (£) 19 Otago Street (tel & fax: 03 573 8553). As the name implies, this homely and welcoming bed and breakfast has good views across Picton from its perch on the hillside.

Marlin Motel (£–££) 33 Devon Street (tel: 03 573 6784; freephone: 0800 100 784; fax: 03 573 6987). Quietly located motel, handy for the ferry, with spacious and well-maintained units.

THE WEST COAST

Fox Glacier

Fox Glacier Hotel (££) Cnr Cook Flat Road and SH6 (tel: 03 751 0839; fax: 03 751 0868). Nice old hotel with 50 warm and cosy rooms with full facilities.

Glacier Country Hotel (££) SH6 (tel: 03 751 0847; free-phone: 0800 730 847; fax: 03 751 0822). Modern hotel with 51 rooms with all the usual facilities. Restaurant, bar lounge with open fire.

The Homestead (££) Lake Matheson Road (tel: 03 751 0835). 500m from the town-ship, B&B accommodation in a 100-year-old farmhouse. Just two bedrooms both with en suite facilities.

Franz Josef Glacier

Château Franz (£) 8 Cron Street (tel & fax: 03 752 0738). Convivial back-packers' lodge near the village centre, with double/twin rooms as well as bunk rooms.

Glacier View Motel (££) SH6 (tel: 03 752 0705; fax: 03 752 0761). 2.5km north of Franz Josef, the only motel in the area with views of the glacier. 14 self-contained ground floor units.

Rata Grove Motel (£–££) Cron Street (tel & fax: 03 752 0741). Close to the main street, this friendly motel has some of the most comfort-able rooms (from studios to family units) in the township.

Westwood Lodge (££) SH6 (tel & fax: 03 752 0111; freephone: 0800 741 111). 1km north of the township, with superb views, the lodge has six rooms and a large guest lounge.

Greymouth

Oak Lodge (££) Coal Creek, Main North Road (tel: 03 768 6832; fax: 03 768 4362). An upmarket B&B/homestay furnished throughout with antiques (some bedrooms have four-poster beds, all have en suite facilities). Pool and tennis.

Quality Kings Hotel (££) 32 Mawhera Quay (tel: 03 768 5085; fax: 03 768 5844). In the town centre overlooking the waterfront, the hotel has 100 rooms including superior suites, licensed restaurant and bar.

Lake Brunner

Lake Brunner Lodge (£££) Mitchells, RD1, Kumara (tel & fax: 03 738 0163). South-east of Greymouth, a lodge on the forested shores of Lake Brunner. Nine bedrooms, plainly decorated but spacious (front ones overlook the lake). Fishing, hiking, biking, hunting and bird-watching.

Hokitika

Southland Hotel (£–££) 111 Revell Street (tel: 03 755 8344; fax: 03 755 8258). Near the seafront in the towncentre, accommodation ranging from budget rooms to self-contained units with spa baths.

Teichelmann's B&B Guest House (£) 20 Hamilton Street (tel & fax: 03 755 8232). Friendly B&B accommodation, quiet location near the town centre. Six rooms, five en suite.

Tudor Motel (££) 123 Tudor Street (tel: 03 755 8193; freephone: 0800 775 555; fax: 03 755 8194). In a peaceful location close to the town centre, spacious fully self-contained units.

Paparoa National Park

Punakaiki Cottage Motels (£–££) SH6, Punakaiki (tel: 03 731 1008). In an enjoyable area with very few places to stay, the Punakaiki Cottage Motels offer comfortable studios or more spacious units (all with kitchens) right on the beach and just 500m from the blowholes.

Westport

AA Host Motel (££) Marine Parade, Carters Beach (tel: 03 789 8002; fax: 03 789 6732). 6km from the town centre, and close to the Cape Foulwind seal colony and Walkway, this is a better option than staying in Westport itself. Beach and golf course near by.

CANTERBURY

Akaroa, Banks Peninsula

Akaroa Village Inn (££–£££) Beach Road (tel: 03 304 7421; fax: 03 304 7423). A sprawling and not particularly attractive complex, but with a wide selection of rooms (some sleeping up to eight), honeymoon and waterbed suites. Indoor pool and licensed restaurant.

Grand Hotel (£) 6 Rue Lavaud (tel: 03 304 7011; fax: 03 304 7304). Built in 1860, the hotel has been refurbished to high standards, with just 12 rooms. Three bars, beer garden, licensed restaurant.

L'Hôtel (££) 75 Beach Road (tel: 03 304 7559; fax: 03 304 7455). Very attractive rooms and waterfront studios overlooking the harbour. Eight units (all en suite) sleeping one to four.

Wai-Iti Motels (££–£££) 64 Rue Jolie (tel: 03 304 7292). New motel right on the water's edge, with safe swimming off the quay. Spacious grounds. Dinghies and fishing gear available. 12 self-contained units (sleeping up to eight).

Christchurch

Alexandra Court Motel (££) 960 Colombo Street (tel: 03 366 1855; fax: 03 379 8796). 1km north of the city centre and ten minutes from the airport. Quiet location, spacious units (sleeping up to six) all with kitchens.

Eliza's Manor House (££) 82 Bealey Avenue (tel: 03 366 8584; fax: 03 366 4946). This wonderful old mansion (1860s) has been carefully restored and features a kauri staircase, wood-carvings and antiques. Ten bedrooms (eight with en suite facilities) show the same attention to detail. Cosy bar and a restaurant.

The George Hotel (£££) 50 Park Terrace (tel: 03 379 4560; freephone: 0800 100 220; fax: 03 366 6747). Close to the centre with views over Hagley Park and the River Avon, a 'boutique' hotel offering 54 tastefully furnished rooms and suites with the usual facilities. Bar, two licensed restaurants.

The Grange Guesthouse (££) 56 Armagh Street (tel: 03 366 2850; fax: 03 366 2115). Close to the city centre, this charming Victorian mansion offers superior B&B accommodation.

Pacific Park (££) 263 Bealey Avenue (tel: 03 379 8660; fax: 03 366 9973). 2km away from the city centre, this attractive hotel has 66 rooms and three suites.

Parkroyal Christchurch (£££) cnr Durham and Kilmore Street (tel: 03 365 1974; fax: 03 365 0082). The city's most exclusive hotel, in a superb position overlooking Victoria Square. 297 rooms with all the facilities you would expect. Several restaurants and bars, gym, sauna.

Windsor Hotel (££) 52 Armagh Street (tel: 03 366 1503; fax: 03 366 9796). This rambling old hotel has pleasantly decorated rooms (with shared bathrooms).

Hanmer Springs

Greenacres Motel (££) 86 Conical Hill Road (tel: 03 315 7125; fax: 03 315 7125). To the north of the resort, five minutes' walk from the thermal pools. One and two-bedroom villas plus four five-star apartments, all with full facilities.

Hanmer Resort Motel (£–££) 7 Cheltenham Street (tel: 03 315 7362; freephone: 0508

369 963; fax: 03 315 7581). Right in the centre of Hanmer Springs, opposite the thermal pools. Studio, family or executive units, most with individual courtyards or balconies, all with fully equipped kitchens.

Mount Cook National Park

THC Hermitage Hotel (£££) Mount Cook Village (tel: 03 435 1809; fax: 03 435 1879). The grand old lady of the National Park, with unsurpassable views of Mount Cook and the surrounding mountains. The monopoly enjoyed by this hotel for many years has allowed it to set prices way above those commensurate with its facilities; while comfortable, the rooms offer a lot less than many a decent motel.

Mount Cook Chalets (££–£££) Mount Cook Village (tel: 03 435 1809). Under the same ownership as the Hermitage, these comfortable chalets are the only mid-priced alternative in the Mount Cook Naitonal Park itself – unfortunately, they are not open year-round. There are 18 units, sleeping up to five people.

Mount Hutt

The Homestead, Mount Hutt Station (££) RD 12, Rakaia Gorge, Methven (tel: 03 302 8102; fax: 03 302 8179). Very comfortable and peaceful accommodation on this up-country station, now mostly devoted to deer farming. Fishing, hunting and other activities available. Restaurant and house bar.

Timaru

Bay Motel (£) 9 Hewlings Street (tel: 03 684 3267; fax: 03 684 3267). Close to Caroline Bay and in a quiet location off the main road. Four fully equipped units.

The Grosvenor Hotel (££–£££) Cains Terrace (tel: 03 688 3129; freephone: 0800 106 102; fax: 03 684 8381). Refurbished grand old hotel close to the main shopping area and the waterfront. 50 rooms, all en suite. Bars, restaurant.

THE DEEP SOUTH

Dunedin

Bentley's Hotel (££–£££) 137 St Andrew Street (tel: 03 477 0572; fax: 03 477 0293). One block from the Octagon, this hotel offers above average rooms (38) and suites (four) with all facilities. Cocktail bar, restaurant.

Cargills Motor Inn (££–£££) 678 George Street (tel: 03 477 7983; freephone: 0800 737 378; fax: 03 477 8098). 1½km from the Octagon, built around a courtyard garden. Superior motel-type rooms (some with waterbeds or spa baths) to executive suites. Lounge bar, restaurant.

Leviathan Hotel (£–££) 27 Queens Gardens (tel: 03 477 3160; freephone: 0508 773 773; fax: 03 477 2385). Old-fashioned hotel which has long been a Dunedin landmark, not flash but very good value for basic rooms or self-contained studio units. Executive suites also.

Wains Boutique Hotel (££) 310 Princes Street (tel: 03 477 1155; freephone: 0800 501 155; fax: 03 477 7737). Superb Victorian hotel renovated to very high standards. 38 individually decorated bedrooms (with all facilities) and four suites. Gym, bar and restaurant. Close to the Octagon.

Invercargill

Ascot Park Hotel (££–£££) cnr Tay Street and Racecourse Road (tel: 03 217 6195; fax: 03 217 7002). In a peaceful location in park-like surroundings five minutes' from the city centre, the hotel has 70 de luxe rooms and 24 above average motel units. Bar, brasserie.

Grand Hotel (£) 76 Dee Street (tel: 03 218 8059; fax: 03 218 8053). Centrally located and tastefully refurbished; 57 rooms with all facilities. Bar and restaurant.

Queenstown

A-Line Hotel (££) 27 Stanley Street (tel: 03 442 7700; freephone: 0800 807 700; fax: 03 442 7755). Alpine-style hotel five minutes' walk from the centre, with views over the lake. All 82 rooms are comfortable and well appointed: best value are the spacious two-storey units at the front, with fine views.

Earnslaw Lodge (££) 53 Frankton Road (tel: 03 442 8728; fax: 03 442 7376). One of a series of motels and lodges on the Frankton Road, the Earnslaw Lodge is an inviting, modern complex with 19 studio units (five with kitchens). Rooms on upper levels have the best views.

Gardens Parkroyal (£££) cnr Marine Parade and Earl Street (tel: 03 442 7750; fax: 03 442 7469). De luxe hotel on the waterfront and next to the Queenstown gardens – a superb location.

Millbrook Resort (£££) Malaghans Road, Arrowtown (tel: 03 441 7000; fax: 03 442 1145). 19km from Queenstown and 1km from Arrowtown, this new resort has large two-storey villas in the middle of a championship 18-hole golf course. The elegant two-bedroom suites are fully equipped.

Parkroyal Queenstown (£££) Beach Street (tel: 03 442 7800; fax; 03 442 8895). The resort's premier hotel, with many rooms overlooking the lake. All 139 rooms and suites have de luxe facilities.

Queenstown House (££) 69 Hallenstein Street (tel: 03 442 9043; fax: 03 442 8755). This refurbished B&B is 500m from the town centre with eight rooms (some en suite). Peaceful, good views.

Queenstown Lodge (£–££) Sainsbury Road, Fernhill (tel: 03 442 7107; fax: 03 442 6498). 1.6km from the town centre (courtesy shuttle), this unusual lodge has stunning views over the lake from panoramic windows. Accommodation ranges from shared bunk rooms to private rooms with en suite facilities. Games room, bar, restaurant.

Stewart Island

Shearwater Inn (£) Halfmoon Bay (tel: 03 219 1114; fax: 03 219 1120). A few minutes' walk from the seafront, this complex offers hostel accommodation, single, double and family rooms. Restaurant.

South Sea Hotel (£–££) Halfmoon Bay (tel: 03 219 1059; fax: 03 219 1120). This old-fashioned hotel is in the hub of the township and its bars and restaurants are the focus of community life on the island. The 16 rooms all have shared facilities but are very reasonably priced.
Stewart Island Holiday Homes (£) Elgin Terrace, Halfmoon Bay (tel: 03 217 6585). Peaceful setting five minutes' walk from the centre. Two self-contained units sleeping up to ten.

Te Anau

Edgewater XL Motel (£–££) 52 Lakefront Drive (tel: 03 249 7528; fax: 03 249 8099). Adjacent to the lake, 15 units with full kitchen facilities, very reasonably priced. Free canoes.
Te Anau Motor Park (£–££) Te Anau–Manapouri Road (tel: 03 249 7457; fax: 03 249 7653). Well-located motor park almost on the lake shore a few minutes from the town centre, offering a range of accommodation from de luxe motel units to basic tourist flats, backpackers' bunkhouse and tent and campervan sites. Good value.
Te Anau Travelodge (£££) Te Anau Terrace (tel: 03 249 7411; fax: 03 249 7947). Right in the centre, 112 rooms all with private facilities. Pool, spa, sauna, two restaurants and two bars.

Wanaka

Te Wanaka Lodge (££) 23 Brownston Street (tel: 03 443 9224; fax: 03 443 9246). This cosy lodge (built from traditional materials) in the town centre has 12 comfortable units at reasonable prices. Two guest lounges, wood fire, cooking facilities.
Wanaka Motor Inn (££–£££) Mount Aspiring Road (tel: 03 443 8216; fax: 03 443 9108). Very well-run inn with 32 studio units with en suite facilities, 2km from the town centre with lake and mountain views. Restaurant and bar.

RESTAURANTS

£ = NZ$20 or less
££ = NZ$20–$30
£££ = NZ$30 plus

North Island

AUCKLAND

Auckland

Cin-Cin on Quay (££–£££) Auckland Ferry Building, 99 Quay Street (tel: 09 307 6966). Popular and busy restaurant with a long-standing reputation as one of Auckland's best. Outdoor area overlooking the harbour. The menu encompasses cordon bleu dishes as well as pizzas from the wood-burning oven.
Collins House (£££) 20 Greenhithe Road (tel: 09 413 9322). Converted from one of the oldest cottages in Auckland, an attractive restaurant in a rural setting in Greenhithe, in north Auckland. The chef trained at Cin-Cin (see above) and specialises in French food.
Grapevine Wine Bar (£–£££) 1 Victoria Road, Devonport (tel: 09 445 0085). Spacious wine bar with wood décor and views over the harbour. Interesting food and extensive wine list as well as local and imported beers.
Hammerheads (££–£££) 19 Tamaki Drive, Mission Bay (tel: 09 521 4400). Large and popular seafood restaurant and bar with a wide-ranging and tempting menu; spicy tuatua fritters, char-grilled lamb and fish and shellfish.
Kermadec (££–£££) 1st floor, Viaduct Quay, Lower Hobson Street (tel: 09 309 0412). The owners promise the freshest fish possible in this interesting new restaurant – it should be fresh, since they own a fishing fleet. Oysters, sashimi and skilfully prepared fish.
The Loaded Hog (£–££) Viaduct Quay, Hobson and Quay Streets (tel: 09 366 6491). Busy 'brewery restaurant' and bar – their own beers are brewed on the premises. Fun food and a lively atmosphere.
Metropole (££–£££) 223 Parnell Road (tel: 09 379 9300). Trendy eaterie in Parnell, casual but stylish. Menu ranges from interesting bar snacks to classic dishes and less traditional fare such as grilled salmon in soy sauce.
Mexican Café (£–££) 67 Victoria Street West (tel: 09 373 2311). Fun and friendly Mexican cantina, offering great margaritas and a good selection of vegetarian dishes.
Poppadom (££) 55 Customs Street East (tel: 09 379 8601). Award-winning Indian restaurant with traditional dishes and a full Tandoori menu; lunchtime buffets are good value.
Union Fish Co (££–£££) 16 Quay Street (tel: 09 379 6745). In one of Auckland's oldest waterfront buildings, this spacious fish restaurant serves consistently good food. Crayfish a speciality.

NORTHLAND

DOUBTLESS BAY

Mangonui

Mangonui Fish Shop (£) The Wharf (tel: 09 406 0478). Fresh shellfish, fish and chips, seafood salads.

BAY OF ISLANDS

Paihia

Bistro 40 Restaurant and Bar (£££) Bayswater Inn, 40 Marsden Road (tel: 09 402 7444). Attractive restaurant in a converted homestead (1884) with an outside patio. Wide-ranging menu. Evenings only.
The Colonial Restaurant (££–£££) Bay of Islands Motel, Tohitapu Road (tel: 09 402 6640). Award winning restaurant with a set menu as well as daily blackboard specials.
Fish Pot Seafood Café (££) Selwyn Mall (tel: 09 402 7653). Cosy restaurant serving seafood chowder as well as fish burgers or just plain old fish and chips.

Russell

Duke of Marlborough (£–££) The Strand (tel: 09 403 7829). There are several

options in this historic waterfront hotel, with pub food in the bar or more elegant dining in Somerset's Restaurant. Sunday brunch with live jazz every week.
The Gables (££) The Strand (tel: 09 403 7618). Popular restaurant on the seafront (reservation recommended). New Zealand produce and seafood.

Whangarei
Killer Prawn Bar and Restaurant (£–£££) Strand Plaza, 26–8 Bank Street (tel: 09 430 3333). Trendy hang-out in the town centre, built from old bricks and wooden beams. Wide-ranging menu described as'international with a splash of California'; prawns are of course a speciality, but bar snacks and breakfasts (weekends only) are also available.
Reva's Pizza Parlour (£–££) 15 Dent Street (tel: 09 438 8969). Popular hang-out with international yachties, plenty of choice from pizzas to Mexican and seafood. Live music Wed, Thu, Fri.

FROM CORO-MANDEL TO THE WAIKATO

COROMANDEL
Coromandel Town
Coromandel Hotel (£–££) Kapanga Road (tel: 07 866 8760). Historic pub 300m from the town centre, open for lunches as well as 'bistro dining' every evening.
Star and Garter Café (£) 24 Wharf Road (tel: 07 866 7157). Pleasant little café with a garden, open all day for home cooking, pizzas and a selection of coffees.

Pauanui
Puka Park Lodge (£££) Mount Avenue (tel: 07 864 8088). The lodge has an award-winning restaurant with an innovative menu of NZ/international cuisine. Bistro food in the Puka Café.

Thames
Brian Boru Hotel (£–££) 200 Richmond Street (tel: 07 868 6523). Atmospheric dining room with a fairly basic menu. Local flounder is a speciality.
Majestic Family Restaurant (£–££) 640 Pollen Street (tel: 07 868 6204). Specialises in seafood and steak, as well as take-aways.

Whitianga
CC Restaurant (£–£££) 20 Esplanade Road (tel: 07 866 4833). Beachfront location with a terrace. Huge menu features everything from bar snacks to pheasant, salmon, rabbit, seafood and vegetar-ian meals.
Snapper Jacks (£) cnr Albert and Monk Streets (tel: 07 866 5482). Popular fish and seafood restaurant with a take-away section and fresh seafood sales as well.

BAY OF PLENTY
Rotorua
Aorangi Peak Restaurant (£££) Mountain Road, Mount Ngongotaha (tel: 07 347 0046). A ten-minute drive from the city, with panoramic views across the lake and the township. Wide-ranging menu with specialities such as steak, venison teriyaki and scallop tempura as well as vegetarian dishes. A great place for a special night out.
Cobb & Co (££–£££) Grand Hotel, 55 Hinemoa Street (tel: 07 348 2089). Part of a chain of 'coach-house' type restau-rants found in nearly every major city, Cobb & Co specialise in straightforward meals such as steaks, grills, pies, chicken and fish. Service is efficient but with the high throughput of cust-omers, standards can vary.
Fish Pot Café (£–££) 161 Fenton Street (tel: 07 349 3494). Fresh fish and seafood as well as steaks and a dessert menu. Licensed/BYO.
Gazebo Café/Restaurant (£–££) 45 Pukuatua Street (tel: 07 348 1911). Café by day, restaurant by night, this non-smoking, plant-filled place has a range of well-prepared dishes; blackboard specials.
Orchid Gardens Café (£–££) Government Gardens, Hinemaru Street (tel: 07 347 6182). In a plant-filled conservatory, this pleasant café serves breakfasts, light meals and snacks from early morning onwards.
Rumours (£££) 81 Pukuatua Street (tel: 07 347 7277). Sophisticated restaurant with a creative menu of well-presented dishes.

Tauranga
Bella Mia (££) 73a Devonport Road (tel: 07 578 4996). Cosy pizzeria/ ristorante, pasta dishes, pizzas, meat and fish.
Cherokee Red (££) Goddards Centre, 25 Devonport Road (tel: 07 577 0067). South-west American cuisine served in a relaxed atmo-sphere; unusual dishes include Mexican grilled rabbit, Hopi grilled pork and seafood stew with ginger, citrus and pineapple.
Fish Pot Café (£–££) 11 Avenue Plaza (tel: 07 578 5729). Good selection of dishes include catch of the day, snapper dishes, steaks and children's menu. Licensed and BYO. Part of a well-managed chain.
Harbourside Brasserie and Bar (££–£££) Old Yacht Club Building, Strand extension (tel: 07 571 0520). Bright, brasserie overlooking the harbour. Excellent seafood and grills; desserts and coffee until midnight.

THE WAIKATO
Hamilton
Eldorado's (£–££) 10 Alma Street (tel: 07 838 1013). Atmospheric Mexican restaurant with a huge menu and equally huge portions. A fun place to eat, good value.
Gino's Portofino (££–£££) 8 Bryce Street (tel: 07 834 0000). Popular restaurant with a good selection of Italian and continental dishes. Pizzas from the wood-burning oven.
Montana (££–£££) 131 Victoria Street (tel: 07 839 3459). Long-established, unpretentious restaurant. Extensive menu including fish, steaks, salads, vege-tarian dishes and desserts.
Valentines (£–££) cnr Anglesea and Clarence Streets (tel: 07 839 1990). Licensed 'buffet restaurant'

with a smorgasbord of over 120 dishes to choose from at a fixed price (higher for dinner than lunch).

EAST COAST

Hastings

St Vinees Wine Bar & Café (£–££) 108 Market Street South (tel: 06 878 8596). Pleasant little wine bar with an open fire and terrace. Open six days a week for bar snacks or more substantial meals.

Vidal Winery Brasserie (££–£££) 913 St Aubyn Street East (tel: 07 876 8105). On the Vidal Estate winery to the south of town, this popular brasserie has a rustic decor and a relaxed atmosphere. Light meals, steaks, blackboard specials. Jazz brunch on Sundays. Wine tastings and sales.

Napier

Bayswater on the Beach (££–£££) Hardinge Road, Ahuriri (tel: 06 835 8517). Stylish waterfront restaurant with an imaginative men. A la carte dining for brunch, lunch and dinner; reservation advisable.

Bucks Great Wall Restaurant (££–£££) A & B Building, Marine Parade (tel: 06 835 0088). Housed in a magnificent Art Deco building, this sophisticated Chinese restaurant has an extensive menu featuring mostly Cantonese cuisine.

Cottage Arms (£) 209 Marine Parade (tel: 06 835 3766). English-style pub with a good selection of beers and wines; snacks and steaks. Garden courtyard.

Gumnuts (££) The Provincial Hotel, cnr Emerson Street and Clive Square (tel: 06 835 6934). Imaginative vegetarian menu although they do also serve steaks, lamb and seafood. Children's menu and tempting desserts.

Pierre sur le Quai Restaurant (£££) 62 West Quay, Ahuriri (tel: 06 834 0189). Slightly out of town on the quayside, this elegant restaurant is rated as one of Napier's top dining out venues. Reservations essential.

CENTRAL NORTH ISLAND AND THE WEST COAST

Lake Taupo

Echo Cliff Restaurant (££) 5 Tongariro Street (tel: 07 378 8539). On the lakeside with good views. The usual NZ fare (lamb, fish, chicken, beef) is complemented by Dutch Indonesian dishes.

Edgewater Restaurant (£££) Manuel's Motor Inn, Lake Terrace (tel: 07 378 5110). One of Taupo's top restaurants, imaginative and well-presented New Zealand dishes. The plush dining room overlooks the lake.

Hudders Licensed Café (££–£££) 22 Tuwharetoa Street (tel: 07 378 5919). 'Hollywood theme café' with an interesting and varied menu, good music and a lively atmosphere.

Margarita's (££) 63 Heu Heu Street (tel: 07 378 9909). Right in the town centre, a lively Mexican restaurant with Aztec-style décor, cocktail bar and live music.

New Plymouth

Gareth's (£££) 182 Devon Street East (tel: 06 758 5104). Elegant restaurant with a long-standing reputation for freshly prepared, imaginative dishes, fine wines and good service. Baked lamb fillets are a speciality, as is Bombe Taranaki – a dessert in the shape of the neighbouring mountain.

Wanganui

Cables (££–£££) cnr Victoria Avenue and Ridgeway Street (tel: 06 345 6891). In the heart of the city, an tmospheric restaurant offering a range of interesting dishes. Open evenings only and Sunday brunch.

Cameron House (£££) 281 Wickstead Street (tel: 06 345 2690). Characterful restaurant inside a converted historic home, surrounded by gardens. Classic dishes include noisettes of lamb, salmon and beef fillets.

Liffiton Castle Restaurant (££–£££) 26 Liffiton Street (tel: 06 345 7864). Amusing venue (complete with moat and antique fittings) with a lively atmosphere and good food. Steaks are a speciality.

The Quay Bar and Café (£–££) cnr Victoria Avenue and Taupo Quay (tel: 06 345 4631). Good value lunch and dinner menus with a range of entertainments at night.

SOUTHERN NORTH ISLAND

Wellington

Brasserie Bellezar (££–£££) 41 Courtenay Place (tel: 04 801 8001). An atmospheric brasserie features a limited but well-presented menu with dishes such as grilled cervena (venison) and tenderloin steak. Imaginative starters. Reservations recommended.

Bengal Tiger (££) Level 2, the Majestic Centre (tel: 04 472 8706). Long-established and popular Indian restaurant with a particularly good-value evening buffet.

Chevy's (££) 97 Dixon Street (tel: 04 384 2724). The neon cowboy outside advertises the essentially American nature of this diner. Spare ribs, burgers, nachos, chicken wings and steaks.

Dockside (££–£££) Shed 3, Queen's Wharf (tel: 04 499 9900). A busy and trendy eating place on the waterfront, *Dockside* serves everything from breakfasts through to late-night snacks (open every day 7am–3am).

Shed 5 Restaurant (£££) Shed 5, Queen's Wharf (tel: 04 499 9069). One of a clutch of waterfront restaurants, Shed 5 also has a wet fish market alongside the cavernous restaurant and bar area. Seafood specials as well as NZ lamb and venison, pasta and poultry. Good wine list. A great place for brunch at weekends.

Scorpio's (££) 163 The Parade, Island Bay (tel: 04 383 7563). In a city which offers almost every possible cuisine, there is always something new to discover – in this case a Welsh restaurant serving traditional cooking in a friendly atmosphere.

South Island

NELSON AND MARLBOROUGH

Blenheim

Paddy Barry's Irish Pub (£–££) 51 Scott Street (tel: 03 578 7470). Friendly pub with a pleasant veranda, offering reasonably priced pub food.
Paysanne Café and Bar (£–££) 1st floor, Forum Building, Blenheim (tel: 03 577 6278). Handily located just above the Information Centre, this convivial wine bar serves light snacks and meals, with daily blackboard specials.
Seymours (££–£££) Blenheim Country Lodge' cnr Alfred and Henry Streets (tel: 03 578 5079). Elegant restaurant near the centre, with specialities including gourmet Marlborough foods: the wine list has over 70 Marlborough wines.

Kaikoura

White Morph Restaurant (££–£££) 94 The Esplanade (tel: 03 319 5676). Atmospheric restaurant in a historic home, with fish and seafood straight off the local boats plus Devonshire cream teas served all day.
Caves Restaurant (££) Main Highway South (tel: 03 319 5023). Local seafoods as well as snacks and light meals, reasonable value.

Nelson

La Bonne Vie (£££) 75 Bridge Street (tel: 03 548 0270). Seafood restaurant with a wide-ranging à la carte and blackboard menu featuring oysters, mussels, crayfish, salmon and more; meat and vegetarian dishes also available. Licensed and BYO.
Chez Eelco (£) 296 Trafalgar Street (tel: 03 548 7595). Snacks and light meals including soups, burgers, toasted sandwiches. Popular local meeting place with a cheerful atmosphere.
Pomeroy's (£–££) 276 Trafalgar Street (tel: 03 548 7524). Centrally located café/wine bar open from 10am for croissants, cakes and coffee, plus delicious snacks and light meals later on. Extensive wine list.
Victorian Rose (£–££) 281 Trafalgar Street (tel: 03 548 7631). 'Old English'-style pub with a good range of beers. Meals and snacks (vegetarian, pasta and steaks). Live entertainment.

Motueka

Gothic Gourmet Restaurant (££–£££) 208 High Street (tel: 03 528 6699). This unmistakable pink-painted converted church in the High Street has an interesting menu; perennial favourites include scallops, steaks and medallions of lamb. Also a 'casual' menu and one for children.
Hot Mamas (£–££) 105 High Street (tel: 03 528 7039). Busy bistro with live bands at weekends, serving breakfasts, light lunches and Mexican food alongside traditional NZ fare 'at café prices'.

Picton

The 5th Bank (£££) 33 Wellington Street (tel: 03 573 6102). One of Picton's best restaurants, with a sophisticated atmosphere. Crayfish, cervena, mussels, steak.

THE WEST COAST

Fox

Fox Glacier Hotel (£–££) Fox township (tel: 03 751 0839). A licensed restaurant specialising in local delicacies such as whitebait, salmon and venison; bar with bar snacks.

Franz Josef

Blue Ice (£–£££) Main Street (tel: 03 752 0707). Cheerful restaurant with mountain views, jazz music. Cosmopolitan menu featuring Westland salmon, venison casserole, lobster and vegetarian dishes. Tasty desserts and great espresso coffee.
Glacier Store and Tearooms (£–££) Main Street (tel: 03 751 0868). Self-service cafeteria offering sandwiches, soups, salads and pastries.

Hokitika

Filling Station Café (£–££) Revell Street (tel: 03 755 8344). A good place for sandwiches, light meals, coffee and pizza. NZ wines by the glass or bottle plus naturally brewed beers.
Tasman View Restaurant (££–£££) Southland Hotel, Revell Street (tel: 03 755 8344). Overlooking the windswept Tasman Sea, this upmarket restaurant specialises in 'West Coast foods'. Friday smorgasbord specials are good value.
Trappers (££) Revell Street (tel: 03 755 5133). Very unusual restaurant which grew out of the Hokitika Wildfoods Festival, with a changing menu which features wild venison, chamois, thar and wild boar, plus exotic meats such as crocodile, kangaroo and water buffalo.

CANTERBURY

Akaroa, Banks Peninsula

Astrolabe (£–££) 71 Beach Road (tel: 03 304 7656). Café/bar open from 10.30am until late. Pizzas, brunch, French pastries, coffee, fully licensed.
C'est la Vie (£–££) 33 Rue Lavaud (tel: 03 304 7314). Intimate little café/bistro specialising in French food as well as cakes and desserts.
La Rue Restaurant (££–£££) 6 Rue Balguerie (tel: 03 304 7658). Long-established and popular restaurant on the waterfront which has won many awards. Crayfish (in season), lamb, venison and fish appear on the menu in many different guises.

Christchurch

Canterbury Tales (£££) Christchurch Parkroyal, cnr Kilmore and Durham Streets (tel: 03 365 7799). Formal restaurant with a medieval theme, winner of many awards and generally considered one of the best in the South Island. The accent is on the freshest Canterbury produce, complemented by an extensive wine list.
Death by Chocolate (£–££) 209 Cambridge Terrace (tel: 03 365 7323). Chocaholics will love this little restaurant which serves nothing but

chocolate-based meals accompanied by chocolate bread with chocolate butter!
Dux de Lux (£–££) cnr Hereford and Montreal Streets (tel: 03 366 6919). Close to the Arts Centre, this popular place has an excellent self-service vegetarian restaurant (considered one of the best in Christchurch) as well as a Tapas Seafood bar and the Tavern Bar with beers brewed on site Courtyard and regular live music.
Lone Star Café (££) 26 Manchester Street (tel: 03 365 7086). Tex-Mex food in a carefully contrived 'Wild West' atmosphere. Lots of fun, reasonable value. Branches in Dunedin, Invercargill and Queenstown.
Mainstreet Café and Bar (£–££) cnr Colombo and Salisbury Streets (tel: 03 365 0421). Popular vegetarian restaurant and bar, with an innovative menu.
Sign of the Takahe (£££) Dyers Pass Road, Cashmere Hills (tel: 03 332 4052). In a mock-baronial castle 20 minutes drive from the city centre, this restaurant is best known for its crayfish, which are brought in live from Lobster New Zealand's Christchurch base. The menu is rounded out with other seafood specialities, such as whitebait, mussels and scallops.
Strawberry Fare (£–££) 114 Peterborough Street (tel: 03 365 4897). Divine desserts are the speciality of this restaurant, served at any time of day. They also have savoury meals from brunch through to dinner. There is another branch in Wellington.
Thomas Edmonds Restaurant (££–£££) cnr Cambridge Terrace and Manchester Street (tel: 03 365 2888). In a delightful setting on the riverbank inside a converted band rotunda. New Zealand specialities are complemented by home-made desserts and an extensive wine list.

THE DEEP SOUTH

Dunedin

Bacchus Wine Bar and Restaurant (££–£££) 1st floor, 12 The Octagon (tel: 03 474 0824). Centrally located and overlooking the Octagon, this smart wine bar serves good food plus an extensive selection of imported and NZ wines.
City Limits Restaurant (£–££) 412A George Street (tel: 03 477 2463). This unusual restaurant has a barrel-vaulted kauri ceiling and is furnished with period touches. Open for lunch and dinner, generous portions and good food.
Palms Café (£–££) 18 Queens Gardens (tel: 03 477 6534). Cosy café in an atmospheric old building with a blackboard menu as well as staples such as chicken, lamb and fish. BYO.
Wharf Street (££–£££) cnr Birch and Wharf Street (tel: 03 477 4455). At the top of the Port Otago Building, this restaurant is most notable for its location, with great views of the harbour and city especially by night.

Queenstown

Berkels Gourmet Burgers (£–££) 19 Shotover Street (tel: 03 442 6950). Straightforward burger joint with burgers as simple or as complicated (with Camembert, horseradish, chilli and more) as you want them. Licensed, with a wide range of beers and wines.
Boardwalk Seafood Restaurant & Bar (££–£££) Steamer Wharf (tel: 03 442 5630). On the first floor of the Steamer Wharf complex, this stylish restaurant specialises in fresh seafood and New Zealand produce such as venison, lamb and beef.
Fishbone Bar & Grill (££) 7 Beach Street (tel 03 442 6768). One of Queenstown's best-value fish restaurants, with char-grilled seafoods and other delicacies straight from the slab. There is also a fresh fish counter. Licensed and BYO.
HMS *Britannia* (££) The Mall (tel: 03 442 9600). Rigged out as an old English galleon, with booths running down either side of a central gangway. Varied menu, including fresh food, crayfish and venison dishes.
Lone Star Café (££) 14 Brecon Street (tel: 03 442 9995). Char-grilled steaks, Cajun dishes, Dixie chicken and spare ribs are just some of the southern specialities on offer in this popular chain restaurant. Generous portions, fun atmosphere.
McNeills (££) 14 Church Street (tel: 03 442 9688). Open fires add atmosphere in this cosy micro-brewery, bar and restaurant where their award-winning beers are complemented by a menu of 'innovative European cuisine'.
Minami Jujisei (££–£££) 45 Beach Street (tel: 03 442 9854). By reputation one of the best Japanese restaurants in New Zealand, with a sushi bar, traditional Tatami room, and Western-style dining room.
Pot au Feu (££) 24 Camp Street (tel: 03 442 8333). Imaginative, well-presented food with a Mediterranean influence. Good selection of wines by the glass.
Promenade (£££) Gardens Parkroyal, Marine Parade and Earl Street (tel: 03 442 7750). A smart restaurant with excellent service and a menu of NZ fare which includes a wide variety of lamb dishes.
Reflections (£) Holiday Inn, Salisbury Road, Fernhill (tel: 03 442 6600). Good value Sunday buffet (11.30–2): as much as you can eat with both hot and cold choices for NZ$15 per person.
Skyline Restaurants (££–£££) Brecon Street (tel: 03 442 7860). Fabulous views from the gondola complex, with a choice of a an international-style menu in the brasserie (evenings only) or a huge spread (including carvery) in the buffet. Lounge bar – great for sundowner cocktails – and a cafeteria.

Index

Author's Acknowledgements

The author, Nick Hanna, would like to thank the following for their assistance: The Palzer family, Ocean View Chalets, Marahou; Grant and Judie Smith, Wanaka Motor Inn, Mount Hutt Station; Stefanie and Brent Ritchie, Punakaiki Cottage Motels; Jean and Don Goldschmidt, Aachen House, Remuera; Kevin and Lois Kelly, Taipororo House, Tauranga; Lake Plaza Hotel, Rotorua; Clint and Jill Tauri, Te Anau Motor Park; Garrick and Maureen Workman, Hobbit Motor Lodge, Ohakune; Bart and Theresa Blommaert, Ascot Parnell; Bernadette Walker, Wains Boutique Hotel, Dunedin; The Wairakei Resort, Lake Taupo; Mercury Bay Beachfront Resort, Whitianga; Bruce and Aileen Stone, Cheviot Park Motor Lodge, Whangarei; Napier Travel Inn, Hawke's Bay; Harry Sellarsby, A-Line Hotel, Queenstown; Russell and Rosalie Mathews, Grandvue, Picton; Ellenor and Leslie King, Rata Grove Motel, Franz Josef; Avenue Motor Inn, Wanganui. Also thanks to Peter Peck of Fjordland Travel, Queenstown; Neil Ross, Dart River Safaris, Queenstown; Graham Allen of Mount Cook Line, London; Karen Jones, New Zealand Rail, London; Kiwifruits Bookshop, London. Finally, thanks to Angela Becket and Adrienne Wilde in Tauranga and to Graham and Jill Hubble in Auckland for their generous hospitality.

Publisher's Acknowledgements

The Automobile Association wishes to thank the following photographers, libraries and associations for their assistance in the preparation of this book:
ALEXANDER TURNBALL LIBRARY, WELLINGTON 76/7; **ALLSPORT UK LTD** 146a (M. Hewitt), 146b (S. Bruty), 147a (S. Dunn), 147b (S. Bruty); **AUCKLAND CITY ART GALLERY** 51a; **AUCKLAND INSTITUTE AND MUSEUM** 34b; **BRUCE COLEMAN COLLECTION** 34a (M. Carwardine), 98b (G Cubitt), 105a (F. Furlong), 105b (F. Furlong), 156 (M. Carwardine), 167 (M. Carwardine), 216/7 (L. Lee Rue), 223b (G. Cubitt), 236a (F. Furlong), 236b (G. Cubitt); **MARY EVANS PICTURE LIBRARY** 32a, 39b, 218/9; **FOCUS NEW ZEALAND PHOTO LIBRARY** 13, 17, 18b, 20, 20/1, 22/3, 22, 23, 24b, 44, 46b, 54, 59, 60, 64/5, 74/5, 80, 86, 88, 92, 101, 102/3, 104, 106/7, 107, 111, 118/9, 127, 138, 145, 154/5, 163, 166a, 185b (carved by Neil Brown), 187a, 187b, 244, 250; **FIORDLAND TRAVEL** 235; **FOOTPRINTS COLOUR LIBRARY (Nick Hanna)** 136b, 224, 234b; **GREENPEACE COMMUNICATIONS LTD** 19 (Miller); **L. C HAZLEY** 228/9; **HULTON GETTY** 27b, 31, 33a, 37, 40, 42a, 43, 45, 150, 171, 237; **THE MANSELL COLLECTION LTD** 30b, 32b, 35, 36a, 38a, 38b, 39a, 40/1, 41, 137, 218;**NATIONAL MARITIME MUSEUM, LONDON** 32/3, 116a, 116b, 117; **NATURE PHOTOGRAPHERS LTD** 213 (B. Burbidge); **NEW ZEALAND TOURISM BOARD PHOTO LIBRARY** 114, 185a; **OTAMATEA KAURI AND PIONEER MUSEUM** 77; **PICTOR INTERNATIONAL, LONDON** Back flap; **POPPERFOTO** 42/3, 99, 112/3, 112b; **THE RONALD GRANT ARCHIVE** 57c; **SPECTRUM COLOUR LIBRARY** 46a, 120, 149, 176/7, 180/1, 182a, 182b, 223a; **TAHI DESIGNS** 57; **TE PAPA TONGAREWA MUSEUM OF NEW ZEALAND** 151; **ZEFA PICTURES LTD** 133.
The remaining photographs are held in the Association's own library (AA PHOTO LIBRARY) and were taken by Paul Kenward with the exception of page 14/15a which was taken by Adrian Baker and pages 195, 202, 227, 242, 259 taken by Nick Hanna.

Contributors

Designer: Philip Barfoot
Joint series editor: Josephine Perry **Copy editor**: Barbara Mellor
Verifier: Michael Mellor **Indexer**: Marie Lorimer